Legislating Morality in America

Legislating Morality
in America

Debating the Morality of
Controversial U.S. Laws and Policies

Donald P. Haider-Markel, Editor

BLOOMSBURY ACADEMIC
NEW YORK • LONDON • OXFORD • NEW DELHI • SYDNEY

BLOOMSBURY ACADEMIC
Bloomsbury Publishing Inc
1385 Broadway, New York, NY 10018, USA
50 Bedford Square, London, WC1B 3DP, UK
29 Earlsfort Terrace, Dublin 2, Ireland

BLOOMSBURY, BLOOMSBURY ACADEMIC and the Diana logo
are trademarks of Bloomsbury Publishing Plc

First published in the United States of America by ABC-CLIO 2020
Paperback edition published by Bloomsbury Academic 2024

Library of Congress Cataloging-in-Publication Data
Names: Haider-Markel, Donald P., editor.
Title: Legislating morality in America : debating the morality of controversial U.S. laws
and policies / Donald P. Haider-Markel, editor.
Description: Santa Barbara, California : ABC-CLIO, 2020. |
Includes bibliographical references and index.
Identifiers: LCCN 2019026987 (print) | LCCN 2019026988 (ebook) |
ISBN 9781440849701 (hardback) | ISBN 9781440849718 (epub)
Subjects: LCSH: Law—Moral and ethical aspects—United States. | Crimes without victims—
Law and legislation—United States. | Sex and law—United States. |
Law—Social aspects—United States. | Law—Political aspects—United States.
Classification: LCC KF380 .L44 2020 (print) | LCC KF380 (ebook) | DDC 172.0973—dc23
LC record available at https://lccn.loc.gov/2019026987
LC ebook record available at https://lccn.loc.gov/2019026988

ISBN: HB: 978-1-4408-4970-1
PB: 979-8-7651-2520-5
ePDF: 978-1-4408-4971-8
eBook: 979-8-2161-1045-3

To find out more about our authors and books visit www.bloomsbury.com
and sign up for our newsletters.

Contents

Introduction

Many of the early European colonists to America were fleeing religious persecution or otherwise seeking greater freedom and individual autonomy. Few of those early colonists recognized the moral hypocrisy of occupying and transforming a land already inhabited by Native Americans in order to pursue greater freedom. Nor did many colonists object to the dehumanizing treatment of Africans kidnapped and shipped to the colonies to live out their lives as slaves to the colonists. However, resistance to these early violations of human rights provided some of the foundations by which both religious and secular morality have come to shape American society, politics, and public policy.

This book attempts to outline some of the ways moral concerns have been embedded within political issues that Americans have struggled with over the last 200-plus years. The issues include everything from abortion to education to torture. In each of the cases examined, one or more sides in the debate have attempted to frame the issue in moral terms, usually in an attempt to gain greater political leverage by appealing to a high-order notion of right and wrong. At times, these moral appeals are successful in producing shifts in public opinion and social and policy changes, but other times they fail.

WHAT WE MEAN BY MORALITY

Morality is often defined by a set of (typically religious but also secular) principles or values. Moral value or belief systems help us to evaluate whether behaviors, actions, or conditions should be assessed as good, right, or correct and for many people are established at a relatively early age. Of course, behaviors, actions, or conditions can be presented in different ways, making it possible to manipulate how individuals apply values in order to understand a given situation or issue. Efforts at such manipulation, or issue framing, get to the heart of the role of morality in American politics and the policy-making process.

ISSUE FRAMING AND MORALITY POLITICS

In social science literature, we have come to understand issue framing in terms of the multiple dimensions of any given issue. Social issues that enter into political discourse always have several dimensions, even though political actors may choose to focus on only one or two dimensions. For example, guns and gun ownership can be presented as issues in which the most essential considerations orbit around individual rights and freedom, constitutional rights, and self-protection, but they can also be presented as threats to public safety and health (including that of our children), a potential challenge to legitimate authorities, and a grim indication of societal priorities.

Indeed, how conditions in society and the broader environment are defined or framed can influence the likelihood that these conditions will enter a public or political debate—and subsequently, whether the condition is defined as a public problem that governmental resources should be mobilized to address (Stone, 1989). This also means that issues can be redefined or reframed over time. Issue definitions are not static and provide a fundamental basis by which political and policy change can occur (Baumgartner & Jones, 1993).

Issue framing is used as a rhetorical device to prime an audience to focus on one dimension of the issue over others by arguing that that dimension is more important than other possible dimensions of the issue. The speaker thus hopes to gain political advantage by appealing to underlying values or beliefs held by the receiver of the message (Chong & Druckman, 2007). So a speaker who frames an issue in moral terms hopes to appeal to the receiver's underlying morally based values, which could be grounded in secular- or religious-based morality. For example, in discussing the issue of abortion, a speaker may refer to a right to life or the notion that all life is sacred in framing a moral argument against abortion. Meanwhile, a speaker in support of allowing abortion might frame the issue in terms of the right of women to control their own bodies and to assert that violating that right is morally wrong (Burns, 2005). Both frames can potentially activate underlying values in the audience, mobilizing political support or opposition (Haider-Markel & Joslyn, 2001). Framing issues in moral terms has a measurable effect on attitudes. Indeed, even fictional representations of moral framing on abortion have been shown to influence attitudes (Mulligan & Habel, 2011).

Walter Fisher takes the idea of framing a step further when he argues that moral values can be used to frame any issue. Fisher wrote that "public moral argument is moral in the sense that it is founded in ultimate questions—of life and death, of how persons should be defined and treated, of preferred patterns of living" (Fisher, 1984: 12). As such, any issue can be potentially framed in moral terms. Indeed, Christian Spielvogel argues that "[w]hen used in political discourse, frames rooted in moral values invite audiences to interpret political issues and programs based on their own deeply rooted cultural standards of what is considered right or wrong in human conduct, action, and character" (Spielvogel, 2005: 551). He demonstrates, for example, how President George W. Bush framed the War on Terrorism and the Iraq War in explicitly religious moral terms (a battle between good and evil) during the 2004 presidential election, which aided in his reelection. Other studies have demonstrated a similar effect of moral framing on attitudes about climate change and conservation, especially among conservative respondents (Wolsko, Ariceaga, & Seiden, 2016), but examples can be found throughout the social sciences in a variety of issue contexts (Knill, 2013; Permoser, 2019).

A bit grander in scope relative to issue framing is Amitai Etzioni's development of the Moral Dialogue model, which combines perspectives from across the social sciences. Moral dialogues are:

> social processes through which people form new shared moral understandings. These dialogues typically are passionate, disorderly, and without a clear starting point or conclusion (in contrast to elections or debates in a legislature). However, moral dialogues often do lead to profound changes in the moral positions of those who are engaged in them. (Etzioni, 2018: 6)

Etzioni's description of Moral Dialogue suggests these are metalevel debates that can shape our understanding of a particular issue or a set of issues based on our emotional understandings of the principles at stake rather than facts or statements of logic. Etzioni uses same-sex marriage as an example. He suggests that the baseline moral dialogue about same-sex marriage prior to the 1990s saw same-sex unions as wrong, with marriage between a man and a woman as right. Several focusing events—or what he calls sociological dialog starters, including court decisions—helped to ensure that this dominant moral understanding was enshrined in state and federal law in the 1990s. But additional legislative and court action in favor of same-sex unions in the early 2000s, which had backlash effects, also changed the focus of the debate to allow for a broader recognition of same-sex love and families. Campaigns for state constitutional bans on same-sex marriage, a number of court decisions in favor of same-sex marriage, and an increasing number of positive representations of gay people and couples in popular culture media led many Americans to reconsider the merits of the bans. These events and trends also demonstrated to some Americans that same-sex marriages did not lead to the apocalyptic societal outcomes that opponents had suggested. All of this helped to shift the emotional responses of many people to same-sex marriage, which paved the way for significant attitude change and subsequent policy change. The new moral dialogue was one where a majority of the public supported same-sex unions (Etzioni, 2018).

However, Etzioni's Moral Dialogue model is not predictive: It can explain how new moral dialogues have emerged in the past, but it cannot predict the likelihood of a new moral dialogue supplanting an existing one in the future or explain what conditions are necessary for such a transition to occur. For example, he suggests that the rapid emergence of transgender issue rights in the 2010s may be indicative of a new emerging moral dialogue around transgender issues (Etzioni, 2018), but setbacks for transgender military service and the rejection of transgender civil rights protections in some states suggest that a tipping point has not been reached (Haider-Markel et al., 2019).

MORALITY POLITICS AND POLICY LITERATURE

Throughout this volume, the authors reference examples from a subfield of the literature often referred to as Morality Politics, Morality Policy (Easterly, 2019; Haider-Markel & Meier, 1996; Meier, 1994; Mooney & Lee, 1995; Sharp, 2005), or sometimes Social Regulatory Policy (Tatalovich, Daynes, & Lowi, 2014). Much of this research is focused on the traditional culture war issues, such as abortion and gay rights. At its core, the theoretical perspective suggests that Theodore Lowi's policy typology has merit—the type of policy being considered determines the pattern of politics involved in the policy formulation, adoption, and implementation process (Lowi, 1969). At its core, Morality Policy involves any issue where at least one set of actors defines an issue in terms of morality—often based in religious principles (Meier, 1994). This process of framing centers the struggle around core values, which tends to make conflict more intense and also to make compromise more difficult. Because core values are at stake, factual or technical information becomes less relevant, and attitudes are shaped by the emotional connection to the core values involved (Mooney, 2000). The emotional connection for citizens makes engagement and participation in the political process more likely (Haider-Markel & Meier, 1996). As citizens are mobilized around the issue, political parties are forced to stake out positions, often polarizing, that help to define the perceptions of the parties (Lindaman & Haider-Markel, 2002). In such cases of high citizen participation and party polarization, the relative power of interest groups and government bureaucrats becomes less relevant in determining policy outcomes (Easterly, 2019; Haider-Markel et al., 2019).

THE SCOPE OF THIS PROJECT

This volume consists of contributions by scholars from many disciplines who explore the role of morality in politics across dozens of thematic issue areas throughout American history. Some of these issues remain in the headlines today, while others have largely fallen out of the public discourse. Throughout, the authors have done their best to present the debates objectively. Our goal is to trace these histories in order to better understand how framing issues in moral terms advances as well as inhibits public debate in a democracy. In terms of coverage, we felt compelled to include the standard issues that have comprised the core elements of the culture wars since the 1980s: abortion and reproductive rights, religion in the public space, LGBT (lesbian, gay, bisexual, and transgender) issues, and guns. Other areas, such as animal rights, sex education, and surveillance would be less obvious to the casual observer of American politics, but as we show, each of these issues has also been peppered with attempts to frame public understanding in moral terms—and often to create a new, shared, moral understanding of the issue or underlying principles. Our hope is that each of the essays will provide readers with an introduction to the issue, some of the main ways it has been framed along a moral dimension, and inspire further investigation.

FURTHER READING

Baumgartner, Frank R., & Bryan D. Jones. 1993. *Agendas and Instability in American Politics*. Chicago: University of Chicago Press.
Burns, Gene. 2005. *The Moral Veto: Framing Contraception, Abortion, and Cultural Pluralism in the United States*. New York: Cambridge University Press.

Chong, Dennis, & James N. Druckman. 2007. "Framing Theory." *Annual Review Political Science*, *10*: 103–126.

Easterly, Bianca. 2019. *The Chronic Silence of Political Parties in End of Life Policymaking in the United States*. Lanham, MD: Lexington Books.

Etzioni, Amitai. 2018. "Moral Dialogs." *The Social Science Journal*, *55*(1): 6–18.

Etzioni, Amitai. 1988. *Moral Dimension: Toward a New Economics*. New York: Free Press.

Fisher, Walter R. 1984. "Narration as Human Communication Paradigm: The Case of Public Moral Argument." *Communication Monographs*, *51*(1): 1–22.

Haider-Markel, Donald P., & Kenneth J. Meier. 1996. "The Politics of Gay and Lesbian Rights: Expanding the Scope of the Conflict." *Journal of Politics*, *58*(2): 332–349.

Haider-Markel, Donald P., Jami Taylor, Andrew Flores, Daniel Lewis, Patrick Miller, & Barry Tadlock. 2019. "Morality Politics and New Research on Transgender Politics and Public Policy." *The Forum*. https://doi.org/10.1515/for-2019-0004

Hurka, Steffen, Christian Adam, & Christoph Knill. 2017. "Is Morality Policy Different? Testing Sectoral and Institutional Explanations of Policy Change." *Policy Studies Journal*, *45*(4): 688–712.

Knill, Christoph. 2013. "The Study of Morality Policy: Analytical Implications from a Public Policy Perspective." *Journal of European Public Policy*, *20*(3): 309–317.

Kreitzer, Rebecca J. 2015. "Politics and Morality in State Abortion Policy." *State Politics & Policy Quarterly*, *15*(1): 41–66.

Lindaman, Kara, & Donald P. Haider-Markel. 2002. "Issue Evolution, Political Parties, and the Culture Wars." *Political Research Quarterly*, *55*(1): 91–110.

Lowi, Theodore. 1969. *The End of Liberalism*. New York: Norton.

Meier, Kenneth J. 1994. *The Politics of Sin: Drugs, Alcohol and Public Policy*. Armonk, NY: M. E. Sharpe.

Mooney, Christopher Z. 2000. "The Decline of Federalism and the Rise of Morality-Policy Conflict in the United States." *Publius* (Winter–Spring): 171–188.

Mooney, Christopher Z., & Mei-Hsien Lee. 2000. "The Influence of Values on Consensus and the Contentious Morality Policy: U.S. Death Penalty Reform, 1956–1982." *Journal of Politics*, *62*(1): 223–239.

Mooney, Christopher Z., & Mei-Hsien Lee. 1995. "Legislating Morality in the American States: The Case of Pre-*Roe* Abortion Regulation Reform." *American Journal of Political Science*, *39*(3): 599–627.

Mooney, Christopher Z., & Richard G. Schuldt. 2008. "Does Morality Policy Exist? Testing a Basic Assumption." *Policy Studies Journal*, *36*(2): 199–218.

Mulligan, Kenneth, & Philip Habel. 2011. "An Experimental Test of the Effects of Fictional Framing on Attitudes." *Social Science Quarterly*, *92*(1): 79–99.

Oldmixon, Elizabeth Anne. 2005. *Uncompromising Positions: God, Sex, and the U.S. House of Representatives*. Washington, DC: Georgetown University Press.

Patton, Dana. 2007. "The Supreme Court and Morality Policy Adoption in the American States." *Political Research Quarterly*, *60*(3): 468–488.

Permoser, Julia Mourão. 2019. "What Are Morality Policies? The Politics of Values in a Post-secular World." *Political Studies Review*. https://doi.org/10.1177/1478929918816538

Pierce, Patrick A., & Donald E. Miller. 2004. *Gambling Politics: State Government and the Business of Betting*. Boulder, CO: Lynne Rienner.

Sharp, Elaine B. 2002. "Culture, Institutions, and Urban Officials' Responses to Morality Issues." *Political Research Quarterly*, *55*(4): 861–844.

Sharp, Elaine B. 2005. *Morality Politics in American Cities*. Lawrence: University of Kansas Press.

Smith, T. Alexander, & Raymond Tatalovich. 2003. *Cultures at War: Moral Conflicts in Western Democracies*. Peterborough, ON: Broadview.

Spielvogel, Christian. 2005. "'You Know Where I Stand': Moral Framing of the War on Terrorism and the Iraq War in the 2004 Presidential Campaign." *Rhetoric & Public Affairs*, *8*(4): 549–569.

Stone, Deborah A. 1989. "Causal Stories and the Formation of Policy Agendas." *Political Science Quarterly*, *104*(2): 281–300.

Tatalovich, Raymond, Byron W. Daynes, & Theodore J. Lowi. (4th ed.). 2014. *Moral Controversies in American Politics*. New York: Routledge.

Taylor, Jami Kathleen, Daniel C. Lewis, & Donald P. Haider-Markel. 2018. *The Remarkable Rise of Transgender Rights*. Ann Arbor: University of Michigan Press.

Wolsko, Christopher, Hector Ariceaga, & Jesse Seiden. 2016. "Red, White, and Blue Enough to Be Green: Effects of Moral Framing on Climate Change Attitudes and Conservation Behaviors." *Journal of Experimental Social Psychology*, *65*: 7–19.

Abortion

Abortion has become a fixed item in the agenda of American politics. In the last 50 years, proponents and opponents of abortion rights have argued their case in front of Congress, in the courts, and in the streets of the United States. With morality at its heart, the abortion controversy has mobilized and polarized the nation along prolife and prochoice lines. Prolife activists have sought to restrict abortion access as a means to protect prenatal life. Prochoice advocates, on the other hand, have defended a woman's right to decide matters of maternity. As both sides have articulated their position, questions of bodily autonomy, self-determination, women's health, and personhood have featured prominently in the abortion debate. With undying attention from legislative bodies and the public, the seemingly intractable issue of abortion is deeply embedded in today's American culture.

From the mid-19th century until the early 1970s, the deliberate termination of a pregnancy in the United States was a criminal offense. Nevertheless, until the end of World War II, abortion was common and rarely prosecuted relative to the number of performed procedures (Solinger, 1996, 1998). In the post–World War II era, pregnancy and abortion became widely interpreted as moral issues, where women had the responsibility to be vessels for life, and intentional terminations were deemed immoral (Solinger 1998, 2000). By the 1950s, fewer doctors agreed to perform even medically necessary abortions for fear of prosecution. The scarcity, demanding requirements, and cost of legal abortion care, which frequently required sterilization as a condition to treatment, drove many women to rely on self-induced or back alley abortions (Solinger, 1998, 2000). Women's experiences with illegal abortions in the 1960s and 1970s highlight the scarcity of timely, affordable, and safe care, resulting in delayed termination and heightened anxiety (Gold-Steinberg & Stewart, 1998: 361). Similarly, women were often fearful of arrest and dubious medical care, as well as the common medical complications of illegal abortions (Gold-Steinberg & Stewart, 1998).

ROE V. WADE

Motivated by women's experiences with unwanted pregnancies and illegal abortions, many abortion rights activists organized to amend the law. Abortion advocates began to mobilize their interests to repeal the abortion ban in state legislatures. Although this strategy yielded some success, with the states of Hawaii, New York, and Washington legalizing abortion in the early 1970s, the movement soon redirected its efforts to pursuing a federally recognized constitutional right to abortion (Wilder, 1998). In 1973, the Supreme Court decision in *Roe v. Wade* transformed American abortion politics. Before *Roe*, most American states banned abortion at all points of fetal development unless the procedure was necessary to save the life of a pregnant woman.[1] The Court ruled that a ban on abortion is unconstitutional and violates women's right to privacy, arguing that individual privacy is protected against the interference of state law under the Constitution. Citing precedence of this protection in contraception and child rearing rulings, the Court extended this protection to women's abortion decisions. *Roe v. Wade* established that states could not ban or regulate abortion procedures during the first trimester of pregnancy. States could regulate abortion only during the second and third trimesters to preserve a woman's health and during the third trimester to protect the life of the fetus.[2] The Court also maintained that, although states could continue to ban abortion after fetal viability, understood as the time at which a fetus can survive outside the womb, exceptions must be allowed to preserve the life of the mother.

The so-called trimester model outlined by the Court in *Roe v. Wade* effectively distinguished between stages of fetal development during pregnancy. The Court's decision determined that prenatal life does not constitute a person and thus cannot receive legal protection. Only when prenatal life can exist independently from a woman may it be safeguarded by the law. Prochoice advocates applauded this change, which they described as freeing women from the undue perils of illegal abortions and recognizing women's right to govern their own bodies. The victory for prochoice activists, however, was short-lived. The Court's decision in *Roe v. Wade* propelled prolife activists into action.

Antiabortion activists were motivated by what they saw as an erroneous and fatal interpretation of prenatal life. In stark opposition to the fetal viability model advanced by the Court and many prochoice activists, prolife advocates believe human life is a continuum and begins at conception. From the moment a woman's egg is fertilized, forming a zygote, the zygote has all 46 chromosomes that make it a unique organism. Prolife advocates believe that a zygote is both human, as it has human DNA, and alive, as a zygote is a diploid cell, and cells are the smallest unit of life in living organisms. Accordingly, antiabortion activists argue that a

---

1. The terms "pregnant woman" and "mother" are used interchangeably in this chapter. Both terms have been politicized in the abortion debate context. "Pregnant woman" is often used by prochoice activists, while prolife activists prefer the term mother."
2. The terms "fetus" and "unborn child" are used interchangeably in this chapter. Both terms have been politicized in the abortion context. "Fetus" is often used by prochoice activists, while prolife activists prefer the term "unborn child."

zygote is a living human being and remains a living human being throughout all stages of development until death. For some prolife activists, by virtue of being human, the zygote is a unique, living, separate being. Inspired by Biblical references,[3] many prolife advocates also assert that God views the unborn as people. Furthermore, they believe that, as persons, developing human beings in the womb have intrinsic humanity and personhood that grant them individual human rights. Paramount among these rights is the right to life, which is violated in abortion.

According to the prolife position that the fetus has personhood, abortion implies the intentional termination of a human life and the death of a person. This perspective deems abortion an unjust and immoral choice akin to murder. Antiabortion activists argue that because abortion purposefully ends the life of a person, it should be prohibited and condemned by the law. Furthermore, they believe it is imperative to legally recognize and protect the full rights of unborn persons. Although prolife advocates recognize a person's right to make decisions about her own body, they argue that a person's right to life supersedes another's right to make medical decisions.

The argument of fetal personhood to assert the immorality of abortion has been challenged by abortion advocates and others. Personhood, they argue, is not an inherent quality of human life. Instead, personhood requires a level of consciousness, self-awareness, and thought that is only developed after birth. Therefore, asserting that a fetus is both human and alive does not support the claim that it is a person or that it has individual human rights. In *A Defense of Abortion*, American moral philosopher Judith Jarvis Thomson argued that the fetus "is no more a person than an acorn is an oak tree" (Thomson, 1971). Consequently, a fetus is not a person but rather has the potential to become a person after birth. At the same time, a fetus has no legal or moral rights; these are acquired only after birth or, in some cases, adulthood. Although many prochoice advocates subscribe to this logic, they also recognize the unviability of the fetus as a condition for abortion. Unless continuing a pregnancy would endanger a woman's well-being, few prochoice advocates sanction third trimester abortions.

Consistent with the ruling in *Roe v. Wade*, the prochoice perspective also denounced government intervention in women's wombs as a violation of their freedom and autonomy. Prochoice advocates assert that, because pregnancy and child care overwhelmingly disrupt a woman's body and life, women should have the moral authority to decide whether to carry a pregnancy to term. This position denounces the lack of self-determination women have over their own bodies and their inability to make decisions that would impact their future. The prochoice perspective holds that requiring women's bodies to support the development of a fetus with no regard for the women's wishes, health, employment, education, or family life equates to valuing a woman's biological abilities over her personhood and violates women's bodily integrity. Proponents of abortion argued that forcing a woman to continue a pregnancy against her wishes is akin to forcing someone to

---

3. Some of the most common biblical references noted by prolife activists include Psalm 139: 13–16, Jeremiah 1:5, Psalm 127: 3–5, Job 31: 15, Psalm 22: 10, Isaiah 49: 15.

donate a kidney or undergo a life-altering surgery without giving consent (Jarvis Thompson, 1971). Continuing a pregnancy, they argued, is no different from any other medical decision a person makes, and it is therefore morally wrong to force that decision without a woman's consent.

In opposition to this position, prolife advocates state that a woman's right to bodily integrity cannot supersede the right to life of the unborn child. In their eyes, women's temporary imposition during pregnancy cannot compare to the suffering and death of the fetus caused by abortion and cannot justify the termination of a human life. From the prolife perspective, women's personhood rights also apply to the unborn fetus. Thus, the unborn have the moral rights to life and to bodily integrity that cannot be violated by women's own rights.

SHIFTING ARGUMENTS AND STRATEGIES

The growing tensions between prolife and prochoice positions following *Roe v. Wade* preluded the incremental changes that would take place across the country. In 1976, Congress enacted the Hyde Amendment, banning the use of federal Medicaid funds to provide abortion services. This would be the first of many post-*Roe* legislative changes to restrict access to abortion. Following the Court's ruling that states could regulate abortion to safeguard a woman's health in the second and third trimesters, many states adopted a series of procedural obstacles to abortion access under the premise of protecting women's health. These included mandatory waiting periods for women seeking abortion, spousal notification prior to the procedure, and parental consent to abortion access for minors. Abortion rights activists contested these requirements, charging that they circumvented stipulations outlined in *Roe v. Wade* and thus violated the Court's ruling.

In 1992, the Supreme Court considered the question in a landmark case that would transform the standard for legislating abortion. *Casey v. Planned Parenthood* affirmed that abortion should remain legal in most cases, yet it also granted states power to regulate and limit abortion access in broader circumstances. The ruling in *Casey* eliminated the trimester model established in *Roe v. Wade* by granting states permission to legislate abortion throughout pregnancy to preserve the health of women, as long as regulations do not pose a substantial obstacle for women seeking abortion. The new so-called undue burden model formulated in Casey incited a flurry of legislative activity to restrict abortion rights in the United States.

In the 1990s, prolife arguments also began to shift their focus from the "unborn child" to the pregnant woman. With the goal of convincing the American public that abortion harms both the fetus and women's physical and emotional heath, prolife arguments began to highlight women's vulnerability when facing an unexpected or difficult pregnancy (Siegel, 2008). This argument suggests that women are often coerced or deceived into having an abortion, unaware of the long-term impact of the procedure. Prolife activists increasingly argued that abortion causes a woman to betray "her very nature as a mother to protect her child" (Siegel, 2008: 1653), resulting in deep emotional trauma and regret following the termination of the pregnancy. Therefore, there is a moral imperative to ban abortion to protect women from the psychological and physical injuries caused by abortion, as well as their "natural intrinsic right to a relationship with [their] child" (Siegel, 2008: 1654). This psychological trauma is often referred to as post abortion syndrome (PAS) by antiabortion activists. Although PAS is not recognized as a medical condition by the American Medical Association (AMA) and has been discredited in scientific studies, it reflects the lived experiences of many women in the prolife movement (Doan & Ehrlich, forthcoming; Munk-Olsen, Laursen, Pedersen, Lidegaard, & Mortensen, 2011).

Prolife activists successfully used this protection of the woman argument to influence the Supreme Court's decision in the 2007 *Gonzales v. Carhart* case, which upheld the Partial-Birth Abortion Ban Act of 2003. In this case, the argument was presented in an amicus brief introduced by the Justice Foundation, a prolife legal organization. The brief documents the testimony of 180 women who reported struggling with regret, depression, interpersonal relationships, motherhood, and religiosity in the aftermath of abortion (Doan & Ehrlich, 2017). The brief was cited by Justice Anthony Kennedy in the opinion of the Court, which stated:

> Respect for human life finds an ultimate expression in the bond of love the mother has for her child. . . . While we find no reliable data to measure the phenomenon, it seems unexceptionable to conclude some women come to regret their choice to abort the infant life they once created and sustained. . . . Severe depression and loss of esteem can follow. (Justice Kennedy, 2007)

Despite the admitted lack of scientific evidence to corroborate the assertion, the ruling in *Gonzales v. Carhart* legitimized post abortion syndrome and bolstered the women-protective antiabortion argument. Subsequently, several states adopted additional measures to "protect" women from abortion (Vanderwalker, 2012). By 2017, 35 states had adopted informed consent laws requiring women to receive counseling before an abortion (Guttmacher Institute, 2016a). Many of these laws also established longer mandatory waiting periods between the counseling session— the delivery of information about fetal development and the alleged risks of abortion publicized by prolife organizations in relation to mental health, fertility, and breast cancer—and the abortion procedure (Guttmacher Institute, 2016a). Similarly, 25 states also regulated the provision of ultrasounds to abortion patients (Guttmacher Institute, 2016b). Informed consent laws were not the only measures that proliferated in the states to protect women's health. By 2017, legislation requiring abortion providers to have some affiliation with a local hospital has been adopted in 11 states, while specific requirements for procedure rooms and corridors in abortion clinics have been adopted in 20 states (Guttmacher Institute, 2016c).

Proponents of abortion rights argue that these requirements pose an undue burden on women wishing to terminate their pregnancy. Laws requiring abortion providers to have admitting privileges at local hospitals or clinics to comply with ambulatory surgical centers can be prohibitive, and they have caused several clinics to close, leaving women in some areas without abortion access. Furthermore, restrictions to abortion care affects women inequitably. Low-income women have fewer means to afford the extended travel or multiple trips required to receive care outside of their communities. Job insecurity and lack of child care resources can also deter women from seeking or delaying abortion care, which can increase the overall cost of the procedure.Since 2011, legislation introduced under the premise of protecting women has once again been challenged at the Supreme Court level, resulting in a more favorable ruling for abortion rights advocates. In 2016, the Court ruled in the case of *Whole Woman's Health v. Hellerstedt*, finding that Texas regulations requiring abortion physicians to have admitting privileges to a nearby hospital and to maintain ambulatory surgical center–level facilities did not benefit women's health and placed an undue burden on women seeking abortions. This decision strengthens *Casey*'s undue burden model after decades of erosion and imposes greater limits on states' ability to restrict abortion access (Greenhouse & Siegel, 2016).

Carolina Costa Candal

FURTHER READING

Doan, A. E. 2007. *Opposition & Intimidation: The Abortion Wars & Strategies of Political Harassment.* Ann Arbor: University of Michigan Press.

Doan, A. E., & S. Ehrlich. 2017. "Teaching Morality by Teaching Science: Religiosity and Abortion Regret." In L. Campo-Engelstein & P. Burcher (Eds.), *New Challenges and Conversations in Reproductive Ethics*, 117–136. Berlin: Springer.

Gold-Steinberg, S., & A. J. Stewart. 1998. "Psychologies of Abortion, Implications of a Changing Context." In R. Solinger (Ed.), *Abortion Wars: A Half-Century of Struggle 1950–2000*, 356–373. Berkeley: University of California Press.

Greenhouse, L., & R. Siegel. 2016. *The Difference a Whole Woman Makes: Protection for the Abortion Right After Whole Woman's Health* (SSRN Scholarly Paper No. ID 2838562). Rochester, NY: Social Science Research Network. Retrieved from https://papers.ssrn.com/abstract=2838562

Guttmacher Institute. 2016a. "Counseling and Waiting Periods for Abortion." March 14. Retrieved from https://www.guttmacher.org/state-policy/explore/counseling-and-waiting-periods-abortion

Guttmacher Institute. 2016b. "Requirements for Ultrasound." March 14. Retrieved from https://www.guttmacher.org/state-policy/explore/requirements-ultrasound

Guttmacher Institute. 2016c. "Targeted Regulation of Abortion Providers." March 14. Retrieved from https://www.guttmacher.org/state-policy/explore/targeted-regulation-abortion-providers

Jefferis, J. L. 2011. *Armed for Life: The Army of God and Anti-abortion Terror in the United States.* Santa Barbara, CA: Praeger.

Justice Kennedy. *Gonzales v. Carhart* (Justice Kennedy, Opinion of the Court), U.S. (U.S. Supreme Court 2007). Retrieved from https://www.law.cornell.edu/supct/html/05-380.ZO.html

Munk-Olsen, T., T. M. Laursen, C. B. Pedersen, Ø. Lidegaard, & P. B. Mortensen. 2011. "Induced First-trimester Abortion and Risk of Mental Disorder." *New England Journal of Medicine, 364*(4): 332–339.

Roberts, D. E. 1997. *Killing the Black Body: Race, Reproduction, and the Meaning of Liberty* (1st ed.). New York: Vintage Books.

Rose, M. 2011. "Pro-Life, Pro-Woman? Frame Extension in the American Antiabortion Movement." *Journal of Women, Politics & Policy, 32*(1): 1–27. https://doi.org/10.1080/1554477X.2011.537565

Siegel, R. B. 2008. "The Right's Reasons: Constitutional Conflict and the Spread of Woman-protective AntiAbortion Argument." *Duke Law Journal, 57*(6): 1641–1692.

Siegel, R. B. 2007. "The New Politics of Abortion: A Quality Analysis of Woman-Protective Abortion Restrictions." *University of Illinois Law Review, 2007*: 991.

Solinger, R. 1996. *The Abortionist: A Woman Against the Law.* Berkeley: University of California Press.

Solinger, R. (Ed.). 1998. *Abortion Wars: A Half Century of Struggle, 1950–2000.* Berkeley: University of California Press.

Solinger, R. 2000. *Wake Up Little Susie* (2nd Routledge pbk. ed.). New York: Routledge.

Thomson, J. J. 1971. "A Defense of Abortion." *Philosophy & Public Affairs, 1*(1): 47–66.

Vanderwalker, I. 2012. "Abortion and Informed Consent: How Biased Counseling Laws Mandate Violations of Medical Ethics." *Mich. J. Gender & L., 19*: 1.

Wilder, M. J. 1998. "The Rule of Law, the Rise of Violence, and the Role of Morality, Reframing America's Abortion Debate." In R. Solinger (Ed.), *Abortion Wars: A Half-Century of Struggle 1950–2000*, 73–94. Berkeley: University of California Press.

Wilson, J. C. 2013. *The Street Politics of Abortion: Speech, Violence, and America's Culture Wars.* Stanford, CA: Stanford Law Books, an imprint of Stanford University Press.

Alcohol Restrictions

Debate over the production, distribution, and use of alcohol in the United States has long had a moral component and easily fits what has been called morality politics (Meier, 1994). Political fights over the development of so-called blue laws (e.g., ordinances prohibiting the sale of alcohol on Sundays), society's response to drunk driving, the disagreement regarding drinking while pregnant, and underage drinking have all sparked political debates with a pronounced morality dimension. Even today, many counties in the United States still ban the retail sales of alcohol and allow only "by the drink" sales in bars and taverns as a means to restrict access to "demon rum" and other alcoholic beverages. Access to bars and taverns is also sometimes restricted to so-called members. However, these restrictions have as much to do with class, professional, ethnic, and racial segregation as they have to do with localized moral policing.

EARLY BLUE LAWS AND PROHIBITION

In early colonial times, the Puritans were responsible for laws preventing people from performing work on the Sabbath (Sunday) that would interfere with church attendance. Over time, these bans became known as blue laws, and many additional religious communities, such as Evangelical Christians, overwhelmingly supported them. Blue laws were designed to prevent "immoral" activities on Sundays, and over time the definition of immoral expanded to include such activities as "travel, smoking, drinking, gaming or sporting, all manner of labor, and . . . sleeping in church" (Hanson & Hanson, 2012). However, as new immigrants arrived in the United States, Catholics, Jews, and political progressives organized in opposition to blue laws, arguing these laws joined church and state (NABCA, 2018). The constitutionality of blue laws was not challenged until 1885 when the Supreme Court ruled that Sunday laws were good for the laborer, in *Soon Hing v. Crowley*. The highest court upheld blue laws as late as 1961, in *McGowan v. Maryland*, based on nonreligious reasoning. Despite criticism that blue laws violated the separation between church and state, the courts have ruled to uphold them under the notion that government intervention in this area has broader societal benefits.

Blue laws spread across the Eastern and Southern states with migration, but most territories and states stopped them at the Rockies. Texas is the westernmost state limiting Sunday sale, while Minnesota's blue laws were uniquely strict in the Midwest region (until 2017, when Minnesota repealed a long-standing law prohibiting liquor sales on Sundays). In the early 20th century, the Anti-Saloon League joined forces with the Woman's Christian Temperance Union urging local officials to pass prohibition laws based on the immorality of alcohol consumption but also on the public health harm caused by alcohol abuse (Kerr, 1996). These were the two most notable single-issue groups that eventually earned national influence to help elect enough supportive politicians to Congress to amend the Constitution.

The 18th Amendment to the Constitution, which prohibited the manufacture, sale, and transportation of alcohol in the United States, took effect in 1920. Supporters of a national prohibition on alcohol believed it would clean up crime-infested industrial cities, reduce the tax burden of prisons and poorhouses, improve health and hygiene, and return God to daily life. However, criminalizing alcohol—Prohibition—came with serious side effects. "Alcohol became more dangerous to consume; crime increased and became 'organized'; the court and prison systems were stretched to the breaking point; and corruption of public officials was rampant" (Thornton, 1991: 1). During the roughly 13 years of prohibition, in fact, poisoning from toxic batches of alcohol soared, and American organized crime flourished. As the country realized the magnitude of these unintended consequences, public opinion turned against Prohibition, and politicians took heed. In 1933, with support from President Franklin Roosevelt, the 21st Amendment was ratified, and the manufacture, sale, and consumption of alcohol became legal in America once again.

Since the end of Prohibition, many states have liberalized their bans on Sunday sale of liquor, but as of 1990, 29 states and the District of Columbia still banned the Sunday sale of alcohol (Lowenheim & Steefel, 2011). In the most recent wave of liberalization, Minnesota became the 39th state allowing the sale of alcohol on Sundays in 2017, just in time for Super Bowl LII in Minneapolis (Distilled Spirits Council, 2017). Indiana, which had a unique list of blue laws, even banning carryout sale, repealed its laws in 2017 (Clairborne, 2018). Interestingly, efforts to change Indiana's blue laws were blocked by the lone state Senator Ron Alting for nearly a decade, until the Indiana Association of Beverage Retailers got behind the proposed legislation (Cook & King, 2018).

Although most blue laws were supported by religious groups arguing that alcohol is an immoral vice, secular reasons for keeping blue laws are still popular in some areas. Some observers have argued that eliminating these laws could have an adverse effect on public health and safety, could increase consumption, and increase cost to local businesses (*New York Times*, 1984). Meanwhile, the push to liberalize blue laws has come from a coalition of consumers desiring convenience, retailers; from public officials pursuing new tax revenue with higher taxes on "sin" items like alcohol; and from a significant decline in public debate over the morality of alcohol use (NABCA, 2018).

DRINKING WHILE PREGNANT

Alcohol has regularly been targeted as a social problem in the United States, although during colonial times, Puritan clerics actually hailed alcohol as "the Good Creature of God" (Levine, 1983). This view of alcohol lasted into the early 1800s, when the antidrinking reform movement emerged in response to increases in crime, poverty, diseases, and the distortion of traditional family life due to rapid industrialization (Armstrong & Abel, 2000). A century later, the turbulent 1960s resulted in antialcohol/antidrug crusades attributing the evils of crime to a breakdown in public morality (Engs, 1997). The media heralded this development as the "new temperance" movement, the "sobering of America" movement, or the "new abstinence" movement (Reinarman, 1988). Whatever the terminology used to label this new wave of morality, long-standing issues associated with alcohol abuse, such as child abuse/neglect and the victimization of children by those consuming alcohol, has garnered growing attention (Best, 1990). This focus on the harms done by alcohol to children was exemplified by the growing awareness of fetal alcohol syndrome (FAS). FAS emerged as an umbrella term for a variety of birth defects, including brain damage and stunted growth and development, associated with an infant's exposure to alcohol during the mother's pregnancy. The new temperance movement showed religious overtones as well. The effects of alcohol on the fetus have been known to experts since Biblical and Greco-Roman times (Abel, 1997), and modern society was criticized for failing "to heed the wisdom of our forefathers" (Hill & Tennyson, 1980). In the early 1980s, the U.S. Surgeon General began advising pregnant women not to drink alcohol, and in 1988, the United States became the first and only country to require warning labels on every alcohol container (Public Law 100-690). The panic surrounding pregnancy and alcohol had evolved into a crusade by the 1980s through the use of phrases such as "bruised before birth" (Steacy, 1989) and "child abuse in the unborn fetus" (Apolo, 1995).

The crusades against drunk driving and drinking while pregnant rested on similar underlying ideologies. Both these movements reacted to the turbulent 1960s' radical challenge to traditional norms with a renewed focus on the individual, personal responsibility, and lifestyle choices (Reinarman, 1988). Much of the moral arguments marshaled during this period centered on women making poor or uneducated choices while pregnant. Likewise, persons who drank alcohol and drove began to be portrayed as individuals lacking moral character.

DRUNK DRIVING

Prior to the late 1960s, most Americans, politicians, and judges did not view drunk driving as a criminal activity. During this time, alcohol consumption was considered part of the "good life" (Lerner, 2011), and social stigmas against drunk driving ranged from mild to nonexistent (Fella & Vosa, 2006). The federal government initiated programs to deal with intoxicated driving, however, after the U.S. Department of Transportation presented its 1968 report *Alcohol and Highway Safety*. This study identified drunk drivers as "problem drinkers" and a danger to public safety (USDOT1958).

During the last three years of the 1960s, Doris Aikens, a journalist, reported on two fatalities caused by an intoxicated driver (Lerner, 2011). She was disgusted by the courts' reluctance to prosecute DUI cases and formed Remove Intoxicated Drivers (RID), a precursor to Mothers Against Drunk Driving (MADD), advocating for driver sobriety (Loewit-Phillips & Boldbas, 2013). In 1980, after a serial drunk driver killed Candy Lightner's daughter in a California bike lane, Lightner created MADD to advocate for tougher sentencing of first-time offenders (Bartelli & Richardson, 2012). Aikens and Lightner soon began collaborating on bringing attention to drunk driving by staging public protests and publicizing the names of lenient judges and prosecutors (McCoy et al., 2012).

In the decades since MADD was founded, its grassroots advocacy against intoxicated driving has been a huge factor in shifting public perceptions about the seriousness of drunk driving (Fella & Vosa, 2006). The organization and its allies have even been cited as an important factor in reducing road fatalities. Between 1980 and 2010, alcohol-related traffic fatalities decreased from 30,000 (NHTSA, 2004) to 10,228 (CDC, 2013). Through its advocacy for sober driving, MADD has effectively changed impaired driving policies in the United States (Loewit-Phillips & Boldbas, 2013).

Much of the strengthening in drunk driving laws and policies across the United States took place during the 1980s and 1990s. Congress provided states with incentives to reduce impaired driving and set a blood alcohol content (BAC) of 0.10 or greater (Fella & Vosa, 2006) In 1982, President Ronald Reagan established the Presidential Commission Against Drunk Driving (PCDD) to formulate recommendations that would curb the drunk driving epidemic (Executive Order 12358). Two years later, he signed a federal law setting the minimum legal drinking age (MLDA) at 21 across the nation (U.S. Code § 158). MADD's influence on alcohol politics is best exemplified in its ability to convince President Reagan to choose the MLDA over 38 other recommendations from the PCDD to reduce drunk driving occurrences (Choose Responsibility, 2018b). Further, in 1990 the U.S. Supreme Court upheld the constitutionality of random sobriety checkpoints in *Michigan v. Sitz*. The advocacy work continued, and in 1996, President Bill Clinton signed a federal law requiring states to lower their BAC levels to 0.08 or lose federal highway funds. "To create global change, MADD's grassroots initiative had attacked the problem from several angles, including preventive efforts as well as advocating for the increase in the consequences of drunk driving" (Loewit-Phillips & Boldbas, 2013).

One of MADD's greatest achievements is the establishment of Victim Impact Panels. During these panels, victims and families share their stories with offenders to effectively communicate the devastating loss, trauma, anger, frustration, and financial loss they have suffered as a result of drunk driving. These panels are mandated for drivers convicted of driving under the influence of alcohol (DUI) in every state across the country (MADD, 2013). MADD has been uniquely successful in its mission due to its multipronged approach of educating the public, encouraging stricter drunk driving laws and prosecution of offenders, pressuring manufacturers to modifying their advertising, supporting increased taxation on alcohol products, and limiting the sale hours of alcoholic beverages (Fella & Vosa, 2006). MADD has also collaborated with Students Against Drunk Driving (SADD), although efforts to consolidate the two organizations failed due to MADD's philosophical position of jailing first-time DUI offenders (Bartelli & Richardson, 2012). For all of these reasons, Candy Lightner's MADD has had a transformative impact on American attitudes toward drunk driving. From the simple beginning of curbing the negative impact of drunk driving, this organization has played an important role in changing how society deals with—and views—drunk drivers.

UNDERAGE DRINKING

The remaining temperance movement successfully changed drinking policies in the 1980s by urging Congress to pass, and the president to sign, age limit legislation forcing states to increase the legal drinking age to 21. Six years after President Reagan signed the National Minimum Drinking Age Act (NMDAA) in 1984, every state in the country had changed their local age limits to meet the new requirement (Carpenter & Dobkin, 2011).

In the decade preceding the adoption of NMDAA, 39 states had set their drinking ages at 18, 19, or 20. These states saw a significant rise in motor vehicle fatalities (Wagenaar and Toomey, 2002). Although most of the moral focus regarding underage drinking has been on preventing youth from gaining access to alcohol, the Amethyst Initiative has recently called for reexamining the drinking age (Carpenter & Dobkin, 2011). The 21-year-old drinking age limit places the United States in company with repressive countries such as Equatorial Guinea, Mongolia, Oman, Pakistan, Sri Lanka, and the United Arab Emirates (Hines, 2018). Since a majority of the world's countries—more than 65 percent (WHO, 2004)—allow people 18 or older to purchase alcohol, the Amethyst Initiative has advocated for a reexamination of U.S. age limits on alcohol consumption. In the summer of 2008, over 120 chancellors and presidents of universities and colleges across America signed a public statement that irresponsible binge drinking was a significant problem on many campuses, made worse by a high minimum age (Amethyst Initiative, 2018b). Their goal is to reopen the debate surrounding the MLDA and the age 21 limit, due to current realities and the lack of effectiveness of the current law. Chancellors and presidents have witnessed students making choices that erode their respect of the law, when using fake IDs to engage in underage drinking (Amethyst Initiative, 2018a). President Emeritus John M. McCardell Jr. of Middlebury College founded Choose Responsibility in 2006 (Choose Responsibility, 2018a). These two organizations are the main advocacy groups seeking to lower the current minimum legal drinking age policy.

CONCLUSION

Many issues involving alcohol, such as blue laws, drunk driving, drinking while pregnant, and underage consumption, were not politically salient until after it was clear that the national prohibition of alcohol could not be sustained. The moral arguments concerning alcohol failed as religion took a less prominent role in public life. However, other attempts to moralize about the evils of alcohol have continued to manifest themselves in American political discourse.

Alexander Jorgensen

FURTHER READING

Abel, Elizabeth. 1997. "Was the Fetal Alcohol Syndrome Recognized in the Ancient Near East?" *Alcohol & Alcoholism*: 3–7.

Amethyst Initiative. 2018a. "Statement." Retrieved from http://www.theamethystinitiative.org/statement

Amethyst Initiative. 2018b. "Welcome to the Amethyst Initiative." Retrieved from http://www.theamethystinitiative.org

Apolo, J. O. 1995. "Child Abuse in the Unborn Fetus." *International Pediatrics*: 214–217.

Armstrong, Elizabeth, & Ernest Abel. 2000. "Fetal Alcohol Syndrome: The Origins of a Moral Panic." *Alcohol & Alcoholism*: 276–282.

Bartelli, A. M., & L. E. Richardson. 2012. "The Behavioral Impact of Drinking and Driving Laws." *Policy Studies Journal*: 545–569.

Best, J. 1990. *Threatened Children: Rhetoric and Concern About Child Victims.* Chicago: University of Chicago Press.

Carpenter, Christopher, & Carlos Dobkin. 2011. "The Minimum Legal Drinking Age and Public Health." *The Journal of Economic Perspectives*: 133–156.

CDC. 2013. *Centers for Disease Control and Prevention: Injury Prevention and Control: Motor Vehicle Safety.* Retrieved from www.cdc.gov/motorvehiclesafety/impaired_driving/impaired-drv_factsheet.html

Choose Responsibility. 2018a. Choose Responsibility. Retrieved from http://www.chooseresponsibility.org/about

Choose Responsibility. 2018b. History. Retrieved from http://www.chooseresponsibility.org/history

Clairborne, Matthew. 2018. "Last State to Bar Sunday Beer, Wine and Liquor Carryout Poised to Raise a Glass." *ABC News*, February 23.

Cook, Tony, & Robert King. 2018. "It's Official: You Can Now Buy Alcohol at Stores on Sunday in Indiana." *IndyStar*, February 28.

Distilled Spirits Council. 2017. "Distilled Spirits Council Applauds Minnesota Legislature for Ending Sunday Alcohol Sales Ban." March 2. Retrieved from https://www.distilledspirits.org/news/distilled-spirits-council-applauds-minnesota-legislature-for-ending-sunday-alcohol-sales-ban

Dorris, Michael. 1989. *The Broken Cord.* New York: Harper & Row.

Edman, Johan. 2015. "Temperance and Modernity: Alcohol Consumption as a Collective Problem, 1885–1913." *Journal of Social History*, *49*(1): 20–52.

Engs, R. C. 1997. "Cycles of Social Reform: Is the Current Anti-Alcohol Movement Cresting?" *Journal of Studies on Alcohol*: 223–224.

Executive Order 12358. 1982. *Presidential Commission Against Drunk Driving.* Washington, DC: Office of the Federal Register, 4–14.

Fella, J. C., & R. B. Vosa. 2006. "Mothers Against Drunk Driving (MADD): The First 25 Years." *Traffic Injury Prevention*: 195–212.

Hanson, Tina, & Robin Hanson. 2012. "State Blue Laws." In Wilbur R. Miller (Ed.), *The Social History of Crime and Punishment in America*, 1707–1710. Thousand Oaks, CA: Sage Publications.

Hill, R. M., & L. M. Tennyson. 1980. "An Historical Review and Longitudinal Study of an Infant with the Fetal Alcohol Syndrome." In F. S. Messiha and G. S. Tyner (Eds.), *Alcoholism: A Perspective*, 177–201.Westbury, NY: P.J.D. Publications.

Hines, Nickolaus. 2018. "The Legal Drinking Age in Every Country." February 2016. Retrieved from https://www.supercall.com/culture/legal-drinking-age-every-country

Kerr, Austin. 1996. "Temperance and Prohibition: Why Prohibition?" Retrieved from https://prohibition.osu.edu/why-prohibition

Lerner, B. H. 2011. "Drunk Driving, Distracted Driving, Moralism, and Public Health." *New England Journal of Medicine*: 878–881.

Levine, H. G. 1983. "The Good Creature of God and the Demon Rum: Colonial and 19th Century American Ideas About Alcohol, Accidents, and Crime." In R. Room & G Collins (Eds.), *Alcohol and Disinhibition*, 111–161. Washington, DC: National Institute on Alcohol Abuse and Alcoholism.

Loewit-Phillips, Patricia Melody, & Abbie Boldbas. 2013. "Mothers Against Drunk Driving (MADD): History and Impact." *International Journal of Childbirth Education*: 62–67.

Lowenheim, Michael, & Daniel Steefel. 2011. "Do Blue Laws Save Lives? The Effect of Sunday Alcohol Sales Bans on Fatal Vehicle Accidents." *Journal of Policy Analysis and Management*: 798–820.

MADD. 2013. Victim Impact Panels. Retrieved from https://www.maddvip.org

McCoy, T., P. Salinas, J. Walker, & L. Hignite. 2012. "An Examination of the Influence of Strength of Evidence Variables in Prosecution's Decision to Dismiss Driving While Intoxicated Cases." *American Journal of Criminal Justice*: 562–579.

McGirr, Lisa. 2015. *The War on Alcohol: Prohibition and the Rise of the American State.* New York: W.W. Norton.

McGowan v. Maryland. 1961. 366 U.S. 420 (SCOTUS, May 29).

Meier, Kenneth. 1994. *The Politics of Sin: Drugs, Alcohol, and Public Policy.* New York: Routledge.

Michigan v. Sitz. 1990. 496 U.S. 444 (US Supreme Court, June 14).

Mooney, Christopher. 2001. "The Public Clash of Private Values: The Politics of Morality Policy." In Christopher Mooney (Ed.), *The Public Clash of Private Values: The Politics of Morality Policy*, 3–18. Chatham, NJ: Chatham House.

Mooney, Christopher. 2000. "The Decline of Federalism and the Rise of Morality—Policy Conflict in the United States." *Publius*: 171–188.

NABCA. 2018. *National Alcohol Beverage Control Association: Sunday Alcohol Sales: History and Analysis.* Retrieved from https://www.nabca.org/sunday-alcohol-sales-history-and-analysis

New York Times. 1984. "The Crazy Quilt of Blue Laws." August 29: 6.

NHTSA. 2004. *Traffic Safety Facts 2002: A Compilation of Motor Vehicle Crash Facts from the Fatality Analysis Reporting System and the General Estimates System.* DOT HS 809 620, Washington, DC: National Center for Statistics and Analysis.

Plant, M. 1997. *Women and Alcohol: Contemporary and Historical Perspectives.* London: Free Association Books.

Public Law 100–690. 1988. 27 USC 201–211.

Reinarman, Craig. 1988. "The Social Construction of an Alcohol Problem: The Case of Mothers Against Drunk Drivers and Social Control in the 1980s." *Theory and Society*: 91–120.

Sandbrook, Dominic. 2012. "How Prohibition Backfired and Gave America an Era of Gangsters and Speakeasies." *The Guardian*, August 25. Retrieved from https://www.theguardian.com/film/2012/aug/26/lawless-prohibition-gangsters-speakeasies

Soon Hing v. Crowley. 1885. 113 U.S. 703 (SCOTUS, March 16).

Steacy, A. 1989. "Bruised Before Birth: Alcoholic Mothers Damage Their Babies." *Mclean's*, 48.

Thornton, Mark. 1991. *Alcohol Prohibition Was a Failure.* Policy Analysis No. 157, Cato Institute.

U.S. Code § 158. 1984. "National Minimum Drinking Age." U.S.C.

U.S.C. 105–178. 1996. "Transportation Equity Act for the 21st Century." U.S.C.

USDOT. 1968. *Alcohol and Highway Safety.* Washington, DC: U.S. Department of Transportation, Government Printing Office.

Vergari, Sandra. 2001. "Morality Politics and the Implementation of Abstinence-Only Sex Education: A Case of Policy Compromise." In Christopher Mooney (Ed.), *The*

Public Clash of Private Values: The Politics of Morality Policy, 201–210. Chatham, NJ: Chatham House.

Wagenaar, Alexander, & Traci Toomey. 2002. "Effects of Minimum Drinking Age Laws: Review and Analyses of the Literature from 1960 to 2000." *Journal of Studies on Alcohol*: 206–225.

Waldman, H. B. 1989. "Fetal Alcohol Syndrome and the Realities of Our Time." *Journal of Dentistry for Children*: 435–437.

WHO. 2004. *Global Status Report: Alcohol Policy.* Geneva: World Health Organization.

Animal Rights and Welfare

Following the 1975 publication of philosopher Peter Singer's highly influential book, *Animal Liberation: A New Ethics for Our Treatment of Animals*, the modern animal rights and welfare movement in the United States began to develop into a more prominent and significant social movement. In the decades since, the animal rights and welfare movement has attempted to raise national consciousness about the treatment and use of animals. Today, the animal protection movement is characterized by a wide diversity of groups, activists, and ethical and philosophical beliefs about how animals should be treated. Within the movement, issues of concern surround the key areas of vivisection (medical research on animals), the use of animals for food and clothing, animals used for entertainment, and the treatment of companion animals and wildlife, among other concerns.

GROWTH OF THE CONTEMPORARY ANIMAL PROTECTION MOVEMENT

The animal protection movement is characterized by a vast diversity of people and beliefs and encompasses groups ranging from the moderate to the extreme. During the 1980s, the United States experienced a marked increase in the number of animal protection groups; hundreds of new organizations were founded, many at the grassroots level. The 1980s also saw the birth of what would later become the world's most well-known and visible animal protection group, People for the Ethical Treatment of Animals (PETA). In 1980, Alex Pacheco and Ingrid Newkirk established PETA on the founding principle that "animals are not ours to eat, wear, experiment on, or use for entertainment." Although PETA works to eliminate animal cruelty and exploitation in all forms, it focuses most of its attention on the plight of animals in factory farms, research laboratories, the fur business, and the entertainment industry. PETA's first significant accomplishment came in 1981 when Alex Pacheco performed undercover investigative work at the Institute for Behavioral Research, an animal research facility in Silver Spring, Maryland. Dr. Edward Taub, the facility's lead researcher, had received federal grant money to research injured limbs on monkeys and in doing so severely abused 17 monkeys under his care. Pacheco secretly collected evidence of Taub's activities and handed it over to the Silver Spring police, who raided the facility, arresting Taub for animal cruelty. Eventually Taub was convicted of six counts of animal cruelty for his mistreatment of the monkeys. Although his convictions were later overturned on appeal when courts ruled that Maryland's animal cruelty law did not apply to researchers operating under federal funding, the case was still monumental. It was the first time in the United States that law enforcement raided a scientific laboratory and arrested a person who experimented on animals for animal cruelty. Pacheco's experience motivated other animal protection activists to perform undercover investigative work to support the movement's goals. PETA's involvement in the Silver Spring monkeys case thus helped jump-start the contemporary animal rights movement in the United States (Finsen & Finsen, 1994: 62).

Today PETA is the world's largest animal rights organization, with more than 5 million members and supporters. In addition to the work of PETA, there are hundreds of other animal protection organizations in the United States, both national and regional in focus. These organizations represent a wide variety of approaches and perspectives about tactics and focus, including the American Anti-Vivisection Society, Fund for Animals, Animal Legal Defense Fund, Last Chance for Animals, and the Humane Society of the United States.

ISSUES AND PHILOSOPHICAL BELIEFS OF THE ANIMAL PROTECTION MOVEMENT

With the sudden interest in animal protection issues in the 1970s and 1980s came a division in the larger movement between advocates who supported "animal welfare" and those who supported "animal rights." For people from both of these groups, ethical questions about animal treatment center on when it is acceptable to use animals for human purposes. Animal welfare advocates believe that humans have a moral obligation to treat animals humanely and to properly feed, water, and house them. Yet they also believe that animals may be used for human purpose and that their interests can be justifiably ignored when doing so benefits humans. Animal welfare advocates hold the position that animals "may be killed or subjected to suffering based on some consequential consideration" (Francione, 1996a: 42). Generally, animal welfare advocates view animals as means to an end rather than as ends in themselves. They find the raising and slaughtering of animals for human consumption to be ethical provided it is done in a humane fashion and animals do not suffer needlessly in the process (Singer, 1996: 17). Animal welfare organizations work to regulate the humane use of animals and are generally seen as the more traditional, conservative, and mainstream groups within the animal protection movement. These traditional organizations focus on ending "the unnecessary suffering of animals: the beating or starvation of pets by cruel owners; the use of carriage horses in extreme heat; the inadequate anesthetization of animals in scientific experiments; [and] the conditions of animals raised for food" (Jasper, 1996: 130), among other goals.

Whereas animal welfare activists advocate for the humane treatment of animals, animal rights advocates seek the total elimination of animal use by humans for any purpose, including food, entertainment, medical testing, and clothing. The advocates on the animal rights side of the larger movement believe that animals have intrinsic, basic rights that are equivalent to human rights and that treating animals solely as means to human ends violates the animals' rights and should not be tolerated, regardless of any potential human benefit. Because of this ethical view, animal rights proponents often utilize the legal language of rights to support their call for change, as have many other American social movements (e.g., the movements for civil rights, women's rights, LGBTQ rights) (Jasper, 1996: 136).

In contrast to the welfare-oriented organizations within the movement, the rights-oriented organizations focus on issues where the animals do not "always suffer obvious physical hardship" (Jasper, 1996: 131), such as confining animals in zoos, using animals as performers in circuses, using fully anesthetized animals for research purposes, and sheering sheep for their wool (Jasper, 1996: 131). Animal rights advocates often have anthropomorphic views about the suffering of animals based on their own observations of the ways in which humans suffer. They focus not only on animals' physical suffering but on their psychological and emotional pain as well (Sutherland & Nash, 1994: 180). While animal welfare groups are often seen as the more traditional groups within the animal protection movement, animal rights groups are viewed as more fundamental, extreme, or radical (Jasper, 1996: 136, 138). Some scholars have suggested that the ideological and psychological beliefs of many animal rights advocates about the proper treatment of animals function as a sort of quasi-religion in their moral crusade (Jamison, Wenk, & Parker, 2000; Sutherland & Nash, 1994).

REFORM STRATEGIES OF THE ANIMAL PROTECTION MOVEMENT

The diversity of the animal protection movement is often considered to be one of its strengths, and the movement is usually able to incorporate both animal rights and animal welfare beliefs without conflict (Ryder, 1996: 178). In fact, many supporters of animal protection measures "regard the rights/welfare distinction as involving a tedious and irrelevant philosophical distraction" from the overall goal of helping animals (Francione, 1996a: 42). Yet the distinction between animal welfare and animal rights "becomes problematic when it causes divisions [within the movement] over strategy" for bringing about change (Garner, 1996: xiii).

Even among animal rights advocates themselves, many disagree on what political strategy their organizations should use in order to reach their goal of ending the exploitation of animals, and advocates have diverged into a reformist arm of the movement and a radical arm (Jamison, Wenk, & Parker, 2000: 308). In the reformist arm, animal rights advocates believe that "any welfarist measure must be seen as a desirable stop along the road to animal rights" because of the great difficulty and significant obstacles in bringing about any change in the animal protection movement (Finsen & Finsen, 1994: 269). These advocates believe that in

order to be effective, they must focus their efforts on attainable goals (Finsen &
Finsen, 1994: 265), understanding that it is difficult enough to persuade key decision makers to adopt animal welfare measures, let alone measures for animal rights
(Garner, 1996: xiv). For them, animal welfare measures are a practical and necessary part of America's progress toward total animal liberation because of the realities of public opinion, coalition building, and political process (Francione, 1996a: 45).
Instead of outwardly working toward the goal of ending animal exploitation, they
focus on gaining improvements in the vivisection of research animals and in
establishing more humane methods of slaughter and better conditions for factory
farm animals, as well as many other improvements in the treatment of animals (Finsen & Finsen, 1994: 259). These compromises are celebrated as progress, not a
betrayal of the cause (Ryder, 1996: 192).

Some animal rights advocates disagree with the view that focusing on animal
welfare measures is a desirable and necessary step in the struggle toward animal
rights and argue instead that advocates should focus exclusively on ending the
exploitation of animals (Francione, 1996b). These advocates reason that securing
piecemeal reforms of the system instead of its outright abolition is "blatantly incon-
sistent with respecting the moral inviolability of those animals who are exploited
today" (Finsen & Finsen, 1994: 262).

Advocates within the animal protection movement are also split regarding the
use of violence to achieve their goals. The Animal Liberation Front (ALF), which
came into existence in the late 1970s, is an extremist and amorphous animal rights
organization with no public structure. It is composed of secretive cells of like-
minded people committed to helping animals through illegal acts. The ALF seeks
to directly help animals by breaking into research labs and farms to release animals and by engaging in damaging property belonging to people or businesses that
exploit animals. In some cases, ALF activists have caused millions of dollars in
damage. Within the movement, opinion about ALF's tactics is varied. Many dis-
approve of its violent and illegal activities, fearing public backlash against the animal protection cause. Yet other advocates and even some more mainstream animal
protection organizations have refused to condemn ALF's violent tactics (Masci,
1996: 686–687).

ANIMAL PROTECTION AND ENVIRONMENTALISM

The animal protection movement has often been compared to the environmental movement, as both movements seek to change people's attitudes from ones of
misuse and exploitation to ones of respect for the world and its inhabitants. In addition, wildlife conservation and the preservation of endangered species are important issues for both movements. Because the well-being of animals is interrelated
with the well-being of the environment, animal protection advocates and environmentalists are often natural allies working together. Yet there are also some fundamental divisions and contradictions between animal rights and environmentalism.
For animal rights activists, animals are believed to have intrinsic rights of their own,
making the individual animal of supreme importance. Animal rights advocates do

not believe in using animals to achieve human ends, despite any significant benefit to society as a whole. In contrast, for some environmentalists and most deep ecologists, giving up the lives of some animals to protect an ecosystem or for the benefit of the environment as a whole is acceptable and part of the Deep Ecology philosophy. Another difference between the two movements can be found in their views on vivisection, or animal testing, which is stringently opposed by animal rights advocates. Environmentalists still widely use animal testing to conduct risk analysis and to determine, for example, the toxicity of chemicals. Despite their commonalities, a primary difference between environmentalists and animal rights activists is that while environmentalists work to protect habitat, biosystems, and animal species, animal rights activists work to protect individual animals.

CONFLICTING IDEOLOGIES: ANIMAL PROTECTION ADVOCATES AND THEIR OPPONENTS

Some people do not feel an emotional connection to animals and hold different perspectives from those of animal protection activists about the basic nature of human–animal interactions. Opponents of animal protection often see human nature differently than animal protection advocates and view humans as "fundamentally predatory." They believe that in the struggle of life, humans need to look out for their own interests (Lawrence, 1994: 176). Humans are seen as unique among animals because of their "distinctive reasoning ability," and some opponents of the animal protection movement reason that humans should embrace their separation and otherness from other animals (Lawrence, 1994: 177). Countergroups also use quality-of-life and standard-of-living arguments to oppose animal protection advances, many of which they view as having deleterious economic impacts, especially on "long-suffering farmers and country folk" who rely on livestock to support themselves and their families (Munro, 1999: 48, 50). Many members of the farm employment community, especially those working in modern confinement-based, industrialized agriculture settings, often challenge the intellectual arguments of the animal protection movement and participate in intense lobbying campaigns against it (Rollin, 2010). For animal protection advocates, these types of farming practices are seen as a violation of the "practice of reciprocity and symbiosis between animals and people" (Rollin, 2010: 13). Yet animal welfare advocates, hoping to improve the conditions of farm animals and small local farmers, are sometimes natural allies, forming alliances around their mutual goal of preserving traditional animal husbandry, fighting against changes in the nature of agriculture, and eliminating modern concentrated animal feeding operations, commonly called factory farms (Rollin, 2010: 8).

Historically, animal protection advocates have had great difficulty in bringing about any political change in the movement. In all political arenas, they face difficult barriers and have found it challenging to turn increasing public support for animal protection into state and federal legislation or court victories. Well financed and organized lobbyists representing industries with a financial interest in the continued use of animals, such as the agribusiness industry, fur industry, biomedical industries, pet and entertainment industries, cosmetic and pharmaceutical industries, and hunting, fishing, and gun manufacturer interests, have all lined up in opposition to the passage of animal protection laws.

Even the limited policy protections for animals have spurred an enormous backlash from the animal use industry, which has created groups with misleading names such as the Wildlife Legislative Fund of America but also groups whose name makes their mission clear, such as the National Association for Biomedical Research. These groups have worked to enact policies to enhance their legal standing, increase their resources, and forestall future animal protection campaigns. Some of the opponents' policy strategies include limiting which animals and activities are covered by protective laws, placing the enforcement of legislation in the hands of agencies that are aligned with the industries they are monitoring, not providing agencies with enough funding or staff to do their jobs well, and allowing industry to self-regulate rather than operate under government regulation.

Along with constraining and subverting policies to extend protections to animals, opponents of animal protection measures also have initiated policies of their own in order to forestall future animal protection progress. For example, the Animal Enterprise Protection Act of 1992 made it a federal crime to cause physical disruption to the functioning of an animal enterprise resulting in economic damage and has been used to convict animal protection advocates of animal enterprise terrorism. In 2006, Congress passed the Animal Enterprise Terrorism Act, which expands the range of activities prohibited under the Animal Enterprise Protection Act, modifies the definition of animal enterprise to include pet stores and breeders, and increases penalties for offenses. Some states have also passed antiwhistleblower laws (commonly called ag-gag laws) that criminalize the exposure of animal abuse or cruelty on industrial farms. The fight against these ag-gag laws has united some animal protection advocates with people working in food safety, such as meat inspectors, who also oppose the laws and feel they prevent them from fully performing their jobs.

CONCLUSION

Individuals have been advocating for the liberation and protection of animals for thousands of years, and today the animal protection movement has become one of the "great moral struggle[s] of our time" (Pollan, 2002: 60). While the movement's early leaders and activists were often antiestablishment and sought to bring about social change by working outside the realm of traditional politics, the contemporary movement has matured politically and now routinely engages in sophisticated political tactics. The contemporary animal protection movement in the United States is more than just a political campaign; it describes itself as a moral crusade that seeks a revolution in the way we treat and relate to animals (Armstrong & Botzler, 2016; Garner, 2016). In the past several decades, it has achieved both social and political relevance, focusing primarily on campaigns against animals used for food and clothing, the treatment of domestic animals and wildlife, and the use of animals for scientific and medical research (Garner, 2016). The continued success of the animal protection movement rests on its willingness and ability to establish a clear understanding of its goals, to bring together a broader base of advocates, to sharpen its political and legal skills, and to frame its issues for the broadest possible appeal to morality (Palmer, 2008).

Mahalley D. Allen

FURTHER READING

Armstrong, Susan J., & Richard G. Botzler. (Eds.) (3rd ed.). 2016. *The Animal Ethics Reader.* New York: Routledge.

Beers, Diane L. 2006. *For the Prevention of Cruelty: The History and Legacy of Animal Rights Activism in the United States.* Athens: Swallow Press/Ohio University Press.

Finsen, Lawrence, & Susan Finsen. 1994. *The Animal Rights Movement in America: From Compassion to Respect.* New York: Twayne Publishers.

Francione, Gary L. 1996a. "Animal Rights: An Incremental Approach." In Robert Garner (Ed.), *Animal Rights: The Changing Debate*, 42–60. New York: New York University Press.

Francione, Gary L. 1996b. *Rain Without Thunder: The Ideology of the Animal Rights Movement.* Philadelphia: Temple University Press.

Francione, Gary L. 2000. *Introduction to Animal Rights: Your Child or the Dog?* Philadelphia: Temple University Press.

Garner, Robert. 1996. *Animals, Politics and Morality.* Manchester: Manchester University Press.

Garner, Robert (Ed.). 2016. *Animal Rights: The Changing Debate.* New York: New York University Press.

Jamison, Wesley V., & William M. Lunch. 1992. "Rights of Animals, Perceptions of Science, and Political Activism: Profile of American Animal Rights Activists." *Science, Technology, and Human Values, 17*: 438–458.

Jamison, Wesley V., Caspar Wenk, & James V. Parker. 2000. "Every Sparrow That Falls: Understanding Animal Rights Activism as Functional Religion." *Society and Animals, 8*(3): 305–330.

Jasper, James M. 1996. "The American Animal Rights Movement." In Robert Garner (Ed.), *Animal Rights: The Changing Debate*, 129–142. New York: New York University Press.

Jasper, James M., & Dorothy Nelkin. 1992. *The Animal Rights Crusade: The Growth of a Moral Protest.* New York: Free Press.

Lawrence, Elizabeth Atwood. 1994. "Conflicting Ideologies: Views of Animal Rights Advocates and Their Opponents." *Society and Animals, 2*(2): 175–190.

Masci, David. 1996. "Fighting over Animal Rights." *CQ Researcher, 6*: 675–696.

Munro, Lyle. 1999. "Contesting Moral Capital in Campaigns Against Animal Liberation." *Society and Animals, 7*(1): 35–53.

Palmer, Clare (Ed.). 2008. *Animal Rights.* London: Routledge.

Pollan, Michael. 2002. "An Animal's Place." *New York Times Magazine*, November 12, 58–64, 100, 110.

Regan, Tom. (updated ed.). 2004. *The Case for Animal Rights.* Berkeley: University of California Press.

Ricard, Matthieu. 2014. *A Plea for the Animals: The Moral, Philosophical, and Evolutionary Imperative to Treat All Beings with Compassion.* Boulder, CO: Shambhala Publications.

Rollin, Bernard E. 2010. "Farm Factories: The End of Animal Husbandry." In Daniel Imhoff (Ed.), *The CAFO Reader: The Tragedy of Industrial Animal Factories*, 6–14. Berkeley: University of California Press.

Ryder, Richard D. 1996. "Putting Animals into Politics." In Robert Garner (Ed.), *Animal Rights: The Changing Debate*, 166–193. New York: New York University Press.

Scully, Matthew. 2002. *Dominion: The Power of Man, the Suffering of Animals, and the Call to Mercy*. New York: St. Martin's Press.

Silverstein, Helena. 1996. *Unleashing Rights: Law, Meaning, and the Animal Rights Movement*. Ann Arbor: University of Michigan Press.

Singer, Peter. 2009. *Animal Liberation*. New York: HarperCollins (First Harper Perennial Edition).

Singer, Peter. 1996. "Animal Liberation." In Robert Garner (Ed.), *Animal Rights: The Changing Debate*, 7–18. New York: New York University Press.

Sunstein, Cass R., & Martha C. Nussbaum. (Eds.). 2004. *Animal Rights: Current Debates and New Directions*. New York: Oxford University Press.

Sutherland, Anne, & Jeffrey E. Nash. 1994. "Animal Rights as a New Environmental Cosmology." *Qualitative Sociology, 17*: 171–186.

Border Security and Immigration

National borders are a distinctively moral category. By their very definition, borders exist to separate. Borders separate the imagined "us" from the imagined "them." In other words, they are among the clearest distinctions made by a nation between inclusivity and exclusivity. As such, borders—and discourse surrounding borders—offer a unique window into the moral life of a nation. Borders lay bare the differences between those whom a country values and those who are not valued. Borders also expose contradictions in the morality of a country by juxtaposing a country's ideals with its actions. The United States prides itself on being a nation of immigrants, a country open to the "huddled masses" of the world. However, critics assert that this vainglorious sentiment is too often betrayed by restrictionist policies that seek to limit admission, reserving entry to only those who display the "right" moral, ethnic, religious, and other characteristics.

Borders are multifaceted ideas (Fassin, 2011; Menjívar, 2014). Borders are most commonly conceptualized as external, that is, as a physical boundary separating two or more nation-states. However, borders can also be internal, existing in the form of legal distinctions that impose the border on the everyday lives of those who have already crossed the physical border by defining their status in society relative to citizenship (Menjívar, 2014). Both forms of the border operate with their own mutually reinforcing security regimes and their own moral categories. Security is a value Americans identify with. The securitization of the border is wrapped up in the classic liberal idea that the state has the moral obligation to protect its citizens from threats. Yet the meaning of security has shifted over time. In the post–Cold War era, the meaning of security has changed to be one less of military security to societal security (Ackleson, 2005). This has translated into border security as well.

ATTACHING MORALITY CONSIDERATIONS TO BORDER ENFORCEMENT

Border enforcement has historically been linked with the moral character of those wishing to enter. For instance, the first U.S. immigration legislation, the

1875 Immigration Act, barred prostitutes and criminals from entry (Tichenor, 2002: 3). Later immigration laws barred polygamists, anarchists, "lunatics," and those deemed likely to become a "public charge," and eventually banned Chinese and other Asian immigrants (Tichenor, 2002: 3). As immigration laws became more complex and more restrictive, the need for these new laws to be enforced became clear. To enforce the country's new immigration laws, a border patrol force was established in 1924 with the mandate "to protect the national interest by enforcing federal immigration laws" (Hernandez, 2010: 17). The Border Patrol, as the main personification of the U.S. immigration enforcement bureaucracy, is an active agent in the creation of moral frameworks surrounding immigrants and border security (Rodriguez & Paredes, 2014). Prior to 1924, the United States paid very little attention to border security along the southern border. Indeed, only 60 Bureau of Immigration agents were stationed along the entire U.S.–Mexico border before that time (Lee & Yung, 2010: 250). And even when the U.S. government established the Border Patrol in an attempt to enforce new immigration policies, Border Patrol agents "were mostly concerned with stopping Asians and Europeans from entering without inspection" and "only selectively applied immigration laws to Mexican migrants" (Lee & Yung, 2010: 251). This selectivity was driven by the economic needs of employers in the Southwest who relied heavily upon Mexican laborers who crossed the border to work during the agricultural season and returned south after the harvest. Indeed, this seemingly transitory movement of Mexican laborers was one of the major ways in which agribusiness in the Southwest eased the fears of nativists who might have otherwise regarded them as threats. Mexican immigrants at the time were framed as "at least temporary if not contained, and their transitory presence in the fields of the southwest would benefit agribusiness without having any major or long-term impact upon American society" (Hernandez, 2010: 31). The idea that this migration was or should be circular was even later institutionalized through the implementation of the Bracero Program, a binational agreement between the United States and Mexico that allowed millions of Mexican laborers to work in American fields under short-term labor contracts (Calavita, 2010).

This arrangement existed for several decades, and it remained remarkably stable. However, the political and policy context surrounding the border began to change dramatically beginning in the 1960s and 1970s toward one of increased restriction. For instance, in 1965 the United States imposed quotas on the number of migrants who could get visas from countries in the Western hemisphere. The number of visas allotted to Mexico was set at 20,000, down from 50,000 in the 1950s (Massey et al., 2002). Additionally, the new policy did not offer any temporary working visas, which was a big departure from the 450,000 temporary work visas offered in the 1950s (Massey et al., 2002). Likewise, entrepreneurial policy makers began to frame immigration as "legal" or "illegal," thus constructing a new category of "illegal immigrant." So-called illegal immigrants were "invading" America, posing a threat to security, and providing an opportunity for terrorists and drug traffickers to enter the United States and cause harm. Public opinion also shifted, driven largely by media representations and elite discourse and framing around immigration. Around this time, the media constructed an illegal "Latino threat" narrative on the Southern border (Chavez, 2001, 2008). Media regularly depicted immigration from the south as a "flood" or "crisis" or "invasion" (Massey & Pren, 2012), even though immigration declined in the 1960s.

Accompanying changes in immigration policy and public sentiment, the United States also began to change its approach toward enforcing the border by militarizing border security operations (Dunn, 1996). The 1980s saw President Ronald Reagan's War on Drugs, which sought to crack down on drug users and traffickers. This new war also profoundly shaped the direction of the Border Patrol. Transforming border security into drug control "transformed the U.S.–Mexico border into an increasingly unpredictable, militarized, and violent worksite" (Hernandez, 2010: 230). By 2016, the border, once sparsely patrolled, resembled a demilitarized zone with approximately 17,500 border agents along the Southwest Border Sectors (U.S. Government Accountability Office, 2016), as well as a variety of surveillance and military technology such as drones, night vision equipment, surveillance cameras, and heat- and motion-detecting devices (Wilson, 2014). But perhaps the most visible manifestation of border militarization has been the construction and expansion of a border fence along the U.S.–Mexico border.

These measures have occurred not just by happenstance; they have been driven by enforcement policy and by Border Patrol operations. Specifically, two Operations—1993's Operation Blockade/Hold-the-Line and 1994's Operation Gatekeeper—forcefully increased border security along the U.S.–Mexico border. Operation Blockade/Hold-the-Line established the Border Patrol's current enforcement strategy of "prevention through deterrence," which actively sought to deter border crossers by diverting migration flows to the most hostile terrain (Dunn, 2009: 2). Further, Operation Gatekeeper, implemented by the Clinton administration, saw a considerable increase in the amount of money, border agents, technology, and fencing constructed in order to more efficiently divert would-be border crossers (Nevins, 2010). During this significant change in the U.S. approach to the border, however, "annual border-crossing deaths more than doubled" (Dunn, 2009: 2). All told, authorities reported more than 4,600 border crossing deaths between 1994 and 2007. The great irony of this increased security surrounding the border, however, is that some observers believe that it does little to actually deter border crossings while actually de-incentivizing the return of Mexicans to their home soil (Massey, Durand, & Pren, 2016: 1565).

Law enforcement agencies, the Border Patrol included, must maintain some form of legitimacy in order to operate. The Border Patrol's moral authority emanates from what has been dubbed its "bureaucratic ideology" (Rodriguez and Paredes, 2014). The ideological influence and power that the U.S. Border Patrol has over the border is witnessed by the fact that the U.S.–Mexico border is constructed primarily as belonging to the United States. In other words, U.S. immigration bureaucracy creates the view that securing the border is the moral duty and responsibility of the United States and that the "Mexican concern for maintaining the border pales in comparison with U.S. enforcement concerns" (Rodriguez & Paredes, 2014: 66). In other words, the Border Patrol is an active agent in creating the view that America and its border are under threat from Mexico. This construction serves to legitimate the work of the Border Patrol and its methods, as well as to justify its continued existence and funding. The Border Patrol's moral authority also protects its actions, no matter how much "collateral damage," such as increased border deaths, it produces, either directly or indirectly, as a result of its actions. According to one critical analysis:

> One of the functions that this ideological posturing serves is to preempt or deflate criticisms against the coercive bureaucracy when enforcement activities, or actions of bureaucratic agents, become excessive and lead to the deaths of unauthorized migrants. Because the bureaucracy has constructed a strong moral image of itself, whatever goes wrong from enforcement activity—including the deaths of migrants—should never be thought to be a nefarious or malicious action, as the bureaucracy casts itself as incapable of such action. (Rodriguez & Paredes, 2014: 70)

DEBATING THE MORALITY OF ICE ACTIONS AND POLICIES

However, the Border Patrol is no longer the only enforcement actor in immigration, and the physical border is no longer the only border that is being enforced. Increasingly, immigration enforcement is being delegated to local police departments as the border shifts inward. The U.S. Immigration and Customs Enforcement Agency (ICE) has developed and implemented programs, such as 287(g) and the former Secure Communities program, to enter into agreements with local municipal police departments. The goal of these programs, according to its advocates, is to conscript local police into the role of de facto immigration agents by enforcing immigration law during otherwise routine procedures such as traffic stops. This strategy was implemented most clearly in Arizona's now repealed SB 1070, which had required local police to inquire about anyone's immigration status during traffic stops or other interactions. However, the result was widespread racial profiling as police essentially had to operate on the basis of "those who 'seem American' and those who 'seem foreign'" (Glaser, 2015: xi). This has exacerbated an already existing situation in which immigration status is now comparable to race, class, and gender in terms of impactful social categorizations (Massey, 2007). Critics contended that such laws and programs also undermine trust in the local police as documented and undocumented immigrants increasingly fear deportation and no longer feel safe calling the police, even if they are victims of a crime (Becerra et al., 2016).

Despite the proliferation of new immigration enforcement mechanisms, as well as the increase in resources given to securing the border, perceptions of government inaction on the border persist. Driven by the narrative that America is under attack from a secret invasion from the South, this has led to the emergence and proliferation of vigilante groups, the most prominent of these groups being the Minutemen. These "moral entrepreneurs" seek to create fear and block the movement of immigrants in an attempt to redefine the borderlands as a moral, nationalistic space (Taylor, 2010). However, even some of those who do not feel compelled enough to join such a paramilitia group respond to appeals of lax border enforcement, as can be illustrated by the support Donald Trump received during the 2016 presidential election for his now infamous campaign pledge to build "an impenetrable physical wall on the southern border" and to make Mexico pay for it.

The primary moral actors defining border security and immigration are the president and his political party. The Border Patrol and other federal law enforcement agencies implement policies, but other moral actors are involved in immigration. Certain churches and faith workers have responded to the border and border violence with more of a social justice framing. To be sure, not every church responds this way. But the faith-based social justice perspective provides a counterframing to the border that is outside the main security framing that is dominated by the Border Patrol. Many faith workers' responses to the border draw on universalizing themes such as the dignity of all people and the right of all people to have access to life, food, shelter, education, mutual respect, and collaboration These faith workers draw upon interpretations of Scripture to make the case that Christ's journey is reflective of the journey many immigrants take; indeed, they portray Jesus as an outsider having crossed many different types of borders during his time on Earth (Menjívar, 2007: 119). This universalizing, social justice–based narrative often clashes with the security narrative, often in very visible ways, along the physical border. For instance, many of these faith workers take action in the form of setting up water stations for border crossers or patrolling the dessert looking for immigrants in distress (Menjívar, 2007: 115). These actions do not go unnoticed, and many of these water stations are vandalized or destroyed by the Border Patrol and private citizens (Border Action Network, 2008).

Morality is embedded within all laws and policies. But this is particularly true when it comes to immigration. Morality has an opposite: immoral, unrighteous, indecent. Recent political actions, specifically the series of executive orders signed in the early days of the Trump administration, represent a marked increase and expansion not only of the rhetoric of morality but of the corresponding border security policies.

Daniel R. Alvord

FURTHER READING

Ackleson, Jason. 2005. "Border Security Technologies: Local and Regional Implications." *Review of Policy Research, 22*(2): 137–155.

Becerra, David, M. Alex Wagaman, David Androff, Jill Messing, & Jason Castillo. 2016. "Policing Immigrants: Fear of Deportations and Perceptions of Law Enforcement and Criminal Justice." *Journal of Social Work*. doi:https://doi.org/10.1177/1468 017316651995

Border Action Network. 2008. "Supplemental Submission of Border Action Network on Its Petition Regarding Victims of Anti-Immigrant Activities and Vigilante Violence in Southern Arizona." Petition No. P-478-05. Retrieved from https://law.arizona.edu /sites/default/files/Border%20Action%20Network%20Second%20Supplemental %20Submission%20to%20IACHR.pdf.

Calavita, Kitty. 2010. *Inside the State: The Bracero Program, Immigration, and the I.N.S.* New York: Quid Pro Books.

Chavez, Leo. 2001. *Covering Immigration: Popular Images and the Politics of the Nation.* Berkley: University of California Press.

Chavez, Leo. 2008. *The Latino Threat: Constructing Immigrants, Citizens, and the Nation.* Stanford, CA: Stanford University Press.

Dunn, Timothy J. 1996. *The Militarization of the U.S.–Mexico Border: 1978–1992*. Austin: University of Texas Press.

Dunn, Timothy J. 2009. *Blockading the Border and Human Rights: The El Paso Operation That Remade Immigration Enforcement*. Austin: University of Texas Press.

Fassin, Didier. 2011. "Policing Borders, Producing Boundaries. The Governmentality of Immigration in Dark Times." *Annual Review of Anthropology, 40*: 213–226.

Glaser, Jack. 2015. *Suspect Race: Causes and Consequences of Racial Profiling*. New York: Oxford University Press.

Hernandez, Kelly Lytle. 2010. *Migra! A History of the U.S. Border Patrol*. Berkley: University of California Press.

Lee, Erika, & Judy Yung. 2010. *Angel Island: Immigrant Gateway to America*. New York: Oxford University Press.

Massey, Douglas S. 2007. *Categorically Unequal: The American Stratification System*. New York: Russell Sage Foundation.

Massey, Douglas S., & Karen A. Pren. 2012. "Unintended Consequences of US Immigration Policy: Explaining the Post-1965 Surge from Latin America." *Population and Development Review, 38*(1): 1–29.

Massey, Douglas S., Jorge Durand, & Nolan J. Malone. 2002. *Beyond Smoke and Mirrors*. New York: Russell Sage Foundation.

Massey, Douglas S., Karen A. Pren, & Jorge Durand. 2016. "Why Border Enforcement Backfired." *American Journal of Sociology, 121*(5): 1557–1600.

Menjívar, Cecilia. 2007. "Serving Christ in the Borderlands: Faith Workers Respond to Border Violence." In Pierrette Hondagneu-Sotelo (Ed.), *Religion and Social Justice for Immigrants*, 104–121. New Brunswick, NJ: Rutgers University Press.

Menjívar, Cecilia. 2014. "Immigration Law Beyond Borders: Externalizing and Internalizing Border Controls in an Era of Securitization." *Annual Review of Law and Society, 10*: 353–369.

Nevins, Joseph. 2010. *Operation Gatekeeper and Beyond: The War on "Illegals" and the Remaking of the U.S.–Mexico Boundary*. New York: Routledge.

Rodriguez, Nestor, & Cristian Paredes. 2014. "Coercive Immigration Enforcement and Bureaucratic Ideology." In C. Menjívar & D. Kanstroom, *Constructing Immigrant "Illegality:" Critiques, Experiences, and Responses*, 63–83. New York: Cambridge University Press.

Taylor, Lawrence J. 2010. "Moral Entrepreneurs and Moral Geographies on the US/Mexico Border." *Social & Legal Studies, 19*(3): 299–310.

Tichenor, Daniel J. 2002. *Dividing Lines: The Politics of Immigration Control in America*. Princeton, NJ: Princeton University Press.

U.S. Government Accountability Office. 2016. Southwest Border Security. Retrieved from http://www.gao.gov/assets/680/675522.pdf

Wilson, Dean. 2014. "Border Militarization, Technology and Crime Control." In S. Pickering and J. Ham (Eds.), *The Routledge Handbook on Crime and International Migration*, 141–154. New York: Routledge.

Civil Rights and Free Speech

Most Americans think of civil rights as those rights that guarantee equal treatment and opportunity in society for all citizens, including the right to speak freely, to exercise the vote, and be allowed due process in governmental proceedings. Of course, not all American citizens have always been treated equally, and the struggle for black Americans to defy racist beliefs and institutions and secure their full constitutional rights has largely come to define how we think of civil rights. Martin Luther King Jr. argued that it was a moral imperative that America fully recognize the civil rights of African Americans. By civil rights, King meant that African Americans should be able to enjoy the full rights and responsibilities of citizenship in the United States as provided for by the Constitution and its amendments. In King's 1965 words, "the arc of the moral universe is long, but it bends toward justice." During the long civil rights struggle of the 1950s and 1960s in the American South, however, some white preachers with racist and prosegregationist views used the Bible to morally justify the continuation of racial segregation and white supremacy. Each side appealed to moral considerations and practiced the American right to freedom of speech. Both sought to mobilize followers in a moral crusade and to demobilize those they viewed as on the wrong side of a moral red line. Today, Americans continue to evoke the power of morality as they debate the rights of citizens and who can lay claim to those rights.

The successes of the black Civil Rights movement have inspired other marginalized groups to seek civil rights protections, including women, Latinos, Native Americans, lesbian, gay, bisexual, and transgender (LGBT) people, and Americans with disabilities. Each of these groups has framed its claims to equal rights as a moral necessity, but only some of them have faced opposition on moral grounds.

The denial of basic civil rights dates back to the American colonies, the establishment and use of slavery, and the forcible takeover of lands from Native Americans. European colonists saw themselves as battling savages in a civilized crusade to tame the non-Christian peoples of the Americas. Indeed, many viewed the Native population as a subhuman species that should not be afforded the same human rights as white Europeans. As European colonists pursued their belief in so-called Manifest Destiny—the idea that white American dominion over the midsection of the North American continent was inevitable and divinely ordained—Native tribes continued to face suffering and death. Their lands eventually were taken by force and through laws such as the Indian Removal Act of 1830. Tribes were herded onto reservations and faced forcible assimilation in Indian boarding schools. The logic behind these assimilation efforts was, "Kill the Indian, Save the Man." The reservation system established by the Dawes Act of 1887 solidified the second-class citizen status of Native Americans even as it established them as individuals with property rights rather than granting rights to tribes. Other acts of Congress allowed for the establishment of tribal governing systems and access to public services and representation in Congress, but on most reservations these services, including education and health care, have not measured up to those available in nonreservation communities.

EMANCIPATION

The American colonies practiced slavery as a means for creating economic wealth and expanding Europe's reach within the Americas. By its nature, slavery denies a person her civil rights, and many Europeans viewed this practice as fundamentally immoral. However, some interpreters of Christian theology suggested that slavery could be morally justified through the notion of original sin. Since all persons are born with original sin, their humanity and related rights could be denied until they became Christians. Slaves in the Americas were largely Africans kidnapped from the northern and western portions of the continent, but some Europeans, including the Irish, were also forced to become slaves at least for a time in the American colonies.

The American Abolitionist movement began as the first colonists began making use of slaves. The early movement was founded in the religious traditions of Quakers and German Mennonites, who began speaking out against slavery in the 1680s. They argued that slavery violated the basic moral tenets of Christianity. By the American Revolution era, the Abolitionist movement had grown in the northern colonies-turned-states to the point that they took steps to formally ban slavery and adhere to the notion that slavery violated what Thomas Jefferson referred to as "natural rights." Most of these states followed Pennsylvania's example from 1780 with laws that would provide gradual emancipation to slaves or their children. In 1806, Jefferson asked Congress to criminalize the slave trade, telling them to "withdraw the citizens of the United States from all further participation in those violations of human rights . . . which the morality, the reputation, and the best of our country have long been eager to proscribe" (Jefferson, 1806). Effective in 1808, the United States made the importation or exportation of slaves a crime.

By the 1830s, abolitionists increasingly rejected the notions of white supremacy that were touted by Southern slave owners and accepted some notion of black equality with whites. This shift was partly enabled by the Second Great Awakening among Evangelical Christians, who aligned themselves directly with free persons of color who were fighting against slavery. They rejected the argument that slavery could be justified through a notion of "original sin," which had been previously held by many Christians (Tomek, 2004).

During this shift in beliefs among white abolitionists, the movement began to practice moral suasion in which they attempted to convince supporters of slavery of the "evils of the system" and encourage them to turn away from the practice (Tomek, 2004). In the 1850s, new laws and Supreme Court decisions expanded the possibility of slavery extending to territories that had previously been established as free from slavery and enhanced the right of slave owners to retrieve escaped slaves from anywhere in the country. In the 1857 case *Dred Scott v. Sanford*, the U.S. Supreme Court ruled that the Constitution did not recognize the rights of African Americans. Chief Justice Roger Taney wrote that black people were "a subordinate and inferior class of beings" with "no rights which the white man was bound to respect." These new policies and laws effectively denied citizenship to free blacks and convinced many in the North that slave owners were determined to expand the institution.

The moral outrage over slavery began to erupt in violence as settlers moved into the Kansas territories during the 1850s in order to vote on whether it would be a slave state or free state upon achieving statehood. As violence between the two factions escalated across what came to be known as Bleeding Kansas, the famous abolitionist John Brown joined his sons in the territory, where he justified violence and the killing of slavery supporters as a legitimate response to the fundamental immorality of slavery. In 1861, the Civil War began as a number of slave states withdrew from the Union to form the Confederacy and protect slavery. As a political move during that war, President Abraham Lincoln issued the Emancipation Proclamation, which freed all slaves in the Confederate states. Additional changes in law at the national and state levels freed slaves in other states and in Washington, D.C. However, slavery was not constitutionally banned until the adoption of the 13th Amendment in 1865. The civil rights of African Americans were more firmly protected from discrimination by the adoption of the 14th Amendment in 1868, which also ensured due process under the law for all American citizens.

Even with the end of slavery and the passage of new constitutional protections, however, the civil rights of African Americans were limited. This was especially true in the South, where a multitude of so-called Black code laws that limited the rights of African Americans to travel and work were passed by white lawmakers. The ideology of white supremacy that had been embedded in the institution of slavery motivated whites to resist black equality. First came the violent uprising of the Ku Klux Klan and white mobs against blacks trying to exercise their rights and against federal government officials during Reconstruction. Then came the so-called Jim Crow laws, which sought to segregate African Americans from whites and deny them the vote. Southern states also banned interracial marriage with statutes that stood until 1967, when the U.S. Supreme Court ruled in *Loving v. Virginia* that such bans were unconstitutional.

In 1890, Mississippi was the first state to pass laws that made it more difficult for blacks to vote, including statutes mandating literacy requirements and poll tax requirements that were specifically crafted to disenfranchise blacks. Other Southern states adopted similar laws, and the number of African Americans voting began to quickly decline. For example, in 1896 there were over 130,000 African Americans registered to vote in Louisiana, but by 1904 that number had declined to 1,342 (Menand, 2019). The U.S. Supreme Court upheld Southern segregation laws in a decision for *Plessy v. Ferguson* (1896), which established the principle that racial segregation is not inherently unequal.

Faced with the discrimination and restrictions of the Jim Crow South, many African Americans migrated north to find more economic and social opportunities. But in the North they faced a population that accepted some of the precepts of the moral guidelines of white supremacy that allowed for forms of de facto segregation in housing and schools. This form of institutionalized racism allowed whites in some areas to draw school and election boundaries to restrict black access to predominately white schools and neighborhoods, while also reducing their impact at the ballot box. In housing, banks and insurance companies, as well as some federal housing programs, followed a practice known as redlining, that is, the rejection of loan requests and other services, making it difficult for African Americans to move into white neighborhoods.

Modest efforts to reduce discrimination against African Americans occurred at the national, state, and local levels during the 1930s and 1940s. For example, the Works Projects Administration (WPA) during the Great Depression sought to reduce discriminatory practices in WPA programs. Perhaps most notably, after World War II, President Harry Truman came to view black civil rights in moral terms, describing the struggle as such in a 1947 speech to the National Association of Colored People (NAACP). Shortly after delivering that speech, President Truman issued Executive Order 9981, which desegregated the U.S. Armed Forces.

The racial discrimination codified in Jim Crow laws and upheld by *Plessy* largely stood until the 1954 Supreme Court decision in *Brown v. Board of Education*, which overturned school segregation laws in Kansas and across the country. The Court held that laws requiring racial separation were inherently unequal and thus a violation of the 14th Amendment. Evidence considered by the Court during arguments included social science evidence that African American children are psychologically harmed by segregation into believing that whiteness is superior. President Dwight Eisenhower hesitated to enforce the Court decision but by 1957 had to use federal troops in Little Rock, Arkansas, to force the integration of a high school. Eisenhower also signed into law watered-down measures in 1957 and 1960 to protect the voting rights of African Americans. The 1957 Civil Rights Act authorized the federal prosecution of anyone who tried to deny a citizen's right to vote and created a Civil Rights Division in the Justice Department to pursue prosecutions.

As the Civil Rights movement gained strength across the South, white violence against the activists—in the form of police violence, Ku Klux Klan terrorism, and hate-filled mobs of ordinary white citizens—shocked and disgusted many whites across the country. The sacrifices of black activists showed the violent immorality of racial discrimination and finally inspired Congress and the White House to take more decisive action. The integration of universities in the South began in 1963 with the aid of American troops. On June 11, 1963, President John F. Kennedy addressed the nation in a televised speech on the issue of black civil rights, framing the issue as a moral one. In part he said:

We are confronted primarily with a moral issue. It is as old as the scriptures and is as clear as the American Constitution. The heart of the question is whether all Americans are to be afforded equal rights and equal opportunities, whether we are going to treat our fellow Americans as we want to be treated. If an American, because his skin is dark, cannot eat lunch in a restaurant open to the public, if he cannot send his children to the best public school available, if he cannot vote for the public officials who represent him, if, in short, he cannot enjoy the full and free life which all of us want, then who among us would be content to have the color of his skin changed and stand in his place? Who among us would then be content with the counsels of patience and delay? One hundred years of delay have passed since President Lincoln freed the slaves, yet their heirs, their grandsons, are not fully free. . . . Those who do nothing are inviting shame as well as violence. Those who act boldly are recognizing right as well as reality.

President Kennedy's speech helped to reshape the discussion of civil rights in a moral dimension, in line with the arguments of Martin Luther King, Jr. and the Civil Rights movement.

The year 1963 thus marked a shift in tone, and, following the assassination of Kennedy in 1963, President Lyndon Johnson continued to frame civil rights as a moral issue. This line of argument proved helpful in convincing Congress to pass the Civil Rights Act of 1964. The 1964 Act made it illegal to discriminate on the basis of race, color, religion, sex, or national origin in education, voting requirements, employment, and public accommodations. That same year, the 24th Amendment was ratified, making the use of any tax in order to vote in a federal election illegal. Voting rights were further strengthened in 1965 with the passage of the Voting Rights Act, which was designed to reinforce the 15th Amendment and remove all existing state and local laws that had been erected to prevent African Americans from exercising their legal right to vote.

The struggle for black civil rights continues today, with activists and supporters continuing to frame their efforts as a moral imperative. Efforts to ensure an equitable playing field in society, such as Affirmative Action programs in hiring and education access, have been justified as morally necessary (Taylor, 2012). But some have argued that Affirmative Action programs go too far and violate the moral principle of equality by elevating one person or group over another (Fish, 2007).

FREE SPEECH

The first of the first ten amendments to the Constitution that were passed into law by America's Founding Fathers addressed speech, the news media, and religion. The First Amendment's limitations on the government's ability to regulate speech in the public square gave citizens the right to speak freely on the issues of the day without fear of official censure or punishment. Freedom of the press ensured that the media could speak for those without a voice and provide independent coverage of events and issues without government censorship. Freedom from government-endorsed religion further pushed back on a likely source of restriction on speech.

Of course, this liberty does not come without a cost or potential moral trade-off. Hateful speech, especially when directed at specific groups of people, is especially challenging in the context of a Constitution that prohibits government from restricting speech but also provides for the civil rights of individuals. Espousing the hate of a group and a desire to limit the rights of group members clearly violates the moral code of religious traditions as well as humanist logic. However, legal decisions in the United States have protected this right—provided that the intent of the speech is not to inspire violence against others. Since the 1969 Court decision in *Brandenburg v. Ohio*, which protected speech by a Ku Klux Klan member, courts have consistently followed *Brandenburg*'s assertion that "the constitutional guarantees of free speech and free press do not permit a state to forbid or proscribe advocacy of the use of force, or of law violation except where such advocacy is directed to inciting imminent lawless action and is likely to incite or produce such action." In other words, *Brandenburg* established an "imminent danger" of incitement to unlawful action test to which hate speech has been subject.

The desire for the law to reflect moral outrage over offensive ideas has continued. The only types of laws that have survived judicial scrutiny and that satisfy civil rights proponents are typically referred to as hate crime laws. Hate crime laws focus on the motives of those committing criminal acts and allow for crime classification and penalty enhancements in cases where a crime is deemed motivated by bias toward a group—typically a specific racial, gender, ethnic, religious, or sexual minority group.

CONCLUSION

Birthed out of the institution of slavery, the civil rights tradition in the United States has been most clearly associated with the struggle for African American civil rights. But the moral arguments central to the black Civil Rights movement has also been a pillar of the women's, Latino, Native American, LGBT, and disability rights movements. All have claimed that unequal treatment is immoral and must be corrected in a country founded on the basis of equality for all.

However, like the black Civil Rights movement, these campaigns have faced opposing morality-based arguments that their demands are immoral and violate "the natural order of things." Perhaps the women's movement and LGBT rights movements, with their challenges of gender norms and traditional definitions of institutions such as marriage, have faced the greatest opposition from defenders of traditional morality and "family values."

Efforts to restrict free speech, even when the speech seeks to restrict the rights and equality of others, have faced sharp resistance, even though most would agree that espousing hate for other groups is immoral. Even so, some states and the national government have signaled that hate is not valued by providing greater punishment for crimes motivated by bias toward groups.

Donald P. Haider-Markel

FURTHER READING

Altman, Andrew. 1993. "Liberalism and Campus Hate Speech: A Philosophical Examination." *Ethics*, *103*(2): 302–317.
Dred Scott v. Sanford, 1857.

Fish, Stanley. 2007. "Revising Affirmative Action, with Help from Kant." *New York Times*, November 14. Retrieved from https://opinionator.blogs.nytimes.com/2007/01/14/how-kant-might-view-affirmative-action/

Garber, Mark A. 2011. "Foreword: Plus or Minus One: the Thirteenth and Fourteenth Amendments." *Maryland Law Review, Special Issue: Symposium—the Maryland Constitutional Law Schmooze, 71*(1): 12–20.

Gardner, Michael A. 2002. *Harry Truman and Civil Rights: Moral Courage and Political Risks*. Carbondale: Southern Illinois University Press

Gates, Henry Louis, Jr. 2019. *Stony the Road: Reconstruction, White Supremacy, and the Rise of Jim Crow*. New York: Penguin Group.

Gates, Henry Louis, Jr., Anthony P. Griffin, Donald E. Lively, & Nadine Strossen. 1996. *Speaking of Race, Speaking of Sex: Hate Speech, Civil Rights, and Civil Liberties*. New York: New York University Press.

Gopnik, Adam. 2019. "How the South Won the Civil War." *The New Yorker*, April 1. Retrieved from https://www.newyorker.com/magazine/2019/04/08/how-the-south-won-the-civil-war

Jefferson, Thomas. 1806. "Sixth Annual Message to Congress." December 2. Retrieved from http://avalon.law.yale.edu/19th_century/jeffmes6.asp

Kennedy, John F. 2019. "John F. Kennedy's Address on Civil Rights." *American Experience*. Retrieved from https://www.pbs.org/wgbh/americanexperience/features/president-kennedy-civil-rights

Kennedy, Joseph E. 2009. "The Jena Six, Mass Incarceration, and the Remoralization of Civil Rights." *Harvard Civil Rights–Civil Liberties Law Review, 44*(2): 477–510.

Menand, Louis. 2019. "The Supreme Court Case That Enshrined White Supremacy in Law." *The New Yorker*, January 28. Retrieved from https://www.newyorker.com/magazine/2019/02/04/the-supreme-court-case-that-enshrined-white-supremacy-in-law

Mucciaroni, Gary. 2011. "Are Debates About 'Morality Policy' Really About Morality? Framing Opposition to Gay and Lesbian Rights." *Policy Studies Journal, 39*(2): 187–216.

Newman, Richard S. 2002. *The Transformation of American Abolitionism: Fighting Slavery in the Early Republic*. Chapel Hill: University of North Carolina Press.

Orozco, Cynthia E. 2010. *No Mexicans, Women, or Dogs Allowed: The Rise of the Mexican American Civil Rights Movement*. Austin: University of Texas Press.

Plessy v. Ferguson, 1896.

Starkey, Armstrong. 2002. *European and Native American Warfare 1675–1815*. New York: Routledge.

Taylor, Aaron N. 2012. "Retain Affirmative Action—Because It's the Morally Right Thing to Do." *The Chronicle of Higher Education*. October 8. Retrieved from https://www.chronicle.com/article/Retain-Affirmative/134914

Tinker, George E. 1993. *Missionary Conquest: The Gospel and Native American Cultural Genocide*. Minneapolis, MN: Fortress Press.

Tomek, Beverly. 2004. "Antislavery Movement, 1700s–1830s." In Immanuel Ness (Ed.), *The Encyclopedia of American Social Movements*, 3–17. Armonk, NY: M. E. Sharp

Waldron, Jeremy. 2012. *The Harm in Hate Speech*. Cambridge, MA: Harvard University Press.

Walker, Samuel. 1994. *Hate Speech: The History of an American Controversy*. Lincoln: University of Nebraska Press.

Wildcat, Daniel R. 2014. "Why Native Americans Don't Want Reparations." *The Washington Post*, June 10. Retrieved from https://www.washingtonpost.com/posteverything/wp/2014/06/10/why-native-americans-dont-want-reparations

Climate Change

Climate change may not initially appear to be a morality issue. However, both sides of the climate change debate have purposefully integrated morality in an effort to convince the public and decision makers that their perspective is right. This integration is facilitated by the ability of climate change to influence many of the issue domains that frequently involve morality debates. Unlike many morality debates, climate change does not involve the trading of accusations regarding the morality of the opposing factions. Instead, morality is used on the peripheral of the climate change debate to justify both action and inaction. As early as 1992, when then Senator Al Gore appeared on *The 700 Club* to discuss climate change, advocates on both sides of climate change have attempted to evoke morality to justify their positions. There exist three core arguments that require public support before decision makers are likely to legislatively address climate change. These revolve around the debate over whether climate change is real, whether it is actually a bad thing, and whether it is caused by human activity.

IS CLIMATE CHANGE REAL?

The most fundamental issue associated with climate change is whether it is actually happening. The scientific community has overwhelmingly accepted that climate change is happening. Numerous scientific organizations around the globe agree that it is a reality, and studies indicate that approximately 97 percent of climate scientists actively publishing in peer-reviewed journals agree that the scientific evidence overwhelmingly indicates that the planet's climate is changing (Cook, 2016). Evidence in support of climate change has been found through examinations of global and regional temperature change over time, ocean temperature change over time, regional climates, and a host of other indicators. In short, the scientific evidence suggests that the planet's temperature has been steadily increasing over time. The scientific evidence also finds that ocean temperatures have been increasing. Additionally, research has shown that large areas of land have been witnessing localized climate shifts. These shifts include situations where farmland or forests become deserts, while other areas are seeing an increase in annual rainfall. Scientists argue that these changes are happening too quickly to be naturally occurring and that human activity is the source. Despite repeated presentations of this strong scientific evidence, a substantial portion of the American public does not believe that anthropogenic climate change is occurring. Some skeptics believe that climate scientists are pushing the idea of climate change because they want to get more grant money from the government and are therefore conducting research that is biased toward "proving" that climate change is real. Others describe climate change warnings as a conspiracy to justify the expansion of the government through further regulation of the environment and the economy.

These false claims can be heard most ardently within the Republican party, including elected officials from the highest levels of government (U.S. House of Representatives Committee on Science, Space, & Technology, 2017) and are treated as plausible on the Fox News channel and other conservative media outlets. These concerted efforts to attack the credibility of climate scientists is relatively unique within the scientific community (Bromley-Trujillo et al., 2014). These climate change doubters have seized on the views of a small group of researchers—many of them industry funded—who assert that climate change is not happening, allowing those who support this perspective an opportunity to point to scientific research in support of their argument. (Recent research has revealed, however, significant methodological problems with all of the replicated research that suggests climate change is not happening [Benestad et al., 2016].) Regardless of why they do not believe in climate change, public opinion surveys conducted between 2010 and 2017 generally found that anywhere between 30 and 50 percent of the American public viewed the severity and risks of climate change to be exaggerated. While a substantial portion of the public continues to reject the idea of climate change, this number has decreased in recent years.

Although climate change might appear to be a primarily scientific debate, there have been efforts on both sides to marshal moral considerations for their cause. However, it is worth noting that morality is evoked differently for an issue like climate change than for issues like abortion or gay rights. For example, Pope Francis has officially recognized the existence of climate change and has declared it one of the most important issues facing humanity. He has made an effort to encourage Catholics to accept the scientific consensus on climate change. Meanwhile, many evangelical Christian leaders, like Reverend Pat Robertson, have rejected the idea that climate change could possibly occur in the belief that God would not allow such a thing to happen. He and others argue that climate change is like a religion and that climate scientists are religious fundamentalists. The implication is that if climate change is a religion, it is a false religion.

POTENTIAL BENEFITS OF CLIMATE CHANGE?

While scientists agree that climate change is happening, there is not a consensus on what will happen and on whether everything that will happen will be bad. According to the International Panel on Climate Change, a United Nations–funded organization dedicated to studying climate change, far too many implications are associated with climate change to discuss in this overview. The scientific literature indicates that climate change will cause sea levels to rise as the ice caps melt, more frequent and extreme weather events (like stronger hurricanes and longer seasons of drought), and human health issues due to species migration and the release of bacteria that were previously frozen in the ice caps and permafrost. These are three of the more commonly discussed negative implications. Meanwhile, other research reveals that some plant life, at least that not in areas of extended drought, will flourish with warmer temperatures and higher levels of carbon dioxide. Some regions will see higher levels of rainfall, which will potentially boost crop yields in those areas. Despite some regional benefits associated with climate change, however, scientists tend to agree that the overall impact of climate change is a negative for the planet.

Those who generally do not believe climate change is happening tend to emphasize the contradictory nature of the scientific research. They emphasize the benefits, while discounting or even rejecting the negatives. For example, many members of Congress frequently point to the research saying that plant life will thrive in a warmer climate (recent research suggests that plants that grow in these environments do not contain as many nutrients, which may have health implications in the future [Myers et al., 2014]), and they will use this information to justify not legislating on this issue. Others will argue that the United States and other nations will be able to adapt to any of the potential negative repercussions of climate change by taking mitigation measures, such as building sea walls to counter rising sea levels.

There are several morality arguments concerning this core argument. As noted, Pope Francis has argued that it is the duty of Catholics to fight to protect the planet from climate change. Indeed, religious leaders adopting this perspective also argue that God created this planet and that we have a moral obligation to treat it well and to be responsible stewards of other life and the ecosystems on which they depend. Those who disagree with this moral perspective have introduced a number of arguments. One approach is to argue that if climate change is happening, then it is God's will. If it is God's will and God is infallible, then we should not do anything about it. Another argument is that God would never allow something so calamitous to occur. Perhaps the most common response to all of the warnings is, "God never gives us more than we can handle." This suggests that everything will work out in the end, as God sees fit. Additionally, events that scientists believe are linked to climate change, such as particularly strong hurricanes and tornadoes, are reframed as acts of God punishing the communities ravaged by these storms for some reason. In other words, it is not that climate change may be making these storms worse; it is that God is angry and is punishing them.

CLIMATE CHANGE AND MORAL STEWARDSHIP OF THE PLANET

If the public accepts that climate change is happening and that it is generally a negative development, one might expect decision makers to begin legislating on climate change. However, before decision makers can begin drafting public policy, they need to know what is causing climate change. Scientists need to understand how virtually all the bodies of scientific knowledge interact with one another to begin to predict the causes of climate change and understand how climate change will impact the planet. Before policy can be written, consensus must be reached on the precise nature of the problem and on the steps that can be taken to mitigate or ameliorate the impact.

The scientific community emphasizes that climate change is caused by an excess of greenhouse gases in our atmosphere. Greenhouse gases, which include carbon dioxide, methane, water vapor, nitrous oxide, and ozone, trap heat from the sun within the atmosphere. Changes in the concentrations of greenhouse gases will directly impact the amount of heat trapped. Since the Industrial Revolution, the atmosphere has seen an unprecedented increase in the concentration of carbon dioxide, which has been produced in ever growing volumes by industrial activity ranging from burning coal and gas to generate electricity to consuming gas to operate trucks, automobiles, and planes. Consequently, scientists have identified carbon dioxide emissions as the primary cause of climate change.

Once identified as a cause, scientists needed to identify the source of the increase in carbon dioxide levels. By examining carbon dioxide levels going back several million years (using ice core samples and tree ring data), scientists have been able to determine that the rate of change in carbon dioxide levels measured since the late 1700s is abnormal by planetary standards. In other words, scientists were able to rule out natural processes that might explain the increase in carbon dioxide. Without an explanation, the only realistic alternative is human behaviors. To test this hypothesis, scientists measured carbon dioxide emissions from various industrial processes. With these measurements on hand, scientists were able to map the creation, adoption, and spread of these carbon dioxide–producing systems over time. When carbon dioxide levels were mapped over human activities that produced carbon dioxide, scientists found that human activity explained the rise in carbon dioxide levels very well. As a result of all of this research, the scientific community has identified humans as the primary cause of climate change. This is referred to as anthropogenic climate change.

This creates a problem for decision makers and the public. If climate change is happening, is bad, and is caused by humans, then it would be necessary to pass appropriate legislation. This, though, would likely necessitate significant changes to the standard of living in the United States, as it would require the public and industry to drastically alter their behaviors to limit carbon dioxide emissions. This means abandoning reliance on fossil fuels, substantially reducing the use of energy and potentially ending the use of certain products. It would require completely overhauling the economy of the world.

In light of these realities, a good proportion of those who believe climate change is happening do not believe it is caused by humans. The most common argument against anthropogenic climate change is that everything that is happening is caused by natural forces. The typical culprit is the sun, where many argue that changes in sun spot activity impacts the climate. Others point to natural occurrences like El Niño, which impact ocean currents and can change sea temperatures.

Morality plays an important role in this debate as well. Those who believe climate change is caused by humans are quick to point out that humans have a moral imperative to protect the environment. They argue that this is the only planet we have and that we have to take care of it, even if this means making sacrifices in terms of economic growth or material comforts. The moral imperative argument has become increasingly common as a method of justifying the changes that scientists believe are necessary to prevent or limit the impact of climate change on the global ecosystem.

Meanwhile, the morality argument against anthropogenic climate change does not deviate much from the previous core arguments. However, some argue that if climate change is caused by human actions, then God will provide a means to fix the problem, if God deems it necessary.

James W. Stoutenborough

FURTHER READING

Benestad, R. E., D. Nuccitelli, S. Lewandowsky, K. Hayhoe, H. O. Hygen, R. van Dorland, & J. Cook. 2016. "Learning from Mistakes in Climate Research." *Theoretical and Applied Climatology, 126*(3–4): 699–703.

Bromley-Trujillo, R., J. W. Stoutenborough, K. J. Kirkpatrick, & A. Vedlitz. 2014. "Climate Scientists and Environmental Interest Groups: The Intersection of Expertise and Advocacy." *Politics, Groups, and Identities, 2*(1): 120–134.

Cook, J., et al. 2016. "Consensus on Consensus: A Synthesis of Consensus Estimates on Human-caused Global Warming." *Environmental Research Letters, 11*(4) (April 13).

Francis, P. 2015. "'Encyclical Letter Laudato Si' of the Holy Father Francis on Care for Our Common Home." Vatican, May 5. Retrieved from http://w2.vatican.va/content /dam/francesco/pdf/encyclicals/documents/papa-francesco_20150524_enciclica -laudato-si_en.pdf

Intergovernmental Panel on Climate Change. 2014. *Climate Change 2014: Impacts, Adaptation, and Vulnerability. Part A: Global and Sectoral Aspects. Contribution of Working Group II to the Fifth Assessment Report of the International Panel on Climate Change* (C. B. Field, V. R. Barros, D. J. Dokken, K. J. Mach, M. D. Mastrandrea, T. E. Bilir, M. Chatterjee, K. L. Ebi, Y. O. Estrada, R. C. Genova, B. Girma, E. S. Kissel, A. N. Levy, S. MacCracken, P. P. Mastrandrea, & L. L. White [eds.]). New York: Cambridge University Press.

Intergovernmental Panel on Climate Change. 2014. *Climate Change 2014: Impacts, Adaptation, and Vulnerability. Part B: Regional Aspects. Contribution of Working Group II to the Fifth Assessment Report of the International Panel on Climate Change* (V. R. Barros, C. B. Field, D. J. Dokken, M. D. Mastrandrea, K. J. Mach, T. E. Bilir, M. Chatterjee, K. L. Ebi, Y. O. Estrada, R. C. Genova, B. Girma, E. S. Kissel, A. N. Levy, S. MacCracken, P. P. Mastrandrea, & L. L. White [eds.]). New York: Cambridge University Press.

Myers, S. S., A. Zanobetti, I. Kloog, P. Huybers, A. D. B. Leakey, A. J. Bloom, E. Carlisle, L. H. Dietterich, G. Fitzgerald, T. Hasegawa, N. M. Holbrook, R. L. Nelson, M. J. Ottman, V. Raboy, H. Sakai, K. A. Sartor, J. Schwartz, S. Seneweera, M. Tausz, & Y. Usui. 2014. "Increasing CO_2 Threatens Human Nutrition." *Nature, 510*(7503): 139–142.

Oreskes, N. 2004. "Beyond the Ivory Tower: The Scientific Consensus on Climate Change." *Science, 306*(5702): 1686.

Rosenberg, S., D. F. Vedlitz, D. F. Cowman, & S. Zahran. 2010. "Climate Change: A Profile of U.S. Climate Scientists' Perspectives." *Climatic Change, 101*(3–4): 311–329.

Tashman, Brian. 2017. "Pat Robertson: Climate Scientists Are Religious Fundamentalists." *Right Wing Watch*, February 1. Retrieved from http://www.rightwingwatch.org/post /pat-robertson-climate-scientists-are-religious-fundamentalists

U.S. House of Representatives Committee on Science, Space, & Technology. 2017. "Former NOAA Scientist Confirms Colleagues Manipulated Climate Records." Press Release, February 5. Retrieved from https://science.house.gov/news/press-releases /former-noaa-scientist-confirms-colleagues-manipulated-climate-records

Cloning

The cloning of Dolly the sheep—the world's first cloned mammal—was announced in 1997 and sparked celebration among scientists, who applauded the breakthrough as a means to understanding human disease and eventually developing cures. The news, however, prompted religious groups and other concerned people to express grave concern that the breakthrough might ultimately lead to the cloning of human beings. They immediately acted to ban research on human cloning in order to forestall what they feared would be the widespread creation and destruction of early-stage human embryos. Though scientists did not intend to use cloning for reproductive purposes, some in the public worried that, once cloned human embryos could be created, they might be used clandestinely to make a baby instead of therapeutically for the development of cures. It was also argued that cloning would be dangerous for any potential offspring due to the unknown safety and efficacy of the as yet untested procedure. Critics arose from many corners, but champions of traditional family values argued that creating cloned embryos could lead to children being treated as manufactured products and sow confusion about kinship and parental roles. Concern was also expressed across the political/ideological spectrum that cloning could lead to the promotion of genetic engineering or eugenics. Scientists supportive of the technology took issue with such slippery slope arguments and strenuously resisted any state or federal attempts to ban or restrict their research. Such prohibitions, they argued, would be at odds not only with American ideals of individual and intellectual freedom but with the freedom of the market as well, since the scientific enterprise of cloning research held the promise of opening and expanding lucrative markets in health care.

The scientists who first accomplished mammalian cloning—Ian Wilmut and Keith Campbell—saw it as a means to the desired end of genetic engineering, which could be used for a wide variety of purposes, including creating animal models for the study of disease, developing new sources for transplant organs, and preventing genetic childhood diseases like sickle cell anemia or cystic fibrosis. But in the midst of enthusiasm for human enhancement and the potential for vanquishing disease, some saw the potential for a fundamental altering of the human species—the beginning of an "age of biological control" (Wilmut, Campbell, and Tudge, 2001) or an ominous "post human future" that could lead to neoeugenics and human rights violations (Fukuyama, 2002). Leon Kass, who became chairman of the President's Council on Bioethics during the George W. Bush administration, championed this cautionary view of cloning. Kass, who had objected to in vitro fertilization as a means of assisted reproduction after its introduction in 1978, generally opposed unnatural procreation and medical enhancement, especially if it employed genetic or reproductive technology. While some shared his view of cloning as "repugnant" and an affront to human dignity (Kass & Wilson, 1998), others argued that it should be used not only for its therapeutic potential but as a treatment for infertility or a way for same-sex couples to have biologically related children, as a matter of pro-creative liberty (Robertson, 2002).

THE SPECTRE OF HUMAN CLONING

The technological advance of cloning technology was unprecedented, and public debate quickly focused on the possibility of human cloning rather than on the health care advances that might result from the technology. Indeed, the legislative debates it unleashed fell very much along the lines of the familiar moral controversy of abortion. Both involved concern for nascent human life—the embryo or fetus—in conflict with other, competing interests, such as the health, well-being, and autonomy of women (in the case of abortion) and with the fate of any patients who could be cured by therapies and treatments derived from cloning research. The independence of scientists in researching therapies and of medical doctors in accessing treatments was also considered to be under threat by proposed laws to curb cloning. The predominant groups opposing cloning were the same as those who had long fought to outlaw or restrict abortion in the United States: the Catholic Church, the National Right to Life Council, and the Family Research Council. Research universities and those in the biotech industry, on the other hand, were vocal in their resistance to efforts to limit what they could do in the lab. While their efforts were mostly characterized in terms of freedom and the benefits of technological advance, morality-based objections to the placement of restrictions on cloning research were also leveled by patient advocacy groups. These organizations represented individuals and families who might someday benefit from the expected development of cures for an array of conditions including heart disease, Parkinson's disease, paralysis, Alzheimer's disease, and multiple sclerosis.

Within a month of learning about the birth of Dolly the sheep, President Bill Clinton issued an executive order banning the use of federal funds for human cloning research and called for a voluntary moratorium on the use of private funds for that purpose. He declared that "any discovery that touches upon human creation is not simply a matter of scientific inquiry" but "a matter of morality and spirituality as well" (CNN Interactive, 1997). He also warned against the temptation of scientists to "play God" (Weiss, 1997). Clinton tasked his National Bioethics Advisory Council to study the issue and make a recommendation for action. Over the course of the next year, two dozen states introduced legislation to ban human cloning, and 15 states ultimately enacted such bills into law. Attempts at federal measures to prohibit human cloning failed repeatedly from 1998 through 2016, however, despite broad consensus among the U.S. public that reproductive cloning should not be allowed. The biggest point of contention in crafting a federal ban was over whether so-called therapeutic cloning should also be banned. In the process of therapeutic cloning, also known as somatic cell nuclear transfer (SCNT), cloned human embryos would be created for the purpose of extracting stem cells from them that could be used to develop personalized cures rather than for implantation in a surrogate for pregnancy.

Clinton's National Bioethics Advisory Council took the position that while reproductive cloning could be dangerous, cloning should not be banned for research and therapeutic purposes, where it held some promise for the development of cures and the advancement of knowledge. Motivated by a similar reasoning, the state of California placed a five-year moratorium on reproductive cloning but placed no strictures on SCNT research. Governor Pete Wilson, when signing Senate Bill 1344 into law in October of 1997, said, "We must not hinder the bona fide work of researchers and scientists as they unlock the important secrets of nature" (Hand, 1998). In state legislatures throughout the United States, it was argued that criminalizing SCNT would run counter to "the spirit of discovery that fuels scientific advancement" (Stabile, 2009). From manifest destiny to the mission to the moon, the idea that Americans have a right and a responsibility to expand frontiers is a core value that many lawmakers did not want to be seen as suppressing.

But the idea of American exceptionalism is also characterized by a tendency to engage in moralistic crusades (Lipset, 1997), and those who opposed cloning the most vehemently undertook their efforts with religious zeal. Fundamentalist and Evangelical Christians shared the position of Catholic doctrine that creating and destroying embryos for research or any other purpose is immoral (Stabile, 2010). Family Research Council President Tony Perkins opposed federal legislation supporting embryo research, saying it would lead to "a market for creating and cloning more human embryos for the express purpose of killing them" (Kirkpatrick, 2007). Roman Catholic bishops identified "five 'nonnegotiable' issues" that they said should determine how Catholics vote: "abortion, euthanasia, embryonic stem cell research, human cloning and same sex marriage" (Steinfels, 2007). So in state legislatures and the U.S. Congress, religious opponents framed their votes in favor of bills to ban cloning as a reflection of their deep respect for human life.

STARKLY DIFFERENT OUTLOOKS ON STEM CELL RESEARCH

Some critics even ascribed sinister motives to proponents of therapeutic cloning research, a term that would later come to be used interchangeably with "stem cell research." Kansas State Representative Mayans (R-Wichita) called one cloning ban bill an effort to "prevent researchers from playing God" since "technology in the hands of evil people could create a 'master race'" (Milburn, 2002, quoted in Stabile, 2009). *New York Times* columnist William Safire went so far as to say,

"Down that monstrous human-cloning road lies production of slaves for organs, demographic manipulation and notions of master races" (Safire, 2001). Allusions to evil were not uncommon in testimony or media discussion of cloning, which also made mention of science fiction scenarios evoking Mary Shelley's *Franken-stein* or Aldous Huxley's *Brave New World* as cautionary tales. President George W. Bush himself referenced "human beings created in test tubes in what he [Huxley] called a hatchery" in a 2001 speech in which he rejected federal financing of stem cell research (Bush, 2001).

Bush's landmark speech declared embryonic stem cell research to be "at the leading edge of a series of moral hazards," which he said included "growing human beings for spare body parts" (Bush, 2001). Yet in that same address, he acknowledged "the promise and potential of stem cell research" to one day lead to cures for a wide range of ailments and diseases. That potential led him to allow limited federal funding of research using existing stem cell lines, thus demarcating a moral cutoff point: As of the date of his declaration, no new embryos could be created using federal funds for the purpose of extracting their stem cells. The decision was described by supporters as "Solomonic"—a biblical reference to a wise but difficult choice—but it nonetheless troubled both research opponents who considered it to be too permissive and research advocates who found it overly restrictive.

Proponents of regenerative medicine, which includes SCNT and stem cell research, sought its advancement for the stated purpose of alleviating human suffering. Scientists, medical doctors, researchers, and patient groups claimed a moral high ground in employing science to seek cures. Some faith traditions also explicitly spoke in favor of the research, notably the largest Orthodox Jewish organizations in the United States (Cooperman, 2002). And, despite the official position of the U.S. Conference of Catholic Bishops, there was evidence that some sizable number of U.S. Catholics and other Christians were not convinced that embryos in a petri dish had the same moral status as an actual baby; they rejected the idea that pursuing potentially curative therapies through the new technology was evil (Stabile, 2009). Sympathetic public figures like Christopher Reeves, a handsome actor who had portrayed Superman in the movies and subsequently suffered a spinal cord injury rendering him a paraplegic, and Michael J. Fox, a popular actor afflicted with Parkinson's disease, put a sympathetic face on appeals for public support of stem cell research. Former First Lady Nancy Reagan's plea in 2004 for legislation to allow for ethical therapeutic cloning research was especially powerful, coming as it did from the wife of a popular president who had been ardent in his opposition to abortion and had banned fetal tissue research. Her firsthand experience of his protracted suffering from Alzheimer's disease had led her to experience a change of heart on the issue.

Moral debate over cloning's potential for good or evil took place alongside arguments strongly asserting its potential to promote economic growth. Among states that passed laws pertaining to human cloning between 1997 and 2005, those with greater biotechnological capacity were more likely to craft legislation that allowed the research to go forward (Stabile, 2007). While organizations such as the Coalition for the Advancement of Medical Research (CAMR) clearly had an ethical stake in advancing cures through this avenue of research, their interests in doing so were also material. The industry and university groups that made up CAMR and other such coalitions, like MassCURE (Massachusetts Citizens United for Research Excellence), sought to advance state preeminence in the field. Research and development budgets in the billions of dollars and involving tens of thousands of jobs were argued to be at stake. In 2004, the state of California passed a bond referendum—Proposition 71—dedicating $3 billion over 10 years to support stem cell research and therapeutic cloning in a move explicitly intended to establish market dominance. Even in states not as commonly associated in the public mind with scientific advancement, such as Kansas, restrictive legislation was averted by the argument that it would contribute to the state being seen as antiscience and anti-industry, with negative repercussions for its bottom line.

In 2006, researchers at Kyoto University in Japan developed the ability to reprogram regular cells back to a state at which they have the potential to become any cell in the human body. The existence of these "induced pluripotent stem cells" (iPCSs) may reduce or even eliminate the need to use either existing or cloned embryos for stem cell research and therapies, thus allowing researchers to sidestep a significant source of moral and political controversy.

Bonnie B. Stabile

FURTHER READING

Bush, George W. 2001. "The President's Decision; Bush's Address on Federal Financing for Research with Embryonic Stem Cells." *The New York Times*, August 10. Retrieved from http://www.nytimes.com/2001/08/10/us/president-s-decision-bush-s-address -federal-financing-for-research-with.html

CNN Interactive. 1997. "Clinton Bars Federal Funds for Human Cloning Research." Retrieved from http://www.cnn.com/TECH/9703/04/clinton.cloning

Cooperman, Alan. 2002. "2 Jewish Groups Back Therapeutic Cloning." *The Washington Post*, March 13. Retrieved from https://www.washingtonpost.com/archive/politics /2002/03/13/2-jewish-groups-back-therapeutic-cloning/7e11e22b-e77f-41d5-b176 -4a9d5969c176

Fukuyama, Francis. 2002. *Our Posthuman Future: Consequences of the Biotechnology Revolution.* New York: Farrar, Straus & Giroux.

Hand, Nancy. 1998. "Breasts, Bars and Bans; A Slew of New Laws Hits the Books January 1." *Monterey County Weekly*, January 8. Retrieved from http://www.mont ereycountyweekly.com/news/local_news/a-slew-of-new-laws-hit-the-books-jan /article_c51df07e-ee5e-5f00-adcb-fec791e73842.html

Kass, Leon R., & James Q. Wilson. 1998. *The Ethics of Human Cloning.* Washington, DC: AEI Press.

Kirkpatrick, David D. 2007. "Stem Cell Bill Sails Through the House." *The New York Times,* January 12. Retrieved from http://www.nytimes.com/2007/01/12/washington /12stem.html?sq=stem%20cell%20bill%20sails%20through%20house&st=cse&scp =1&pagewanted=print

Lipset, Martin. 1997. *American Exceptionalism: A Double-Edged Sword.* New York: W. W. Norton.

Milburn, John. 2002. "House Advances Anti-Cloning, Human Embryo Bills." *The Topeka Capital-Journal*, March 22. Retrieved from http://cjonline.com/stories/032202/bre _embbill.shtml#.We90hNPysWo

Robertson, John. 2002. "Cloning as a Reproductive Right." In Glenn McGee (Ed.), *The Human Cloning Debate*, 42–57. Berkeley, CA: Beverly Hills Books.

Safire, William. 2001. "Stem Cell Genie." *The New York Times,* July 16. Retrieved from http://www.nytimes.com/2001/07/16/opinion/essay-stem-cell-genie.html

Stabile, Bonnie. 2007. "Demographic Profiles of States with Human Cloning Laws: Morality Policy Meets Political Economy." *Politics and the Life Sciences, 26*(1): 43–50.

Stabile, Bonnie. 2009. "What's the Matter with Kansas? Legislative Debates over Stem Cell Research in Kansas and Massachusetts." *Politics and the Life Sciences, 28*(1): 17–30.

Stabile, Bonnie. 2010. "Stem Cells, Cloning and Political Liberalism." *World Medical & Health Policy, 2*(1): 301–315.

Steinfels, Peter. 2007. "Catholic Bishops' Taxing Task: Election-Year Statement." *The New York Times*, October 27. Retrieved from http://www.nytimes.com/2007/10/27/us/27beliefs.html?scp=1&sq=cloning+catholic+bishops&st=nyt

Weiss, Rick. 1997. "Clinton Forbids Funding of Human Clone Studies." *The New York Times,* March 5. Retrieved from https://www.washingtonpost.com/archive/politics/1997/03/05/clinton-forbids-funding-of-human-clone-studies/3b2f831f-f23e-4457-8611-6c9bda0b8ebf

Wilmut, Ian, Keith Campbell, & Colin Tudge. 2001. *The Second Creation: Dolly and the Age of Biological Control*. Cambridge: Harvard University Press.

Death Penalty

Capital punishment has historically been among the most hotly debated topics in criminal justice. Many have weighed in on the issue, from philosophers to politicians, criminologists to economists. The nature of the debate has shifted over time, but several elements of the issue have consistently been salient, including the constitutionality of the death penalty, its financial costs, and whether it is effective in deterring violent crime. Key moral and ethical components of the debate, meanwhile, include questions about rights and retribution, racial and socioeconomic biases, wrongful convictions, and society's obligations to the families and friends of murder victims.

MODERN TRENDS IN CAPITAL PUNISHMENT IN AMERICA

Capital punishment has been part of American culture since colonial times, but the modern era of the death penalty dates back to the 1970s. In 1972, the United States Supreme Court ruled in the case, *Furman v. Georgia*, that capital punishment laws violated the Eighth Amendment to the U.S. Constitution, which prohibits punishments that are considered "cruel and unusual." In effect, this ruling put a moratorium, or temporary prohibition, on the death penalty. After the Court's decision, the U.S. Congress and many states rewrote their capital punishment laws to address the problems outlined in the *Furman* decision. In 1976, the Supreme Court again examined these statutes in the case *Gregg v. Georgia*. The Court ruled that the new death penalty laws in Georgia, Florida, and Texas were constitutional, thus reinstating the practice. Within a few years of the *Gregg* decision, more than 30 states enacted new capital punishment laws.

At first, few people were executed under the new death penalty statutes. However, executions began to increase in the mid-1980s, a trend that continued until 1999, when 98 people were executed in the United States. However, after 1999 the number of executions across the country decreased consistently; in 2015, 28 people were executed, and in 2017 the number dwindled further to 23. As of 2018, 30 states still have capital punishment laws, although few actually carry out executions. Furthermore, eight states have abolished or overturned their death penalty laws since 2006, and four states currently have moratoria on the practice (DPIC, 2018). This trend away from using capital punishment, along with decreased support among the public, has prompted some commentators to suggest that we may have reached the "beginning of the end" of the death penalty in the United States (Dow, 2014; Mangino, 2016).

LEGAL AND PRACTICAL CONSIDERATIONS

A constant question regarding the death penalty is its constitutionality, specifically, whether it violates the Eighth Amendment's restriction on cruel and unusual punishment. Overall, the Supreme Court has never ruled that the death penalty is intrinsically a violation of the Constitution. However, despite reinstating the practice in 1976, the Court has restricted its use through a series of important cases. In *Woodson v. North Carolina* (1976), the Court ruled that the death penalty could not be a mandatory sentence but that it must be handled on a case-by-case basis to take into account the individual offender and crime. The Supreme Court has also ruled that the death penalty is unconstitutional for people convicted of rape of an adult victim (*Coker v. Georgia*, 1977), insane prisoners (*Ford v. Wainwright*, 1986), offenders suffering from mental retardation (*Atkins v. Virginia*, 2002), juvenile offenders under 18 years old (*Roper v. Simmons*, 2005), and people convicted of child rape (*Kennedy v. Louisiana*, 2008). Debates continue over the constitutionality of capital punishment; for example, some people argue that using lethal injection, the primary method used to execute offenders, may be cruel and unusual, although the Supreme Court has not yet ruled as such.

In terms of practical considerations, two important issues regularly come up in conversations about the death penalty. The first involves its cost. Critics of capital punishment regularly point out that, as administered in the United States, the death penalty costs significantly more money than a similar case that results in a long-term prison sentence. These costs stem from all aspects of the cases but are largely due to more expensive trials, a longer appeals process, and the increased expense of housing inmates on death row, which is usually the most secure and thus most expensive sector of a prison in which to hold inmates. Importantly, these costs can be extensive. For example, a recent study in Oregon found that death penalty cases cost an average of $2.3 million each, while similar cases with noncapital sentences cost $1.4 million each (Hernandez, 2016). In Pennsylvania, estimates suggest that a death penalty case costs about $2 million more than a similar nondeath case and that the state may have spent as much as $1 billion on capital punishment since 1978 (Migdail-Smith, 2016). Similarly, California spent approximately $4 billion on its death penalty system since reinstatement (Alarcon & Mitchell, 2011), and studies in a number of states have found figures in line with these. On the other hand, proponents of the death penalty suggest that these costs are due to the bloated and overcomplicated nature of capital cases, and thus the process should be streamlined to save money rather than be abolished.

A second practical consideration is a utilitarian one, asking whether the death penalty is a useful tool for deterring, or preventing, murder. Capital punishment clearly incapacitates individual offenders convicted of murder by physically preventing them from committing additional crimes. Death penalty supporters also often argue that it deters others from committing violent crimes, for fear of being apprehended and punished with death. On the other hand, many opponents argue that the death penalty does not deter crime any more than other forms of punishment. Historically, some have even argued that it does the opposite, that is, that the death penalty creates a "brutalization" effect that actually increases violence in society by showing that it is acceptable. This issue—the effect of capital punishment on crime rates—has been perhaps the most widely researched aspect of the death penalty. The vast majority of studies suggest that the death penalty leads to neither a reduction nor an increase in murder rates. However, recent research conducted by economists has found somewhat mixed results; a few studies have found evidence that executions reduce murders, while many others find no such impact. Thus, while the overall body of research suggests that the death penalty does not have a major effect on murder rates, we cannot draw definitive conclusions.

MORAL AND ETHICAL CONSIDERATIONS

Moral arguments for and against the death penalty can take a variety of forms. For some proponents of capital punishment, the moral justifications are clear: A person who makes the decision to commit murder, taking the life of another human being, forfeits his or her own right to life. This perspective is very much rooted in retribution, or the application of equal punishment on those who deserve it as a response to their actions. In death penalty debates, this perspective is often framed using the phrase "an eye for an eye." The idea here is simple: In committing a murder, a person deserves punishment in kind, or the death penalty. Critics, on the other hand, may point out that equal punishment may not be possible or reasonable, depending on the situation. For example, "If a mass murderer kills ten people, then taking his single life is technically not punishment in kind" (Fieser, 2008). Furthermore, opponents of capital punishment point out that we use this retributive justification only for murder but not for other crimes: "We don't punish rapists by raping them" (Fieser, 2008). Finally, many opponents suggest that the death penalty is simply unacceptable from a moral standpoint. Specifically, it is simply wrong to end the life of another human being, even when that person has committed a heinous crime and even when the execution is done on behalf of the state.

A related justification for the death penalty is that some crimes are just so heinous, or so obscene, that death is the only appropriate response on the part of the state. Indeed, for practical purposes, capital punishment in the United States applies only to some who are convicted of murder. In other words, it is reserved for "the worst of the worst." Opponents of capital punishment often dispute this, suggesting that it is not actually applied to the worst offenders but rather is driven by the same racial biases and socioeconomic inequalities that influence all aspects of the justice system. Indeed, unequal application of the death penalty based on race has been a key issue since its reinstatement in 1976.

The issue of racial bias came to a head in 1987 in the Supreme Court case, *McCleskey v. Kemp*. The defense relied on research by law professor David Baldus, which showed that in Georgia during the 1970s (when McCleskey committed his crime), murderers were 4.3 times more likely to be sentenced to death if the victim was white and that in those cases, black offenders were more likely to receive a capital sentence than white offenders. While the Court ruled against McCleskey and he was executed, the case raised several important issues related to racial bias in the death penalty that are still debated today. According to the Death Penalty Information Center, as of November 2016, there are approximately equal proportions of white and black defendants on death row, and whites make up more than half of all defendants executed since 1976, while blacks make up just under 35 percent. In terms of victims, more than 75 percent of the cases that resulted in execution involved a white victim, while approximately 15 percent involved a black victim, even though black Americans are the most likely to be the victims of homicide (Sugarmann, 2014). For opponents of capital punishment, this suggests that, if the death penalty is truly reserved for the "worst of the worst," then we consider murders the worst only when the victim is white. In other words, we place a higher value on a white life than a black one. Many supporters of capital punishment do acknowledge a bias against black victims, but there is a different interpretation regarding the race of offenders. Supporters may argue that the preceding figures actually show a bias against white offenders; that is, most murders are intraracial, meaning they occur within the same racial group. Since the death penalty is less likely when the murder victim is black, and the person who kills that victim is most likely to also be black, overall the system actually punishes black murderers less severely than white murderers (McAdams, 2006).

Closely related to racial bias is inequality based on socioeconomic status. Those from lower classes are at a disadvantage throughout the criminal justice system, which includes capital punishment. As famed lawyer and activist Bryan Stevenson wrote, "Death sentences are imposed in a criminal justice system that treats you better if you are rich and guilty than if you are poor and innocent." Stevenson continued:

> Embracing a certain quotient of racial bias and discrimination against the poor is an inexorable aspect of supporting capital punishment. This is an immoral condition that makes rejecting the death penalty on moral grounds not only defensible but necessary for those who refuse to accept unequal or unjust administration of punishment. (Stevenson, 2004)

Biases and inequalities are related to yet another important issue: wrongful convictions, or the convictions of people who did not commit the crime for which they were convicted and punished. Although errors were always a part of the justice system, only in recent years has the issue become a prominent part of the death penalty debate. Indeed, innocence has become the leading frame or theme in the public death penalty debate and is often credited as a key reason for the declining support for and use of the death penalty in the United States (Baumgartner, De Boef, &

Boydstun, 2008). The argument is straightforward: How can a system that executes innocent people be useful, and how can we morally support such a system?

According to the Death Penalty Information Center, between 1973 and 2018, 164 people have been exonerated from death row in the United States on the basis of innocence (DPIC, 2019). These cases have sparked concerns about the possibility that the government might mistakenly execute an innocent person, which is among the most compelling arguments against capital punishment. Furthermore, several high-profile cases in recent years have involved executions despite serious questions about guilt or innocence, such as the cases of Cameron Todd Willingham in Texas and Troy Davis in Georgia. On the other hand, proponents of capital punishment tend to suggest that wrongful executions do not occur; when someone is exonerated, according to this view, it is a sign of the system catching its mistakes before it is too late. And if the system does make mistakes on occasion, many death penalty supporters suggest that they are so rare as to not warrant abolishing the practice. As several have written, many social practices—medicine, construction, and many others—involve innocent deaths, yet those practices are continued. Ultimately, the debate about how often innocent people are convicted and sentenced to death may never be resolved, but the most scientific estimate we have suggests that 4.1 percent of those sentenced to death may be innocent (Gross et al., 2014).

A final ethical consideration worth mentioning deals with the families of murder victims. For some supporters, the families deserve justice, and killing the offender who murdered their loved one is the only way to provide it. For example, Fred Romano, whose older sister was murdered in 1987, waited 15 years for the killer to be executed in Maryland. He said it wasn't about revenge; his wife, Vicki, said, "Revenge would be going out and killing one of [the murderer's] family members." Nor was it about closure. "It's justice," Fred said (Kane, 2003).

Despite Romano's claim that it was not about closure, some supporters of capital punishment believe that execution is the only way to truly bring closure to the family members of a murder victim. Whether this is true depends on the person and on what is meant by closure. As professor Nancy Berns said, "If they're defining closure as, 'This is an end to the trial itself,' then yes, maybe they can find closure. But if they're thinking that closure means, "Oh, my grief is done,' then absolutely not" (Marsh, 2015). In fact, the research on this topic has produced mixed results. For example, one study examined the public statements made by victims' loved ones in 150 cases and found that they reported feeling relief in only 17 percent of them and closure in only 2.5 percent of them; on the other hand, they said they did not feel closure or healing in 20 percent of the cases (Vollum & Longmire, 2007). Another study compared murder victims' loved ones in Texas (where those convicted received the death penalty) and Minnesota (where they received life in prison without parole) and found that the loved ones in Minnesota were healthier in the long run and expressed more satisfaction with the justice system (Armour & Umbreit, 2012). Even Fred Romano, who wanted his sister's murderer to be executed, said, "It won't bring closure. Dawn [his sister] will never be back. I'm not looking for closure" (Kane, 2003). Thus, the answer to the question of whether the death penalty can bring closure to murder victims' families is murky at best.

Robert J. Norris

FURTHER READING

Alarcon, Arthur L., & Paula M. Mitchell. 2011. "Executing the Will of the Voters? A Road-map to Mend or End the California Legislature's Multi-billion-dollar Death Penalty Debacle." *Loyola of Los Angeles Law Review, 44*: S41–S224.

Allen, Ronald J., & Amy Shavell. 2005. "Further Reflections on the Guillotine." *Journal of Criminal Law and Criminology, 95*: 625–636.

Armour, Marilyn Peterson, & Mark S. Umbreit. 2012. "Assessing the Impact of the Ultimate Penal Sanction on Homicide Survivors: A Two State Comparison." *Marquette Law Review, 96*: 1–131.

Baumgartner, Frank R., Suzanna L. De Boef, & Amber E. Boydstun. 2008. *The Decline of the Death Penalty and the Discovery of Innocence*. New York: Cambridge University Press.

Cassell, Paul G. 2000. "We're Not Executing the Innocent." *Wall Street Journal*, June 16.

DPIC. Death Penalty Information Center. 2018. "States With and Without the Death Penalty." Retrieved from https://deathpenaltyinfo.org/states-and-without-death-penalty

DPIC. Death Penalty Information Center. 2019. "Innocence and the Death Penalty." Retrieved from https://deathpenaltyinfo.org/innocence-and-death-penalty

Dow, David R. 2014. "The Beginning of the End of America's Death-penalty Experiment." *Politico*, July 25. Retrieved from http://www.politico.com/magazine/story/2014/07/the-beginning-of-the-end-of-americas-death-penalty-experiment-109394

Durlauf, Steven N., Chao Fu, & Salvador Navarro. 2013. "Capital Punishment and Deterrence: Understanding Disparate Results." *Journal of Quantitative Criminology, 29*: 103–121.

Eberhardt, Jennifer L., P. G. Davies, Valerie J. Purdie-Vaughns, & Sheri Lynn Johnson. 2006. "Looking Deathworthy: Perceived Stereotypicality of Black Defendants Predicts Capital-Sentencing Outcomes." *Psychological Science, 17*: 383–386.

Fieser, James. 2008. "Capital Punishment." Retrieved from https://www.utm.edu/staff/jfieser/class/160/7-cap-pun.htm

Garland, David. 2010. *Peculiar Institution: America's Death Penalty in an Age of Abolition*. Cambridge, MA: Belknap Press.

Gibson, James, & Corinna Barrett Lain. 2015. "Death Penalty Drugs and the International Moral Marketplace." *Georgetown Law Journal, 103*: 1215–1274.

Gross, Samuel R., & Barbara O'Brien. 2008. "Frequency and Predictors of False Conviction: Why We Know So Little, and New Data on Capital Cases." *Journal of Empirical Legal Studies, 5*: 927–962.

Gross, Samuel R., Barbara O'Brien, Chen Hu, & Edward H. Kennedy. 2014. "Rate of False Conviction of Criminal Defendants Who Are Sentenced to Death." *Proceedings of the National Academy of Sciences, 111*: 7230–7235.

Hernandez, Tony. 2016. "How Much Does the Oregon Death Penalty Cost? New Study Examines 100s of Cases." *The Oregonian*, November 16. Retrieved from http://www.oregonlive.com/portland/index.ssf/2016/11/how_much_does_the_oregon_death.html

Hodgkinson, Peter, ed. 2016. *Capital Punishment: New Perspectives*. London: Routledge.

Johnson, Robert. 2014. "Reflections on the Death Penalty: Human Rights, Human Dignity, and Dehumanization in the Death House." *Seattle Journal for Social Justice, 13*: 583–598.

Kane, Gregory. 2003. "To Murder Victims' Families, Executing Killers Is Justice." *The Baltimore Sun*, February 5. Retrieved from http://www.baltimoresun.com/news/maryland/bal-md.kane05feb05-column.html

Kennedy, Janice. 2005. "Forgive . . . but Don't Forget: No Matter How Heinous the Crimes, Sister Helen Prejean Wants Victims to Spare Themselves—by Reconciling." *The Ottawa Citizen*, May 22.

Mangino, Matthew T. 2016. "The End of the Inevitability of the Death Penalty." *Hannibal Courier-Post*, October 21. Retrieved from http://www.hannibal.net/news/20161021 /matthew-t-mangino-end-of-inevitability-of-death-penalty?start=10

Marsh, Jason. 2015. "Does the Death Penalty Bring Closure?" *CNN*, May 20. Retrieved from https://www.cnn.com/2015/05/20/opinions/marsh-tsarnaev-forgiveness/index .html

McAdams, John. 2006. Statement of John McAdams, Professor of Political Science, Marquette University, Milwaukee, Wisconsin, *An Examination of the Death Penalty in the United States, Hearing Before the Subcommittee on the Constitution, Civil Rights and Property Rights of the Committee on the Judiciary of the United States Senate.* Retrieved from https://www.gpo.gov/fdsys/pkg/CHRG-109shrg29599/pdf /CHRG-109shrg29599.pdf

Migdail-Smith, Liam. 2016. "Executing Justice: A Look at the Cost of Pennsylvania's Death Penalty." *Reading Eagle*, June 19. Retrieved from http://www.readingeagle.com /news/article/executing-justice-a-look-at-the-cost-of-pennsylvanias-death-penalty

Prejean, Sister Helen. 1993. *Dead Man Walking: An Eyewitness Account of the Death Penalty in the United States.* New York: Vintage.

Sheffer, Susannah. 2013. *Fighting for Their Lives: Inside the Experience of Capital Defense Attorneys.* Nashville, TN: Vanderbilt University Press.

Stevenson, Bryan. 2004. "Close to Death: Reflections on Race and Capital Punishment in America." In Hugo Bedau & Paul Cassell (Eds.), *Debating the Death Penalty: Should America Have Capital Punishment? The Experts on Both Sides Make Their Best Case*, 76–116. New York: Oxford University Press.

Sugarmann, Josh. 2014. "Murder Rate for Black Americans Is Four Times the National Average." *Huffington Post*, January 31. Retrieved from http://www.huffingtonpost .com/josh-sugarmann/murder-rate-for-black-ame_b_4702228.html

Sundby, Scott E. 2005. *A Life and Death Decision: A Jury Weighs the Death Penalty.* New York: Palgrave Macmillan.

Van den Haag, Ernest. 1986. "The Ultimate Punishment: A Defense." *Harvard Law Review*, *99*: 1662–1669.

Vollum, Scott, & Dennis R. Longmire. 2007. "Co-victims of Capital Murder: Statements of Victims' Family Members and Friends Made at the Time of Execution." *Violence and Victims*, *22*: 601–619.

Disability

America is a politically polarized society. At the core of polarization are two, often implicit but strikingly different conceptions of justice. Social justice competes with an idea of an allegedly "true" market-based justice. Foundations and think tanks are mobilized to defend one idea or the other. Political advertising and social movements exert influence on one side or the other. In political theory, conceptions of social democracy or social liberalism are principal carriers of social justice, while neoliberalism and libertarianism are carriers of market-based justice.

Social justice is concerned with securing minimal conditions of self-development and equal citizenship for all citizens. Among these conditions are constitutionally rooted civil, political, and social rights. Individual freedom and political participation depend upon the cultivation of a set of human capabilities (Dewey, 1923; Nussbaum, 2007, 2011; Sen, 1999, 2009). For this to occur, social rights, cashed out as tax-supported, government-provided education, health care, and other supports and services, must be guaranteed to all citizens. Thus some level of economic redistribution is required. By contrast, for neoliberals and libertarians, there is no such thing as "social" justice. It is a "fraudulent" idea based upon "quasi-religious superstition" (Hayek, 1976). There are no social rights, and true justice is about the just or unjust conduct of individuals. Subsequently, true freedom is not about self-development or equal citizenship; rather, it refers to a private space wherein individuals, within the constraints of the law, can choose what to do (or be) without interference from other individuals or government. In essence, individuals, separately and alone, are responsible for what they achieve or become. Taxation for the purpose of redistribution is unjust, and voluntary market transactions provide the only just distribution (Hayek, 1944, 1960).

DISABILITY AND DISABILITY POLICY

Just as current conceptions of justice range from market-based, neoliberal perspectives to those rooted in social justice, conceptions of disability have changed and even conflicted over time. Conceptions of disability have defined disability either as a problem residing within a person to be remediated or as an outcome of an interaction between the person and his/her physical or community environment. These differing conceptions have shaped the rights of people with disabilities.

Throughout most of modern history, definitions of disability focused on a personal pathological condition requiring remediation. Until recently, this conceptualization dominated the field of intellectual and developmental disability (Wehmeyer et al., 2008). This perspective defines people with intellectual disability as inherently deficient, unworthy of full membership in the community, and incapable of enjoying and exercising the rights of citizenship. It ultimately leads to a position in which such persons are not seen as having "the right to have rights" (Arendt, 1951).

In the late 19th and early 20th centuries, large numbers of people with intellectual and developmental disabilities were separated from society in segregated, state-run institutions. Early in the institutionalization movement, the focus was on state-supported education and rehabilitation. Leaders asserted that people with intellectual disability could be educated and contribute to society if adequate social services were provided. Over time, however, the purpose and focus of these institutions changed. Political shifts, a growing emphasis on eugenics and intelligence testing, and moves toward providing services only to those deemed worthy led to the denial of rights of citizenship to people with disabilities. Institutions grew in size and became focused on a custodial mission designed to eliminate the alleged "menace" to society that people with intellectual and developmental disabilities were viewed as posing (Trent, 1994). These attitudes justified the horrific treatment of people with disabilities, as documented in multiple sources (Blatt & Kaplan, 1966). Involuntary sterilization, for example, was upheld by the U.S. Supreme Court in *Buck v. Bell* (1927). In a eugenic justification of the Court's decision, Justice Oliver Wendell Holmes wrote: "It is better for all the world, if instead of waiting to execute degenerate offspring for crime, or to let them starve for their imbecility, society can prevent those who are manifestly unfit from continuing their kind." This opinion reflected the "otherness" that came to define people with intellectual and developmental disabilities. It reflected not only exclusion from society but also denial of the basic rights of citizenship.

Over time, particularly after the Nazi extermination of people with intellectual disability in the early 1940s and revelations of horrific and inhumane conditions of state-run American institutions in the 1960s and 1970s, attitudes toward eugenics and human warehousing began to change. Parents and advocates asserted that people with intellectual disability were the moral equals of other citizens and that they had needs that the state should address. They argued that as citizens, people with disabilities had a right to an appropriate education. As such, efforts were instituted to eliminate segregated living conditions and to promote integration into community life (by eliminating environmental barriers to participation, for example). Parents and advocates argued for social supports and environmental accommodations to cultivate the capabilities that these citizens possessed.

One major aspect of these changes was a movement away from conceptualizing disability as a problem that resided within a person. Instead, newer frameworks emerged that adopted a social-ecological model of disability. For example, the World

Health Organization replaced the biomedical classification system in its *International Classification of Impairment, Disability and Handicap* (1980) with one in its revised *International Classification of Functioning, Disability, and Health* (2001), asserting that disability is an interaction of personal capabilities and the environment. Essentially, every person has a range of personal capabilities and needs, and disability can occur when there is a mismatch between these capabilities and the individual's social and cultural environments. This view of disability shifted the focus from a pathological condition to how environments can be modified to provide the supports necessary for capability cultivation. It changed the definition of needed services from medicalized rehabilitation to individualized supports for capability development. The same model was incorporated into the definition of intellectual disability forwarded by the American Association on Intellectual and Developmental Disabilities (Luckasson et al., 1992; Schalock et al., 2010).

Prior to the person–environment model, the Disability Rights movement built on the achievements of African Americans and women in the broader civil rights movement (Shapiro, 1993). Recognizing the need for cultural and institutional change to improve the life experiences of people with disabilities, agencies and lawmakers passed new regulations and laws, such as Section 504 of the Rehabilitation Act, P. L. 94–142 (now the Individuals with Disabilities Education Act [IDEA]) and the Americans with Disabilities Act (ADA), with the aim of advancing civil rights for people with disabilities by prohibiting discrimination based on disability in education and employment, among other life domains. These laws acknowledged the need for environmental change and recognized the civil rights of people with disabilities. As stated in the Congressional Findings of the ADA, "physical or mental disabilities in no way diminish a person's right to fully participate in all aspects of society, yet many people with physical or mental disabilities have been precluded from doing so" (42 USC § 12101[a][1]).

The normalization and deinstitutionalization movements brought increased attention to the inherent right of people with intellectual and developmental disabilities to live in the community and participate within its schools and neighborhoods, with systems of supports (Bradley, 1994; Nirje, 1969). These systems of support made it possible for people with intellectual disability to be viewed as moral equals and afforded them both full membership in society and the full rights of citizenship. These movements led to a significant decrease in the numbers of people with intellectual and developmental disabilities living in segregated settings (Braddock et al., 2015), as well as increased access to neighborhood schools (U.S. Department of Education, 2014)—though there is still significant progress to be made.

In recent years, legal challenges to and governmental enforcement of the ADA has led to significant changes in understanding the law's provisions. The Supreme Court decision in *Olmstead vs. L. C.* (1999), for example, clarified that unjustified segregation of people with disabilities was discrimination under the ADA. The Court wrote: "[I]nstitutional placement of persons who can handle and benefit from community settings perpetuates unwarranted assumptions that persons so isolated are incapable of or unworthy of participating in community life," and "[C]onfinement in an institution severely diminishes the everyday activities of individuals including family relations, social contacts, work options, economic independence, educational advancement, and cultural enrichment." Recently, the Department of Justice has expanded the application of Olmstead beyond residential segregation to segregated employment, entering into a consent decree in the state of Rhode Island stating that the state's overreliance on segregated and separate workshops and day programs for people with disabilities violated ADA, again asserting that unjustified segregation diminishes the personhood of people with disabilities.

Legislation within the past 30 years has changed society's understanding of disability and has led to a new recognition of previously denied rights and services and support for people with intellectual and developmental disabilities. Instead of segregation and programs that did not meet the needs and interests of people with disabilities by failing to build on their capabilities, the new conceptualization of disability shifted the focus to an "array" of individualized supports—"resources and strategies that aim to promote the development, education, . . . and personal well-being of a person" and that contribute to individual self-development (Luckasson et al., 1992: 88). There is a moral basis for these supports as they promote inclusion and enhance community integration. Further, they support the active involvement of people with disabilities in determining and managing the systems of supports that meet their needs, based on their rights as citizens.

IMPLICATIONS OF THE TWO IDEAS OF JUSTICE

In reflecting upon this sketch of disability and disability policy, what are the implications for persons with disabilities? How would neoliberals construe the IDEA and the ADA? Would neoliberals view the regulations and mandated services as expressions of basic justice or of public charity or prefer them to be privatized with perhaps some form of minimal government support? Knowing that neoliberals prefer a minimum of government-supported programs of any kind (in order to minimize redistribution) and that market-based provision of essential services is the best outcome, we would need to determine whether those providers would be required to submit to regulations similar to those of the IDEA and ADA. We also know that privatization of public education, the context focused on by the IDEA for its implementation, is the preferred policy. In any case, neither the IDEA nor the ADA would be construed by neoliberals as acts of legislated *social* justice. As such, this implies that the quality of services would depend on the ability of parents of children with disabilities to pay for needed services and programs that are available in the marketplace. Similarly, adults with disabilities would have to depend upon family or private and public charity.

The implications of social democratic or social liberal conceptions of justice for individuals with disabilities are radically different. First, at the root of *social* justice is the idea that all citizens should have opportunity to flourish as human beings and that government should provide the essential material and institutional means of individual self-development (Dewey, 1923; Nussbaum, 2007). Under this conception of justice, disabled individuals are considered citizens and morally equal with other citizens. Second, as citizens, they enjoy "'the right to have rights'—not any single civil, juridical, or even social right, but the [more] primary right of recognition, inclusion, and membership in both political and social society" (Somers and Wright, 2008: 25). As citizens, however, they are entitled to the same civil, political, and social rights. These rights are construed as constitutional rights, which cannot be violated by legislative majorities (Nussbaum, 2007). With regard to the IDEA and ADA, social democrats would argue that these laws are grounded in the basic rights that all citizens are entitled to. Therefore, these laws and the systems of support they mandate cannot be construed as forms of public charity. As constitutionally backed public policy, social democrats would operationalize the rights of disabled citizens, serving to enable their self-development.

Over the past 40 years, disability theory and, to a lesser extent, disability policy have edged toward the social democratic conception of justice, but full adoption of this conceptualization requires constitutional rights and protections for all citizens. Without such constitutional guarantees, the disability community is at risk of losing its current, hard-won statutory rights under the influence of neoliberal Congressional majorities promoting financial liberalization, deregulation, low taxes, limited deficits, and privatization (Dardot & Laval, 2013). For people with disabilities and other minority groups, the combination of decreased tax revenue and limited deficit spending is particularly toxic as it creates fiscal conditions that can be used to justify cutting and/or privatizing discretionary social programs that they depend upon. The projected effects of such policies nationally can be seen today in states like Kansas and Wisconsin, where entrenched governors with legislative majorities and billionaire benefactors pride themselves on strict adherence to neoliberal rationality. In Kansas, for example, substantial tax cuts have created unprecedented revenue shortfalls addressed largely by funding cuts in public education and social programs for the state's most vulnerable citizens—the poor and people with disabilities. This includes, at the governor's urging, privatizing Medicaid and its disability waiver program for individuals with intellectual and developmental disabilities, among other impairments, by shifting most service provision responsibilities to three, managed care firms that operate with little state supervision. The Centers for Medicare and Medicaid Services (CMS) officials who recently rejected the state's request to extend this privatized arrangement, cited concerns about its lack of transparency, effectiveness, and oversight. CMS charged the state with failing to meet federal and state standards and using practices that make it difficult for enrollees to understand, use, and assess their benefits, deficiencies that under conditions of limited state oversight, they concluded, ultimately risked the health and safety of enrollees (Lowery & Woodall, 2017).

As there is no such thing as social justice for neoliberals and libertarians, the recognition of citizens' social right to supports and services required to cultivate their human capabilities is absent. Far from this ideal, however, an emboldened neoliberal political culture is pulling established disability policy and programs in the opposite direction, toward a market-based form of justice in which separate, independent individuals are solely responsible for what they achieve or become. Premised on the "myth of autonomy" (Fineman, 2004), market-based justice has dire consequences for society as a whole, given the inherent interdependency of its members. However, this type of justice is especially dire for those members who, owing to age, health, and/or ability, may require additional or even extensive support from others temporarily or permanently, including citizens with intellectual and developmental disabilities.

Karrie A. Shogren, J. Robert Kent, and Thomas M. Skrtic

FURTHER READING

Arendt, Hannah. 1951. *The Origins of Totalitarianism.* New York: Harcourt Brace.

Blatt, Burton, & Fred Kaplan. 1966. *Christmas in Purgatory.* New York: Allyn & Bacon.

Braddock, David, Richard Hemp, Mary C. Rizzolo, E. Shea Tanis, Laura Haffer, & Joy Wu. 2015. *State of the States in Intellectual and Developmental Disabilities: Emerging from the Great Recession.* Washington, DC: American Association on Intellectual and Developmental Disabilities.

Bradley, Valerie J. 1994. "Evolution of a New Service Paradigm." In V. J. Bradley, J. W. Ashbaugh, & B. C. Blaney (Eds.), *Creating Individual Supports for People with Developmental Disabilities: A Mandate for Change at Many Levels*, 11–32. Baltimore: Brookes

Dardot, Pierre, & Christian Laval. 2013. *The New Way of the World: On Neoliberal Society.* London: Verso.

Dewey, John. 1923. *Democracy and Education: An Introduction to the Philosophy of Education.* New York: Macmillan.

Fineman, Martha A. 2004. *The Autonomy Myth: A Theory of Dependency.* New York: The New Press.

Hayek, F. A. 1944. *The Road to Serfdom: A Classic Warning Against the Dangers to Freedom Inherent in Social Planning.* Chicago: University of Chicago Press.

Hayek, Friedrich A. 1960. *The Road to Serfdom.* Chicago: University of Chicago Press.

Hayek, Friedrich A. 1976. *Law, Legislation and Liberty, Vol. 2: The Mirage of Social Justice.* Chicago: University of Chicago Press.

Lowery, Bryan, & Hunter Woodall. 2017. "Criticizing Kansas, Feds Deny Extension of KanCare Privatized Medicaid Program." *The Kansas City Star.* Retrieved from https://www.kansascity.com/news/politics-government/article127424309.html#storylink=cpy

Luckasson, Ruth, Sharon Borthwick-Duffy, Wil H. E. Buntinx, David L. Coulter, Ellis M. Pat Craig, Alya Reeve, Robert L. Schalock, Matha E. Snall, Deborah M. Spitalnik, Scott Spreat, & Marc J. Tasse. (9th ed.). 1992. *Mental Retardation: Definition, Classification, and Systems of Supports.* Washington, DC: American Association on Mental Retardation.

Nirje, Bengt. 1969. "The Normalization Principle and Its Human Management Implications." In R. B. Kugel and W. Wolfensberger (Eds.), *Changing Residential Patterns for the Mentally Retarded*, 179–195. Washington, DC: President's Committee on Mental Retardation.

Nussbaum, Martha C. 2007. *Frontiers of Justice: Disability, Nationality, Species Membership.* Cambridge, MA: Harvard University Press.

Nussbaum, Martha C. 2011. *Creating Capabilities: The Human Developmental Approach.* Cambridge, MA: Harvard University Press.

Schalock, Robert L., Sharon A. Borthwick-Duffy, Valerie J. Bradley, Wil H. E. Buntinx, David L. Coulter, Ellis M. Craig, Sharon C. Gomez, Yves Lachapelle, Ruth Luckasson, Alya Reeve, Karrie A. Shogren, Martha E. Snell, Scott Spreat, Marc J. Tasse, James R. Thompson, Miguel A. Verdugo-Alonso, Michael L. Wehmeyer, & Mark H. Yeager. (11th ed.). 2010. *Intellectual Disability: Definition, Classification, and*

Systems of Support. Washington, DC: American Association on Intellectual and Developmental Disabilities.

Schalock, Robert L., Jack A. Stark, Martha E. Snell, David L. Coutler, Edward A. Polloway, Ruth Luckasson, Steven Reiss, & Deborah M. Spitalnik. 1994. "The Changing Conception of Mental Retardation: Implications for the Field." *Mental Retardation, 32*, 181.

Sen, Amartya. 1999. *Development as Freedom*. New York: Anchor Books.

Sen, Amartya. 2009 *The Idea of Justice*. Cambridge, MA: Harvard University Press.

Shapiro, Joseph P. 1993. *No Pity: People with Disabilities Forging a New Civil Rights Movement*. New York: Three Rivers Press.

Skrtic, Thomas M., & J. Robert Kent. 2013. "Rights Needs, and Capabilities: Institution and Political Barriers to Justice for Disabled People." In Arlene S. Kanter & Beth A. Ferri (Eds.), *Righting Educational Wrongs: Disabilities Studies in Law and Education*, 58–101. Syracuse, NY: Syracuse University Press.

Somers, Margaret R., & Olin Wright. 2008. *Genealogies of Citizenship: Markets, Statelessness, and the Right to Have Rights*. Cambridge: Cambridge University Press.

Thompson, James R., Valerie J. Bradley, Wil H. E. Buntinx, Robert L. Schalock, Karrie A. Shogren, Martha E. Snell, & Michael L. Wehmeyer. 2009. "Conceptualizing Supports and the Support Needs of People with Intellectual Disability." *Intellectual and Developmental Disabilities, 47*, 135–146.

Trent, James W., Jr. 1994. *Inventing the Feeble Mind: A History of Mental Retardation in the United States*. Berkley: University of California Press.

U.S. Department of Education. 2014. *36th Annual Report to Congress on the Implementation of the Individuals with Disabilities Education Act*. Washington, DC: DOE.

Wehmeyer, Michael L., Wil H. E. Buntinx, Yves Lachapelle, Ruth A. Luckasson, Robert L. Schalock, Miguel A. Verdugo, & Sharon Borthwick-Duffy. 2008. "The Intellectual Disability Construct and Its Relation to Human Functioning." *Intellectual and Developmental Disabilities, 46*: 311–318.

World Health Organization. 1980. *The International Classification of Impairment, Disability and Handicap*. Geneva: WHO.

World Health Organization. 2001. *International Classification of Functioning, Disability, and Health*. Geneva: WHO.

Discrimination in K–12 Education

America's public schools have a complicated relationship with discrimination. In some ways, schools are the most egalitarian institutions we have, and, in other ways, they are the ultimate perpetuators of social injustice. Foundational ideas about what it means to be an American can be traced directly to the public schools, which are emblematic of the belief that with a good education anyone in America can get ahead. Schools, though, have also been places of suffering and humiliation for some marginalized people. To understand how this is true, it is necessary to examine the way schools make decisions about who will be served, what will be taught, and how learning will happen. Schools are subject to policies, laws, and regulations from the federal government, state governments, local municipal governments, and school boards. At each of those levels, policy makers can make decisions that affect students' day-to-day lives. In fact, policies often have emotional, social, financial, and academic impacts, so they are frequently described as having a moral component.

EDUCATION POLICY AND PRACTICE

It is more typical to describe morality as a belief system, but in the world of schools and students, it is the action, not the belief, that matters. Schools are places of activity and, like most institutions in the United States, are run according to policy prescriptions that guide and constrain the actors within the institution. The attention to moral concerns brought by educators and other policy makers who set the rules are distinct but combine to create the ethical outlines of students' school experiences.

Public schools and the professionals who work in them are subject to multiple agencies that have regulatory and policy-making power. Federal policy comes from both Congress and the Supreme Court and has widespread impact on the more local policy-making bodies. For instance, the Individuals with Disabilities Education Act (IDEA) and the *Brown v. Board of Education* decision both created federal guidelines with which all public schools in the United States are mandated to comply and that impact policy decisions in almost every aspect of educational decision making. States also have state-specific laws for public schools, and each state has a State Education Agency (SEA) tasked with licensing teachers, monitoring schools, and deciding how schools in the state will earn accreditation, among other things. Local municipalities also impact education, often in the form of tax policies, which typically have a significant effect on school funding. The next level of policy resides at the district level, usually in the form of a locally elected school board. School boards have the potential for substantial power in most places because they usually set policy and hire superintendents. Finally, of course, schools often create their own policies about a variety of issues, including school dress codes and who can use school bathrooms.

Each layer of school-related policy making is consequential for somebody, but the degree to which we can uncover the relationships between a policy and the lived experience of a student, parent, teacher, or district administrator is variable. When any given school phenomenon could be accounted for by any number of combinations of federal, state, city, district, and school policies, it becomes hard to lay claim to a line of reasoning that connects a "policy" to a "practice." This confounding of factors results in individuals not having a clear sense of why they are doing some things, which makes individual moral decision making difficult.

For instance, when the federal government included, in the 2004 reauthorization of IDEA—a mandate for states to have policies and procedures that prevent disproportionality (the over- or underrepresentation of minorities in special education) and to collect, examine, and report data to determine significant disproportionate rates—they likely didn't suspect that some states might change their policies to include more lenient definitions of "disproportionate" or that some districts would use the policy as a rationale to underidentify all students with disabilities in order to avoid triggering censure. Some have argued that in an attempt to create more equitable educational environments, Congress actually triggered a cascade effect, in some places, that has resulted in individual students not getting the services they need. Others, however, assert that in this same period there has been a decrease in educational funding in most states, as well as a perpetual underfunding of IDEA by the federal government, and so changes or decreases in special education services are more likely the result of fiscal policies.

Yet another set of scholars and politicians argue that the trends in education are moving toward more inclusive schools and more effective responses to intervention frameworks, which effectively and efficiently keep students from needing special education; thus areas experiencing a decrease in special education referrals are also likely to contain schools that have implemented strong academic support systems. Regardless of the cause, in school districts where fewer children are identified as having disabilities, the mechanisms that make the referral process work tend to get used less and less, thus sustaining the trend. As a result, a teacher who has an African American student with a learning disability may not end up recommending that child for special education, even if doing so is in the child's best interest, because the process of making that recommendation seems overwhelming or foreign or because that teacher is afraid of being "wrong." The underserving of the student, which amounts to discrimination, is a moral failure, but to place the blame on the teacher is misguided; it is the policies informing the teacher's under-standing of the problem that constrained her or his decision making.

The purpose of this example is to illustrate the complicated and nuanced nature of discrimination in public schools. Students who are marginalized in schools are often the victims of forces far outside the school building. The effects of institu-tionalized racism are well documented, although far from being fully or even par-tially addressed. Beyond institutionalized racism, though, a variety of other factors may be keeping students of different races, ethnicities, gender identities, sexual ori-entations, religions, ability levels, and socioeconomic statuses from fully access-ing their potential. These factors create the constraints within which moral choices must be made. Thus, the moral parameters available to any individual within the system are predetermined by the policies that have combined to create the envi-ronment. The moral choices of the policy makers, however, are bound by a differ-ent and generally less restrictive set of factors. It is worthwhile, then, to examine the ways in which people think about and frame the issue of discrimination in schools when they embark on policy creation.

DEBATING THE PURPOSE OF PUBLIC EDUCATION

Education scholar David Labaree has theorized that America's public schools exist to serve one of three purposes, depending on the dominant political agenda of the era and the local context surrounding decision making and education. For some, the purpose of education is to prepare *citizens*, people who can participate effectively in a democracy in which the goal is equality. For others, the goal of schools is to train *workers*, people who can step into the marketplace and contrib-ute effectively to our economic system. His final contingent is made up of people who believe schools are the engine of social mobility, meaning the purpose of edu-cation is to prepare people to compete for *social positions* (Labaree, 1997). Policy makers, whether they know it or not, are always privileging one of these purposes when they make decisions about schools.

As an example, today's policy makers have been increasingly forced to reckon with the resegregation of America's public schools. This phenomenon, in which schools that were desegregated post–*Brown v. Board of Education*, have, over time, become resegregated due to complicated and often preexisting factors in the wider region or community (like real estate redlining and racist banking practices), has been widely criticized by people of every political stripe. But how to address the criticism? For some people—and especially those who are most likely to subscribe to the idea that the goal of public education is to create equality-minded citizens—the answer is to reinstitute bussing and other purposeful policies that "force the hand" of local school districts to educate all students, regardless of their background. People who see the role of schools as places to produce valuable workers attempt to address the problem through higher academic standards and increased account-ability. For policy makers who turn to these measures, the issue isn't the people those students go to school with but instead the focus is on what skills those stu-dents have learned by the time they graduate.

The final group, which emphasizes the social mobility goal, are the policy makers who promote school choice, charter schools, and private school vouchers because in their view the ultimate purpose of education is either to escape low circumstances or to maintain privileged status, both of which can best be accomplished by maintaining a variety of educational options. It is worth noting that these "solutions" are not complementary, but instead each pushes schools into very different methods of survival. They also determine the environment in which teachers and school leaders operate, regardless of whether they agree with that system and set of priorities.

Labaree's framework isn't the only way to contextualize policy maker's choice making, however. Another approach is to frame policy as the mediation of a *problem*, and the lens through which people view the problem is determined by the scope of the problem instigators. Specifically, policy can be aimed at "fixing" a problem with individuals, groups, institutions, society, or global issues. To illustrate this framework, it is useful to examine school discipline, which is historically meted out unevenly. Minorities and boys tend to suffer the most severe consequences of school discipline policies in general, and to date no magic bullet has been found for overcoming the myriad of problems students can come up with to challenge school administrators. Thus, school discipline has routinely become a part of policy conversations at multiple levels.

Policy makers who view poor school discipline as a problem rooted primarily in individual students tend to favor rules and consequences allowing for disciplinary actions that are specific to the person and thus relatively subjective. However, if the prevailing view in the policy-making space is that discipline is a manifestation of group dynamics, policy makers are more likely to champion solutions like implementing a Restorative Justice program or foregrounding peer role models in public spaces. If school discipline is considered an institutional-level problem, policy is more likely to include an investment in school-wide initiatives, like a Positive Behavior Intervention and Supports (PBIS) system. Yet another perspective is that school discipline is a manifestation of societal problems, which leads policy makers to turn to family training programs, community-building activities, and "marketing" of proschool ideologies intended to counteract negative school messaging, which is perceived to be more prevalent. Finally, a policy maker who envisions school discipline as a global problem is likely to focus on things like effecting change through school-wide nutrition and exercise programs or on implementing meditation routines in schools. In each scenario, the policy prescriptions attempt to address the problem of "school discipline," but each "solution" is going to produce different results because the problem definition is different.

Regardless of the way that issues of disproportionality, segregation, and discipline are framed, each of these has captured policy makers' attention because the problem is indicative of inequitable educational opportunities and experiences. For many people, each represents discrimination in some form, but few people claim that educators purposefully perpetuate any of them to *create* discriminatory practices. Some claim, however, there are other examples in which school policies seem to do just that.

For instance, in recent years there has been a national conversation about who should be allowed to use public bathrooms. This is especially salient in schools because the issue of gender and bathrooms has been grounded in both identity politics and in a discussion of safety, both of which are particularly pertinent to school-aged children. If the issue is framed as a human rights or civil rights issue, who uses which bathroom is a question of fundamental rights. People viewing the issue from this perspective maintain that if people are not allowed this fundamental right, that constitutes a battle against their identity, which is a moral choice many find unconscionable. On the other hand, for people who frame the issue based on their understanding of public safety, letting anybody use any bathroom is equivalent to setting the stage for a crime, which is equally unconscionable. The bathroom debate is unique in that it has engaged policy makers at every level of the educational policy spectrum, but the framing has been relatively static.

Unlike the bathroom issue, controversy over school curricular materials has been an ongoing debate for decades. Since the 1970s, critics of Euro-centric school curricula have been calling for revisions in what is considered canonical. The desire of advocates for more diverse texts and perspectives is considered by some to be a reasonable response to the repression of minority voices and experiences and non-Western concepts and worldviews. For others, it is a disparaging of traditional ideals and foundational concepts that are central to our society. Again, we can look at how the framing of the argument clarifies the moral grounding of the participants; for some, our priority as a society should be to foreground the voices of multiple cultures, and for others it is more important to fully explore the roots of the dominant culture.

It is interesting to note that few of the major issues involving discrimination and education have ever been successfully addressed through policy at a large scale. There have been dramatic changes, to be sure. Unlike earlier periods, in contemporary America all children have a right to attend public school. Beyond this basic right, however, policy prescriptions have alternately made inroads and created detours toward the goal of equitable educational opportunities and learning environments. Furthermore, the educational landscape continues to get more complicated, ensuring that future educators and policy makers will face increasingly difficult choices as they try to navigate a path they find morally appropriate. Teachers and students often find themselves at the nexus of these controversial and morally contentious issues, but rarely do they have the power to enact any kind of change or reset the framing of the debates. Perhaps, however, policy makers will take note of their perpetual inability to find solutions and look to new places and people for help.

Elizabeth Meitl

FURTHER READING

Banks, James A. 1991. "A Curriculum for Empowerment, Action, and Change." *Empowerment Through Multicultural Education* (1991): 125–141.

Drakeford, William. 2004. *Racial Disproportionality in School Disciplinary Practices.* Denver, CO: National Center for Culturally Responsive Educational Systems.

Labaree, David F. 1997. "Public Goods, Private Goods: The American Struggle over Educational Goals." *American Educational Research Journal*, *34*(1): 39–81.

Lewis, A. E., & J. B. Diamond. 2015. *Despite the Best Intentions: How Racial Inequality Thrives in Good Schools* (Transgressing Boundaries: Studies in Black Politics and Black Communities). Oxford: Oxford University Press.

Rosiek, Jerry, & Kathy Kinslow. 2015. *Resegregation as Curriculum: The Meaning of the New Racial Segregation in US Public Schools*. New York: Routledge.

Serpell, Zewelanji N. 2010. "Disproportionality in Special Education." In *Encyclopedia of Cross-Cultural School Psychology*, 382–385. New York: Springer US.

Driving Under the Influence

Law enforcement typically sees an increase in the number of driving under the influence (DUI) arrests between Christmas Eve and New Year's Day. The California Highway Patrol (CHP) reported, for example, that they arrested 530 drivers on New Year's Eve in 2016 (Tatro, 2017). To combat the number of arrests and fatalities that occur over the holidays, Mothers Against Drunk Driving (MADD), in partnership with the National Football League (NFL), developed a program where individuals can volunteer to be the designated driver for their friends. The National Highway Traffic Safety Administration (NHTSA) also had a Drive Sober or Get Pulled Over holiday campaign in an effort to educate the public about the dangers of drunk driving.

Drunk driving, to many, is a clear-cut example of a crime, but it is also considered by some to be a moral failure. Individuals who are impaired and knowingly place themselves behind the wheel of a vehicle put both themselves and innocent drivers and passengers at risk. This viewpoint often collides with Americans' love of alcohol, their enthusiasm for driving, and their zeal for defending individual liberties.

CHANGING ATTITUDES ABOUT DRUNK DRIVING

The problem of drunk driving has been an issue in the United States ever since the creation of the automobile. For many decades, however, little effort was made to combat the issue, which was couched as an issue of private behavior rather than of public health. In the 1970s, however, citizen activists, churches, and interest groups began to successfully lobby state government regulations to reduce the incidence of drunk driving and publicly shame violators. This shift was largely due to the political and cultural climate that allowed moralistic campaigns driven by the media to redefine the problem of drinking and driving. Activists were able to successfully redefine drinking and driving as a public problem by publicizing drunk driving accidents that took the lives of children and other innocent people, which in turn prompted shifts in public attitudes about alcohol use and regulation.

The Anti–Drunk Driving Movement

Drunk driving is a leading cause of deaths and injuries on American roads and highways. In 1982, when the NHTSA started keeping statistics of alcohol-related crashes through the Fatality Analysis Reporting System (FARS), the number of alcohol-related fatalities totaled 21,113 (Mothers Against Drunk Driving, 2014). In 2014, alcohol-impaired driving fatalities accounted for 9,967 deaths, 31 percent of overall driving fatalities (National Highway Traffic Safety Administration, 2018). This 52 percent decline from 1982 to 2014 has been widely attributed to the efforts of Mothers Against Drunk Driving (MADD) and other anti–drunk driving supporters.

Although many associate the anti–drunk driving movement with MADD, the first group to organize efforts supporting anti–drunk driving efforts was Remove Intoxicated Drivers (RID). RID was founded in 1978 by Doris Aiken in Schenectady, New York, after two children were killed by a drunk driver. Aiken was motivated to form the group after she was informed that the district attorney would not prosecute or take away the license of the driver. The district attorney's reasoning was that "this was an accident, he didn't mean to do it" (Lerner, 2011: 76). Other organizations involved in the anti–drunk driving movement included the Alliance Against Intoxicated Motorists (AAIM), Boost Alcohol Consciousness Concerning the Health of University Students (BACCHUS), and Students Against Driving Drunk (SADD). MADD, however, ultimately became the most prominent and powerful organization of the anti–drunk driving movement.

One of the main triggering events that brought the DUI problem in the United States to light was the death of Candy Lightener's 13-year-old daughter by an intoxicated driver who had a previous record of DUI; Lightener used this experience to found MADD in 1980. Lightener's family tragedy and MADD's activity personalized the problem of DUI and changed public perceptions toward understanding DUI as a social harm rather than as simply foolish behavior. When MADD was first founded, an estimated 25,000 people were killed in drunk driving crashes each year across the United States. Since then, that figure has been cut by over half (NHTSA, 2018), in large part because of the passage of anti–drunk driving, victim rights, and underage drinking prevention laws (National Institutes of Health, 2018).

The anti–drunk driving movement knew that it was making headway in changing public perceptions about the issue in the 1980s, when *Newsweek* described DUI as a "socially accepted form of murder" and President Ronald Reagan condemned the "slaughter" caused by drunk driving and created a presidential commission to study the problem (Lerner, 2011. The success of groups like MADD and RID can be attributed to changing the public perception of drunk driving in general and to elevating drinking and driving to become a public policy problem that legislatures had an electoral incentive to address.

The success of the anti–drunk driving movement in changing public perception has in large part been due to the way the movement framed the policy problem, in particular the way the movement focused on drunk driving as a moral failure. By framing the act as both selfish and criminal, the anti–drunk driving movement was able to increasingly define drunk drivers as "killer drunks" who drink and drive irresponsibly and claim the lives of "innocent victims." Focusing on the individual "blameworthy driver," the movement created a dominant paradigm that socially constructed drunk drivers as "deviants" and that established negative connotations in the mind of the public about individuals who drive intoxicated.

Another way in which the anti–drunk driving movement has been able to make progress in reducing the drunk driving problem is by emphasizing the need to establish and enforce laws to protect innocent victims—especially young children. Indeed, both RID and MADD were founded in response to events in which a child was killed by a drunk driver. During the early mobilization of the anti–drunk driving movement in the 1980s, the press coverage of drunk driving, specifically accidents involving innocent victims, increased dramatically, highlighting an often hidden issue (Lerner, 2011). By giving families an opportunity to tell their stories about how drunk driving impacted them, the organizations not only mobilized and expanded their memberships but also were able to effectively lobby to change drunk driving policies in numerous states.

In many ways, the anti–drunk driving movement received broad support because it was perceived as a grassroots victims' movement and had support from both liberals and conservatives. In fact, their efforts to care for victims through support groups, new laws to compensate victims, and other means attracted bipartisan support.

Opposition to the Anti–Drunk Driving Movement

The success of the anti–drunk driving movement relied upon a message that advocated for victims of drunk driving and that framed drunk drivers as threats to innocent family members. Their efforts, though, were perceived as a threat by some business interests related to the alcohol industry and to people who expressed concern about the rights of the individual drivers. Most of these individuals and groups framed their opposition to groups like MADD and RID as based on concern that the groups were filled with "neoprohibitionists," people opposed not to just drunk driving but to drinking any alcohol before driving and to the consumption of alcohol more broadly.

During the initial organization of MADD, framing the anti–drunk driving movement as "neoprohibitionists" was difficult considering that many of the leaders of MADD, including Candy Lightener, were avid drinkers (Lerner, 2011). MADD was not against drinking but against drunk driving. Shortly after Candy Lightener left MADD in 1985, the philosophy of MADD began to shift from a focus on drunk driving to a position that opposed all drinking and driving, whether legally intoxicated or not. This philosophical shift became evident when in 1992 MADD president Milo Kirk sent out a direct-mail fund-raising solicitation focusing on how the advertising of the alcohol industry had contributed to drinking and driving (Marshall & Oleson, 1994).

MADD argued that the alcohol industry's own advertising guidelines "are either ineffectual or are simply ignored" and that the alcohol industry must "accept more responsibility for its role in our drunk driving tragedy and its solution." It also told lawmakers that "the industry must be held accountable" (Marshall & Oleson, 1994: 54). This turn toward attacking alcohol use and drinking by MADD occurred even as RID faded from the public view largely because the group advocated regulating the alcohol industry. Even Candy Lightner questioned the philosophical shift in an article where she claimed, "[MADD has] become far more neo-prohibitionist than I had ever wanted or envisioned. I didn't start MADD to deal with alcohol. I started MADD to deal with the issue of drunk driving" ("MADD Struggles . . . ," 2002).

Those opposed to the anti–drunk driving movement have also attempted to frame their opposition to MADD and other anti–drunk driving organizations by arguing that the policies for which they advocate are discriminatory. One policy in particular that alarmed opponents of the anti–drunk driving movement was the effort to bring the nationwide blood-alcohol threshold for alcohol-impaired driving down to 0.08 from 0.10. Critics argued that a majority of the alcohol-related fatalities involved blood-alcohol levels of 0.14 or higher and that focusing on drivers between the 0.08 and 0.10 level "was diluting law enforcement efforts against truly dangerous drivers" (Lerner, 2011: 128). Many academics questioned the premise laws because many felt the punishment did not fit the crime. In the minds of the opposition to the anti–drunk driving movement, it was "essential to maintain the distinction between drunk driving and drinking driving" (Jacobs, 1989: 43).

A Profound Shift in Public Attitudes About Impaired Driving

The anti–drunk driving movement has been successful in advocating their policy positions by framing drivers who drive drunk as sinful and deviant. Put simply, it is hard to be against policies that try to reduce drunk driving. This success has led to countless policies meant to target those who drink and drive, including laws that require those previously convicted of impaired driving to install interlock devices in their vehicles that require the driver to blow in a measurement device before the vehicle's engine will start.

Advocates of MADD and the anti–drunk driving movement have always pointed to public education programs, victim assistance, and legislative activism as their primary goals. Regardless of these debates, MADD and the other organizations of the anti–drunk movement have managed to make drunk driving a major public health issue that many state legislatures feel obligated to address, out of genuine concern for either community safety, moral conviction, or their own political careers.

Steven Sylvester

FURTHER READING

Fell, James C., & Robert B. Voas. 2006. "Mothers Against Drunk Driving (MADD): The First 25 Years." *Traffic Injury Prevention*, 7: 195–212.

Gore, Andrew. 2010. "Know Your Limit: How Legislatures Have Gone Overboard with Per Se Drunk Driving Laws and How Men Pay the Price." *William & Mary Journal of Women and the Law, 16*: 423–447.

Greenfield, Thomas K., Suzanne P. Johnson, & Norman Giesbrecht. 2004. "The Alcohol Policy Development Process: Policymakers Speak." *Contemporary Drug Problems, 31*: 627–654.

Gusfield, Joseph R. 1996. *Contested Meanings: The Construction of Alcohol Problems.* Madison: University of Wisconsin Press.

Gusfield, Joseph R. 1981. *The Culture of Public Problems: Drinking-Driving and the Symbolic Order.* Chicago: University of Chicago Press.

Hamilton, Wendy J. 2000. "Mothers Against Drunk Driving—MADD in the USA." *Injury Prevention, 6*: 90–91.

Jacobs, James B. 1989. *Drunk Driving: An American Dilemma.* Chicago: University of Chicago Press.

Lerner, Barron H. 2011. *One for the Road: Drunk Driving Since 1900.* Baltimore: Johns Hopkins University Press.

"MADD Struggles to Remain Relevant." 2002. *Washington Times.* Retrieved from http://www.washingtontimes.com/news/2002/aug/6/20020806-035702-2222r

Marshall, Mac, & Alice Oleson. 1994. "In the Pink: MADD and Public Health Policy in the 1990s." *Journal of Public Health Policy, 15*: 57–70.

McCarthy, John D. 1996. "Resource Mobilization by Local Social Movement Organizations: Agency, Strategy, and Organization in the Movement Against Drinking and Driving." *American Sociological Review, 61*: 1070–1088.

Meier, Kenneth J. 1994. *The Politics of Sin: Drugs, Alcohol, and Public Policy.* Armonk, NY: M. E. Sharpe.

Mothers Against Drunk Driving (MADD). 2013a. "About Drunk Driving." Retrieved from http://www.madd.org/drunk-driving/about

Mothers Against Drunk Driving (MADD). 2013b. "Information by State." Retrieved from http://www.madd.org/drunk-driving/state-stats

Mothers Against Drunk Driving (MADD). 2013c. "Status of State Ignition Interlock Laws." Retrieved from http://www.madd.org/drunk-driving/ignition-interlocks/status-of -state-ignition.html

Mothers Against Drunk Driving (MADD). 2014. "Campaign to Eliminate Drunk Driving." Retrieved from http://www.madd.org/drunk-driving/campaign

National Highway Traffic Safety Administration (NHTSA). 2018. "Drunk Driving." Washington, DC. Retrieved from https://www.nhtsa.gov/risky-driving/drunk-driving

National Institutes of Health. 2018. "Alcohol Related Traffic Deaths." Washington, DC: U.S. Department of Health and Human Services. Retrieved from https://report.nih .gov/nihfactsheets/ViewFactSheet.aspx?csid=24

Ross, H. Laurence. 1992. *Confronting Drunk Driving: Social Policy for Saving Lives.* New Haven, CT: Yale University Press.

Sylvester, Steven M., & Donald P. Haider-Markel. 2016. "Buzz Kill: State Adoption of Dui Interlock Laws, 2005–2011." *Policy Studies Journal, 44*: 491–509.

Tatro, Samantha. 2017. "DUI-related Fatalities on San Diego Roads Down over New Year's Eve: CHP." *NBC San Diego.* Retrieved from http://www.nbcsandiego.com/news /local/DUI-Arrests-Fatalities-Report-in-San-Diego-County-CHP-409175685 .html

Drones and Unmanned (Smart) Weapons Systems

Successful combat missions are often reliant on successful surveillance techniques. While armies' utilization of spies to gather information prior to military engagement with an adversary is as ancient as the premodern Israelites' reconnaissance of Canaan, the covert collection of intelligence can be costly and frequently yields an incomplete interpretation of the battlefield and of the capabilities of adversarial forces. The introduction of air power into warfare enriched militaries' surveillance capabilities, as aerial photo surveillance could produce a wider view of the battlefield and the adversarial threat potential. The downing of American pilot Francis Gary Powers' U-2 spy plane over Soviet Russia in 1960 increased public awareness of U.S. surveillance methods but also spurred new government investments in surveillance technologies that would reduce the threat to human life.

THE HISTORY OF UNMANNED AERIAL DRONES

Unmanned aerial vehicles (UAVs) seemed to be an answer to this dilemma. Photo and video capabilities advanced, allowing for clearer visual surveillance, and devices could be operated from greater distances, allowing for the reduced threat to human pilots. UAVs were successfully utilized by the United States military for the duration of the Vietnam War and continued to be of interest to the Department of Defense in the waning years of the Cold War for the purposes of "reconnaissance and surveillance, target acquisition, target spotting, command and control, meteorological data collection, nuclear biological and chemical detections, and lastly, disruption and deception" (Blom, 2010: 73). While the United States military worked on its own UAV capabilities, the U.S. Navy purchased the Israeli-developed Pioneer UAV system in 1986, which was utilized in the Persian Gulf during Operation Desert Storm to direct sea-to-land naval gunfire against Iraqi targets. This deployment proved very successful as 18,000 pounds of explosives were leveled against Iraqi targets on February 3, 1991, alone.

The successful use of UAVs in the Persian Gulf led to the development and deployment of the widely used Predator system for aerial reconnaissance in 1994. The Predator was a valuable surveillance asset during the Bosnian Conflict in 1995. The Predator used UHF satellite technology to convey images to its operators, allowing "for real-time still images to be transmitted back to the ground terminals" (Blom, 2010: 93). General Wesley Clark, supreme allied commander Europe during the Bosnian Conflict, was very impressed with the Predator's utility in military operations and advocated for its continued development. In an interview with academic James der Derian, he described the ability of UAVs' surveillance to integrate with other strategic technologies and practices to locate targets:

> What you needed was integration of the digitized images from the unmanned aerial vehicle flying overhead, your map coordinates, and the geolocations of the enemy from the GPS, and to project it all on the thermal viewer, to use it as a computer, so the driver and the gunner know when they get to the top of the hill, they'll know that the son-of-a-bitch is going to be right there. (der Derian, 2009: 188–189)

Predators were especially valuable in the Bosnian War because they could fly between 3,000 and 25,000 feet for about 24 hours at a time and possessed radar that could penetrate clouds. These technological advances permitted lengthy surveillance, in variable weather, with little threat of being shot down from the ground, and essentially no danger to the pilot (Lambeth, 2001).

Although surveillance remains the primary objective of UAVs, the integration mentioned by General Clark was further developed in final months of the Clinton administration and proved vital in the George W. Bush administration's Global War on Terror. In February of 2001, Predators equipped with precision-guided munitions completed their first successful tests. On October 7, 2001 (the first night of Operation Enduring Freedom in Afghanistan), an armed Predator completed its first successful combat strike. The attack was successful and "killed several members of the Taliban leader Mullah Omar's security detail in an attempt to flush him out of a nearby building" (Plaw, Fricker, & Colon, 2016: 21). The early successes of weaponized UAVs in counterterrorism efforts prompted greater use of this technology in Afghanistan, Iraq, Yemen, Libya, Somalia, Syria, and elsewhere.

Arming Predators enables sustained surveillance of targets with the ability to launch strikes on targets quickly and without ground troops in the immediate vicinity. This capacity has been especially valuable in conflicts featuring difficult terrain, such as Afghanistan, in which combatants can take refuge and that traditional ground troops and munitions have difficulty traversing in pursuit of adversaries. In a 2001 speech given to military cadets at the Citadel, President Bush extolled the value of the Predator:

> This unmanned aerial vehicle is able to circle over enemy forces, gather intelligence, transmit information instantly back to commanders, then fire on targets with extreme accuracy. Before the war, the Predator had skeptics, because it did not fit the old ways. Now it is clear the military does not have enough unmanned vehicles. We're entering an era in which unmanned vehicles of all kinds will take on greater importance—in space, on land, in the air, and at sea. (Bush, 2001)

The increased use of UAVs in combat and counterterrorism scenarios has refreshed the ages-long ethical debates regarding warfare ethics and has prompted technology-centric debates about methods of target selection and combatant distinction. While the drone literature is continuously expanding, ethical debates surrounding drone warfare can be divided into legal and philosophical discussions.

ETHICAL CONSIDERATIONS IN DRONE DEPLOYMENT

First, the legality of strikes is a central point of ethical contention surrounding the utilization of weaponized drones. The importance of international law to wartime conduct is vital to the protection of all parties within the legal practice of war. The International Committee of the Red Cross (ICRC) details six principles that make up the Law of Armed Conflict and establishes international expectations for the execution of warfare: distinction, proportionality, military necessity, limitation, good faith, and humane treatment and non-discrimination (2002). The two areas of the Law of Armed Combat that scholars are most interested in when determining the legality of weaponized drone use in military engagement are the *jus in bello* (justice in war) principles: proportionality and distinction.

Proportionality is intended to determine and evaluate the balance between the military advantage achieved as a result of attacking a target and the amount of potential and/or realized collateral damage (the impact on nonmilitary targets) associated with it. The Law of Armed Conflict states that "when military objectives are attacked, civilians and civilian objects must be spared from incidental or collateral damage to the maximum extent possible" (ICRC, 2002: 12–14). The precision associated with weaponized UAVs cause proportionality to be an expected outcome. Scholars Daniel Brunstetter and Megan Braun (2011) suggest that the use of UAVs increases adherence to the principle of proportionality due to its use of precision-guided missiles and the limitation of force necessary to neutralize threats. Journalist Jane Mayer (2009) also reports that "predator drones . . . have a better track record for accuracy than fighter jets" and that "the drone's smaller Hellfire missiles are said to cause far less collateral damage."

However, the general expectation of precision results in reduced tolerance of collateral damage. One of the fiercest critics of American drone tactics in Pakistan comes from Amnesty International (AI), an international human rights organization. In a 2013 report, AI cautions the United States that in order to abide by international expectations of proportionality, the United States military must do "everything feasible . . . to verify that targets are military objectives . . . and to halt attacks if it becomes apparent they are wrongly-directed or disproportionate" (46). Conducting strikes that will "cause excessive incidental civilian loss, injury or damage," AI warns, "is a war crime" (46).

The principle of distinction requires that militaries "distinguish between combatants and civilians" (ICRC, 2002: 12). Committed to protecting civilians (or noncombatants) present in conflict, international law permits "only members of a state's armed forces during armed conflict or persons taking a direct part in hostilities" to be targeted (O'Connell, 2010: 21). Because drone warfare is waged from a great distance and through a video camera, a person's role in the conflict may not be immediately clear to a UAV pilot who is surveying the scene from above. Making matters of distinction even more difficult is the fact that "suspected militant leaders wear civilian clothes. Even the sophisticated cameras of a drone cannot be certain that a suspect being targeted is not a civilian" (O'Connell, 2010: 23). While the role of targets may not be immediately clear from a live video feed on a screen, some legal scholars suggest that the sustained surveillance provided by UAVs increases the potential for discrimination between combatants and noncombatants (Vogel, 2011).

A chief area of contention surrounding the drone strike program under the Barack Obama administration was the utilization of a target-selection procedure known as signature strikes. Such attacks are leveled against targeted individuals whose identities are unknown but whose monitored activities "match a pre-identified 'signature' of behavior that the US links to militant activity, rather than targeting a specific person" (Greenfield, 2013). Because President Obama initially found signature strikes to be legally risky and ethically distasteful, he and his military advisors created a "kill list" of known, targeted affiliates with the Taliban and al-Qaeda to guide drone strikes (Becker & Shane, 2012; Bowden, 2013). Ultimately, however, the CIA convinced President Obama that signature strikes were strategically efficacious because "you could take out a lot more bad guys when you targeted groups instead of individuals" (Klaidman, 2012: 41).

Some scholars contend that the potential ambiguity of identifying targets and carrying out strikes based on behavior seem to trouble the distinction principle of the law of armed conflict. For example, University of Amsterdam Professor Kevin Heller leveled tough criticism on the Obama administration for its reliance on signature strikes: "The United States considers any military-age male in the area of known terrorist activity and any individual who 'consorts' with 'known militants' to be a lawful target—a standard that bears little resemblance to long-standing principles of [International Humanitarian Law]" (Heller, 2013: 105). A 2013 humanitarian report on drone strikes also suggested that "the legality of so-called 'signature strikes' is highly suspect" (Stanford International Human Rights and Conflict Resolution Clinic and the Global Justice Clinic at NYU School of Law, 2013). This is primarily due to the secrecy surrounding drone strikes and their produced damage and casualties. Accordingly, Amnesty International concludes that the American drone program would alleviate the concerns of human rights activist and the international community if it were to "disclose the legal and factual criteria for identification of targets, including for placement on so-called 'kill lists,' and criteria for so-called . . . 'signature strikes'" (58).

While Heller is critical of the legality of the Obama administration's practice of signature strikes, he does provide a list of "adequate signatures" that he believes are necessary for signature strikes to align more closely with international law. He suggests that individuals who can be proven to be "planning attacks," "transporting vehicles," and/or "handling explosives" would be displaying adequate signatures of combat. Additionally, known "Al-Qaeda compounds" and "Al-Qaeda training camps" that are consistently used for combative purposes are also well within the bounds of international humanitarian law (Heller, 2013: 94–97).

The second area of ethical debate surrounding the utilization of weaponized drones in combat is philosophical in nature and is couched within the Just War theory tradition. Just War theorists who study drone warfare are attempting to root new, technologically advanced tactics of warfare in premodern ethical categories. For scholars who support the continued engagement with and application of Just War theory, the principles associated with the theory present a framework by which they might better understand and thus talk about war's ethical conduct. These principles also translate from the philosophical to the pragmatic, suggesting a standard of justice that is expected before, during, and after war and providing a vocabulary necessary to explain how occurrences of civilian casualties might be expected even in the course of a justly fought war.

From the perspective of Just War theory, drone warfare is primarily situated within the categories of *jus in bello* (justice during war) that are mirrored in international law: proportionality and discrimination. Because the categorical language is similar, a helpful distinction between international law and the Just War tradition involves the questions asked by the respective approaches in regard to the ethical dilemma. Scholars utilizing international law would ask is the act in accordance with legal code? Just War theorists, on the other hand, would ask is the act just or right?

Concerning the use of UAVs in warfare, the Just War perspective is primarily interested in the protection of civilians during strikes. Just War theorist Michael Walzer, for example, maintains the importance of considering the condition of noncombatants who are caught up in the crosshairs of conflict. He notes that noncombatants "do not forfeit their rights when their states wrongly go to war." Instead, noncombatants are to be considered "men and women with rights [who] cannot be used for some military purpose" (2006: 137). Walzer argues that, according to Just War principles, "noncombatants cannot be attacked at any time" (2006: 151). However, international relations theorist Marcus Schulzke (2016) points out that occasionally civilian deaths do result from military actions but are not intended by the soldier. This is known as the principle of double effect, which understands that both positive and negative consequences can result from acts of war (Steinhoff, 2007; Van Damme & Fotion, 2002). For example, "Actions performed by a soldier can lead not only to the death of enemy soldiers but also to the death of by-standers . . . the destruction of buildings, damage to the environment, and so on" (Van Damme & Fotion, 2002: 137).

The humanitarian reports on drone strikes, *Will I Be Next?* (Amnesty International, 2013) and *Living Under Drones* (Stanford International Human Rights and Conflict Resolution Clinic and the Global Justice Clinic at NYU School of Law, 2013), detail the insecurity and existential threats experienced by noncombatants in areas that are regularly targeted by UAVs. While the Obama administration reported in 2016 that 64 to 116 noncombatants had been killed by American drone strikes over the duration of Obama's presidency, the humanitarian reports suggest that this number is much higher (Savage & Shane, 2016). Due to the covert nature of missions and their persistent status as classified, the casualty numbers of drone strikes are almost impossible to confirm. However, the deaths of civilians resulting from drone strikes have established a crucial area of concentration for Just War theorists and have likely increased during the Trump administration as strikes in Yemen and Somalia have increased dramatically (FDD's Long War Journal, 2018).

The question of UAV strikes and double effect remains poignant and contentious. Himes explains that noncombatant casualties generally result from one of two human errors when conducting a drone strike: "the unobserved nearness of civilians to the locale of an airstrike, or ground troops calling for a strike when mistakenly thinking civilians were enemy combatants" (2016: 137). Just War theorist Alex Bellamy argues, however, that more can and should be done in the planning stages in order to prevent the principle of double effect from being realized as a result of drone strikes and highlights a trade-off between troop safety and noncombatant casualties. "Reliance on air power [is] designed to lower risks to coalition forces by removing them from harm's way. The result is that we must accept higher noncombatant casualties" (Bellamy, 2005: 292).

It is clear that weaponized UAVs provide an impressive surveillance and tactical advantage for the American military. Their effectiveness has caused them to be indispensable in contemporary battlefields and in non–battlefield strikes. However, questions about their legal and moral adequacy continue to badger policy makers, academics, human rights activists, and legal professionals. While the ethical debates surrounding weaponized UAVs will persist, it is important that questions and critiques be continually posed and thoughtfully regarded.

Terilyn Johnston Huntington

FURTHER READING

Amnesty International. 2013. *"Will I Be Next?" US Drone Strikes in Pakistan.* London: Amnesty International Publications. Retrieved from https://www.amnestyusa.org/pdfs/asa330132013enExecutiveSummary.pdf

Becker, Jo, & Scott Shane. 2012. "Secret 'Kill List' Proves a Test of Obama's Principles and Will." *New York Times*, May 29. Retrieved from http://www.nytimes.com/2012/05/29/world/obamas-leadership-in-war-on-al-qaeda.html?_r=1

Bellamy, Alex. 2005. "Is the War on Terror Just?" *International Relations*, *19*(3): 275–296.

Bergen, Peter L., & Daniel Rothenberg. 2015. *Drone Wars: Transforming Conflict, Law, and Policy.* New York: Cambridge University Press.

Blom, John David. 2010. *Unmanned Aerial Systems: A Historical Perspective.* Occasional Paper 37. Fort Leavenworth, KS: Combat Studies Institute Press.

Bowden, Mark. 2013. "The Killing Machines: How to Think About Drones." *The Atlantic*, September. Retrieved from http://www.theatlantic.com/magazine/archive/2013/09/the-killing-machines-how-to-think-about-drones/309434

Brunstetter, Daniel, & Megan Braun. 2011. "The Implications of Drones on the Just War Tradition." *Ethics and International Affairs*, *25*(3): 337–358.

Bush, George W. 2001. "President Speaks on War Effort to Citadel Cadets." *The White House: President George W. Bush*, December 11. Retrieved from http://georgewbush-whitehouse.archives.gov/news/releases/2001/12/20011211-6.html

Chamayou, Gregoire. 2015. *A Theory of the Drone.* Trans. Janet Lloyd. New York: New Press.

der Derian, James. (2nd ed.). 2009. *Virtuous War.* New York: Routledge.

FDD's Long War Journal. 2018. "US Airstrikes in the Long War." Retrieved from https://www.longwarjournal.org/us-airstrikes-in-the-long-war

Greenfield, Dayna. 2013. "The Case Against Drone Strikes on People Who Only 'Act' Like Terrorists." *The Atlantic*, August 19. Retrieved from http://www.theatlantic.com /international/archive/2013/08/the-case-against-drone-strikes-on-people-who -only-act-like-terrorists/278744

Gusterson, Hugh. 2016. *Drone: Remote Control Warfare.* Cambridge, MA: MIT Press.

Heller, Kevin Jon. 2013. "'One Hell of a Killing Machine': Signature Strikes and International Law." *Journal of International Criminal Justice*, *11*: 89–119.

Himes, Kenneth R. 2016. *Drones and the Ethics of Targeted Killing.* Lanham, MD: Rowman & Littlefield.

International Committee of the Red Cross. 2002. *The Law of Armed Conflict: Basic Knowledge.* Geneva: ICRC.

Klaidman, Daniel. 2012. *Kill or Capture.* New York: Houghton Mifflin Harcourt.

Lambeth, Benjamin S. 2001. *NATO's Air War for Kosovo: A Strategic and Operational Assessment.* Santa Monica, CA: RAND.

Mayer, Jane. 2009. "The Predator War." *The New Yorker*, October 26: 36–45.

O'Connell, Mary Ellen. 2010. "Unlawful Killing with Combat Drones: A Study of Pakistan, 2004–2009." *Notre Dame Law School Legal Studies Research Paper*, 09-43: 1–26.

Plaw, Avery, Matthew S. Fricker, & Carlos R. Colon. 2016. *The Drone Debate.* Lanham, MD: Rowman & Littlefield.

Savage, Charlie, & Scott Shane. 2016. "U.S. Reveals Death Toll from Airstrikes Outside War Zones." *New York Times*, July 1. Retrieved from https://www.nytimes.com /2016/07/02/world/us-reveals-death-toll-from-airstrikes-outside-of-war-zones.html ?_r=0

Singer, P. W. 2009. *Wired for War.* New York: Penguin Books.

Stanford International Human Rights and Conflict Resolution Clinic and the Global Justice Clinic at NYU School of Law. 2013. *Living Under Drones.* Retrieved from http:///www.livingunderdrones.org; http://chrgj.org/wp-content/uploads/2012/10 /Living-Under-Drones.pdf

Steinhoff, Uwe. 2007. *On the Ethics of War and Terrorism.* Oxford: Oxford University Press.

Van Damme, Guy, & Nicholas Fotion. 2002. "Proportionality." In Bruno Coppieters and Nicholas Fotion (Eds.), *Moral Constraints on War*, 129–139. Lanham, MD: Lexington Books.

Vogel, Ryan J. 2011. "Drone Warfare and the Law of Armed Conflict." *Denver Journal of Law and International Policy*, *39*(1): 102–138.

Walzer, Michael. (4th ed.). 2006. *Just and UnJust Wars.* New York: Basic Books.

Drug Use and Policy

Some people see the use of any substance that alters your mood, personality, and/or consciousness as an immoral act or a demonstration of moral failing. For others, moral judgment falls only on those who abuse or who are addicted to drugs, seeing these individuals as morally weak and corrupt, as well as linked to crime and other social ills. However, besides alcohol, many mind-altering substances were available and legal in the United States until early in the 20th century. Elements of marijuana, cocaine, opium, and even heroin were commonly used in a variety of ways, and components of these drugs could be found in some regularly used products and medicine, including Coca-Cola. It wasn't until the alcohol prohibition movement grew strong in the late 19th and early 20th centuries that the use of these substances fell under greater scrutiny.

Many of the attempts to criminalize drugs, their distribution, and use since the 1910s in the United States could be described as moral panics, in which a rapid alarm over a perceived problem that is believed to threaten the moral fabric of society brings quick and harsh response from government with little thought about the long-term consequences of such expansive increases in state power (Goode & Ben-Yehuda, 2010). However, even in the 1880s, many religious figures and social reformers were decrying the widespread use of psychoactive drugs in widely available pain relievers, cold medicines, and other everyday products. By 1906, temperance reformers, aided by Upton Sinclair's 1904 novel *The Jungle*, which described in graphic fashion the revolting sanitary conditions in Chicago's meatpacking plants, were able to bring about the passage of the Pure Food and Drug Act, which required product labeling of food ingredients, including drugs like opium. Likewise, elements of the Temperance movement were behind the significant restriction in opiates and cocaine in products, with some exceptions for prescriptions, which came with the Harrison Narcotic Act of 1914 (Cherry, 2006).

The first wave of antidrug legislation was certainly inspired by class, ethnic, and racial bias, since the users of street drugs such as opium were often portrayed as Chinese or urban blacks (Courtwright, 1992). However, opposition to opium and cocaine use grew in the 1920s and 1930s as more young white men became users of cocaine. Extremists portrayed addicts as such lost causes that some extremists "even proposed firing squads as a permanent solution for the drug problem, on the theory that the only abstinent addict was a dead one" (Courtwright, 1992: 17). Young men who frequented bars and pool halls were viewed as morally suspect and susceptible to indulgence with drugs like cocaine, which would only lead to a spiral of moral decline, criminality, and ruin (Courtwright, 1992). This portrayal inspired a strong law enforcement application of the Harrison Act in many urban areas.

The first wave of moral panic about marijuana began as early as the 1910s when several states begin to regulate cannabis products. But federal intervention regarding marijuana and the harms it was causing to American youth took off in the 1930s, initially with the creation of the Federal Bureau of Narcotics, the first federal drug regulatory agency, in 1930. A second milestone was the 1937 imposition of one form of tax on medical marijuana and another tax on marijuana for recreation use. Then, one year later, the film *Reefer Madness*, which portrayed marijuana-using youth as crazed psychotics, was released. The movie helped fashion a dark picture of the drug and its users that lasted for the next several decades. By 1970, marijuana was illegal in national law, but a slow and incomplete process of decriminalization began in fits and starts shortly thereafter at the local and state levels. This shift came in response to more positive (or at least less negative) representations of marijuana in popular culture, as well as growing skepticism about the morality and public health arguments that had long been wielded against it (Ferraiolo, 2014).

Shocked by the glorification of marijuana and LSD in the 1960s counterculture and the perceived damage to the moral fabric of the country, President Richard Nixon initiated the first American War on Drugs when he called drug abuse "public enemy number one." In 1973, the Nixon administration merged the office for Drug Abuse Law Enforcement, the Bureau of Narcotics and Dangerous Drugs, and the Office of Narcotics Intelligence to create the Drug Enforcement Agency (DEA). Antidrug efforts were largely focused on heroin, with cocaine and marijuana being less of a priority. Nixon's war was as much a public health crusade as it was a war against the immorality of drugs and the counterculture that helped to create an abuse problem.

The national government's orientation toward drugs did not decline significantly in the 1970s, but by the 1980s the focus began to shift more dramatically away from drug treatment and prevention and toward criminalization and punishment for drug-related offenses. President Ronald Reagan continued Nixon's efforts at criminalization but took these steps further, pushing for harsher penalties and drug interdiction activities in parts of Latin America that were trafficking drugs to the United States. From a framing perspective, it was relatively easy to portray Latin American drug traffickers as morally corrupt criminals who were attempting to make a profit by getting Americans addicted to drugs. This framing enhanced Reagan's ability to militarize the war on drugs and make use of government resources beyond the DEA. The administration's efforts became especially concentrated on cocaine, especially its derivative crack, which had begun to spread through urban areas in the United States as an inexpensive alternative. The shift in enforcement meant that the targets were more likely to be less affluent nonwhites than affluent whites who were the more typical users of regular cocaine.

The targeted enforcement of drug laws subsequently resulted in growing charges that the war on drugs, as it was being prosecuted by the Reagan administration and so-called law-and-order politicians, was an immoral, racialized attack on black America. As evidence, critics pointed to the 1986 Congressional passage of the Anti-Drug Abuse Act, which increased funding for antidrug education efforts but also significantly enhanced penalties for crack cocaine (which was more predominant in black communities) over other illegal drugs (more popular in white communities) when it imposed mandatory minimum sentences for convicted offenders.

President Reagan's War on Drugs was reinforced by first lady Nancy Reagan's 1985 Just Say No campaign, which used private funds and the bully pulpit of the White House to suggest to school-aged children that drug use and abuse was a failure of morals (Sirin, 2011). Reagan's DARE (Drug Abuse Resistance Education) program was premised on the notion of just saying no, but research throughout the 1980s and 1990s concluded that the DARE program did not decrease the use of drugs or alcohol among youth. The moral sermonizing of Reagan has continued, with Attorney General Jeff Sessions saying in 2017: "I think we have too much tolerance for drug use—psychologically, politically, morally. We need to say, as Nancy Reagan said, 'Just say no'" (Joseph, 2017).

In the 1990s, however, evidence for the medical benefits of marijuana began to grow, and moralizing about the use of the drug began to decline. States such as California began to experiment with allowing marijuana for medical use, compelled in part because advocates of legalization emphasized its positive impact on those suffering from medical conditions such as AIDS in 1996 (Hollander & Patapan, 2017). Other states followed California's example in the 2000s, and the legalization of recreational marijuana came to pass through ballot measures passed in Washington and Colorado in 2012. Several other states have also allowed recreational marijuana through ballot measures since then, although North Dakota voters rejected such a measure in 2018. However, the rejection appears to have been more a result of law enforcement opposition than moral arguments against legalization (MacPherson & Kolpack, 2018).

Shifting perceptions about drug use in the early 2000s were also fed by growing recognition among both liberals and conservatives of the sentencing inequalities within the criminal justice system regarding drug-related cases. The 2010 Fair Sentencing Act reduced minimum sentencing requirements for crack cocaine, and several other measures sought to reduce the jail time for nonviolent offenders at the national and state levels.

Even though the war on drugs has scaled back relative to earlier decades, proponents of the decriminalization of all drugs have consistently argued that many antidrug laws and measures are themselves immoral. First, they point to deaths and injuries caused by an illegal drug black market where only violence can enforce contracts. Second, they highlight a criminal justice system overloaded with drug cases, giving police and prosecutors significantly less time and resources to pursue even the most egregious crimes, such as murder. And finally they point to the relatively high percentage of Americans who violate drug laws, which contributes to a belief that the existing social order is suspect and need not be adhered to.

NEEDLE EXCHANGE PROGRAMS

Those addicted to drugs such as heroin often use syringes to inject the drugs. Often addicts engaged in the reuse and sharing of syringes (needles), which in the 1980s helped to rapidly increase the spread of HIV/AIDS, hepatitis C, and other blood-borne diseases. To reduce the spread of disease and reduce the risk posed by used needles in public spaces, many began calling for the establishment of publicly funded needle exchange programs and even the creation of safe injection sites. Some activists even began conducting needle exchanges on their own, even at risk of arrest. They framed these actions as ones based on compassion and concern for the public good. In New York City, local activists known as the Needle Eight ran afoul of laws that banned the distribution of syringes. But the judge in their case recognized their actions as civil disobedience in 1991 and said, "This court is satisfied that the nature of the crisis facing the city, coupled with the medical evidence offered, warranted the defendants' action" (Schumaker, 2019).

Those opposed to these programs argued that they were morally suspect because the programs enabled addicts to use drugs rather than forcing them to deal with the consequences of their addiction. The abstinence-only approach to intravenous drug use was fueled by a disgust for the practice and a conviction that illegal drug use reflected a profound moral failing (Wolf, Russell, & Rich, 2006). This viewpoint prevailed through the darkest periods of the AIDS crisis. Many states and localities banned any nonmedical distribution of syringes, and the national government banned funding for these programs in 1988 (Bowen, 2012).

By the 1990s, many states outside of the South were establishing needle exchange programs, and those programs have been shown to be effective at reducing disease and getting addicts into treatment programs. However, these programs have been and still are typically small-scale and can usually be found only in urban areas.

In 2017, drug overdose deaths in the United States rose to record 70,000, outpacing deaths from gun violence, vehicle crashes, and HIV/AIDS. About 49,000 of those deaths were caused by opioids (Schumaker, 2019). One group believes that the opioid crisis is so bad and that so many lives are at risk of overdose, that it has chosen to violate federal and state laws and independently provide clean needles and related materials to people with addictions to heroin and fentanyl (abuse of prescription pain relief medicines is the other major element of the opioid crisis). They call themselves the Church of Safe Injection and operate in 18 branches in eight states. The founder is a former drug user, Jesse Harvey. The organization also offers the drug Narcan, which can reverse an overdose, along with an inclusive gospel arguing that people who use drugs don't deserve to die (Gaita, 2019). By claiming a religious faith, the group hopes eventually to be exempt from laws regarding syringe distribution.

The church has only three rules: "Congregations are required to welcome people of all faiths, atheists included; to serve all marginalized people; and, most importantly, to support harm reduction, which involves keeping drug users safe and healthy, instead of focusing solely on getting them into addiction treatment" (Schumaker, 2019). Jesse Harvey is quoted as saying:

All too often today, people who use drugs are offered only two choices. . . . get sober or die. Jesus would have rejected this shameful and lethal binary. He'd have been on the front lines providing the third option that Maine and the United States so desperately need: harm reduction. Naloxone, safe injection sites, sterile syringes, the works. (Schumaker, 2019)

CONCLUSION

Concerns over drug use and drug abuse have been common in American history, with underling moral perceptions often driving debate and government action. In times of moral panic over drugs, the United States has sought to reduce drug use through punitive measures, with lessor efforts directed to prevention and treatment. Opponents of punitive policies point to the immoral outcomes of an aggressive criminal justice program that does little to curb demand or to reduce the harms caused by a black market.

Needle exchange programs and other efforts designed to assist the addicted versus criminalizing drug users get to the heart of the moral dilemmas over drugs. Those trying to assist the addicted are accused of facilitating the moral failures of drug users. Those that seek punitive action against drug users are seen as immoral for not reducing human suffering where possible and for perpetuating the racial and economic inequalities in society and the criminal justice system.

Donald P. Haider-Markel

FURTHER READING

Ben-Yehuda, Nachman. 1990. *The Politics and Morality of Deviance: Moral Panics, Drug Abuse, Deviant Science, and Reversed Stigmatization*. Albany, NY: SUNY Press.

Bowen, Elizabeth A. 2012. "Clean Needles and Bad Blood: Needle Exchange as Morality Policy." *Journal of Sociology & Social Welfare*, 39(2): 121–142.

Cherry, Andrew L. 2006. "Drug Abuse." In James Ciment (Ed.), *Social Issues in America: An Encyclopedia*, 570–583. Armonk, NY: M. E. Sharp.

Courtwright, David T. 1992. "A Century of American Narcotic Policy." In Dean R. Gerstein and Henrick J. Harwood (Eds.), *Treating Drug Problems: Volume 2*, 1–62. Washington, DC: National Academies Press. Retrieved from https://doi.org/10.17226/1971

Ferraiolo, Kathleen. 2014. "Morality Framing in US Drug Control Policy: An Example from Marijuana Decriminalization." *World Medical & Health Policy*, 6(4): 347–374.

Gaita, Paul. 2019. "'Church of Safe Injection' Hopes to Save Lives Through Needle Exchange." *The Fix*, January 16. Retrieved from https://www.thefix.com/church-safe-injection-hopes-save-lives-through-needle-exchange

Goode, Erich, & Nachman Ben-Yehuda. 2010. *Moral Panics: The Social Construction of Deviance*. New York: John Wiley & Sons.

Gstrein, Vanessa. 2018. "Ideation, Social Construction and Drug Policy: A Scoping Review." *International Journal of Drug Policy*, 51(January): 75–86.

Hollander, Robyn, & Haig Patapan. 2017. "Morality Policy and Federalism: Innovation, Diffusion and Limits." *Publius: The Journal of Federalism*, 47(1): 1–26.

Joseph, Rebecca Bergenstein. 2017. "We Can't Just Say No." *Health Policy Musings*, April 9. Retrieved from https://sites.tufts.edu/cmph357/2017/04/09/we-cant-just-say-no

Mackey-Kallis, Susan, & Dan F. Hahn. 1991. "Questions of Public Will and Private Action: The Power of the Negative in the Reagans' 'Just Say No' Morality Campaign." *Communication Quarterly*, 39(1): 1–17.

MacPherson, James, and Dave Kolpack. 2018. "Marijuana, Ethics Measure, House Seat Add to ND Ballot." *U.S. News and World Report*, November 7. Retrieved from https://www.usnews.com/news/best-states/north-dakota/articles/2018-11-06/marijuana-ethics-measure-house-seat-add-to-nd-ballot

Meier, Kenneth J. 1999. "Drugs, Sex, Rock, and Roll: A Theory of Morality Politics." *Policy Studies Journal, 27*(4): 681–695.

Ostrowski, James. 1990. "The Moral and Practical Case for Drug Legalization." *Hofstra Law Review, 18*(3): 607–702.

Schumaker, Erin. 2019. "New 'Church' Wants to Save Lives—By Offering a Safe Place to Shoot Up." *The Huffington Post*, January 1. Retrieved from https://www.huffingtonpost.com/entry/church-of-safe-injection_us_5c2650c1e4b08aaf7a901462

Sirin, Cigdem V. 2011. "From Nixon's War on Drugs to Obama's Drug Policies Today: Presidential Progress in Addressing Racial Injustices and Disparities." *Race, Gender & Class, 18*(3–4): 82–99.

Vitellone, Nicole. 2017. *Social Science of the Syringe: A Sociology of Injecting Drug Use.* New York: Routledge.

Wolf, Francis, Phillip Russell, & Josiah D. Rich. 2006. "Needle Exchange Programs." In James Ciment (Ed.), *Social Issues in America: An Encyclopedia*, 1222–1234. Armonk, NY: M. E. Sharp.

Economic Inequality

How much economic inequality is too much? Does the gap between the rich and the poor matter if the poor have enough to begin with? If people are wealthy, they must have worked hard to get that way, right? Is it fair that some of the fruits of their labor be redistributed to those who have less? Or are great concentrations of wealth too often the result of simple good fortune (such as inheritances of wealth) or skewed societal values (such as salaries of professional athletes and movie stars compared to those of schoolteachers). These difficult questions—along with their moral underpinnings—are central to the politics of economic inequality in contemporary America.

In seeking the U.S. 2016 Democratic presidential nomination, self-professed democratic socialist Senator Bernie Sanders made economic inequality the cornerstone of his campaign platform. Mainstream news outlets and the center-left Democratic party establishment largely ignored the Vermont senator until his rallies began turning up thousands—and eventually tens of thousands—of people. Sanders's rhetoric on income inequality was terse and unflinching—he decried the greed of elites and the fundamental unfairness of the American economic system. Also unflinching was his advocacy for the rights and dignity of lower-income and working-class people. Vanessa Williamson of the center-left Brookings Institution tied Sanders's dogged emphasis on income inequality to his popular success. "Sanders' single-minded focus on economic inequality may help a new generation of Democrats speak the language of economic populism," she noted. "Given that nearly half of Americans now identify as working or lower class, it's a language that has the potential for widespread appeal" (Williamson, 2016).

Although Sanders was ultimately defeated by Hillary Clinton for the Democratic Party's presidential nomination, his campaign's focus on income inequality and class in America—along with grassroots social movements like Occupy Wall Street and even the presidential victory of Donald Trump—helped reinvigorate a long-standing public debate around issues of social justice, economic inequality, and the rights of working people in the United States (Bartels, 2016).

A GLOBAL LEADER IN INCOME INEQUALITY

The United States is one of the richest countries in the world, with an average of about $57,000 gross domestic product (GDP) per capita. This means that the value of all of the products and services in the United States was divided by the country's population, each person would produce about $57,000 worth of goods and services (Pasquali, 2016). The story does not end here, however. This measurement says nothing about how these economic resources are *distributed* within the country—it actually assumes that they are distributed equally. When unequal distribution is taken into account (using what is called a Gini coefficient, named after the Italian economist who first calculated it), the results indicate that, despite its prosperity, the United States is in fact a remarkably *unequal* country, especially compared to other prosperous democracies around the world. The Gini index ranks countries on a scale where a 0 would be perfect equality (everyone makes exactly the same amount of money) and 100 would be perfect inequality (one person makes all the income and everyone else makes nothing). As of 2010, the United States had a Gini coefficient of 38. This counts taxes and redistribution programs, which tend to lower the number—without these factored in, the United States comes in just below 50. This makes it the second most unequal country among similarly developed countries, with others like Germany (28), Canada (32), Japan (33), and Britain (34) coming in with significantly lower Gini coefficients (DeSilver, 2013). Countries with similar Gini coefficients to the United States are Cameroon, Peru, Nigeria, Iran, and Jamaica (Central Intelligence Agency, 2016).

There are two major "schools of thought" on the issue of economic inequality in America. It is helpful to think of these as on a continuum. At one extreme is a school of thought that prizes equality as a fundamental organizing principle of society—economic inequalities are harmful, unjust, and immoral. At the other extreme are those who say that there is nothing morally wrong with inequality—or even with extreme inequality. Those who subscribe to the latter view assert that if people have significantly more wealth than others, they have clearly earned it and that it is wrong to take away that wealth. Finally, in the middle are those who say that economic inequality is expected and acceptable within certain limits. This position takes arguments from the other two positions but changes them significantly: It holds that while the rich should not be penalized for being successful, they should not be permitted to make their fortunes by exploiting others. It also asserts that the country should not have great masses of people who are homeless or hungry. Each of these positions exists within a moral framework, and each of these frameworks motivates different types of legislation to address issues of inequality.

EGALITARIAN PERSPECTIVE

American economist and social critic Henry George, author of *Progress and Poverty* (1879), described inequality as "an immense wedge . . . being forced, not underneath society, but through society. Those who are above the point of separation are elevated, but those who are below are crushed down" (8). This position is deeply proequality, holding that inequality is socially harmful and morally wrong.

While seemingly radical, this school of thought has been a fundamental driving force in American politics almost since the nation's beginning. After all, as school-children across the country learn, the opening of the Declaration of Independence holds as self-evident the truth that "all men are created equal," which seems to suggest that the principle of equality is a fundamental part of the American experiment. Inspired by such diverse thinkers as Karl Marx, Robert Owen, and Henri de Saint-Simon, proponents of this view have been extraordinarily influential in agitating for workers' rights and a general redistribution of wealth and economic resources.

As the George quote indicates, the main concern animating those who are pro-equality is not the existence of inequality per se but the tendency for one person's wealth to come at the expense of another's misery. Inequality, they argue, is fundamentally unfair. Why, asked 19th-century political economist Henry George, does the creation of great wealth often come along with the growth of great poverty? His answer is that such great wealth can be created only by the rich taking public resources like land for themselves and through their exploitation of working people to gain more for themselves (George, 1879). One of George's contemporaries, sociologist and philosopher Karl Marx, argued that the exploitation of workers was actually the way that wealthy business owners made their wealth. Working people are *forced* to work or else they will starve, not to mention that all of the profit of that work goes to their employer (Marx, 1967). A factory worker producing computers or designer clothing worth thousands of dollars may only make a few dollars per day, while the rest of the money goes to the company's shareholders and executives who have done none of the backbreaking physical work to create the product. We must seek to establish economic equality, these critics say, because by accepting gross inequality, we also tacitly accept the principle that the pursuit of wealth is more important than the human misery it creates.

Although taking a variety of positions and approaches to the issue, today's critics of inequality tend to follow in similar footsteps by decrying the power of corporations over working people and the increasing share of wealth possessed by the very rich. Contemporary debates over inequality often revolve around the ability of those at the top to use the power of the national government to further their own interests. This is evident in the rhetoric of many public voices on the left. Nobel Laureate economist and *New York Times* columnist Paul Krugman criticized the rich for what he called "inequality denial," which persists precisely because "there are powerful groups with a strong interest in rejecting the facts, or at least creating a fog of doubt" around the issue of inequality (Krugman, 2014). The same kind of rhetoric exists in the political realm. Explicitly referring to inequality as "immoral," Senator Bernie Sanders asserted in an interview with *Mother Jones* that "in the last 35 or 40 years, there has been an increasingly aggressive effort on the part of the top 1 percent to take it all" and that the middle and lower classes have suffered as a result (Harkinson, 2015).

Contemporary social science research has tended to support some version of the proequality view. A landmark study supporting this view came from French economist Thomas Piketty, whose book *Capital in the Twenty-First Century* (2014)—explicitly taking on the issue of inequality—became a breakout best seller for its academic publisher. By studying survey responses and tax return data, Piketty showed that, despite a significant increase in living standards for most people around the world, global inequality grew dramatically over the last half of the 20th century largely because the return on investment in capital (rents, financial investments, etc.)—held mostly by the wealthy—has increased at a faster rate than the world economy has grown. In the United States, for instance, inequality has skyrocketed to where the top 1 percent of wealth holders claim over 20 percent of the country's income. Piketty's research bolsters the view that the wealthy are in their positions largely at the expense of the lower classes through "unearned" investments, which are out of reach for most of the poor. Other contemporary proponents of equality temper their tone by arguing that equality benefits everyone, even the rich. Equality isn't necessarily a moral issue, according to this line of argument, but rather a commonsense strategy to increase a society's overall happiness and sustainability. While intuitively correct, there was not much evidence backing these assertions until 2009 when epidemiologists Richard Wilkinson and Kate Pickett published *The Spirit Level*. Their research significantly strengthened this argument, since they found that equality is largely a win-win situation for both the rich and the poor. More equal societies have cleaner air, less crime, and generally happier and healthier people (Wilkinson and Pickett, 2009).

From the creation of the United States Children's Bureau in 1912—an agency founded for the specific purpose of helping raise living standards and health outcomes of mothers and their children—to the 1965 Social Security Act, which expanded health care access to the poor and elderly through the creation of Medicare and Medicaid, the early and mid-20th century is replete with examples of legislation promoting egalitarian ends. One of the most significant periods of this egalitarian sentiment was the Great Depression, during which time President Franklin D. Roosevelt promoted a wide range of so-called New Deal social welfare programs for struggling American families. The signature piece of legislation of this era was the Social Security Act of 1935, which created the modern Social Security and unemployment insurance systems that remain in place today. Edwin Witte, one of the architects of the Social Security Act, made explicit the moral underpinnings of such legislation in a 1955 interview: "It is a fundamental American concept that the standard of living—the conditions of life—should ever be improved," Witte said. "And they should be improved for the poor and the unfortunate as well as for the well-to-do and the successful" (Social Security Administration, 1975: 12). Shortly before his death, President Roosevelt laid out what he called an Economic Bill of Rights inherent in modern, industrialized American society, which has "come to a clear realization of the fact that true individual freedom cannot exist without economic security and independence." Among the rights he proposed were the rights to meaningful employment and fair wages, education, and protection from economic fears of sickness, unemployment, and accident (Roosevelt, 1944).

ANTIEGALITARIAN PERSPECTIVE

On the other side of this debate are those who oppose forced or legislated efforts to increase economic equality. There are many variations of the argument against the egalitarian position, and while not advocating for inequality per se, they tend to center around the idea that *some* inequality is an inevitable consequence of the structure of a society and differences among its people. Many who advocate for this position even see economic inequality as a potential positive—by comparing ourselves to those who have more than us, we are more likely to work harder to get what we want.

The most radical position within the antiequality camp is that economic inequality, no matter how extreme, is justified. Any redistribution of wealth from the rich to the poor is economically harmful and even immoral. The rich have worked for their wealth, and since our capitalist economic system rewards the smartest, most hardworking people with the greatest wealth for their intelligence and hard work, it is wrong to redistribute it to someone who may not have had such good foresight or work ethic. The people who advocate this position tend to identify as libertarians and often reference economists like Friedrich Hayek and Ludwig von Mises or authors such as Ayn Rand. Inequality, according to them, is a natural by-product of differences among people. Some, like professional athletes, simply have talents that other people value, while others like inventors are naturally harder working and more motivated. Any wealth that they earn should be theirs to keep. Trying to force equality between unequal groups is unfair and economically harmful. Citing Friedrich Hayek, Mark Tovey of the libertarian Mises Institute argued that inequality serves a social function. To display their wealth, the rich buy brand-new, extraordinarily expensive items. Their purchases function as a kind of "test market" for goods and services. Companies invest in the most successful products, which become cheaper and are eventually commonplace among the masses. "When there is no class of rich people, as in egalitarian societies," Tovey states, "there is no longer anybody to channel the preferences of tomorrow. Innovators are left in this case to stumble without guidance" (Tovey, 2014). Proponents of this view are resistant to virtually any government regulation and intervention into the economy and to most taxation beyond the amount needed for basic services like emergency response and national defense.

The mainstream conservative position on economic inequality retains many features of the more extreme libertarian view but tempers it with some more egalitarian positions. Many who advocate this position argue that gaining wealth requires work and that the poor should be encouraged to "pull themselves up by their bootstraps" in order to get ahead. People should not be allowed to live off the work of others. Many also hold that, because the rich spend and invest their wealth, they create new jobs for people who pay more taxes and spend their wages on more products, etc. This suggests that the rich are the true drivers of economic growth. The resulting inequality is a necessary by-product of a system that, on balance, is better for everyone. The rich, they argue, ought to keep most of their wealth not only because they earned it but because by using their wealth to invest in companies and create employment, *everyone* is ultimately better off in the long run. This philosophy is best encapsulated in the saying, "A rising tide lifts all boats": that is, some may be richer than others, but even the poorest are better off than they would be in a more equal—but slower growing—economy.

Because it borrows so heavily from ideas that have a long history in America like self-determination and the individualism espoused in the Protestant work ethic, the mainstream antiegalitarian position is a very widely held political philosophy in America. This, of course, goes for conservative Republicans but also among people who identify themselves as liberal Democrats and is imprinted on one of the most significant pieces of legislation of the 1990s, the so-called welfare reform legislation. Signed into law by President Bill Clinton in 1996 and touted as "the end of welfare as we know it," even the bill's title—the Personal Responsibility and Work Opportunity Reconciliation Act—maintains a moral distinction between the "deserving" and "undeserving" poor. The most significant features of the Act are its imposition of time limits for receiving welfare, and its emphasis on work: People cannot receive welfare payments for two consecutive years without working or for more than five years over their lifetime. In a statement released by the White House, President Clinton maintained that, despite some objections he has to it, the bill "provides an historic opportunity to end welfare as we know it and transform our broken welfare system by promoting the fundamental values of work, responsibility, and family" (Clinton, 1996). The moral philosophy behind this legislation lies in the belief that work is virtuous and necessary for success. The bill is predicated on the idea that the extended use of welfare creates dependency on government money. Thus, those who work should not support people who do not demonstrate work initiative.

Alexander J. Myers

FURTHER READING

Bartels, Larry M. 2016. (2nd ed.). *Unequal Democracy: The Political Economy of the New Gilded Age.* Princeton, NJ: Princeton University Press.

Blank, Rebecca M. 2002. "Evaluating Welfare Reform in the United States." *Journal of Economic Literature, 40*(4): 1105–1166.

Central Intelligence Agency. 2016. "The World Factbook: Distribution of Family Income—Gini Index." Retrieved from https://www.cia.gov/library/publications/the-world -factbook/rankorder/2172rank.html

Clinton, William J. 1996. "Statement on Signing the Personal Responsibility and Work Opportunity Reconciliation Act of 1996." August 22. Online by Gerhard Peters and John T. Woolley, The American Presidency Project. Retrieved from http://www .presidency.ucsb.edu/ws/?pid=53219

DeSilver, Drew. 2013. "Global Inequality: How the U.S. Compares." Pew Research Center, updated December 19. Retrieved from http://pewrsr.ch/1bSbQln

Edin, Kathryn J., & H. Luke Shaefer. 2015. *$2.00 a Day: Living on Almost Nothing in America.* New York: Houghton Mifflin Harcourt.

Friedman, Milton. [1962] 2009. *Capitalism and Freedom.* Chicago: University of Chicago Press.

George, Henry. 1879. *Progress and Poverty: An Enquiry into the Cause of Industrial Depressions, and of Increase of Want with Increase of Wealth: The Remedy.* New York: Sterling Publishing.

Harkinson, Josh. 2015. "Bernie Sanders Goes Biblical on Income Inequality." *Mother Jones,* April 2. Retrieved from http://www.motherjones.com/politics/2015/04/bernie -sanders-inequality-president-interview

Krugman, Paul. 2014. "On Inequality Denial." *New York Times,* June 1. Retrieved from http://nyti.ms/1kx5u0x

Marx, Karl. [1867] 1967. *Capital, Vol. 1.* New York: International Publishers.

Pasquali, Valentina. 2016. "The Richest Countries in the World." *Global Finance.* Retrieved from https://www.gfmag.com/global-data/economic-data/richest-countries-in-the -world

Piketty, Thomas, & Arthur Goldhammer. 2014. *Capital in the Twenty-first Century.* Cambridge, MA: Belknap Press of Harvard University Press.

Quadagno, Jill S. 1984. "Welfare Capitalism and the Social Security Act of 1935." *American Sociological Review*, *49*(5): 632–647.

Reich, Robert B. 2016. *Saving Capitalism: For the Many, Not the Few.* New York: Vintage.

Roosevelt, Franklin Delano. 1944. "State of the Union Message to Congress, January 11th, 1944." Online by the Franklin D. Roosevelt Presidential Library and Museum. Retrieved from http://www.fdrlibrary.marist.edu/archives/address_text.html

Social Security Administration. 1975. "The Development of the Social Security Act: An Interview with Edwin Witte." Social Security Administration, Office of Administration, Pub. No. 083-75. Retrieved from https://archive.org/details/development ofsoc00witt

Stiglitz, Joseph E. 2013. *The Price of Inequality: How Today's Divided Society Endangers Our Future.* New York: W. W. Norton.

Tovey, Mark. 2014. "The Social Function of Economic Inequality." *Mises Daily* (blog), The Mises Institute, December 19. Retrieved from https://mises.org/library/social -function-economic-inequality

Wilkinson, Richard, & Kate Pickett. 2009. *The Spirit Level: Why Greater Equality Makes Societies Stronger.* New York: Bloomsbury Publishing.

Williamson, Vanessa. 2016. "Can Sanders Do for Income Inequality What Clinton Did for Healthcare?" *FixGov Blog*, Brookings Institution, May 23. Retrieved from https:// www.brookings.edu/blog/fixgov/2016/05/23/can-sanders-do-for-income -inequality-what-clinton-did-for-healthcare

Education

Guaranteed access to public education has been viewed as a right in the United States since the early 19th century—and since the 1950s as a civil right. However, even in the American colonies, at least some education of children was seen as imperative. For example, the settlers of the Massachusetts colony passed a law in 1642 requiring parents to ensure that their children could read so that they could achieve salvation by reading the Bible (Balliett, 2006). In fact, most early public schools in the colonies focused on religious instruction, starting with the first in 1635. Benjamin Franklin argued that "the proper education of youth" was the most important policy goal of government (Hochschild & Scovronick, 2003). Thomas Jefferson was so convinced that citizens in a democracy had to have access to education that he tried to convince the Virginia legislature in 1779 to pay for all schoolchildren to have access to free education for at least three years, just as schools in New England were already providing. Jefferson was not successful in this particular effort. Under the Ordinance of 1787, however, Congress decreed that all new townships in the Northwest Territories (the modern upper Midwest) had to set aside a plot of land to support public education (Graham, 2007).

In addition to many existing sectarian schools controlled by local churches or other religious organizations, many communities adopted the common school model during the 1800s. This model provided elementary education for all children but required a fee from parents and room and board for the teacher. New York was the first state to appoint a state superintendent over common schools (Davis, 2006). Common schools were not supported by or linked to churches or religious organizations, but many did use a religious-based strategy for teaching basic morals and character to youth (Davis, 2006). This basic model became the basis for public elementary schools, which most states adopted and required students to attend by 1900. Massachusetts was the first to adopt this model in 1837 under a state board of education, and Connecticut and Rhode Island soon followed. Even though Massachusetts had passed a similar law in 1642, in 1852 the state became the first to require every town and city to provide elementary education, which included reading, writing, and arithmetic (Graham, 2007). As this model evolved over time, however, it drew increased criticism. Many Americans objected to the belief that public education must exclude religious instruction or teachings. Opponents of this policy argued that the stance could potentially put schools in conflict with what parents were teaching at home. As the 1800s concluded and new models of public education emerged for the 20th century, the removal of all aspects of religion from public schools was increasingly adopted by educators and education administrators. These education advocates, though, continued to believe that the schools should be partly responsible for the moral development of students, and most states still have legal requirements that public schools teach moral responsibility as part of citizenship and character development (Davis, 2006; Nucci, Krettenauer, & Narváez, 2014). Indeed, John Dewey, the founder of the progressive education movement in the early 1900s, clearly articulated that schools are not in the business of direct moral instruction, but through the education of students for participation in social life, schools teach the ethical principles of the society in which they are embedded, including the extent to which both obedience, individuality, and leadership are valued in the context of the well-being of society (1909). In this sense, schools create a mini version of the society in which they exist, with moral values and principles directly embedded in the structure and lived experience of the institution. In other words, these reformers wanted to create a social life within schools similar to social life within society. However, John Dewey clearly advocated for a nonsectarian system of schooling devoid of religious traditions. He favored instruction on ethics derived from science, reasoning, and democratic deliberation. Other advocates of nonsectarian schooling, including Horace Mann, argued that removing religion from the public schools would ensure religious liberty by reinforcing the separation between church and state (Davis, 2006).

In part, this move away from religion stemmed from that fact that most schools had favored Protestant traditions, focused on prayer and the Bible, and excluded other Christian and non-Christian traditions. In the late 1800s, however, the focus on Protestant traditions led to the emergence of Catholic schools as well as Jewish schools. These were often called parochial schools, and some of them continued to thrive in the 20th century. In an 1890 case brought by Catholics, the Wisconsin Supreme Court even ruled, based on the state constitution, that the Protestant King James bible could not be used in schools (Shiell, 2005). In response to the attempts to remove religious teaching from public schools, many states even adopted new laws requiring religious instruction in the early 20th century (Laats, 2012). The court decision in Wisconsin provided a basis for the arguments used in 1960s Supreme Court rulings on school prayer (Shiell, 2005), *Engel v. Vitale* (1962) and *Abington School District v. Schempp* (1963).

By the 1950s, education advocates from the John Dewey and Horace Mann school of thought were still trying to push religious-based morality out of the classroom in many parts of the country. The challenge of doing so was great, however. Indeed, in most states some portion of the day was set aside in schools for reading the Bible. In 1962, the Supreme Court tried to draw a line with its decision in *Engel v. Vitale*, which together with the Court's decision in *Abington School District v. Schempp* (1963), effectively banned prayers in public schools. A variety of court decisions and state laws have followed since the 1960s that allow for some voluntary religious activities in public schools, including the formation of student organizations, but mandatory or officially sanctioned religious observation in public schools remains unconstitutional.

THE DEBATE OVER SEX EDUCATION

The teaching of moral principles in public schools also became a center of conflict after education professionals began advocating for some form of sexuality education early in the 20th century. Sex education classes were subsequently introduced in fits and starts. The Chicago public schools offered a sex hygiene course briefly starting in 1913, but Catholic leaders in Chicago lobbied public officials and quickly killed the course (Millstein, 2015). By the 1920s, an estimated 20 percent of public schools featured some form of sex education, usually focused on a moralistic approach that highlighted the risk of sexually transmitted diseases from premarital sex and warned about the alleged ills of masturbation, including damage to mental health, memory loss, and even death (Millstein, 2015). As national government agencies and the American Medical Association issued guidance for sex education, growing numbers of high school students received some form of sex and reproduction education in the 1940s and 1950s, especially on the coasts and the Midwest. However, in the 1960s, school-based sexuality education became more widespread and reached preadolescent children in greater numbers. It did not take long for conflict over the moral messages allegedly sent by such education to spread as well (Bay-Cheng, 2003). Groups such as the Christian Crusade labeled sex education programs as "smut" and "raw sex," while the John Birch Society called them a "filthy communist plot" (Baker, 1969). Since the 1960s, schools have continued to receive push-back on sex education programs from politically conservative lawmakers as well as parents, and many states and districts have placed limits on sex education.

At its core, the debate over sex education in schools revolves around the notion of whether teaching children about reproduction and sexuality increases the likelihood that they will engage in immoral (often defined by opponents as premarital) sexual behavior or whether they will instead use the knowledge to learn to respect and understand human sexuality, reproduction, and personal health. These concerns intensified in the 1980s, when panic over the spread of HIV/AIDS mounted across the nation. Many conservatives pointed to the spread of HIV as evidence of weakened sexual mores in society, including the legitimizing of homosexuality. Conservatives began to push abstinence-only sex education, which provides education about reproduction and sexual health, but stresses abstinence from sex until marriage. Many states and local school districts quickly revised their sex education programs toward abstinence-only orientations—in part because some states and the national government provided hundreds of millions of dollars to schools that adopted these programs—but also because these programs stressed that morally correct sex can occur only in the context of marriage (Millstein, 2015). However, even as states moved to the abstinence model, President Ronald Reagan's Surgeon General C. Everett Koop issued guidelines on sex education stating that "our reticence in dealing with the subject of sex, sexual practices, and homosexuality" is preventing young people from having "information that is vital to their future health and well-being. . . . This silence must end. . . . We can no longer afford to sidestep frank, open discussion about sexual practices—homosexual and heterosexual" (Koop, 1986). As evidence accumulated that abstinence-only programs do not decrease teen sexual relations and may even be associated with increased teen pregnancy rates, abstinence-only sex education programs have declined in popularity (Millstein, 2015).

Changing conceptions of gender, gender norms, and sexual orientation have been directly incorporated into conflicts over public school education, often through sexual education and health courses but also through battles over which student groups and social events are allowed on school property. In fact, during the 1980s many states adopted laws that prohibited schools receiving government funds from "promoting homosexuality" (Rosky, 2017). Even with these laws in place, by 1990 all states had adopted some form of sex education that included instruction about the HIV/AIDS disease (Rosky, 2017).

The push to eliminate religion in public schools and to require some form of sex education has led many religious families to enroll their children in private, often religious-based schools or simply to opt out of formal school settings altogether and homeschool their children. Indeed, by 2018 it was estimated that an average of over 2 million children were being homeschooled across the country (although not all for religious reasons) (Firmin et al., 2019).

EQUAL ACCESS AND EQUAL OPPORTUNITY

Even early supporters of public education tended to support education only for white boys and girls up to a point—after which only boys, academically gifted students, and wealthier students were expected to continue. For example, in many states, girls were taught only to read but not write well into the 1800s, and in the South most parents had their children tutored until after the Civil War, when public school models began to be adopted. Nonwhites were excluded or relegated to substandard schools, especially in the American South, until the 1950s and 1960s, when sweeping civil rights legislation struck down segregation and discrimination in schools and other areas of American society as unconstitutional. Nonwhites still face de facto segregation into poorly performing schools today however, due to persistent racial segregation in housing patterns and low funding for schools in less affluent areas.

The progressive vision of public schools espoused by John Dewey early in the 20th century is partly built on the notion that public schools provide the first steps in building and establishing the ideology of and reality for the American Dream. The American Dream suggests that all people are free to pursue opportunities to be successful and that those who fail do so because they did not work hard or lacked the requisite talent. Americans also have the responsibility to be good citizens, help others, and respect differences. As such, public education would provide citizens with this nation-unifying ideology as well as an opportunity to build talent, instill the principle of hard work and just rewards, educate youth about citizenship, and teach respect for others.

Dewey's vision of access to public education as a right with a specific purpose for creating productive citizens has come to be understood as a human right. As such, some argue that the moral right to be educated also comes to the citizen as a moral duty to be educated in order to adequately function within—and contribute to—the broader society (Heslep, 1992; Kerr, 1990).

HIGHER EDUCATION

During America's early years of existence, few could afford college, and few jobs in the nation's agrarian-based economy required a college education. But recognizing that college students were mostly wealth white males, in the 1700s, schools such as Harvard began using their higher tuition from wealthy students as a way to pay for the tuition of students from poor families (about 10 percent of enrolled students) (Moore, 2006).

Attempts to expand access to college were enhanced in 1862 with the passage of the Morrill Act, which granted states access to thousands of acres of land to establish public universities, which came to be known as land grant colleges. Because the Act resulted in only one college for African Americans, a second Morrill Act was passed in 1890. This legislation allowed for the states to create separate colleges for African American and white students. Supported by state funding, many of these land grant universities made higher education accessible to middle-class and lower-middle-class Americans for the first time. But the great expansion of access to higher education did not come until the passage of the GI Bill in 1944. This legislation, which provided a wide range of benefits (including payments for college tuition and living expenses) for returning World War II veterans, allowed more women and nonwhites to attend college than ever before (Meyer, 1996). Likewise, the Higher Education Act of 1965 provided federal money to colleges that developed programs to recruit and retain minority students. In addition, federal student aid programs, like the Pell Grant, have greatly expanded college access for minorities as well as the less wealthy (Moore, 2006). Other programs, such as Title IX (of the Education Amendments Act of 1972), have significantly increased the opportunities for women to attend college and achieve full participation in all aspects of college life (Valentin, 1997).

CONCLUSION

The American system of public schools was born out of a desire to educate children to fulfill the duties of citizenry and was based on models designed for religious education. Over time, Americans have come to believe education is a fundamental right, making it a moral obligation for government to provide access to education. Although much progress has been made toward ensuring access to public education regardless of gender, race, or ethnicity, many socioeconomically disadvantaged families still face low-quality educational opportunities.

Public education has also been at the center of moral conflicts in society, including those involving religious instruction, gender, sexuality, and reproductive health. In part, this conflict has revolved around the role of religious morality in public education. All schools now begin some form of sex and health education in elementary school, but the content of those courses varies by school district and state and is often still a flashpoint, leading some families to turn toward private schools and homeschooling.

Donald P. Haider-Markel

FURTHER READING

Abington School District v. Schempp, 374 U.S. 203 (1963).

Baker, Luther G. 1969. "The Rising Furor over Sex Education." *The Family Coordinator*, *18*(3): 210–217.

Balliett, James Fargo. 2006. "Literacy." In James Ciment (Ed.), *Social Issues in America: An Encyclopedia*, 1022–1033. Armonk, NY: M. E. Sharp.

Bay-Cheng, Laina Y. 2003. "The Trouble of Teen Sex: The Construction of Adolescent Sexuality Through School-Based Sexuality Education." *Sex Education: Sexuality, Society and Learning*, *3*(1): 61–74.

Carter, Julian B. 2001. "Birds, Bees, and Venereal Disease: Toward an Intellectual History of Sex Education." *Journal of the History of Sexuality*, *10*(2): 213–249.

Davis, Derek H. 2006. "Character Education in America's Public Schools." *Journal of Church & State*, *48*: 5–14.

Dewey, John. 1909. *Moral Principles in Education*. New York: Houghton Mifflin.

Di Mauro, Diane, & Carole Joffe. 2007. "The Religious Right and the Reshaping of Sexual Policy: An Examination of Reproductive Rights and Sexuality Education." *Sexuality Research & Social Policy*, *4*(1): 67–92.

Engel v. Vitale, 370 U.S. 421 (1962).

Firmin, Michael W., Felisha L. Younkin, Thomas A. Sackett, Jacqlyn Fletcher, Theresa Jones, & Erik Parrish. 2019. "Qualitative Perspectives of Homeschool Parents Regarding Perceived Educational Success." *Journal of Higher Education Theory and Practice*. Retrieved from https://articlegateway.com/index.php/JHETP/article/view/667

Graham, Patricia Albjerg. 2007. *Schooling America: How the Public Schools Meet the Nation's Changing Needs*. New York: Oxford University Press.

Heslep, Robert D. 1992. "Both the Moral Right and the Moral Duty to Be Educated." *Educational Theory*, *42*(4): 413–428.

Hochschild, Jennifer L., & Nathan Scovronick. 2003. *The American Dream and the Public Schools*. New York: Oxford University Press.

Kerr, Donna H. 1990. "Education in Democracy: Education's Moral Role in the Democratic State." *The Journal of Higher Education*, *61*(6): 702–704.

Koop, C. Everett. 1986. "Surgeon Gen. of the U.S. Pub. Health Serv., Statement About the Release of the Surgeon General's Report on Acquired Immune Deficiency Syndrome 6." October 22. Retrieved from http://profiles.nlm.nih.gov/ps/access/QQBBMW.pdf

Laats, Adam. 2012. "Our Schools, Our Country: American Evangelicals, Public Schools, and the Supreme Court Decisions of 1962 and 1963." *Journal of Religious History*, *36*(3): 319–334.

Meyer, Leisa D. 1996. *Creating GI Jane: Sexuality and Power in the Women's Army Corps During World War II*. New York: Columbia University Press.

Millstein, Seth. 2015. "Sex Education in the United States, 1835 Through Today." *Digg*, July 27. Retrieved from http://digg.com/2015/sex-education-history

Moore, Randy. 2006. "At-Risk Students: Higher Education." In James Ciment (Ed.), *Social Issues in America: An Encyclopedia*, 179–188. Armonk, NY: M. E. Sharp.

Nucci, Larry, Tobias Krettenauer, & Darcia Narváez (Eds.). (2nd ed.). 2014. *Handbook of Moral and Character Education*. New York: Routledge.

Rosky, Clifford. 2017. "Anti-gay Curriculum Laws." *Columbia Law Review, 117*(6): 1461–1542.

Shiell, Tim. 2005. "The Edgerton Bible Case." *Wisconsin Free Speech Legacy.* Retrieved from https://web.archive.org/web/20070927210508/ http://www.uwstout.edu/faculty /shiellt/freespeech1/edgerton/index.html

Valentin, Iram. 1997. "Title IX: A Brief History." *Holy Cross Journal of Law & Public Policy, 2*: 123–138.

Zimmerman, Jonathan. 2002. *Whose America? Culture Wars in the Public Schools*. Cambridge, MA: Harvard University Press.

Energy Production

Although policy analysts and academics approach energy topics in terms of alternatives and their quantifiable consequences, in the political sphere debates over energy production often fall along partisan lines and, as such, are frequently marked by narratives and moral arguments embedded in catchphrases like "Drill Baby, Drill" or "No Pipeline; Water Is for Life." Democrats and liberals respond to and rely on one set of moral virtues in policy debates, while Republicans and conservatives rely on another (Feinberg & Willer, 2015) as they argue past one another in debating energy production issues. In such policy debates, opponents strategically frame the issues to shape arguments, emphasizing particular points of interest over others. Either explicitly or implicitly, these frames have moral dimensions.

Matthew Nisbet (2009) defines morality frames as emphasizing "a matter of right or wrong; or of respect or disrespect for limits, thresholds, or boundaries" (18). This definition alludes to the presence of both virtues (e.g., compassion, loyalty) in establishing right and wrong and an argument construction intended to wall off competing ideas—and moralities. Scholars have proposed sets of moral virtues likely to arise in such arguments, such as care, fairness, in-group loyalty, authority, and loyalty (Haidt et al., 2009) and have argued that moral arguments are likely to take absolutist logics as opposed to consequentialist (Feinberg & Willer, 2015). Consequentialist arguments, like those favored by analysts and academics, draw attention to outcomes of specific actions and tend to present the world in terms of trade-offs, appealing to notions of the greatest good for the greatest number. Absolutist arguments, on the other hand, appeal to unassailable moral maxims, like "Thou shall not kill" and "All life is sacred, not just human." Consequentialist arguments allow consideration of alternatives; absolutist arguments offer only a single—righteous—path (Marietta, 2008). Together, moral virtues and absolutist argumentation offer a way of conceptualizing moral frames in policy debates addressing moral virtue and logic, two characteristics apparent in debates about energy production.

Morality frames are especially important in energy production debates because they bypass or undercut traditional consequentialist energy production frames like economic progress, the environment, or even public accountability (Nisbet, 2009). Moral framing—more so than consequentialist framing—encourages polarization in terms of both what is within the frame (content) and how it is structured (form). Moral frame content, relying on virtues (e.g., compassion, loyalty) that interest primarily those already predisposed to support the narrator, are not persuasive or appealing to others (e.g., Haidt et al., 2009; Feinberg & Willer, 2015). Furthermore, employing an absolutist form within the moral frames in addition to partisan virtues emphasizes partisan preferences, discouraging deliberation while also mobilizing those predisposed to support the moral frame (Marietta, 2008). As a result, debates involving moral frames are not likely to motivate consensus, learning, or preference changes but may increase conflict by increasing activity of the most motivated.

Drawing upon moral frames in energy production policy debates likely has strategic designs. For instance, Baumgartner and Jones (2009) identify a strategy of "noncontradictory arguments" (107), where policy actors sidestep opponents' arguments or talk past one another in order to refocus the debate on different aspects of a policy issue. In this way, moral framing may allow an opponent to sidestep direct conflict with an opposing frame. For example, an argument emphasizing the economic stability associated with having abundant access to fossil fuels might be refocused in a noncontradictory manner to a potentially more broadly supported moral frame, such as a religiously motivated custodian of the environment frame (e.g., Nisbet, 2009). The latter presents a moral absolute, ignoring benefits associated with fossil fuels while drawing upon various virtues like care, in-group loyalty, purity, and authority. This tactic may draw the attention of previously unengaged actors and appeal to potential opponents if virtues are carefully chosen. Partisans center debates on moral virtues appealing to them; for conservatives, this means in-group loyalty and authority dominate, and for liberals, it is care and fairness that are most important (Feinberg & Willer, 2015). This tendency is evidenced in recent energy production debates in the United States at the national, state, and local levels.

TRUMP AND OBAMA ON PRODUCTION MORALITY

Presidential statements provide stark evidence of the partisan nature of energy production debates in America in the 21st century, with both Democrats and Republicans working to frame their policy priorities and prescriptions as morally superior to the priorities and prescriptions of the other side. The presidency of Donald Trump, for instance, marks a pronounced change in the moral emphasis of energy production of Barack Obama's administration. The latter emphasized care of the environment in the face of climate change (e.g., Obama, 2015). For instance, in a statement explaining his position against the Keystone XL pipeline, Obama said:

> As long as I'm President of the United States, America is going to hold ourselves to the same high standards to which we hold the rest of the world. And three weeks from now, I look forward to joining my fellow world leaders in Paris, where we've got to come together around an ambitious framework to protect the one planet that we've got while we still can. (Obama, 2015)

Obama's statement exhibits the classic moral framing techniques of a political liberal. It emphasizes fairness and stewardship of the natural world, virtues associated with liberal policy preferences. His statement also draws upon absolutist logic, offering no room for consideration of other alternatives. In this statement, the virtues of fairness and care dictate the boundaries of appropriate action. Indeed, Obama emphasizes the necessity to act with haste. Trump employs similar moral framing, although his stance is contradictory to Obama's not just on the pipeline itself but also on the associated issue of climate change policy.

Early in his administration, Trump reversed Obama's policy aimed at reducing environmental damage from energy production and encouraging low-carbon sources of energy (Radnofsky & Sweet, 2017). Although natural gas infrastructure grew under Obama, Trump framed additional oil and gas development, such as the controversial Keystone XL pipeline, as a moral imperative (Matthew, Ballhaus, & Steele, 2017). In fact, Trump's campaign platform explicitly promised coal miners a revival of their righteous vocation, as well as robust support for other fossil fuels. In outlining his energy plan, Trump said:

> We will unlock job-producing natural gas, oil, and shale energy. We will produce American coal to power American industry. We will transport American energy through American pipelines, made with American steel. (Trump, 2017)

This quote provides an example of reliance on the in-group virtue and, again, absolutist logic about the path ahead. In this statement, the moral imperative is the obligation of group loyalty and membership. Although he notes the consequence of producing jobs, the narrative remains largely absolute in its construction, restricting the speech to what must be done. Obama and Trump offer illustrations of moral framing of energy production debates at the federal level; however, important energy production debates also occur at the state level.

States have become important subnational players in U.S. energy production policy, especially regarding renewable and unconventional gas development (Hughes & Lipscy, 2013). In Colorado, for example, the Republican state attorney general sued a Democrat-led county government for their multiple-year ban on oil and gas development despite a state law regulating such activity (Paul, 2017). The state's primary oil and gas association supported the attorney general, even participating in the lawsuit against the county. It framed its support for the lawsuit as one grounded in moral respect for the law:

> It's not about drilling, or fracking, or pipelines, it's about the law. And the law is clear: Long-term moratoriums—and this one is over five years now—are illegal. Boulder County shouldn't be surprised that the attorney general cares about the rule of law in Colorado. (Paul, 2017)

The statement appeals morally to the virtue of authority in absolutist terms. The statement brokers no argument: The law is the law, the law should be upheld. In rebuttal, the Boulder County Council issued the following statement in which it also framed its position as one founded on moral concerns:

> The Colorado Attorney General sent a special valentine to the oil and gas industry today by filing a lawsuit against Boulder County for our working to safeguard our community from the industrial impacts of oil and gas development.
>
> Drilling proposals of 20 to 40 wells per site are being proposed near residential neighborhoods, schools, parks and recreational areas up and down the Front Range,

and we believe it is our responsibility to ensure that we have the strongest possible protections in place for the residents of Boulder County and the world-class environment we have worked hard to protect and preserve.

It's a sweetheart deal for the oil and gas industry, but a massive waste of Coloradans' tax dollars for the state to sue us on industry's behalf, and we are prepared to defend our right to safeguard the health, safety, and wellbeing of our constituents. (Chow, 2017)

The County Council's statement draws on the virtues of care and fairness, as might be expected due to its association with the Democratic party. Their absolutist argument structure is less pronounced than in the other illustrations, but the clear accusation that the drilling proposals pose a threat to the well-being of the public intuits limitations on what the council believes are acceptable ways ahead.

The Boulder county commissioner's involvement in halting and subsequently imposing regulations on oil and gas development in the region illustrates the important role local policy actors can play in the moral debates regarding energy production. Another example of regional actors employing moral arguments in energy production policy debates can be found in public opposition to energy production facility siting in Oregon (Boudet et al., 2016). Specifically, Canadian and U.S. interests have long been working to gain regulatory approval for a natural gas liquefaction facility and associated pipeline off the southern Oregon Coast (Boudet et al., 2016). The project, referred to as Jordon Cove, was rejected by the Federal Energy Regulatory Committee (FERC) in 2016, citing landowner concerns associated with the use of eminent domain law (Sickinger, 2017a). Landowners whose property is threatened by the Pacific Connector Pipeline have organized an active opposition to the pipeline, employing moral arguments in the debate over the project:

I've been fighting [the proposed pipeline] since 2005, and I think it's so unfair to take property rights, easements through approximately 400 properties, and they're under the threat of the Natural Gas Act so the company can use eminent domain if they don't agree. (Hoard, 2017)

In this statement, the project opponent draws on the virtue of fairness in morally refuting the project's plans to use eminent domain to obtain needed land for the pipeline. The statement emphasizes the lack of options presented to landowners; if they don't agree to have the land used for the purposes of the pipeline, it will be taken from them, precluding any room for negotiation. In this case, the absolutist logic is presented as necessitated by the actions of their policy opponents. The narrative presented here is morally clear: Their treatment is unfair and should not be tolerated.

As part of this controversy over the Jordan Cove and Pacific Connector pipeline, a ballot measure that would have stopped the project failed, and a group supporting the pipeline, Save Coos Jobs, used moral framing in statements opposing the ballot measure:

This is a radical measure driven by fringe activists who have teamed up with national anti-fossil fuel and anti-capitalist groups. The groups behind it want to stop Jordan Cove and change our free market and local government system, and kill jobs and industry in the process. In fact, they have openly stated that they don't care if local communities are hurt having to defend a measure like this in court. (Save Coos Jobs, 2017)

This statement draws upon the virtues of in-group loyalty, care, and authority. The group mixes the "care" virtue with traditionally conservative virtues, indicating less partisanship than in the other preceding examples. Offering a degree of absolutism, it includes references to nonmoral trade-offs like fossil fuel, capitalism, and the free market. However, the statement still presents the virtues in a light that provides little room for negotiation or discussion: The measure is driven by out-group persons lacking proper authority and will hurt the community. As the group is organized around the issue of jobs, a more traditional consequentialist frame for energy production, it makes sense that they include references to related, nonmoral issues. Statements like this may open the conversation about this proposed development to discussions about the role of local government and capitalism in regional energy production debates.

CONCLUSION

Moral framing is particularly important in energy production policy. There is a great global need for energy—estimates range around $45 billion in investment needed in the near future (International Energy Association [IEA], 2014)—at a time when scientists warn of the impending effects of climate change. Deliberation and public support of policy prescriptions may have important consequences for how policy is made, especially, for instance, as the United States considers its stance on investment in areas such unconventional oil and gas development and infrastructure (IEA, 2014)—investments that impact local communities, states, and the nation as a whole (Melo-Martin et al., 2014). Discussions like these raise questions about how policies targeting energy production affect people, communities, governments, and ecosystems. Moral frames address these concerns. They organize information into policy positions while evoking moral virtues and introducing or limiting opportunities to consider trade-offs. However, the use of morality in energy production debates has the potential to increase political polarization of opinion and limit consideration of relevant alternatives and trade-offs of possible policy actions.

Holly L. Peterson and Michael D. Jones

FURTHER READING

"An America First Energy Plan." 2017. *Whitehouse.gov*, January 19. Retrieved from https://www.whitehouse.gov/america-first-energy

Baumgartner, Frank R., & Bryan D. Jones. (2nd ed.). 2009. *Agendas and Instability in American Politics*. Chicago: University Of Chicago Press.

Boudet, Hilary Schafer, Holly L. Peterson, Brittany Gaustad, & Trang Tran. 2016. "Contentious Politics in Liquefied Natural Gas Facility Siting in Oregon." Paper presented at the International Symposium on Society and Resource Management (ISSRM). Houghton, Michigan, June 2016.

Chong, Dennis, & James N. Druckman. 2007. "Framing Theory." *Annual Review of Political Science*, *10*(1): 103–126. doi:10.1146/annurev.polisci.10.072805.103054

Chow, Lorraine. 2017. "Colorado Attorney General Sues Boulder County to End Fracking Ban." *EcoWatch*, February 16. Retrieved from http://www.ecowatch.com/boulder -county-fracking-ban-2265924844.html

Ditto, Peter H., & Spassena P. Koleva. 2011. "Moral Empathy Gaps and the American Culture War." *Emotion Review*, 3(3): 331–332.

Environmental Protection Agency (EPA). 2017. "Summary of the Energy Policy Act." *Overviews and Factsheets*. Retrieved from https://www.epa.gov/laws-regulations /summary-energy-policy-act

Feinberg, Matthew, & Robb Willer. 2015. "From Gulf to Bridge: When Do Moral Arguments Facilitate Political Influence?" *Personality & Social Psychology Bulletin*, 41(12): 1665–1681.

Haidt, Jonathan. (reprint ed.). 2013. *The Righteous Mind: Why Good People Are Divided by Politics and Religion*. New York: Vintage.

Haidt, Jonathan, Jesse Graham, & Craig Joseph. 2009. "Above and Below Left–Right: Ideological Narratives and Moral Foundations." *Psychological Inquiry*, 20(2–3): 110–119.

Heikkila, Tanya, & Christopher M. Weible. 2016. "Contours of Coalition Politics on Hydraulic Fracturing Within the United States of America." In Christopher M. Weible, Tanya Heikkila, Karin Ingold, & Manuel Fischer (Eds.), *Policy Debates on Hydraulic Fracturing*, 29–52. New York: Palgrave Macmillan US.

Hoard, Emily. 2017. "Jordan Cove open House Attracts Douglas County Stakeholders." *News-Review*, March 24. Retrieved from http://www.nrtoday.com/news/envi ronment/jordan_cove/jordan-cove-open-house-attracts-douglas-county-stakehold ers/article_e9a95bf1-73c6-5c06-8a86-aaf875f0c032.html

Hochschild, Arlie Russell. 2016. *Strangers in Their Own Land: Anger and Mourning on the American Right*. New York: New Press.

Hughes, Llewelyn, & Phillip Y. Lipscy. 2013. "The Politics of Energy." *Annual Review of Political Science*, 16(1): 449–469. doi:10.1146/annurev-polisci-072211-143240

International Energy Association (IEA). 2014. "Energy Policies of IEA Countries—The United States." Retrieved from https://www.iea.org/publications/freepublications /publication/USA_2014.pdf

Jones, Michael D., Elizabeth A. Shanahan, & Mark K. McBeth. 2014. *The Science of Stories—Applications of the Narrative Policy Framework*. Retrieved from http:// www.palgrave.com/la/book/9781137370129

"Keystone XL Pipeline." 2017. *New York Times*. Retrieved from http://www.nytimes.com /topic/subject/keystone-xl-pipeline

Lakoff, George. 2010. "Why It Matters How We Frame the Environment." *Environmental Communication*, 4(1): 70–81. doi:10.1080/17524030903529749

Marietta, Morgan. 2008. "From My Cold, Dead Hands: Democratic Consequences of Sacred Rhetoric." *The Journal of Politics*, 70(3): 767–779. doi:10.1017/s00223816 08080742

Matthews, Christopher M., Rebecca Ballhaus, & Anne Steele. 2017. "Trump Administration Grants Permit to TransCanada for Keystone XL Pipeline." *Wall Street Journal*, March 24. Retrieved from https://www.wsj.com/articles/trump-administration -grants-permit-to-transcanada-for-keystone-pipeline-1490357077

McKibben, Bill. 2013. *Oil and Honey: The Education of an Unlikely Activist*. New York: Times Books.

Melo-Martín, Inmaculada de, Jake Hays, & Madelon L. Finkel. 2014. "The Role of Ethics in Shale Gas Policies." *Science of the Total Environment*, 470–471(February): 1114–1119. doi:10.1016/j.scitotenv.2013.10.088

Nisbet, Matthew C. 2009. "Framing Science: A New Paradigm in Public Engagement." *Understanding Science: New Agendas in Science Communication*, 40–67.

Obama, Barack. 2015. "Statement by the President on the Keystone XL Pipeline." *White-house.gov*, November 6. Retrieved from https://obamawhitehouse.archives.gov/the -press-office/2015/11/06/statement-president-keystone-xl-pipeline

Paul, Jesse. 2017. "Boulder County's Oil, Gas Ban Has Gone on Long Enough, Colorado AG Says in Lawsuit." *The Denver Post*, February 14. Retrieved from http://www .denverpost.com/2017/02/14/boulder-county-oil-and-gas-moratorium-colorado-ag -sues

Pierce, Jonathan J., Holly L. Peterson, & Katherine C. Hicks. 2017. "Policy Change: An Advocacy Coalition Framework Perspective." Paper presented at the Midwest Political Science Association (MPSA). Chicago, April 2016.

Pierce, Jonathan J., Holly L. Peterson, Michael D. Jones, Samantha P. Garrard, & Theresa Vu. 2017. "There and Back Again: A Tale of the Advocacy Coalition Framework." *Policy Studies Journal*, *45*(1): 13–46.

Radnofsky, Louise, & Cassandra Sweet. 2017. "Donald Trump Signs Order Rolling Back Obama's Climate-Change Rules." *Wall Street Journal*, March 28, sec. Politics. Retrieved from https://www.wsj.com/articles/donald-trump-signs-order-rolling -back-obamas-climate-change-rules-1490726471

Save Coos Jobs. "Saveourjobs | Facts." 2017. *Saveourjobs*. Formerly retrieved from https:// www.savecoosjobs.com/facts

Sickinger, Ted. 2017a. "Feds Reject Jordan Cove LNG Terminal." *The Oregonian*, March 11. Retrieved from http://www.oregonlive.com/environment/index.ssf/2016/03/feds _deny_jordan_cove_lng_term.html

Sickinger, Ted. 2017b. "Jordan Cove Spends Heavily to Kill Coos County Anti-LNG Measure." *The Oregonian*, May 6. Retrieved from http://www.oregonlive.com/business /index.ssf/2017/05/jordan_cove_spends_heavily_to.html

Smith, Mitch. 2017. "Standing Rock Protest Camp, Once Home to Thousands, Is Razed." *New York Times*, February 23. Retrieved from https://www.nytimes.com/2017/02 /23/us/standing-rock-protest-dakota-access-pipeline.html

Sovacool, Benjamin K. 2014. "Diversity: Energy Studies Need Social Science." *Nature News*, *511*(7511): 529.

"The Paris Agreement—Main Page." 2017. *United Nations*. Retrieved from http://unfccc .int/paris_agreement/items/9485.php

Trump, Donald. 2017. "Remarks by President Trump at Signing of Executive Order to Create Energy Independence." *Whitehouse.gov*, March 28. Retrieved from https:// www.whitehouse.gov/the-press-office/2017/03/28/remarks-president-trump -signing-executive-order-create-energy

Weible, Christopher M. 2008. "Expert-Based Information and Policy Subsystems: A Review and Synthesis." *Policy Studies Journal*, *36*(4): 615–635.

Weible, Christopher M., & Tanya Heikkila. 2017. "Policy Conflict Framework." *Policy Sciences*, *50*(1): 23–40.

Environmental Protection and Conservation

Conservation and protection of the natural environment have deep roots in the United States, and efforts toward these aims have often been framed in terms of people's moral obligations to the natural world and future generations of humans. This moral framework for environmental issues has come to be seen as politically liberal, with many advocates for environmental protection and conservation emphasizing the morality of such practices. The moral framing of environmental concerns was effective in creating significant environmental policy change in the 1960s through the 1980s, but the politicization of issues such as climate change have made environmental moralizing less appealing, especially to conservatives and Republicans.

CONSERVATION

The American Conservation movement emerged late in the 1800s in response to growing concerns raised about the unsustainable consumption of forests and other natural resources and plummeting populations of some wildlife. Advocates of increased resource protection and regulation urged Americans to develop a new understanding of the relationship between humans and nature. In particular, advocates began to argue that humans should not simply seek to dominate and control nature but instead take a moral responsibility for other forms of life, ensuring the protection of natural biology and systems for future generations, and refrain from the overconsumption of wildlife or sport killing for the sake of entertainment (Jepson & Canney, 2003). In addition, the movement understood that taking moral responsibility included engaging with nature aesthetically and intellectually in order to understand its value and thereby value its protection (Jepson & Canney, 2003). Early advocates convinced Congress to create the first national park, Yellowstone, in 1872. Three writers and philosophers—Ralph Waldo Emerson, Henry David Thoreau, and John Muir—came to embody conservationist philosophy for later generations. John Muir was perhaps the most visible public advocate among this cohort, earning the label of Father of the National Parks. Muir led a group that gained protective status for land in the Sierra Mountains, including Yosemite in 1889 (one year later, Yosemite was designated as a national park). Just two years later, the Sierra Club was created for the purpose of further protecting wild spaces. Early conservationists also helped to pass the Forest Reserve Act, which granted the president the power to place forests in the public domain so that they could not be easily exploited by industry interests.

The values of the early Conservation movement came to be personified by Theodore Roosevelt, who as president from 1901 to 1909 was able to secure the protection of many of America's most scenic landscapes through the establishment of new national parks and forests under the 1906 American Antiquities Act. President Roosevelt witnessed the destruction of natural habits, the decline of big game species through overhunting, and the pollution of natural resources by industry. Angered by this wastefulness, Roosevelt and key figures in his administration like Gifford Pinchot (the nation's first ever U.S. Forest Service chief) provided protection for some 230 million acres of wilderness, including 150 national forests under the oversight of the National Forest Service. "Of all the questions which can come before this nation, short of the actual preservation of its existence in a great war, there is none which compares in importance with the great central task of leaving this land even a better land for our descendants than it is for us," said Roosevelt in 1910. The tradition of setting aside natural treasures to be preserved for future generations in the form of national parks, moments, and other protected areas has generally continued among American presidents. However, the Donald Trump administration has rolled back some of the protected designations made by President Barack Obama.

In addition, in the early 20th century, conservationist groups came to include hunters as well as nature advocates. Both groups sought to preserve wildlife and wildlife habitat not only for themselves but for future generations. Early groups were formed in the late 1800s, including the Audubon Society and were mostly composed of wealthy urban people from the East Coast. Later groups included the Isaak Walton League and Ducks Unlimited, which came to recognize the need to protect threatened migratory bird habitats across the United States. This too followed the tradition of Teddy Roosevelt, an avid hunter whose concern about overhunting and disappearing wildlife habitat had led him to cofound the conservation-oriented Boone and Crockett Club in 1887. Strictly preservationist groups such as the Sierra Club (founded in 1892) and Wilderness Society (1935) also made the protection and expansion of natural areas a major focus of their energies.

The Audubon Society helped to pass the first federal law to protect wildlife, the Lacey Act in 1900, which bans trade in wildlife, fish, and plants that have been illegally taken, possessed, transported, or sold. In 1918, conservationists were able to pass the Migratory Bird Treaty Act, which implemented an agreement between the United States and Canada that sought to protect migratory birds. Later legislation extended the agreement to Mexico, as well as other countries.

At the subnational level, all states have established agencies to protect natural areas and wildlife. Some states began establishing these programs early in the

20th century as part of Progressive Era reforms. These agencies have followed the moral logic of our obligation to future generations by enforcing laws to prevent over-hunting and overfishing. In some states, these actions also serve to protect important elements of the local economies, whether commercial, tourist based, or both.

However, perceived obligations to next generations have sometimes run into conflict with citizen perceptions of infringements on their own rights to the use of public lands. Lands owned by the national government in the states have frequently been the sites of conflict between citizens who believe that there should be little restriction of public use of these lands and those who believe that the government agencies must thoroughly regulate the use of these areas to protect them. These clashes have sometimes escalated to the point where the threat of violence has loomed, such as in a 2014 standoff in Nevada between a rancher and law enforcement representing the Bureau of Land Management, as well as the 2016 occupation of the Malheur National Wildlife Refuge in Oregon by activists who claimed they were reasserting God-given rights over public lands and protecting the rights of ranchers in that state to use public lands for grazing their cattle (Williams, 2016).

ENVIRONMENTAL PROTECTION

Conservationists and nature preservationists had taken the first steps toward what today would be regarded as environmental protection, and while the actors' motives differed, all were partly driven by an appreciation of the beauty of nature. Throughout the early 20th century, a number of public health advocates had also become increasingly vocal about pollution in natural as well as in urban areas, but most of their effects were focused on establishing modern sanitation systems as well as taking steps at the state and local levels to protect drinking water supplies.

It was not until after World War II that public health advocates and conservation advocates began to converge to support passage of early environmental protection laws like the Federal Water Pollution Act of 1948 and the Air Pollution Control Act of 1955. Although very modest in scope, both of these laws sought to regulate pollution created by industry because of its negative impact on human health as well as the natural environment.

The modern environmental movement can trace its roots to the publication of Rachel Carson's book *Silent Spring* in 1962. Carson documented how the widespread use of pesticides in agriculture and for mosquito control was disrupting the natural ecology and killing wildlife. Perhaps most notably, she documented how the use of DDT (dichlorodiphenyltrichloroethane) was causing thin shells in bald eagle eggs, making survival of the offspring less likely and precipitating a dramatic decline in the country's bald eagle population. The threat posed by DDT to bald eagles, the country's national symbol, caught the attention of many. But Carson's documentation of the decline of many bird species galvanized others to a grass-roots mobilization that greatly strengthened the environmental movement and its mission to protect humans and the natural environment from harm (Carter, 2018).

The modern movement found rapid growth and policy success in the 1960s and early 1970s. The landmark Wilderness Act, the language of which was drafted by the Wilderness Society, protected over 9 million acres of wilderness as federal land when it passed in 1964. Four years later, Congress passed the Wild and Scenic Rivers Act to protect the natural status of designated rivers throughout the country. Perhaps most dramatically, in 1970 the National Environmental Policy Act became law. This law required all federal agencies to assess and report on the environmental impact of any action by the agency. New rules, regulations, and funding for virtually every federal government activity became subject to restrictions based on their environmental impact. The law also created the President's Council on Environmental Quality as a division within the Executive Office of the President to coordinate federal agencies on environmental and energy initiatives.

April 22, 1970, was the first Earth Day—a "national day for the environment" devised by Senator Gaylord Nelson (D-WI) to bring attention to environmental issues and to inspire grassroots activism. Senator Nelson saw an overlap between environmental issues, civil rights, and inequality: "Environment is all of America and its problems. It is rats in the ghetto. It is a hungry child in a land of affluence. It is housing not worthy of the name; neighborhoods not fit to inhabit" ("Meet Gaylord Nelson . . . ," 2019).

1970 also saw the creation of the Environmental Protection Agency (EPA) though an executive order signed by President Richard Nixon following a number of high-profile environmental crises in 1969. The EPA oversees the implementation of most environmental laws passed by Congress and signed by the president, including the Clean Water Act, the Clean Air Act, and their amendments. Another important law founded on the principles of stewardship was the Endangered Species Act of 1973, an ambitious law crafted to protect animals and plants at the risk of disappearing from the nation's lands. Through the 1970s and 1980s, most of these early laws were strengthened and expanded. However, attempts to roll back the reach of these laws began during the Ronald Reagan administration and have continued on and off since.

CLIMATE CHANGE

During the 1980s, another front opened in the campaign to protect and preserve the environment. Scientists became increasingly concerned about rising average worldwide temperatures and their negative impact on both human populations and ecosystems. And even though industries that produce the most greenhouse gas emissions had researched and understood the problem, by the 1990s and early 2000s these same industries were sowing disinformation and doubt about climate science and urging policy makers to use caution in forming regulatory responses (Hasemyer & Cushman, 2015).

Because climate change poses an existential threat to humanity, as well as many other species on the plant, it is by its very nature a moral concern. However, like many other environmental issues, climate change has become politically polarizing, with liberals and Democrats tending to line up in favor of environmental regulation and conservatives and Republicans less likely to prioritize environmental issues or support government regulations to reverse, stop, or mitigate negative environmental impacts. This is true even though Republican President Richard Nixon was responsible for creating the Environmental Protection Agency in 1970. This pattern of political polarization began to be evident in the 1980s but has accelerated over time (Pew Research Center, 2019). Indeed, studies indicate that political liberals are more likely to describe environmental issues in moral terms and to morally judge someone who does not act in an environmentally friendly manner than are their conservative counterparts (Feinberg & Willer, 2013). These moral judgments matter because without a sense of moral right and wrong, people are less likely to prioritize environmental protection over other concerns, such as economic interests. As University of Toronto psychologist Matthew Feinberg put it, "[W]e're more likely to contribute to a cause when we feel ethically compelled to" (Feinberg, 2015).

It turns out that terms used in liberal moralizing about environmental protection do not motivate conservatives toward prioritizing the environment. In fact, conservatives suggest that environmentalists are engaged in "moral straitjacketing" of those who would challenge claims about climate change and see themselves as part of a growing "new secular public morality" (Brett, 2014). Liberals do focus on the moral concern of environmental *protection*, but if they want to appeal to conservative moral values to promote proenvironmental attitudes, some researchers suggest that they should appeal to notions of protecting future generations and focus on language that stresses environmental purity as a value (Feinberg & Willer, 2013).

Yet even as scientists point to dramatic examples of the impact of climate change today, including the melting of polar ice sheets, the rise of sea levels, and dramatic shifts in the habitable range for particular animal species, Republican policy makers have often refused to acknowledge the role of humans in changing the climate and instead have delayed or reversed policy efforts to reduce the emission of greenhouse gases (Gottlieb, 2019). Often those rejecting climate change or at least a human role in climate change suggest that the moral threat to freedom from environmentalists is greater than the potential harmful effects of humans on the environment. Vaclav Klaus (2007), former president of the Czech Republic, argued, "I feel obliged to say that the biggest threat to freedom, democracy, the market economy and prosperity now [is] in ambitious environmentalism . . . this ideology wants to replace the free and spontaneous evolution of mankind by a sort of central (now global) planning."

CONCLUSION

Environmental issues, especially environmental protection and preservation, have frequently been framed in moral terms. However, the political and policy advances made by the conservation and environmental movements have often come because of more pragmatic concerns over resource depletion and the practical value of natural resources to humans. Dramatic policy changes since the late 1800s have protected tens of millions of acres of wild spaces on land and in coastal waters of the United States, at least partially preserving these spaces for future generations and providing habitats for thousands of species of animals and plant life.

Moral concerns over the pollution harms of modern industry, agriculture, and energy production have led to policy changes that reversed years of damage and wildlife declines. However, the political polarization of environmental issues, especially climate change, has polluted the public debate to the point where moralizing over environmental protection might no longer provide motivation for policy change.

Donald P. Haider-Markel

FURTHER READING

Brett, Judith. 2014. "Must We Choose Between Climate-change Action and Freedom of Speech?" *The Monthly*, August. Retrieved from https://www.themonthly.com.au /issue/2014/august/1406815200/judith-brett/must-we-choose-between-climate -change-action-and-freedom

Carson, Rachel. 1962. *Silent Spring.* New York: Houghton Mifflin.

Carter, Neil. 2018. *The Politics of the Environment: Ideas, Activism, Policy.* New York: Cambridge University Press.

Feinberg, Matthew. 2015. "Is the Environment a Moral Cause?" *The New York Times*, February 27. Retrieved from https://www.nytimes.com/2015/03/01/opinion/sunday/is -the-environment-a-moral-cause.html

Feinberg, Matthew, & Robb Willer. 2013. "The Moral Roots of Environmental Attitudes." *Psychological Science, 24*(1): 56–62.

Gottlieb, Roger S. 2019. *Morality and the Environmental Crisis.* New York: Cambridge University Press.

Hasemyer, David, & John H. Cushman, Jr. 2015. "Exxon Sowed Doubt About Climate Science for Decades by Stressing Uncertainty." *Inside Climate News*, October 22. Retrieved from https://insideclimatenews.org/news/22102015/Exxon-Sowed-Doubt -about-Climate-Science-for-Decades-by-Stressing-Uncertainty

Ikpe, Ibanga B. 2018. "Science, Morality and Method in Environmental Discourse." *Human Affairs, 28*(1): 71–87.

Jepson, Paul, & Susan Canney. 2003. "Values-led Conservation." *Global Ecology and Biogeography, 12*(4): 271–274.

Klaus, Vaclav. 2007. "Freedom, Not Climate, Is at Risk." *The Financial Times*, June 13. Retrieved from https://www.ft.com/content/9deb730a-19ca-11dc-99c5-000b5df10621

Lytle, Mark Hamilton. 2007. *The Gentle Subversive: Rachel Carson, Silent Spring, and the Rise of the Environmental Movement.* New York: Oxford University Press.

"Meet Gaylord Nelson, Founder of Earth Day." 2019. Retrieved from http://www .nelsonearthday.net/nelson

Pew Research Center. 2019. "Economic Issues Decline Among Public's Policy Priorities." *Pew Research Center*, January 25. Retrieved from https://www.people-press.org /2018/01/25/economic-issues-decline-among-publics-policy-priorities

Rich, Nathaniel. 2019. *Losing Earth: A Recent History.* New York: MCD, Farrar, Straus and Giroux.

Roosevelt, Theodore. 1910. "New Nationalism Speech." *TeachingAmericanHistory.org*, August 31. Retrieved from https://teachingamericanhistory.org/library/document /new-nationalism-speech

Stone, Christopher D. 2010. *Should Trees Have Standing? Law, Morality, and the Environment.* Oxford: Oxford University Press.

Stone, Christopher D. 2003. "Do Morals Matter—The Influence of Ethics on Courts and Congress in Shaping US Environmental Policies." *Environs: Environmental Law & Policy Journal, 27*: 13–52.

Thøgersen, John. 1996. "Recycling and Morality: A Critical Review of the Literature." *Environment and Behavior, 28*(4): 536–558.

Willer, Robb. 2015. "Is the Environment a Moral Cause?" *The New York Times*, February 27. Retrieved from https://www.nytimes.com/2015/03/01/opinion/sunday/is -the-environment-a-moral-cause.html

Williams, Jennifer. 2016. "The Oregon Militia Standoff, Explained." *Vox*, January 26. Retrieved from https://www.vox.com/2016/1/3/10703712/oregon-militia-standoff

Eugenics

Eugenics is the science of enhancing the human gene pool selecting who can reproduce based on the desirability of the traits an individual or group of people possesses. Central to the discussion of eugenics is who decides which traits or behaviors are desirable. The coupling of genetic screening tests with procedures that assist with reproduction and new genetic editing techniques has brought renewed attention to the moral and ethical implications of such practices in the 21st century. Previous eugenic policies, like those implemented during the first half of the 20th century in the United States, sought to achieve ideological goals, like creating a better society, race, or nationality. These policies forced individuals with undesirable traits, like mental illness or criminal tendencies, to be sterilized, thus preventing them from passing their genes to future generations. Modern eugenics differs from government-imposed eugenics in that often the decision makers are women (and their partners), who are either trying to become pregnant or are pregnant, deciding what is best for their children. However, few of these individual decision makers would refer to this process as eugenics in the early 20th-century sense.

Even with the shifting from government eugenic policies to individual decisions to engage in eugenics, the moral dilemmas are similar. Both government-imposed eugenics and modern eugenics seek to provide a better future at the cost of genetic discrimination. Previous eugenic programs were often operated by governments who framed their actions as part of a wider effort to create a better society for future generations, whereas eugenics today tends to occur at a familial level and center around what is best for the family and their children. Additionally, government-imposed and modern eugenics seek to rid humans of our most debilitating diseases. These efforts, however, have raised complex questions about discrimination and societal values.

Society has created protected classes of people based on their characteristics, like mental illness, physical disorders, and race. Although government-imposed eugenics actively used these traits as criteria for selecting who was sterilized, modern eugenics has left the question of genetic discrimination up to the individual decision maker. In vitro fertilization, for example, allows people to select embryos for implantation based on gender. If a common genetic disorder, like Down syndrome, is detected early enough during pregnancy, a pregnant woman can choose to have a selective abortion. Finally, new techniques for modifying genes has the potential to allow parents to manipulate their offspring's genes before birth. Should the protection of groups that have endured a history of discrimination, such as those that are not neurotypical or who are physically disabled, extend to protect embryos? Or should genetic discrimination be permitted up until birth?

THE HISTORY OF EUGENICS

The notion behind eugenics is that by artificially selecting humans based on their traits and behaviors, our species will evolve to become better. Although eugenics is often traced back to Plato's *Republic* and the myths of the metals, Sir Francis Galton (who was Charles Darwin's cousin) was the first to advocate for the use of eugenics to create a better society (Galton, 1909). Central to Darwin's theory of natural selection is the survival of the fittest, which suggests that those who are best equipped to survive in their environment survive to reproduce while those who are unequipped perish along with their genes. Galton believed that human evolution could be guided by selecting who reproduced. Ultimately, such a process would produce a superhuman species that possessed only the most desirable traits (Haller, 1984).

Innate to Galton's beliefs about selective reproduction is neglect for the role of environment in shaping behaviors and traits. Galton believed in genetic determinism—that a person's traits, characteristics, and abilities are wholly determined by the genes they possess (Haller, 1984). Genetic determinism suggests that environmental interventions, like educating children in low-income families, will not provide any enduring changes to an individual's behavior because the behavior is hardwired in the individual's genes. The genetic determinist view that is inherent to eugenics has led some researchers to suggest that early advocates for eugenics sought to maintain social inequalities between the wealthy and poor and decrease the need for social welfare programs that provided assistance to people with less desirable traits (Lewontin, Rose, & Kamin, 1985).

The dogmatic belief in genetic determinism for such traits as intelligence, mental illness, beauty, and criminal tendencies has led eugenicists to support policies that either hinder or encourage reproduction based on their perceptions of the desirability of the traits a person possesses. Negative eugenics policies focus on controlling reproduction by sterilizing and, in some extreme cases, even killing those individuals who possess genes for traits that are deemed undesirable. The genocide committed by Nazi Germany during the Holocaust is an extreme example of a negative eugenics policy. Positive eugenics, on the other hand, seeks to promote reproduction among people with desirable traits. Initially, Galton advocated for the use of positive eugenics policies that provided social welfare assistance and monetary rewards if more educated couples produced offspring (Galton, 1909).

Although eugenics is most often associated with Nazi Germany and the Holocaust, the United States also has a history of implementing eugenic policies. In fact, many of Germany's ideas about how to prevent individuals who possess undesirable traits from reproducing originated in the United States. The eugenic policies in the United States during the early 20th century were focused on preventing people deemed to possess low intelligence, mental illness, sexually deviant behavior, criminal tendencies, or severe medical conditions (such as epilepsy) from reproducing, usually through forced sterilization.

Many of the advocates for the early 20th-century eugenic policies tended to believe in social and racial dominance. Eugenics enthusiasts, for example, tended to support the Immigration Act of 1924. This legislation established a quota system to limit the number of people entering the United States from countries with ethnicities deemed to be inferior to those from Western Europe (Levine, 2010). By supporting the sterilization of the mentally ill and limiting the number of "undesirable" immigrants, proponents of eugenics expressed confidence that they could make America stronger for future generations.

The acceptance of eugenics in the United States peaked with the Supreme Court decision in *Buck v. Bell* (1927). *Buck v. Bell* concerned a eugenics law in Virginia that mandated the sterilization of those found to be below average in intelligence or suffering from a mental health issues. The Supreme Court found the law to be constitutional. Justice Oliver Wendell Holmes showed his support for Virginia's treatment of the mentally ill when he stated, "Three generations of imbeciles are enough" (quoted in Cohen, 2016). Similar policies existed in California and Puerto Rico in the early 20th century, with tens of thousands of forced sterilizations occurring in those jurisdictions. Even as late as the 1970s, it is estimated that at least 25 percent of Native Americans were being sterilized, often without consent (Lawrence, 2000).

Public revelations about forced sterilization policies in the United States increased opposition to eugenics by World War II (Silver, 2003). However, the discovery of concentration camps and the horror of the Holocaust in Germany demarcated the turning point of public support for most eugenics policies in the United States. In spite of the change in public opinion toward eugenics, however, forced sterilization of criminals persisted in several states until the late 1970s.

Eugenics, however, returned to the spotlight in the 1980s with the creation of genetic screening technologies capable of determining whether a person has a genetic mutation that is associated with a particular trait, disease, or disorder. This process is usually referred to as human genetic engineering. Since medical interventions capable of preventing genetic disorders or altering genetic traits have thus far been limited, and national and state laws ban genetic discrimination, there are still significant concerns that individual genetic information can be used against a person (Wolf, 2017).

Unlike previous eugenic policies implemented by governments, eugenics today is viewed by some as the product of an individual's right to make reproductive decisions without government interference (Raz, 2009). Modern genetics also differs from previous eugenic policies in that expecting and soon-to-be expecting parents are choosing to select their offspring based on their genetic profiles. Most often, in vitro genetic testing is used to determine whether an embryo tests positive for any mutations.

Couples with fertility problems can turn to in vitro fertilization (IVF) to become pregnant. Often during IVF procedures, several eggs are harvested and fertilized with sperm, but not all fertilized eggs or embryos are implanted in a woman. In choosing which embryos to implant and which embryos to discard, patients or IVF doctors can engage in eugenics if they screen and select the embryos for implantation based on the traits they possess, often based on the traits of the donors rather than genetic tests. These traits can be socioeconomic status, height, or weight. Often this decision is influenced by the legal rights of the patient and the IVF clinic's policies.

Society can also influence the morality of screening embryos during in vitro fertilization. Scientists, for example, sought to understand why IVF parents can engage in embryonic discrimination in Israel but not in Germany. They found that the social beliefs about the relationship between parents and their children could be influencing the difference in embryo screening policies (Hashiloni-Dolev & Shkedi, 2007).

Modern eugenics can also occur at the hands of expecting mothers who have fetal genetic testing done for common genetic disorders, like Down syndrome. Where previous eugenics policies focused on the good for society, expecting parents are often trying to decide what is best for them, their family, and the fetus when they decide whether to have a selective abortion based on the genetic screen results. Government can also influence whether pregnant mothers will engage in this form of modern eugenics. In the United Kingdom, for example, the National Health Service offers free genetic testing during pregnancy (National Health Service, 2015). This service has resulted in the abortion of 90 percent of fetuses identified with prenatal Down syndrome through genetic screening (Morris & Springett, 2014). Of course, some find the practice of abortion morally repugnant, and advocates for the disabled oppose pregnancy termination on the basis of the disability status of a fetus (Friedman & Owen, 2016).

Although fetal genetic screening and parental decisions to selectively abort a fetus are still limited to a short list of genetic disorders that can severely limit the quality of life, the list of possible genetic characteristics that a fetal genetic screening can find is growing. Advancements in technology, fueled with a growing understanding of which genes are associated with which characteristics, could mean that future fetal genetic screening could examine genetic predispositions for such superficial traits and characteristics as eye color or personality. These traits might then be used as selection criteria by parents.

The future of eugenics may not be contained to selectively implanting embryos with desirable traits and aborting fetuses with undesirable genes. DNA manipulation, or editing, could be the next evolution in eugenics. The technological advances necessary for this new wave of eugenics have already been achieved. CRISPR (clustered regularly interspaced short palindromic repeats) allows scientists a level of precision in editing the human genome that until recently was confined to the realm of science fiction. Currently, scientists using CRISPR technology have focused on curing cancer in adults by knocking out cancerous DNA strands that enable cancer's unchecked growth. Already clinical trials using CRISPR to treat bladder, prostate, and renal-cell cancers are are possible (Cyranoski, 2016), and in

2019 U.S. scientists began the first CRISPR treatments for cancer (Fan, 2019). The technology has also been applied in attempts to make future generations resistant to the human immunodeficiency virus (HIV) by genetically altering embryos (Callaway, 2016).

Although the applications of CRISPR technology to humans thus far has focused on eradicating debilitating diseases, little is stopping scientists from applying CRISPR technology to manipulate physical characteristics. For example, the technology could be employed to manipulate an embryo's genes for metabolism, which could end the obesity epidemic and lower risk for heart disease. The jump from treating cancer to reducing obesity may not be that far-fetched. In a 2015 study, scientists deactivated a gene associated with obesity in mice using CRISP-R (Classnitzer et al., 2015). This intermediary step, however, could lead to even more superficial applications of the technology, like choosing eye color or altering likely personality types. The pull to use the technologies to select more desirable traits in our offspring could be too difficult to overcome.

Stephen P. Schneider

FURTHER READING

Bashford, Alison, & Philippa Levine. 2010. *The Oxford Handbook of the History of Eugenics*. Oxford: Oxford University Press.

Callaway, Ewen. 2016. "Second Chinese Team Reports Gene Editing in Human Embryos." Retrieved from http://www.nature.com/news/second-chinese-team-reports-gene-editing-in-human-embryos-1.19718

Classnitzer, Melina, Simon N. Dankel, Kyoung-Han Kim, Gerald Quon, Wouter Meuleman, Christine Haugen, Viktoria Glunk, Isabel S. Sousa, Jacqueline L. Beaudry, Vijitha Puviindran, Nezar A. Abdennur, Jannel Liu, Per-Arne Svensson, Yi-Hsiang Hus, Daniel J. Drucker, Gunnar Mellgren, Chi-Chung Hui, Hans Hauner, & Manolis Kellis. 2015. "*FTO* Obesity Variant Circuitry and Adipocyte Browning in Humans." *The New England Journal of Medicine*, 373(10): 895–907.

Cohen, Adam. 2016. *Imbeciles: The Supreme Court, American Eugenics, and the Sterilization of Carrie Buck*. New York: Penguin Press.

Cyranoski, David. 2016. "CRISPR Gene-editing Tested in a Person for the First Time." Retrieved from http://www.nature.com/news/crispr-gene-editing-tested-in-a-person-for-the-first-time-1.20988

Fan, Shelly. 2019. "CRISPR Used in Human Trials for the First Time in the US." *Singularity Hub*, May 2. Retrieved from https://singularityhub.com/2019/05/02/crispr-used-in-human-trials-for-the-first-time-in-the-us/

Friedman, Carli, & Aleksa L. Owen. 2016. "Siblings of Disabled Peoples' Attitudes Toward Prenatal Genetic Testing and Disability: A Mixed Methods Approach." *Disability Studies Quarterly*, 36(3). doi: http://dx.doi.org/10.18061/dsq.v36i3.5051

Galton, Francis. 1909. *Essays in Eugenics*. London: Eugenics Education Society.

Green, Ronald M. 2007. *Babies by Design: The Ethics of Genetic Choice*. New Haven, CT: Yale University Press.

Haller, Mark H. 1984. *Eugenics: Hereditation Attitudes in American Thought*. New Brunswick, NJ: Rutgers University Press.

Hashiloni-Dolev, Yael, & Shiri Shkedi. 2007. "On New Reproductive Technologies and Family Ethics: Pre-Implementation Genetic Diagnosis for Sibling Donor in Israel and Germany." *Social Science & Medicine*, 65: 2081–2092.

Lawrence, Jane. 2000. "The Indian Health Service and the Sterilization of Native American Women." *American Indian Quarterly, 24*(3): 400–419.

Levine, Philippa. 2010. "Anthropology, Colonialism, and Eugenics." In Alison Bashford and Philippa Levine (Eds.), *The Oxford Handbook of the History of Eugenics*, 43–61. New York: Oxford University Press.

Lewontin, Richard C., Steven Rose, & Leon J. Kamin. 1985. *Not in Our Genes: Biology, Ideology, and Human Nature.* New York: Pantheon.

Morris, Joan K., & Anna Springett. 2014. "The National Down Syndrome Cytogenetic Register for England and Wales: 2012 Annual Report." Retrieved from http://www.binocar.org/content/annrep2012_final.pdf

National Health Service. 2015. "Screening Test in Pregnancy." Retrieved from http://www.nhs.uk/conditions/pregnancy-and-baby/pages/screening-tests-abnormality-pregnant.aspx

Raz, Aviad R. 2009. "Eugenics Utopias/Dystopias, Reprogenetics, and Community Genetics." *Sociology of Health & Illness, 31*(4): 602–616.

Silver, Michael G. 2003. "Eugenics and Compulsory Sterilization Laws: Providing Redress for the Victims of a Shameful Era in United States History." *George Washington Law Review, 72*: 862–892.

Wolf, Susan M. 2017. "Beyond 'Genetic Discrimination': Toward the Broader Harm of Geneticism." In Sheila A. M. McLean (Ed.), *Genetics and Gene Therapy*, 159–167. New York: Routledge.

Evolution and Creationism

The creationism and antievolution movements in the United States have benefited enormously from a decentralized public education system that grants relative autonomy to local and state school boards composed of elected officials; however, schools have been equally constrained by their status as government-funded institutions subject to the establishment clause, which requires them to avoid supporting any particular religion. For this reason, morality framing in the evolution and creationism debates has been and still is inextricably linked to key legislative rulings and subsequent attempts by creationists to adapt their language in response to court decisions. This dynamic has pushed creationists deeper and deeper into epistemological territory as they fight to uphold their moral convictions while at the same time co-opt scientific language and avoid religious language. During the 1960s, the United States sought to overhaul its science curriculum in response to an increasing need for a scientifically literate and capable population. However, the migration of the debate to a scientific frame has done nothing to reduce its moral salience, and, increasingly, proponents of evolution are framing their stance as a moral one.

THE POPULIST AND MAJORITARIAN VIEWPOINTS

In the United States, early opposition to the theory of evolution by natural selection took the form of populist, majoritarian (rule by the majority) rhetoric. One of the theory's most vociferous critics at the end of the 19th century was William Jennings Bryan, a three-time Democratic nominee for president whose speeches resonated well with the values of Midwestern agrarian communities. Bryan's political platform was built on a belief in the superiority of Christian civic morality, and he saw Christianity as the only way a society could make progress in peace. Bryan professed the nobility of "plain people" and often spoke of the need to protect them from the elite classes (originally the bankers opposing free silver and later the educated scientists and professors advocating that evolution be taught in public schools) (Maddux, 2013).

Through thousands of speeches spanning two decades, Bryan gave clear and unambiguous voice to the moral and ethical arguments for antievolution views in America at the dawn of the 20th century. In one of his earliest antievolution speeches, "The Prince of Peace," Bryan declared, "Religion is the foundation of morality in the individual and in the group of individuals" (Bryan, 1914). In "The Menace of Darwinism," a speech first given in 1921, Bryan declared that religion and belief in God are the "mainspring" upon which man's life depends—"that anything that weakens belief in God weakens man," that "it is the duty of the moral, as well as the Christian world to combat" any influence that threatens belief in God, and that Darwinism "is obscuring God and weakening all the virtues that rest upon the religious tie between God and man." According to Bryan, he was the voice of an American majority that was "trying to protect itself from the effort of an insolent minority to force irreligion upon the children under the guise of teaching science" (Bryan, 1921; Maddux, 2013).

THE FUNDAMENTALIST VIEWPOINT

The Christian fundamentalist movement of the early 1900s arose out of the ruins of a fractured movement (premillennial dispensationalist) that viewed the return of Christ to earth as near. When the end of World War I in 1918 did not result in the return of Christ despite the confident predictions of dispensationalist religious leaders, this failure was capitalized on by an evangelical leader named William Bell Riley. He formed the World's Christian Fundamentals Association, organized the World Conference on Christian Fundamentals, and began publishing a periodical titled *The Christian Fundamentalist* (Evans, 2017).

The fundamentalists adopted an argumentative frame toward evolution that was grounded in empirical reasoning. Throughout the 1920s, fundamentalists (including Riley) engaged professors and experts in the field of evolutionary biology to public debates. In these debates, fundamentalists argued for the scientific implausibility of the theory and used the Bible as an authoritative record of historical fact to contradict scientific explanations. "The first and foremost reason for [evolution's] elimination is the unquestionable fact that evolution is not a science; it is a hypothesis only, a speculation," argued Riley (quoted in Numbers, 1987). This is not to say that they abandoned moral and ethical arguments altogether but that they increasingly attempted to base their arguments on science or a redefining of science, using the methods and norms of scientific discourse to argue their side (Maddux, 2013).

THE SCOPES TRIAL

In 1925 in Dayton, Tennessee, John Thomas Scopes went on trial for violating Tennessee's Butler Act, which prohibited the teaching of evolution by natural selection in the state's school systems. The trial addressed three primary debates, and to this day, these debates continue to frame legal challenges to teaching evolution: (1) a substantive debate of the theory of evolution itself and its scientific merit,

(2) a procedural debate that concerned the question of whether or not ordinary citizens should be able to set curricular policies for public schools, and (3) a debate on the autonomy of teachers in their classrooms (which ironically is now used by creationists to try and allow teachers to teach alternatives to evolution) (Berkman & Plutzer, 2010).

William Jennings Bryan led the prosecution and used the platform to further promote his populist views. The burgeoning Christian fundamentalist movement, however, was at the same time endeavoring to reframe the debate in terms of (1) the alleged weaknesses of the science behind evolutionary theory and (2) the inerrancy of the Bible—the belief that the Bible was free from errors in the realm of science as well as in matters of faith. Bryan, who had taken up the antievolution cause more than 15 years prior, was increasingly ill equipped to engage in public debates of this type, and he found himself inadequately versed in the science of the time and unable to stand up to the defense's cross-examination when Bryan agreed to take the stand as an expert witness for the creationist position. Bryan's most common answers to the interrogations of Clarence Darrow, the lead defense attorney for Scopes, were, "I don't know" and "I have been too busy on things that I thought were of more importance than that." It is this mischaracterization of Bryan as a fundamentalist as opposed to a populist that, scholars argue, is the cause for his ridicule as a fundamentalist fool (Maddux, 2013).

In the end, the court in the Scopes trial steered clear of the substantive debate and upheld a majoritarian position that Scopes, as a public employee, was responsible for teaching in accordance with the desires of the people and the laws established by the Butler Act. Although Scopes's fine did not stand up to appeal, the Butler Act was affirmed by the Tennessee Supreme Court and would have major implications for the next 30 years of antievolution efforts as Arkansas, Louisiana, Mississippi, and Oklahoma passed antievolution bills. By 1929, almost all school biology textbooks had been revised to appease the fundamentalist agenda (Berkman & Plutzer, 2010).

OPPOSITION TO MAJORITARIAN DEMOCRACY

In 1961, a major overhaul of America's science curricula was undertaken in response to the Soviet Union's successful launch of the Sputnik satellite. One outcome of this effort was a series of textbooks published under the auspices of the Biological Science Curriculum Study (BSCS). These textbooks, which included chapters on evolution, were quickly and widely adopted across the nation (Berkman & Plutzer, 2010). However, opposition from conservative Christian parents and leaders was immediate, and they argued that the inclusion of evolution in the textbooks was offensive and undermined their faith. Parents began to protest, and officials in many states requested modifications to the textbooks or pasted disclaimers in the bindings that read "evolution is simply a *theory*" (Berkman & Plutzer, 2010).

In 1965, teachers at Little Rock Central High School recommended a BSCS textbook, and the administration adopted the text for the upcoming school year. This presented second-year biology teacher Susan Epperson with a dilemma. The school had adopted a textbook that included sections on evolution, but an Arkansas law dating from 1928 made it illegal for any teacher at a public school or university to teach that humans "descended or ascended from a lower order of animals."

At the trial, Arkansas's Chancery Court ruled in Epperson's favor for her right to teach evolution, stating that the Arkansas law violated the First Amendment because it "tends to hinder the quest for knowledge, restrict freedom to learn, and restrain the freedom to teach" (quoted in *Epperson v. Arkansas*, 100). This statement by Arkansas's Chancery Court is significant because it legitimizes academic freedom as a viable source of opposition to majoritarian democracy. In fact, the antievolution law in Arkansas was passed by an initiative, that is, citizens had proposed the law, and it was subject to a majority vote in a general election. It was approved by 63 percent of the voters (Gray, 1970). The Arkansas State Supreme Court, however, rejected this argument upon appeal and ruled that banning evolution "is a valid exercise of the state's power to specify the curriculum in its public schools" (quoted in *Epperson v. Arkansas*, 1968: fn. 7). The case then went to the U.S. Supreme Court, which voted 9–0 in Epperson's favor. The Supreme Court ignored arguments for academic freedom and focused on the First Amendment's establishment clause. Abe Fortas, in writing for the majority, noted that "there can be no doubt that Arkansas has sought to prevent its teachers from discussing the theory of evolution because it is contrary to the belief of some that the Book of Genesis must be the exclusive source of doctrine as to the origin of man" (*Epperson v. Arkansas*, 1968: 107).

CREATION SCIENCE, INTELLIGENT DESIGN, AND THE EVOLUTION OF ANTIEVOLUTION LEGISLATION

The *Epperson v. Arkansas* ruling prompted a major shift in creationist framing arguments. With an increasingly educated and secularized public less likely to be swayed by evolution's inherent threat to religion and with all their legislative efforts being shot down by the establishment clause, creationists embarked on what would become a decades-long push to establish scientific evidence that contradicted evolution and supported biblical interpretations of history. This had been done before, but now they were more mindful to avoid religious language and instead stressed the science in purer, albeit increasingly disingenuous ways. For example, the Creation Research Society headed by Henry M. Morris (1918–2006) published a handbook for high school teachers called *Scientific Creationism* (1974). In the handbook, Morris argues that creationism could "be taught without reference to the book of Genesis or to other religious literature or religious doctrines" and that schools should teach only "the basic scientific creation model," stripped of all reference to its biblical origins. This framing of creationism as simply another scientific model for human origins on par with the evolution model became known as the two-model approach, and it would become the primary approach used to persuade school boards to provide space for creation science in the classroom. By the 1980s, laws and policies mandating "balanced treatment" were increasingly common (Numbers, 1992).

After a series of court rulings making it abundantly and unambiguously clear that creationism had no place in school curricula, concerted efforts were undertaken by creationist organizations to purge their rhetoric of creationist language. For example, draft versions of a creationist textbook, *Of Pandas and People*, replaced about 150 instances of variations of the word "creation" with the words "intelligent design" and in one instance actually left the typographical error of "cdesign proponentsists" (Matzke, 2006). Intelligent design, as espoused by the Discovery Institute's Center for Science and Culture, was (and in many ways still is) at the leading edge of efforts to provide a scientific foundation for creationist beliefs. The *Kitzmiller v. Dover Area School District* ruling of 2005 hindered intelligent design efforts when the school district tried to impose a policy that required the teaching of intelligent design and a federal court again appealed to the establishment clause in its decision to rule the policy unconstitutional. Since then, groundbreaking research using new statistical tools (phylogenetics) to study cultural transmission has provided a clear way of tracking the evolution of antievolution policy and legislative proposals. Using these techniques, it has been shown that a 2004 model bill created by the Discovery Institute has been modified by various states in attempts to pass antievolution policies or legislation while at the same time attempting to deny its religious origins (Matzke, 2016).

CONTEMPORARY MORAL ARGUMENTS AND MORALIZED RATIONALITY

A survey of a few of the most prominent creationist organizations including *The Creation Research Institute*, *Discovery Institute*, *Answers in Genesis*, and *The Institute for Creation Research* shows that moral arguments against evolution still play a pivotal role in their worldviews. Answers in Genesis claims, "Most evolutionists adhere to a moral code and believe in the concept of right and wrong. But evolutionists have no rational reason for this position. Thus, only creationists have a rational, logical, and consistent reason for morality" (Purdom & Lisle, 2009). The Discovery Institute lays out a syllogistic argument in its multimedia section discussing the moral implications of Darwinism, claiming that Darwinism makes plausible the idea of atheism, which is incompatible with a traditional, "transcendent" account of morality; in another section, it claims that "the idea that evolution undermines objective moral standards is hardly a recent discovery of sociobiology" (Discovery Institute, 2011).

However, as the creationist movement has had to push deeper and deeper into epistemological territory to remain in the fray, secularists have responded by increasingly taking a moral stance on issues regarding evolution and science. Interestingly, research suggests that the debate can be just as morally salient an issue for evolutionists as it is for creationists. This is a result of the psychological phenomenon of moralized rationality, that is, assigning a high degree of *moralization* to rationality that is statistically independent of the degree of *importance* ascribed to rationality (Ståhl, Zaal, & Skitka, 2016).

Currently, the "new atheists," such as popular scientists Richard Dawkins and Sam Harris, are at the forefront of a social movement that increasingly argues for a moral obligation to adhere to strict standards for rational discourse and empirical scientific methodologies. Instead of engaging in the substantive debate of creationism, the new atheists are actively seeking to frame the argument as a moral one through the tools and language of science, thus attempting to provide moral frameworks and answer moral questions. As such, they present religious beliefs as inherently immoral in a way similar to how early creationists presented scientific beliefs. For example, Sam Harris's book *The Moral Landscape: How Science Can Determine Human Values* is essentially an extended deposition of religion's assumed monopoly on morality and a philosophical treatise on how we can and should derive our morality from science. This attempt by scientists to address the moral foundations of creationists' arguments ushers in a new and exciting era of a now more than 150-year-old debate.

Brandon Bretl

FURTHER READING

Berkman, M., & E. Plutzer. 2010. *Evolution, Creationism, and the Battle to Control America's Classrooms.* New York: Cambridge University Press.

Bryan, W. J. 1921. "The Menace of Darwinism." *In His Image.* New York: Fleming H. Revell.

Bryan, W. J. 1914. *The Prince of Peace.* New York and London: Funk & Wagnalls.

Discovery Institute, The. 2011. "Darwinian Evolution, God, and Morality." Video. Retrieved from https://www.discovery.org/multimedia/audio/2011/06/darwinian-evolution -god-and-morality-2/

Epperson v. Arkansas, 1968.

Evans, R. K. 2017. "A New Protestantism Has Come: World War I, Premillennial Dispensationalism, and the Rise of Fundamentalism in Philadelphia." *Pennsylvania History*, *84*(3), 292–312.

Gray, V. 1970. "Anti-Evolution Sentiment and Behavior: The Case of Arkansas." *Journal of American History*, *57*(2), 352–366.

Kitzmiller v. Dover Area School District, 2005.

Maddux, Kristy. 2013. "Fundamentalist Fool or Populist Paragon? William Jennings Bryan and the Campaign Against Evolutionary Theory." *Rhetoric & Public Affairs*, *16*(3): 489–520.

Matzke, N. J. 2016. "The Evolution of Antievolution Policies After Kitzmiller Versus Dover." *Science*, *351*(6268), 28–30. doi:10.1126/science.aad4057

Matzke, N. J. 2006. "Design on Trial: How NCSE Helped Win the Kitzmiller Case." *Reports of the National Center for Science Education*, *26*(1–2), 37–44.

Numbers, R. L. 1992. *The Creationists.* New York: Alfred A. Knopf.

Numbers, R. L. 1987. "The Creationists." *Zygon*, *22*(2), 133–164.

Purdom, G., & J. Lisle. 2009. "Morality and the Irrationality of an Evolutionary Worldview." *Phi Kappa Phi Forum*, *89*(1), 8–13.

Ståhl, T., M. P. Zaal, & L. J. Skitka. 2016. "Moralized Rationality: Relying on Logic and Evidence in the Formation and Evaluation of Belief Can Be Seen as a Moral Issue." *PLoS ONE*, *11*(11), 1–38.

Extraordinary Rendition

Extraordinary rendition refers to the practice of seizing suspected terrorists in foreign countries and transferring them to a third location for interrogation and torture. It differs from deportation and extradition in both its purpose and legal status. Deportation removes individuals from countries according to domestic laws controlling foreign entry, and extradition transfers individuals from one country to another according to established treaty agreements. While deportation and extradition are both legal processes, extraordinary rendition happens *outside* the law. Whether this makes the practice illegal and immoral or whether some exception to the law makes it justifiable is still sharply contested. With respect to purpose, deportation and extradition are both intended to lead to a just outcome: Deportation is the state's legal remedy for the unlawful presence of an individual, and extradition usually returns an individual to a jurisdiction to face criminal charges there. Admittedly, deportation and extradition sometimes appear to pursue a narrow sense of justice—so a legally valid deportation may be still be morally unjust, and an extradition may deliver someone to a corrupt jurisdiction.

THE CRUX OF MORAL ARGUMENTS ABOUT EXTRAORDINARY RENDITION

Extraordinary rendition, on the other hand, does not pursue justice at all. Instead, it delivers suspected terrorists to jurisdictions where they can be interrogated without the legal restraints and protections that would apply in the United States. Proponents say that extraordinary rendition protects innocent people by extracting important information from terrorists and by removing them from the global battlefield. Opponents counter that the practice leads to torture and other cruel, inhuman, and degrading treatment, either through negligence or by design.

Extraordinary rendition does not have a precise legal definition because it is an exception from rather than a feature of domestic and international laws. International law scholar Ingrid Detter says it is used "to send captured terrorists to another jurisdiction to be questioned there rather than in the home country" (2013: 370). In her view, extraordinary rendition is a "fictitious legal device" designed to "avoid stringent rules and guarantees in U.S. law." Law professor M. L. Satterthwaite notes that the individual is transferred "without the benefit of a legal proceeding" and is, upon reaching the destination, "at risk of torture" (2006–2007: 1183). Constitutional scholar Louis Fisher says that "the President claims the inherent authority to seize individuals and transfer them to other countries for interrogation and torture" (2007–2008: 1406).

Extraordinary rendition emerged at a time when the perceived need for security had displaced concerns about justice. The intended outcome of these transfers was the extraction of information for counterterrorism operations. According to proponents of the practice, due process would have caused unacceptable delays in gathering intelligence and was also unnecessary because renditions were not intended to result in trials. Denying individuals due process is what makes extraordinary rendition *extralegal* and moves people beyond the reach of law. An important area of moral concern, then, is whether or when some people can be denied even the minimum legal protections afforded by the Geneva Conventions, the United Nations Convention Against Torture, and U.S. law.

A second key area of moral concern is the connection of extraordinary rendition with torture and other cruel, inhuman, and degrading treatment. The prominent cases of Maher Arar in Canada, Hassan Mustafa Osama Nasr in Italy, and former Guantánamo detainee Mohamedou Ould Slahi all document American renditions to torture (Commission of Inquiry, 2006; Povoledo, 2012; Slahi, 2015). Facilitating violent interrogation is the reason for using extraordinary rendition instead of the legal methods of apprehension and transfer. This distinguishes it from previous practices and means that any moral judgment of extraordinary rendition must account for its propensity to deliver individuals to be tortured.

However, the history of the extraordinary rendition debate is primarily a legal one. Prisoner transfers were controversial long before extraordinary rendition and its immediate precursor. In the aftermath of World War II, it was important to transfer "war criminals, traitors, and quislings" between countries to face justice but also important to avoid facilitating the elimination of political opponents under the guise of international justice (Hambro, 1952: 3). In theory, war crimes were extraditable offenses, and "political" crimes were not, but it was often difficult to "draw a line of distinction between the inter-allied prosecution of war criminals and the desire to prosecute political enemies" (Hambro, 1952: 3).

By the 1990s, extradition controversies had shifted from the question of political crime to the problem of international terrorism, and the United States had developed an intermediate practice for bringing suspected terrorists and drug lords to justice without using extradition procedures. What might be called ordinary rendition was codified during the Clinton administration. It involved seizing or kidnapping suspects abroad and bringing them to the United States or another country for trials in criminal courts (Mayer, 2008: 108; Fisher, 2007–2008: 1418–1420). Prior to 9/11, this more mundane rendition program tried to neutralize terrorist threats by convicting and jailing them for crimes they had previously committed.

EXTRAORDINARY RENDITION AFTER
THE SEPTEMBER 11 ATTACKS

After 9/11, the purpose and legal orientation of rendition changed, making it "extraordinary." Both the postwar extradition dilemma and the 1990s rendition program took place at least partly within the institutional framework of international law and delivered individuals to judicial systems. Extraordinary rendition, on the other hand, prioritizes security over justice and is not subject to legal constraints. Cases that begin with extraordinary rendition have had difficulty crossing back into the justice system once they are compromised by violations of due process and evidence tainted by torture. Unlike the Clinton-era rendition program, which captured suspects extralegally but which terminated in criminal trials, extraordinary rendition begins outside the law and stays that way.

The G. W. Bush administration justified extraordinary rendition by claiming that the relevant laws did not apply. John Yoo, deputy assistant attorney general and chief legal architect of the post-9/11 extraordinary rendition program, argued that "transferring terrorists" is not subject to extradition or deportation laws. He claimed that extradition does not apply to terrorists outside the United States because "the power to extradite is triggered only when another country requests the extradition of an individual for purposes of criminal prosecution" (Yoo, 2004: 1188). Yoo also insisted that deportation applies only to those already within the United States or at its borders, not to terrorists abroad (1189). He did not explain why officials could not request the extradition of suspected terrorists *to* the United States for trial, but essentially Yoo did not want to use the viewpoint of criminal law at all. Instead, he characterized al Qaeda and the Taliban as unlawful combatants at war with the United States, and he justified extraordinary renditions under the president's commander in chief powers. Those powers give the president almost unlimited authority to transfer terrorists wherever is most suitable, including to allies in the war on terrorism (Yoo, 2004: 1192ff.). Justice is at best a secondary concern and even then is difficult to achieve because of the methods used on rendered detainees (Mayer, 2008: 98–100).

Yoo's approach remains contentious. Louis Fisher argues that the president does *not* have an independent authority to transfer prisoners, noting that "Attorneys General repeatedly held that extradition and rendition require congressional action by statutes or treaties" (Fisher, 2007–2008: 1408). In addition, "Administrations that did depart from those principles" by rendering suspects outside the law "paid a political price" (1411). Similarly, Ingrid Detter (2013: 377) notes that moving detainees to other countries or external areas like Guantánamo does not excuse violations of international law. In broader terms, extraordinary rendition raises questions about the power limitations of each branch of government. It forces one to ask whether executive officials must obey the law and, if the answer is no, what the implications might be for democracy.

If, at one end of extraordinary rendition, the executive is exempted from the law, then at the other end the prisoners are exempted from it too. The second part of Yoo's justification for extraordinary rendition (in his language, "transferring terrorists"), beyond his expansive notion of executive power, was to deny that the Geneva Conventions and the United Nations' Convention Against Torture (CAT) even apply to those captured in the fight with al Qaeda and the Taliban. According to Yoo, the commander in chief powers give the president "sole executive authority to interpret and apply the Geneva Conventions on behalf of the nation" (1227). Taliban prisoners do not qualify because they do not fight for a nation-state and "refuse to obey the laws of war" (1226). Finally, Yoo asserted that the CAT "has no extraterritorial effect" outside the United States and thus has no bearing on prisoners at Guantánamo Bay or in Afghanistan (1229).

The logic of extraordinary rendition, then, is that no laws constrain the president at war, no laws protect suspected terrorists, and no laws apply in certain special and remote places. In Satterthwaite's critical assessment, Yoo and the Bush administration attempted to create a "legal vacuum" in which suspected terrorists could be transferred "without those transfers being unlawful, *because no law applies*" (1400, emphasis added). This view has not garnered much acceptance outside the circles from which it emerged. In general, the idea that certain people and places can be exempted from the minimum legal protections of international law has not attracted a wide following.

Still, one more legal obstacle makes it difficult to address extraordinary rendition in American courts. Torture victims in the United States have repeatedly encountered assertions of the "state secrets" privilege. As a counterterrorist practice, extraordinary rendition cases cannot proceed without "an intolerable risk of disclosure that would threaten national security" (quoted in Natalie, 2012: 1255). As long as courts defer to executive branch claims of state secrets privilege, victims of rendition will struggle to win legal remedies, and officials will not be significantly restrained.

For several reasons, legal issues and events dominate the extraordinary rendition debate and crowd out moral discussions. First, it seems to be an arcane derivative piece of the torture debate. To judge extraordinary rendition morally requires mastering this separate, daunting debate but without reducing the morality or rendition to the morality of torture. The moral questions lurking behind the legal analysts previously cited have to do with what it means to theorize that certain kinds of people are above or below the law, but those questions have yet to materialize explicitly in connection with extraordinary rendition. Second, secrecy has protected extraordinary rendition from moral scrutiny since the policy planning steps, and it continues to do so. What people don't know about cannot stir moral debate, and even when the practice does garner public attention, it is often terminated by secrecy. Secretary of State Condoleezza Rice's public statement on terrorist transfers (2005) ends with an assertion of secrecy, and *Mohamed et al. v. Jeppesen Dataplan, Inc.* (R. Fisher, 2010) was dismissed on an assertion of state secrets. Secrecy is a formidable barrier but not insurmountable—especially outside the United States. The Canadian government and Italian criminal courts were able to engage in fact finding and judgment in several cases (see the following discussion). Overall, though, it is easy to conclude that the locus of activity around rendition is legal.

It may be tempting to extrapolate the absent moral arguments from the more available legal ones. Advocates of extraordinary rendition are likely to believe that security is the greatest good, that terrorists do not deserve even minimal wartime protections, and that widespread knowledge of the practice only endangers the public. Opponents are likely to believe that everyone deserves certain minimum protections even in war, that security loses its meaning without justice, and that secrecy and remoteness are hallmarks of shameful actions. It would be more constructive, however, to resist this temptation and instead treat the moral debate around extraordinary rendition as seriously underdeveloped—which it is. Legal arguments did not generate the broad legitimacy for the practice, as the Bush administration had hoped. Legal arguments also did not prevent extraordinary rendition or generate accountability after the fact. Moral reflection on issues such as why war crime rendition was made separate from political crime rendition in the first place, who may act entirely outside the law, and when and whether certain individuals can be denied the most minimal protections would provide a valuable complement to the somewhat uncertain legal landscape around extraordinary rendition.

Steven E. Torrente

FURTHER READING

Commission of Inquiry. 2006. *Report of the Events Relating to Meher Arar: Analysis and Recommendations.* Commission of Inquiry into the Actions of Canadian Officials in Relation to Meher Arar. Retrieved from http://publications.gc.ca

Detter, Ingrid. (3rd ed.). 2013. *The Law of War.* Burlington, VT: Ashgate Publishing.

Fisher, Louis. "Extraordinary Rendition: The Price of Secrecy." *American University Law Review, 57:* 1405–1452.

Fisher, Raymond C. 2010. *Mohamed v. Jeppesen Dataplan,* 3d Federal Reporter 13515 (United States Court of Appeals for the Ninth Circuit).

Gross, Michael L. 2010. *Moral Dilemmas of Modern War: Torture Assassination, and Blackmail in an Age of Asymmetric Conflict.* New York: Cambridge University Press.

Hambro, Edvard. 1952. "New Trends in the Law of Extradition and Asylum." *The Western Political Quarterly, 5*(1): 1–19.

Kirchgaessner, Stephanie. "Ex-CIA Officer Faces Extradition to Italy After Final Appeal Rejected." *The Guardian,* June 8. Retrieved from https://www.theguardian.com/world/2016/jun/08/ex-cia-officer-sabrina-de-sousa-extradition-italy—appeal-rejected-rendition

Mayer, Jane. 2008. *The Dark Side: The Inside Story of How the War on Terror Turned into a War on American Ideals.* New York: Anchor Books.

Natalie, Daniel Joseph. 2012. "No Longer Secret: Overcoming the State Secrets Doctrine to Explore Meaningful Remedies for Victims of Extraordinary Rendition." *Case Western Reserve Law Review, 62*(4): 1237–1284.

Povoledo, Elisabetta. 2012. "High Court in Italy Backs Convictions for Rendition." *New York Times,* September 19. Retrieved from http://www.nytimes.com/2012/09/20/world/europe/rendition-convictions-of-23-americans-upheld-in-italy.html

Rice, Condoleeza. 2005. "Remarks upon Her Departure for Europe." U.S. Department of State Archive, December 5. Retrieved from http://www.state.gov/r/pa/ei/rls/dos/3797.htm

Satterthwaite, M. L. 2006–2007. "Rendered Meaningless: Extraordinary Rendition and the Rule of Law." *George Washington Law Review, 75:* 1333–1420.

Slahi, Mohamedou Ould. 2015. *Guantánamo Diary*. Edited by Larry Siems. New York: Little, Brown.

Walzer, Michael. (4th ed.). 2006. *Just and Unjust Wars: A Moral Argument with Historical Illustrations*. New York: Basic Books.

Yoo, John. 2004. "Transferring Terrorists." *Notre Dame Law Review, 79*(4): 1183–1235.

Yoo, John. 2009. *Crisis and Command: A History of Executive Power from George Washington to George W. Bush*. New York: Kaplan Publishing.

Farming—Livestock

Although moral issues have always complicated farming, modern agricultural techniques, designed to take advantage of economies of scale to feed increasing numbers of people at a low price, have increased the tension between the moral imperative of providing good and nourishing food to humans on the one hand and moral concerns over the welfare and treatment of farming animals and livestock, as well as the environmental impact of large-scale agricultural operations. So called factory farms can house tens of thousands of animals in small, confined spaces and use drugs and food supplements on livestock to speed and enhance growth and reduce food production costs. Meanwhile, harvesting facilities for large livestock find similar methods for taking advantage of scale to reduce costs. Animal welfare activists have charged such factory growing and harvesting facilities as being morally bankrupt for their exploitation and treatment of animals. In light of these views, they feel justified in their attempts to disrupt agricultural operations. Finally, agribusiness has been harshly criticized for filling their workforce with the inexpensively paid immigrants and refugees, with critics raising moral concerns about whether this labor population is exploited.

WELFARE OF LIVESTOCK

Moral and health concerns about the welfare of livestock in the United States first gained attention upon publication of Upton Sinclair's 1904 novel *The Jungle*, which chronicled the struggles of working in the Chicago stockyards. To write the novel, Sinclair engaged in a several-week undercover investigation of the stockyards, where he documented the abuse of animals and unsanitary and unsafe practices. Publication of *The Jungle* sparked national and international outrage, leading to the first set of laws regulating the food industry and establishing the foundation for the creation of the Food and Drug Administration.

Another concern over animal welfare in the United States that emerged later in the 20th century was the use of animals in laboratory testing and experiments. Most early animal experiments were conducted for medical research and veterinary science but were later expanded to product testing for industries such as cosmetics (Franco, 2013). Early state-level efforts to regulate the treatment of animals in these contexts had limited impact. By the 1960s, moral indignation over media reports of the use of stolen house pets and other animals in painful and even fatal medical lab experiments resulted in the 1966 Animal Welfare Act, which was implemented by the United States Department of Agriculture (USDA). Later amendments to the Act incrementally included regulations regarding the treatment and transport of animals used for any purpose, not just experimentation. However, even the early portions of the law were relevant to animal experiments conducted for the purposes of raising and harvesting livestock.

Although animal advocates had been publically decrying animal abuse throughout the 20th century, it was the publication of Peter Singer's (1975) *Animal Liberation* that finally inspired a modern animal rights movement. Singer provided a moral argument about the rights of animals, arguing that speciesism, or the notion that "humans are superior to nonhuman animals," is morally indefensible and akin to racism and sexism (Singer, 1975: ix). Singer contended that animals are not inferior to humans and should not be exploited unless a greater good can be justified. For example, Singer preferred veganism but understood that it is not always possible. Likewise, Singer said that some medical research on animals could be justified if the possible benefits to humans could not be achieved in another manner. Singer's morality-based argument was supported by decades of research in evolutionary biology, which clearly established that humans are not as distinct from other animals as commonly believed and that we are very closely related to some species. For example, while mice seem vastly different from people, central elements of genetics and functioning are remarkably similar. Ironically, these similarities are what can make some medical testing on animals valuable for medical progress in human health. Singer's arguments inspired a modern animal rights movement that focused much of its attention on animal research and experimentation (Slocum-Schaffer, 2011). By 2009, there were at least 250 animal rights groups with millions of members in the United States, with the largest, People for the Ethical Treatment of Animals (PETA), at close to 2 million members (Slocum-Schaffer, 2011: 229).

Modern vegetarians and vegans following the reasoning and moral stances laid out by Singer argue that all animals have sentience and as such there is a moral imperative not to consume meat products. They argue further that, as a society, we cannot morally justify the killing of sentient beings for our consumption, especially those that can remember long-term events (Deckers, 2016).

Some of the most radical animal rights groups, like Animal Liberation Front, so strongly defend the rights of animals that they illegally break into facilities, destroy equipment and buildings, and rescue animals from agricultural facilities and research labs. Other direct action groups avoid property destruction but do break laws. For example, Direct Action Everywhere (DxE) is an animal liberation group that is notorious for its large-scale actions that sometimes involve illegal tactics such as civil disobedience and trespassing. DxE sees their actions as essential to forwarding their cause of exposing cruelty and injustices in the animal agriculture system.

Direction action groups typically evoke the morality of a necessity defense, arguing that violating a law in the name of a greater moral good is justifiable. An example of this logic suggests that it would be justified to trespass and/or break into and enter a home that was burning in order to save the life of someone inside. Likewise, animal activists say, civil disobedience to rescue exploited animals is necessary to protect their rights and safety.

In response to some activist attempts to change practices on industrial farms through protest, disruption, and animal release, the national government and some state governments have passed laws to protect agricultural industry practices and processes related to animals and to punish protestors. Some laws have even targeted journalists and other people (such as employees) who report on conditions and practices in Concentrated Animal Feeding Operations (CAFOs, a more official term for so-called factory farms). These include the 1992 Animal Enterprise Protection Act (AEPA), which was the first national law to potentially arrest and fine activists who disrupt an animal enterprise if the disruption causes economic damage exceeding $10,000. The passage of this law has meant that even peaceful protestors at agriculture facilities can be arrested if their actions, such as disrupting traffic or other operations, causes significant economic harm to the facility (Yang, Su, & Carson, 2014). The AEPA was strengthened by the Animal Enterprise Terrorism Act of 2006 and elements of the U.S. Patriot Act, which enhance law enforcement surveillance powers. These changes broadened the range of actions subject to arrest or other legal action to include threats and conspiracy to commit disruptive acts, not just actual actions. Critics assert that these specialized laws elevate the status of animal-related businesses above that of other businesses, suggesting that their economic losses are more important than those in other industries.

States have passed similar measures, especially in areas such as the Midwest, where agriculture plays a significant role in the economy. Additionally, a number of states have attempted to criminalize agricultural investigations (undercover recording on site) by activists and journalists without the owner's permission. In Iowa, a 2012 law made it illegal to gain access to a livestock facility under false pretenses, such as animal welfare investigators who take jobs at facilities so that they can record the treatment of animals inside. Such laws are referred to as ag-gag laws and have been adopted by 11 states; in five states, these laws have been overturned or enjoined by courts as of early 2019, but they remained on the books in six other states (Moon, 2019). For example, Iowa's 2012 law was struck down in a 2019 ACLU free-speech suit. Activists say that the types of whistleblowing investigations these laws ban "have become one of the most useful tools for keeping mismanaged farms in check: Many have resulted in significant improvements in animal welfare, prompting boycotts and bankruptcies of the offending facilities, convictions of employees and owners, statewide ballot initiatives banning practices like gestation crates, and the largest meat recall in United States history" (Moon, 2019).

ENVIRONMENTAL IMPACT

Intensive large-scale farming can have a dramatic environmental impact with implications for human health. For example, the large scale use of pesticides is linked to negative health outcomes in humans and animals, as well as a degradation of the natural environment (Carvalho, 2017; Horrigan et al., 2002). With heightened concern over climate change, many people believe that the moral imperative of reducing our nutritional reliance on animal protein has become more apparent. Greenhouse gas emissions from farming equipment, livestock, and transporting agricultural products is a significant contributor (more than 10 percent) of all greenhouse gas emissions in the United States when transportation elements are included (Inventory . . . , 2019). In addition, the demand for tillable land to grow plants to feed humans and livestock contributes to soil erosion and deforestation. These trends have climate implications because forests are important for storing carbon (carbon sinks) rather than releasing it into the atmosphere (van der Zee, 2017)

The sustainable agriculture movement argues that the benefits of industrial farming have been overstated and that the environmental harms have been underestimated. They argue that changing practices can reduce the negative impact of agriculture on human health and the environment and that as caretakers of the planet we have a duty to change (van der Zee, 2017).

LABOR FORCE ISSUES

Agriculture tends to be a labor-intensive industry, even with the considerable mechanization of farming over the last 100 years. But wages to work in crop fields, attend to livestock, or work the line at animal food processing plants are low and typically do not include health insurance or other benefits. As such, the industry often attracts uneducated, low-skilled, and undocumented workers who have little choice but to endure low pay and poor working conditions. Ironically, Upton Sinclair's book *The Jungle* was meant to bring the attention of readers to the dangerous and underpaid plight of immigrant laborers, but instead the public focused on the food safety and animal welfare insights of the novel.

Conditions have improved for agricultural laborers over past 100 years, but the industry continues to face criticism. And industrial farms are not the only businesses that have received scrutiny. For example, one response to industrial agriculture has been a push to support local food systems, where consumers source agricultural products within usually 200 miles of where they are produced. But these local farms, often small and family owned, are just as likely to exploit workers, especially the undocumented, making them work long hours with little pay or days off (Gray, 2013). As one farm worker named Javier told agrifood scholar Margaret Gray, "[W]e live in the shadows. We are treated like unknown people. . . . We are not paid well and cannot ask for more." Another farm laborer said that employers "treat us like nothing; they only want the work. . . . Whether we like it or not, we have to like it" (Gray, 2016).

Efforts to reduce the exploitation of farm workers have been limited, and critics of attempts to make it more difficult to employ undocumented workers say that such efforts harm both the worker and the farm owners by criminalizing them. Long-term solutions will likely lay in immigration reform and worker visa programs, as well as in increasing the ability of agricultural workers to organize.

CONCLUSION

Farming, especially livestock farming, can raise a number of ethical and moral concerns. Modern industrialized agriculture is in many ways safer than in the past for workers and operators but continues to be plagued by concerns about its impact on animal welfare, the natural environment, and the exploitation of laborers. Ongoing efforts at reform and shifts to local sourcing and sustainable practices could offset some of these concerns. However, some will always see the growing and consumption of livestock as morally problematic, even if greater efforts are made to ensure the welfare of animals.

Donald P. Haider-Markel

FURTHER READING

Carson, Jennifer, Gary LaFree, & Laura Dugan. 2012. "Terrorist and Non-terrorist Criminal Attacks by Radical Environmental and Animal Rights Groups in the United States, 1970–2007." *Terrorism and Political Violence*, *24*: 295–319.

Carvalho, Fernando P. 2017. "Pesticides, Environment, and Food Safety." *Food and Energy Security*, *6*(2): 48–60.

Chermak, S. M., J. Freilich, C. Duran, & W. Parkin. 2013. *An Overview of Bombing and Arson Attacks by Environmental and Animal Rights Extremists in the United States, 1995–2010.* Final Report to the Resilient Systems Division, Science and Technology Directorate, U.S. Department of Homeland Security. College Park, MD: Start.

Deckers, Jan. 2016. *Animal (Se)liberation.* London: Ubiquity Press.

Fischer, Joern, Tibor Hartel, & Tobias Kuemmerle. 2012. "Conservation Policy in Traditional Farming Landscapes." *Conservation Letters*, *5*(3): 167–175.

Franco, Nuno. 2013. "Animal Experiments in Biomedical Research: A Historical Perspective." *Animals*, *3*(1): 238–273.

Gonzalez, Carmen G. 2010. "Climate Change, Food Security, and Agrobiodiversity: Toward a Just, Resilient, and Sustainable Food System." *Fordham Environmental Law Review*, *22*: 493.

Gray, Margaret. 2016. "The Dark Side of Local." *Jacobin*, August 21, Retrieved from https://www.jacobinmag.com/2016/08/farmworkers-local-locavore-agriculture-exploitation

Gray, Margaret. 2013. *Labor and the Locavore: The Making of a Comprehensive Food Ethic.* Berkeley: University of California Press.

Harrison, Ruth. 1972. "On Factory Farming." In Stanley Godlovitch, Roslind Godlovitch, & John Harris (Eds.), *Animals, Men, and Morals: An Enquiry into the Maltreatment of Nonhumans*, 31–51. New York: Toplinger.

Horrigan, Leo, Robert S. Lawrence, & Polly Walker. 2002. "How Sustainable Agriculture Can Address the Environmental and Human Health Harms of Industrial Agriculture." *Environmental Health Perspectives*, *110*(5): 445–456.

Inventory of U.S. Greenhouse Gas Emissions and Sinks. 2019. Environmental Protection Agency. Retrieved from https://www.epa.gov/ghgemissions/inventory-us-greenhouse-gas-emissions-and-sinks

Moon, Emily. 2019. "A New Iowa Law Would Criminalize Undercover Investigations at Farms (Again)." *Pacific Standard*, March 13. Retrieved from https://psmag.com /news/a-new-iowa-law-would-criminalize-undercover-investigations-at-farms -again

Singer, Peter. 1975. *Animal Liberation*. New York: Random House

Slocum-Schaffer, Stephanie A. (4th ed.). 2011. "Animal Rights: Subordinate or Equal Species?" In Raymond Tatalovich & Bryon W. Daynes (Eds.), *Moral Controversies in American Politics*, 269–303. New York: M. E. Sharpe.

van der Zee, Bibi. 2017. "Why Factory Farming Is Not Just Cruel—But Also a Threat to All Life on the Planet." *The Guardian*, October 4. Retrieved from https://www .theguardian.com/environment/2017/oct/04/factory-farming-destructive-wasteful -cruel-says-philip-lymbery-farmageddon-author

Vice Videos. 2018. "Animal Rights Extremists: Terrorism vs. Protesters." Retrieved from https://video.vice.com/en_ca/video/animal-rights-extremists-terrorism-vs -protests-dxe/5b107772f1cdb33f9a35cea6

Yang, Sue-Ming, Yi-Yuan Su, & Jennifer Varriale Carson. 2014. *Eco-terrorism and the Corresponding Legislative Efforts to Intervene and Prevent Future Attacks*. Waterloo, ON: Canadian Network for Research on Terrorism, Security, and Society.

Gambling

Society has long seen gambling as a morality policy issue that "generates conflict over first principles or core values, lacks amenability to compromise, and has little technical complexity" (Ferraiolo, 2013). However, this debate has taken on increased urgency, since gambling is on the rise in the United States. The Center for Gaming Research estimates that revenue for the industry totaled over $158.54 billion in 2017 alone. The sector has exploded since the 1960s, when only Nevada allowed legal gambling. By 2018, 42 states have lottery systems, and 48 states permit live gambling. That same year, the Supreme Court removed long-standing legal barriers to online sports betting. Despite its growing popularity, though, gambling remains a controversial issue embedded with moral arguments.

Morality policy cannot be understood simply as a single policy category. Scholar Gary Mucciaroni suggests that morality policy is less about the content of the policy issue at hand and more about how political actors frame the issue. He distinguishes morality frames "according to the kind of behavior that is the focus of moral judgment" (Mucciaroni, 2011: 194), identifying private behavior morality frames, governmental morality frames, and social behavior morality frames as most relevant. This approach proves helpful when considering the moral arguments most commonly associated with gambling in the United States.

PRIVATE BEHAVIOR MORALITY FRAME

Both proponents and critics of gambling utilize private behavior morality frames to make their arguments. Often when considering morality policy, these are the frames one tends to think of, with individual behavior being deemed sinful or immoral.

Within the context of gambling, private behavior morality frames are frequently used by those in opposition. Often, these arguments are rooted in conservative religious principles. Some argue "that lotteries redirect the loyalties of individuals, encouraging them to place their faith in chance or luck as the key determinant of their futures, rather than in the sovereignty of God over human affairs" (Ellison & Nybroten, 1999: 358). Others suggest that gambling promotes a poor work ethic and confuses the natural (and Biblical) relationship between work and reward (Cosgrave & Klassen, 2001). Another camp worries that such behavior fosters greed, idolatry, materialism, and selfishness, while distorting an individual's relationship with money.

> A concern of religious conservatives is that the lottery violates key biblical principles of stewardship and scriptural guidelines regarding the appropriate use of money and property (Christian Life Commission, 1995a, 1995b). Citing numerous scriptural passages, conservative Protestants argue that money and goods are provided by God, for well-defined purposes such as meeting personal or family needs (e.g., 1 Timothy 5:8), aiding others and supporting charities (2 Corinthians 9:6–15), paying taxes (Matthew 22:21; Romans 13:7), or supporting religion (e.g., 1 Corinthians 16:1–3). While wise investments of money are viewed favorably (Matthew. 25:14–30), religious conservatives argue that the Bible does not sanction risky investments with very low probabilities of return. (Ellison & Nybroten, 1999: 359)

Put simply, this perspective argues that gambling is sinful because it alters God's intention for man's relationship with faith and money.

Private behavior morality frames are also used within progambling arguments, although far less frequently. A common argument that maintains its religious undertones suggests that gambling is sinful only *some* of the time. The Catholic Church, for example, "teaches that gambling is morally harmless so long as it is practiced with moderation and remains consistent with the satisfaction of one's obligations" (Murphy, 1998: 123). In other words, the private behavior of individuals can remain moral as long as harm is minimized and consequences short felt.

A second individual-centric argument that takes issue with the idea that all gambling is a form of vice focuses on the values of individualism, freedom, and the American ethic of risk taking. As Aaron Duncan (2016) discusses in his book, gambling reemphasizes the role of luck in the American Dream. Adherents to this argument utilize a sort of public, American morality as opposed to a religious one, something Duncan (2016: 41) attributes to the "declining moral authority of organized religion." This private behavior morality frame appears to be gaining traction as the religious frame becomes less relevant.

GOVERNMENTAL MORALITY FRAMES

Advocates for and against the legalization of gambling often utilize governmental morality frames as well. In these frameworks, governmental entities—whether officials or agencies—are presented as moral or immoral in their stances toward gambling. In this way, advocates who use governmental morality frames do not focus on private, individual behavior; rather, "the focus of moral judgment is governmental behavior" (Mucciaroni, 2011: 194).

Opponents of gambling often assert that the government is sanctioning sin when it treats gambling in any form as a lawful activity. In Kathleen Ferraiolo's 2013 study of legislative records, she found members of Congress actively avoided the individual behavior–based arguments. Specifically, she found that "most opponents who raised concerns claimed that state-sanctioned gambling would send the wrong message to children concerning values, communicate to citizens that hard work and savings were less important than luck and chance, and transform the state into a 'bookie' or a 'huckster' that facilitated or encouraged poor choices" (Ferraiolo, 2013: 225). The government-oriented argument is not limited to public officials. Reverend Nancy Kemper made a similarly framed argument in her criticism of government involvement in the sanctioning of gambling. "Gambling leads to the sort of undoing of our common democracy, where we all pay in an equal and equitable way for what we need as a society," she shares. "And this instead says, 'Let's fleece the suckers and get them to pay for what we aren't willing to pay for ourselves'" (Miller, 2012).

The governmental morality frame is also used by progambling advocates, albeit far less commonly. In Jonathan Miller's *Moral Case for Gambling* (2012), he argues that the ends often justify the means. "[B]y generating desperately needed funds for basic human needs," he shares, "tax-revenue-generating gambling serves an extraordinarily valuable—and yes—a moral purpose for society." Miller does not consider the morality of gambling when the revenue is *not* dedicated to such ethical causes, but he certainly makes a case for the moral potential of expanded gambling opportunities.

SOCIAL BEHAVIOR MORALITY FRAME

By far the least common of the gambling morality frames is the social behavior morality frame. These frames "define issues in terms of individual or group behavior that violates important moral principles or cherished values by the way they treat other individuals or groups" (Mucciaroni, 2011: 194). In other words, this frame involves the immoral behavior of one group causing harm to another.

Gambling is perceived to cause harm in a variety of ways. From personal finance to individual health, antigambling advocates often frame this behavior as having long-term negative effects on participating individuals and their families. Moreover, proponents of the social behavior morality argument often place blame on the private sector for causing the harm. Scholar Mariano Chóliz (2018) blames companies for the rise of gambling addiction and charges them with the responsibility to "create the necessary environmental conditions that permit gambling as an economic activity, but with the primary objective of preventing potential health risks, primarily gambling disorder" (6). He, along with others, rebuke the ethics of casino companies armed with business plans that revolve around fostering addiction. As Jonathan Miller (2012) explains, "[G]ambling levies a disproportionate tax on those who too easily fall victim to the false dreams of effortless riches, as well as on those who are addiction-prone to risky, self-destructive behavior." In short, these critics contend that the gambling *industry* violates moral principles by actively harming their customers and damaging their wider families.

CONTEXT MATTERS

The moral arguments most commonly utilized depend, in part, on the context within which the gambling being discussed operates. Patrick Pierce and Donald Miller (2004) delineate between the moral frames associated with lotteries and those used with casinos. They note that casino politics invite a greater number of participants and therefore a greater variety of moral arguments championed by diverse interest groups. The arguments often involve ethical concerns surrounding the direction of revenue, with anticasino proponents worrying about the redistribution of profits back to the casino corporation itself. The perceived cost of gambling no longer succumbs to the benefit when private corporations are the recipient of profit. That argument is mostly eliminated when considering lotteries. Pro-lottery advocates argue that the societal cost of gambling is outweighed by the societal benefit, as lottery profits are often poured back into public projects, such as education or parks and recreation.

The destination for revenue additionally impacts the moral frame used. Whether considering lottery or casino legislation, policy proponents are able to invoke morality depending on where the money is going. "Issue entrepreneurs supporting an education lottery could claim that the 'education of our children'—rather than the 'sinfulness of gambling' should frame the issue" (Pierce and Miller, 2000: 702). The ethical argument centers on benefiting children, whereas general lotteries attract only one moral argument: the sin of gambling. Similar arguments have been advanced to support casino proposals that would spark urban revival in Atlantic City (Pierce & Miller, 2004: 47). The conversation around the benefit of a casino shifted from a corporate profit focus to one looking at economic growth. Policy entrepreneurs are given the freedom to adjust the moral argument in their favor when gambling revenue goes to what the public perceives as a moral cause.

MOVING AWAY FROM A MORAL FRAME?

Another narrative around gambling ignores morality altogether. Proponents—and to a lesser extent opponents—focus on economics as their chief argument frame rather than morality. Some scholars attribute the decline of the moral argument to the rise of state-sanctioned gaming:

> The historical opposition to gambling activities in western societies, based on forms of moral critique (whether religious or economic), is actually exploited by the state through its assumption of control over the regulation of, and generation of revenues from, such activities. The moral discourse on gambling under these conditions then is more properly understood within the framework of an economistic construction of the phenomenon. This can be seen in the state's interest in problem gambling—which is treated as a cost of doing business—and through social and economic impact studies designed to evaluate the possibilities of further implementation of gambling activities. Morality is subsumed by an economic worldview, which has been freed from earlier religiously grounded economic ethics. (Cosgrave & Klassen, 2001: 11)

They argue that pragmatism overrules morality in today's society and that the stigma of being a gambler has steadily decreased.

A second reason for the decline of the moral argument surrounding gambling is the decline of its greatest adversary: the church. As states have increased their support of gambling, the moral opposition is failing to convert new people to their side. As Reverend Tom Grey, spokesman for the National Coalition Against Legalized

Gambling, opined, "The church's opposition to gambling has not been widely effective because (the church is) not relevant in an irreverent age" (Trotter, 2008: 113).

CONCLUSION

Gambling continues to grow in popularity in the United States. Advocates for and against its growing prevalence use a variety of moral frames to make effective arguments. Through the use of private behavior, governmental, and social behavior morality frames, debaters attempt to sway Americans to agree with their point of view. Although these moral frames certainly are not going away, the conversation around gambling may be shifting from one surrounding morality to one focusing on local economic benefits and on increased funding for education and other popular government programs.

Abigail Vegter

FURTHER READING

Chóliz, Mariano. 2018. "Ethical Gambling: A Necessary New Point of View of Gambling in Public Health Policies." *Frontiers in Public Health*, 6. Retrieved from https://www.ncbi.nlm.nih.gov/pmc/articles/PMC5797763

Cosgrave, Jim, & Thomas R. Klassen. 2001. "Gambling Against the State: The State and the Legitimation of Gambling." *Current Sociology*, *49*(5): 1–15.

Duncan, Aaron. 2016. *Gambling with the Myth of the American Dream*. London: Routledge.

Ellison, C. G., & K. A. Nybroten. 1999. "Conservative Protestantism and Opposition to State-sponsored Lotteries: Evidence from the 1997 Texas Poll." *Social Science Quarterly*, *80*: 356–369.

Ferraiolo, Kathleen. 2013. "Is State Gambling Policy 'Morality Policy'? Framing Debates over State Lotteries." *Policy Studies Journal*, *41*(2): 217–242.

Miller, Jonathan. 2012. "The Moral Case for Gambling." *Huffington Post*. Retrieved from https://www.huffingtonpost.com/jonathanmiller/the-moral-case-for-gambli_b_1234160.html

Mucciaroni, Gary. 2011. "Are Debates About 'Morality Policy' Really About Morality? Framing Opposition to Gay and Lesbian Rights." *Policy Studies Journal*, *29*(2): 187–216.

Murphy, Jeffrie G. 1998. "Indian Casinos and the Morality of Gambling." *Public Affairs Quarterly*, *12*(1): 119–136.

Pierce, Patrick A., & Donald E. Miller. 2000. "Variations in the Diffusion of State Lottery Adoptions: How Revenue Dedication Changes Morality Politics: Version 1." Retrieved from http://www.icpsr.umich.edu/ICPSR/studies/01226/version/1

Pierce, Patrick A., & Donald E. Miller. 2004. *Gambling Politics: State Government and the Business of Betting*. Boulder, CO: Lynne Rienner.

Trotter, Greg. 2008. "Gambling Opponents Say Moral Argument No Longer a Trump." *Christianity Today*, 112–122.

Genetic Engineering

In the past half century, the field of genetic engineering has grown dramatically. At each step, advances in the field have faced concern, criticism, and vigorous debate. Genetic engineering is a multifaceted scientific endeavor that seeks to enhance the genes of people, animals, and plants. The process of defining genetic engineering is a politically difficult one. Most agree that the process of adding or removing genes from organisms in a laboratory setting is genetic engineering. This includes processes like adding bioluminescent genes from algae into fish to make them glow in the dark or adding genes to plants that allow those plants to produce nutrients they otherwise would not provide. Genetic engineering can also include age-old processes such as the selective breeding of plants and animals to enhance certain traits. For example, the world features a great diversity of dog breeds ranging from the Great Dane to the Chihuahua. This great diversity is the result of hundreds, if not thousands of years of selectively breeding these dogs on traits such as size and endurance. However, most debates surrounding genetic engineering focus on research taking place in scientific laboratories around the world. In addition, in most cases, genetic engineering raises profound ethical and moral concerns.

A DEBATE ON THREE FRONTS

There exist three main areas of debate surrounding the application of genetic engineering. Each of these debates centers on a different aspect of genetic engineering—genetic engineering as it pertains to humans, genetic engineering as it pertains to nonhuman animals, and genetic engineering as it relates to plants. Each of these debates features unique moral and ethical quandaries. The arguments for and against genetic engineering, however, are similar regardless of context. Supporters tend to make utilitarian arguments in favor of these advances. Utilitarian morality argues that anything can be moral and ethical if it does the greatest amount of good for the most number of people.

The promise of genetic engineering is endless. Through the process of modifying the genetic information found in humans, animals, and plants, genetic engineers believe they can solve some of the most vexing problems facing humanity and our planet. Devastating genetic diseases, which have plagued humanity, could be eradicated. Domesticated plants and animals could be hardier, allowing agriculture to flourish in unforgiving locations. Modification of those same plants and animals could provide vital nutrients they otherwise would not produce, thus solving the issue of malnutrition in the developing world. We might engineer bacteria to fight off insidious human diseases such as cancer, Alzheimer's disease, and Parkinson's disease. These promising applications of genetic engineering are at the heart of the arguments—moral, ethical, or otherwise—for the continued use and expansion of genetic engineering.

For all of genetic engineering's promise, the technology raises serious moral and ethical concerns. Central to the moral and ethical opposition to the use of genetic engineering is a fundamental concern regarding the degree to which genetic engineering upends natural processes—especially if one views these processes as dictated by a higher power. Even from a secular perspective, we can be concerned over science run amok with no consideration for the potential adverse effects of genetically modified organisms. Critics contend that these effects can be environmentally catastrophic. For instance, rapid declines in monarch butterfly populations has been linked to the introduction of genetically engineered crops that have wiped out much of the milkweed the butterflies require.

Beyond fears of environmental degradation, opponents of genetic engineering claim that people who consume genetically engineered food are at greater risk of cancer and other maladies. The movement to label and ban genetically modified organisms (GMOs) in foods for human consumption is widespread, even though the scientific consensus suggests that GMOs pose little risk and offer great benefits for humans.

From a secular perspective, we can view genetic engineering as an attempt to override millions of years of natural evolution with little to no regard for the environmental and societal consequences of such an abrupt shift in how nature operates. Some go so far as to argue for the rights of animals, suggesting that modifying animal genetic material without consent violates the rights of an animal to be free of human exploitation.

Genetic engineering is an affront to the act of divine creation for a variety of religious traditions. If God created plants and animals the way they are, then human-induced modification is an attempt to "play God."

Where there is overlap between secular and religious opposition to genetic engineering, the arguments tend to be framed in terms of how genetic engineering violates core principles of natural law. However, the moral and ethical opposition to genetic engineering can differ based on the context of genetic engineering. Environmentalists may have moral and ethical objections to genetically engineered plants and animals that could disrupt natural processes in ways that we cannot predict. This risk also may not result in the expected benefit of genetic engineering helping to eradicate human disease.

The moral and ethical concerns are also embedded in existing law, limiting the ability of scientists to, for example, engage in processes to alter the human genome. In particular, the debate over human genetic engineering in the United States has led to many legal limitations to this kind of work. As of now, there are two primary ways to go about human genetic engineering—embryonic genetic engineering and gene therapy. The ethical and moral debates over these processes differ significantly. The first is embryonic human engineering. This process involves modifying the genetic code within a human embryo by either adding or subtracting particular genes using a technology called CRISPR. CRISPR allows scientists to "cut" parts of a gene at the molecular level to remove or add elements. The expectation is that the embryo could then be implanted into a uterus and eventually lead to a live birth. Embryonic genetic engineering is a common practice to modify the genetics of nonhuman animals, but, in the context of human genetic engineering, it is fraught with greater moral and ethical concerns. Gene therapy, on the other hand, has received less criticism on moral and ethical grounds. Unlike embryonic human genetic engineering, gene therapy targets people who suffer from debilitating and life-threatening genetic diseases. These types of experimental treatments work by replacing defective genes either with new genes or by "turning off" genes that cause the disease in question.

Gene Therapy

Although gene therapy is generally not as controversial as human embryonic genetic engineering, some forms of gene therapy arouse greater ethical concerns. If the gene therapy operates through the manipulation of genes in somatic cells (that is, any cell in the body that is not responsible for passing on genetic information to offspring), then many of the moral and ethical concerns dissipate. Germline gene therapy (changing genes in the reproductive cells), on the other hand, elicits many of the same concerns raised about embryonic genetic engineering. Since germline gene therapy targets reproductive cells, any modifications made to these cells are passed on to future generations. In other words, the change becomes permeant. Advocates for such treatments point to the potential for eradicating genetic diseases as being a moral and ethical imperative. For instance, we could eradicate Huntington's disease, a fatal genetic disease passed on to 50 percent of the children born to people carrying the genetic mutation that causes it, via germline gene therapy.

Detractors of such therapies do not deny the potential for disease eradication, but they point to two major moral and ethical concerns surrounding germline gene therapy. First is the issue of consent. Children born as a product of germline gene therapy cannot possibly give consent to having their genetic material altered. Some see this lack of consent as a fundamental violation of human rights, but others point to the fact that no person gives consent to their genetic makeup. Second are significant concerns over potentially harmful effects of such treatments. Given the complex nature of the human genome, there are no assurances that modifications to remove the influence of mutated genes would not themselves cause unforeseen health issues for the person receiving those changes or their offspring. People advocating for such therapies say that parents can grant consent, as they often do for their children, and that fears of the impacts are overblown.

Genetic Engineering in the Womb

The genetic engineering of human embryos also carries much of the same moral and ethical baggage as germline gene therapy. In addition to concerns about the right of consent and unintended consequences of genetic alterations, the prospect of engineering human embryos leads some to worry about the production of so-called designer babies. Given the option of providing their children with genetic advantages regarding health, intelligence, or beauty, parents may choose to provide these benefits to their children. Some fear that this process is little more than eugenics and that, if the practice became widespread enough, nongenetically designed people may become seen as inferior and discriminated against as a result. Furthermore, as traits related to beauty differ throughout time, there is also a risk that parents would select faddish traits for their children. Again, supporters of such genetic engineering see these fears as overstated and typically make utilitarian arguments for such technologies. Therefore, arguments for such technology argue that the benefits of having a healthier, more intelligent population outweigh the risks associated with manipulating the genetic code of embryos.

Given the profound moral and ethical concerns surrounding both germline gene therapy and embryonic genetic engineering, many governments around the world, including the United States, either placed significant restrictions on these technologies or officially prohibited related research. Even countries such as China that have less stringent regulations on such practices have, with one apparently unauthorized example in 2018 (Belluz, 2018), engaged in this kind of research only with nonviable embryos that would not result in a live birth. For all the moral and ethical concerns surrounding human genetic engineering, these concerns do not necessarily translate into the debate over the genetic engineering of animals and plants. Moral and ethical concerns about plant and animal genetic engineering tend to focus on environmental and health-based issues.

Genetically Modified Animals

When most people think about the genetic engineering of animals, their thoughts likely lead them to think about modifications made to livestock. For example, advances in animal genetic engineering have produced animals that produce more meat for human consumption. Some research points to the possibility of modifying dairy cows to produce hypoallergenic milk. Countries around the world, including the United States, have many laws in place restricting human consumption of genetically modified livestock (a genetically modified organism [GMO]). In Europe, there is a full ban on human consumption of genetically engineered livestock, and genetically modified livestock made for human consumption in the United States must receive approval from the Federal Food and Drug Administration. To date, the FDA has approved only the sale of salmon that have been genetically modified to grow larger more quickly than nonmodified salmon.

Although most of the focus on genetically engineered animals is on their use for human consumption, much of the commercial and scientific activity surrounding genetically engineered animals does not concern itself with the production of food. Instead, most genetic alteration of animals is for the sole purpose of scientific research or other practical reasons. In 2016, for instance, a major political debate took place in the Florida Keys regarding the release of genetically modified mosquitos designed to fight off diseases such as the Zika virus and dengue fever. Specifically, these mosquito-borne diseases spread through only one species of mosquito, *Aedes aegypti*. A company genetically modified male mosquitos (only female mosquitos bite people) so that the offspring of these male mosquitos will die. Controlled experiments in South America showed the introduction of these modified male mosquitos led to as much as a 90 percent decrease in *Aedes aegypti* populations with no effect on other mosquito species in the area. The company that designed these mosquitos secured the right to perform a controlled release of the mosquitos on a populated island in the Florida Keys. The elected local board in charge of approving such a test decided to put the proposal up as a referendum in the 2016 general election. The debate over the release of these mosquitos highlighted the ethical and moral dimensions of the genetic engineering debate.

Those in favor of releasing the mosquitos pointed to the societal benefit of reduced *Aedes aegypti* populations. Much like the moral defense of human genetic engineering, defenders of the mosquito release primarily make utilitarian arguments pointing to reduced costs associated with mosquito removal as well as lowered risk levels of mosquito-borne disease outbreaks. For instance, there was a major dengue fever outbreak in Key West between 2009 and 2011. As the Florida Keys rely on tourism as a major economic force, there is a reasonable fear that similar disease outbreaks might lead to an overall decrease in economic activity in the Keys.

Opposition was strong and revolved around the idea that scientists could not fully predict the impact of the release. Although the company running the release attempts to modify only male mosquitos, the system is not perfect, and a small number of modified female mosquitos may be included. As only female mosquitos bite, there was a worry about some of the modified DNA passing on to humans and that these bites from modified mosquitos could pose a potential risk to human health. The local measure failed in Key Haven but passed in the County. Local officials called off the test, but the company behind the original trial proposal has continued to pursue a potential release somewhere in the Florida Keys.

This potential risk to people's health is a central concern for those opposed to genetically modified plants as well. Regarding human consumption, genetically modified plants have faced less scrutiny from governments around the world. Some countries do ban the cultivation and consumption of genetically modified crops, but far more do not have any such restrictions. Scientists genetically modify crops, such as corn, soybeans, and rice, for many reasons. Some scientists attempt to add vital nutrients to plants in order to fight off malnutrition. Other crops are genetically designed to survive harsh environmental conditions or to withstand certain kinds of herbicides. Although opponents have health concerns regarding the consumption of these modified crops, there are also fears these crops will disrupt their ecological environments. Some have pointed to the use of herbicide-resistant crops as a contributing factor in the overall decline of monarch butterfly populations. Proponents of genetically modified crops, though, argue that the societal benefits of these crops far outweigh any potential costs.

The moral and ethical debate about genetic engineering is not likely to end anytime soon. The contours of this debate remain similar regardless of the particular context. Supporters of genetic engineering emphasize the potential for these technologies to save lives and lower food costs as being a moral and ethical imperative. Detractors point to the fact that we know little about the long-term consequences of genetic engineering. There are concerns about the welfare of humans and animals that undergo genetic therapies or that are the product of genetic engineering, and there are concerns about potential adverse effects of consuming genetically engineered foods. There does not seem to be much in the way of stopping the advance of research into genetic engineering, and new debates over this technology will emerge as quickly as the technology itself.

Johnathan C. Peterson

FURTHER READING

Belluz, Julia. 2018. "Is the CRISPR Baby Controversy the Start of a Terrifying New Chapter in Gene Editing?" *Vox*, December 3. Retrieved from https://www.vox.com/science-and-health/2018/11/30/18119589/crispr-technology-he-jiankui

Church, George M., & Ed Regis. 2014. *Regenesis: How Synthetic Biology Will Reinvent Nature and Ourselves*. New York: Basic Books.

Green, Ronald Michael, & David Wood. 2007. *Babies by Design: The Ethics of Genetic Choice*. New Haven, CT: Yale University Press.

Knoepfler, Paul. 2015. *GMO Sapiens: The Life-changing Science of Designer Babies*. Singapore: World Scientific.

Lipkin, Steven Monroe, & Jon Luoma. 2016. *The Age of Genomes: Tales from the Front Lines of Genetic Medicine*. Boston: Beacon Press.

Merino, Noël. 2013. *Genetic Engineering: Opposing Viewpoints*. Farmington Hills, MI: Greenhaven Press.

Mitchell, C. Ben. 2007. *Biotechnology and the Human Good*. Washington, DC: Georgetown University Press.

Parrington, John. 2016. *Redesigning Life: How Genome Editing Will Transform the World*. New York: Oxford University Press.

Sandel, Michael J. 2009. *The Case Against Perfection: Ethics in the Age of Genetic Engineering*. Cambridge, MA: Harvard University Press.

Scott, Sydney E., Yoel Inbar, Christopher D. Wirz, Dominique Brossard, & Paul Rozin. 2018. "An Overview of Attitudes Toward Genetically Engineered Food." *Annual Review of Nutrition, 38*: 459–479.

Homelessness

Every society struggles with inequality and with the tendency to praise those who have gained wealth and success and look down on those who have not. Perhaps the most dramatic example of the tension between the aspiration to affluence and the compassion for the less fortunate is the issue of homelessness. There could be over 660,000 homeless people in the United States (Belmonte, 2019), but the true number of homeless is difficult to measure because many persons without a permanent residence are able to temporarily find shelter with friends and family and do not live on the streets or in shelters full-time.

America's homeless population is sometimes regarded with scorn by more financially secure citizens who see their financial plight as indicative of personal weakness or failings. Other citizens see the homeless with greater sympathy and find it morally troubling that such a large population of people lack the basic security of shelter in a nation as rich as the United States.

At the individual level, homelessness is often viewed from an attributional perspective. Some people look at a homeless person and see a person who has made bad life choices or other mistakes. Others see a person who has faced unfortunate circumstances brought on by a broader series of systemic forces, such as economic, educational opportunities, or other life conditions that are beyond the individual's control. Both kinds of attributions can be made from moral grounds. Those who blame the individual for being homeless see their condition as a moral failing of, for example, being too lazy to work. Indeed, beginning in the early 19th century, some social observers begin to view the homeless as purposely idle and therefore sinful and threatening to the moral values of the nation. Those who see homelessness from a systemic perspective regard society as morally corrupt for not protecting vulnerable people from larger economic forces. This perspective sees the homeless as deserving of help. Many interpretations are possible, each of which lead to specific but very different types of solutions, only some of which involve government action.

Beyond the individual homeless person, we can describe a broader condition of homelessness afflicting society. Our attributions for individual homelessness shape how we view the wider population even if we understand that the reasons for specific individuals being homeless vary from case to case. In addition, the extent to which people view homelessness as a problem that should be addressed might be influenced by whether they observe homelessness in their particular community, in news coverage, or in terms of whether the number of homeless people is growing or shrinking.

GOVERNMENTAL RESPONSES TO HOMELESSNESS

Prior to the 1970s, the number of homeless people in the United States tended follow economic trends, increasing in periods of recession and high unemployment and diminishing in times of growth and prosperity. Many local governments provided some basic assistance for the homeless, such as allowing people to sleep in jails overnight and providing meals. Since the recession of the early 1980s and the partial deconstruction of the social safety net around those with mental health issues, homeless populations, including semipermanent encampments, have become more common around the country, especially in and around large cities. At the same time, many urban areas began to see a daily increase in the number of visible homeless people on the street, engaged in panhandling and other activities to generate funds.

Many nonprofit groups, including religious nonprofits, provide programs and services to assist the homeless because they believe society has a moral obligation to serve this portion of the community. Indeed, most religious traditions have teachings that point to a moral imperative for societies to serve the less fortunate. In Christianity and Islam, for example, helping the poor and providing shelter for those in need is framed as part of a moral code of what it means to be a good Christian or Muslim. However, in many communities facilities to help the poor and homeless are interdenominational. These groups offer food services as well as sleeping and bathroom accommodations. Some of these nonprofits operate with the assistance of local, state, and/or federal grants while others depend entirely on donations and volunteers.

For some advocates, the moral imperative to assist the homeless includes finding ways to get the homeless into permanent housing. These advocates view housing as a basic human right, a right that needs to be fulfilled before other issues can be adequately addressed. Indeed, when home foreclosures soared and homeless encampments became common during the Great Depression, the problem of homelessness began to be viewed by much greater numbers of Americans as rooted in broader economic forces, not in the moral failing of individuals. Support for government intervention to help the homeless subsequently increased, based on a moral belief that helping the homeless was necessary to offset the excesses of capitalism. New Deal programs subsequently funded lodging and training for the homeless, and new programs made mortgage loans more accessible to people.

In the 1960s, some additional efforts at providing low-income housing were made as part of President Lyndon Johnson's Great Society programs, an ambitious slate of projects, policies, and initiatives to end poverty in America. In the 1980s and 1990s, many of these support programs were eliminated or severely restricted to rein in government spending, putting more people at greater risk for homelessness. Many of those who opposed restricting or eliminating these programs suggested that the Ronald Reagan administration was morally bankrupt for gutting the programs.

Homeless populations today tend to disproportionately represent minority groups and are more likely to include women and children than in the past. Homeless families pose particular problems for shelters and social service organizations, even though they are more likely to be viewed as "deserving of help." Of course, some people leave their homes because they face abuse from family members or have been forced out by family. This population is especially vulnerable and includes victims of spousal abuse, physically and sexually abused youth, and LGBT youth. Out on the streets, these demographic groups are especially at risk for exploitation, and the need for food and money drives some into illicit activity.

Local and state attempts to address homelessness are sometimes motivated by moral imperative, but often local governments are simply trying to manage the population to minimize disruptions, most often with police officers rather than with social workers or mental health professionals. Some local officials have sought to criminalize the homeless by adopting laws that ban panhandling, sleeping in public spaces, personal use of shopping carts, accumulation of excessive baggage in public spaces, any form of temporary structure, and even making it illegal to give free food directly to people. Other local governments have allowed for segregated homeless communities, approving designated spaces where the homeless are allowed to erect temporary shelters, use cooking fires, and gain access to food and water. Although this tactic appears less punitive and stigmatizing of the homeless, it is also a means to regulate the homeless and displace them to locations far away from commercial and residential areas. Such policies have been described as tools of containment designed to create what one scholar described as "homeless seclusion" (Herring, 2014).

But even as some localities have allowed for homeless encampments, others have a policy of periodically destroying the camps and removing all the material and persons from the sites. This tension illustrates an additional moral dimension to the homeless debate: Do we have a moral obligation to allow citizens to use public space as they see fit, as long as they are not harming others or property? Some people argue we are obligated to allow the homeless to practice their rights in public space. "Now one question we face as a society—a broad question of justice and social policy—is whether we are willing to tolerate an economic system in which large numbers of people are homeless," wrote scholar Jeremy Waldron. "Since the answer is evidently 'Yes,' the question that remains is whether we are willing to allow those who are in this predicament to act as free agents, looking after their own needs, in public spaces—the only space available to them" (Waldron, 2006: 436).

FORCING ASSISTANCE

A final moral consideration sometimes raised in relation to homelessness is whether it is morally correct to force help on a homeless person. A significant portion of the homeless population is homeless in part because of ongoing mental health issues, issues with addiction, or because they are trying to escape abusers. Even when given an opportunity to seek assistance and shelter, some of these people refuse assistance. At least some argue that we have a moral obligation to force these people into assistance programs for their own well-being, while others argue that it is morally wrong to force people to do things they do not want to do. One moral solution for health professionals, in cases of imminent self-harm, is forced temporary intervention that does not move the person far from the location with which they are familiar (van Leeuwen & Merry, 2018).

CONCLUSION

Homelessness continues to be framed as a moral issue, with some blaming the homeless for their situation, seeing them as moral failures. Others point to the immorality of a society that allows people to live without basic needs being met and suggest that we have an obligation to help shelter the homeless. Assistance for the homeless is provided by nonprofit organizations and governments, but the homeless population remains high.

As Americans debate which problems deserve attention and resources, the debate over a moral obligation to the homeless is a key component of this discussion and is often intertwined with conceptions of individual freedom, mental health, and perceptions of threat. Given the complex array of reasons that people become and remain homeless, moral concerns are likely to continue to shape policies designed to address the issue.

Donald P. Haider-Markel

FURTHER READING

Bailey, Ronald. 1973. *The Squatters*. New York: Penguin.

Bauman, Tristia, Jeremy Rosen, Eric Tars, Maria Foscarinis, Janelle Fernandez, Christian Robin, Eugene Sowa, Michael Maskin, Cheryl Cortemeglia, & Hannah Nicholes. 2014. *No Safe Place: The Criminalization of Homelessness in US Cities*. Washington, DC: National Law Center on Homelessness and Poverty.

Belmonte, Adriana. 2019. "Research Details the 'Rapid Increase in Homelessness' in Certain U.S. Cities." *Yahoo! Finance*, January 13. Retrieved from https://finance.yahoo .com/news/research-details-rapid-increase-homelessness-certain-u-s-cities -190205600.html

Ellen, Ingrid Gould, & Brendan O'Flaherty (Eds.). 2010. *How to House the Homeless*. Washington, DC: Russell Sage Foundation.

Farrugia, David, John Smyth, & Tim Harrison. 2016. "Moral Distinctions and Structural Inequality: Homeless Youth Salvaging the Self." *The Sociological Review, 64*(2): 238–255.

Forte, James A. 2002. "Not in My Social World: A Cultural Analysis of Media Representations, Contested Spaces, and Sympathy for the Homeless." *J. Soc. & Soc. Welfare, 29*: 131–158.

Galley, Catherine C. 2006. "Homelessness." In James Ciment (Ed.), *Social Issues in America: An Encyclopedia*, 867–879. Armonk, NY: M. E. Sharp.

Gerry, Sarah. 2007. "*Jones v. City of Los Angeles*: A Moral Response to One City's Attempt to Criminalize, Rather Than Confront, Its Homelessness Crisis." *Harvard Civil Rights-Civil Liberties Law Review, 42*: 239–252.

Gowan, Teresa. 2010. *Hobos, Hustlers, and Backsliders: Homeless in San Francisco.* Minneapolis: University of Minnesota Press.

Harpin, Scott B., April S. Elliott, & Colette L. Auerswald. 2017. "A Moral Case for Universal Healthcare for Runaway and Homeless Youth." *International Journal of Human Rights in Healthcare, 10*(3): 195–202.

Herring, Chris. 2014. "The New Logics of Homeless Seclusion: Homeless Encampments in America's West Coast Cities." *City & Community, 13*(4): 285–309.

Loftus-Farren, Zoe. 2011. "Tent Cities: An Interim Solution to Homelessness and Affordable Housing Shortages in the United States." *California Law Review, 99*: 1037–1082.

McConkey, Robert C., III. 1995. "Camping Ordinance and the Homeless: Constitutional and Moral Issues Raised by Ordinances Prohibiting Sleeping in Public Areas." *Cumberland Law Review, 26*: 633–668.

Skolnik, Terry. 2019. "Rethinking Homeless People's Punishments." *New Criminal Law Review: In International and Interdisciplinary Journal, 22*(1): 73–98.

Torrey, E. Fuller. 2014. *American Psychosis: How the Federal Government Destroyed the Mental Illness Treatment System.* New York: Oxford University Press.

van Leeuwen, Bart, & Michael S. Merry. 2018. "Should the Homeless Be Forcibly Helped?" *Public Health Ethics, 2*(1), 30–43. https://doi.org/10.1093/phe/phy006

Wagner, David, & Jennifer Barton Gilman. 2012. *Confronting Homelessness: Poverty, Politics, and the Failure of Social Policy.* Boulder, CO: Lynne Rienner.

Waldron, Jeremy. 2006. "Homelessness and the Issue of Freedom." In Robert E. Goodin & Phillip Pettit (Eds.), *Contemporary Political Philosophy*, 432–448. Malden, MA: Blackwell.

Homosexuality

Few issues subject to debates about morality have seen their landscape shift in the last few decades as much as that of homosexuality and gay rights. People living in Western countries, who indicated strong disapproval of homosexuality as late as the early 1990s—largely on moral and religious grounds—now appear to approve of same-sex relationships by decisive margins. The Gallup Poll has asked specifically about the morality of homosexuality since 2001. That year, 40 percent of those surveyed in that year believed that homosexual relations were morally acceptable, and 54 percent asserted that they were morally wrong. By 2018, only 30 percent of Gallup respondents indicated that homosexuality was morally wrong. A strong majority of 67 percent stated that homosexuality was morally acceptable (Gallup, 2019). With few exceptions, one would be hard-pressed to find a more rapid and significant shift in viewpoints related to the morality of specific human behavior.

As public views have shifted, particularly in the United States, so have the public arguments in favor of or against homosexuality. Furthermore, shifts in just what is meant by the concept of homosexuality are important to understanding shifts in arguments in favor of or against same-sex relationships (Gibson, Alexander, & Meem, 2013). To provide an accurate overview, it is best to frame shifts in the arguments used by opponents and proponents of homosexuality in their historical context. These arguments change based on what aspect of homosexuality is being debated in any given time (for instance, the lawfulness of homosexual behavior versus the legal recognition of same-sex marriage). At the same time, arguments and views dominant in past periods can often reoccur among different individuals engaging in a public discourse on homosexuality, especially when their messages are targeted to various subpopulations like evangelical Christians or secular liberals, even as new arguments dominate rhetoric in the mass media (Burack, 2008).

ANCIENT AND BIBLICAL-BASED VIEWS AND ARGUMENTS

Homosexuality was common in ancient Greece, and this general approval segued into similar broad approval of homosexuality in Roman culture. As both of these ancient cultures formed part of Western legal and political systems and were contemporaneous with the drafting of the Christian Bible, manifestations of homosexuality in ancient cultures still undergird current debates about homosexuality (Boswell, 1981).

In contrast to most individuals' experience with homosexuality in contemporary Western culture, morally sanctioned homosexuality in ancient times was *hierarchical* as opposed to *egalitarian*. This matched with the general views of ancient Greco-Roman cultures that gender (male/female) and other social hierarchies (like owner/slave) were both natural and moral—values embraced by ancient Greco-Roman cultures. Homosexuality, as approved of by these ancient Western cultures, tended to mean pederasty—that is, a relationship between an adolescent or preadolescent boy and a mature man. The adult male was dominant in the relationship and provided education and other benefits to the adolescent, in exchange for companionship—a dynamic that set distinct and unequal roles. When the boy came of age, the relationship was no longer considered to be as morally acceptable. This was because any femininity in men was associated with weakness and thus morally suspect in Greek and Roman culture (Gibson et al., 2013). For an adult male to continue to take the receptive position in a same-sex relationship (as was the case in the pederastic relationship) was immoral because taking a passive position during intercourse or in other aspects of the relationship implied femininity (Plato, 1980). Thus, egalitarian same-sex relationships—those that occurred between two equally situated males in terms of age or class in Western culture today—were not considered to be as moral as pederastic relationships, as one male participant had to take the feminine "role" and thereby debase his maleness (Plato, 1980).

This is how same-sex male intimacy expressed itself in these cultures. It is the condemnation of these types of same-sex relationships in the Christian Bible that form the basis for much of the arguments against homosexuality in Western cultures today. Particularly cited are passages in Leviticus 18 and 20 (Leviticus 20:13, "If a man lies with a man as with a women, both of them have committed abomination; they shall surely be put to death; their blood is upon them") and in passages by Saint Paul in Romans 1 (Romans 1: 26–27, "For this cause, God gave them up unto vile affections . . . leaving the natural use of the woman, burned in their lust one toward another; men with men working that which is unseemly, and receiving in themselves that recompense of their error which was met"). Biblical passages like this formed much of the basis for the moral condemnation of homosexuality among ardent Christians in the West. While other more nuanced arguments are often used (and will be discussed), these Biblical condemnations are often the most important sources in defending the immorality of homosexuality. Viewpoints that men and women are different, that they are meant for different social roles such as mother, homemaker, father, or breadwinner, and that these roles are defined by both God and natural law also figure prominently as a basis of arguments supporting the condemnation of homosexuality.

Those from more tolerant denominations claim that homosexuality in the times these passages were written referred only to hierarchical, pederastic homosexual relationships (Gibson et al., 2013). For them, these Biblical condemnations are about condemning the erotic exploitation of adolescents and young adults rather than the gender of those in these relationships. Therefore, advocates of lesbian, gay, and bisexual (LGB) rights argue they do not apply to the egalitarian homosexual relationships between similarly situated males and females that are common today.

FURTHER JUSTIFICATIONS FOR VIEWING HOMOSEXUALITY AS IMMORAL

The word "homosexual" has its origin in the rise of the scientific medical profession in the second half of the 19th century, when the modern understanding of a "homosexual"—someone primarily sexually attracted to members of the same sex—first took hold in medical and legal discourse (Gibson et al., 2013). With this new concept, debates on homosexuality among medical, political, and legal communities became possible. Prior to that, same-sex relations were just something people did. They were not a marker of someone being a member of a social group or a "sexual orientation" linked to an individual. The development of the medical profession and the creation of the concept of "homosexuals"—a group of people different from others based on their sexual orientation—allowed for a shift in debate (Foucault, 1978). Homosexuality conceptually shifted from a sin to a (likely) congenital, unhealthy impairment to human reproductive functioning—a dysfunction under the purview of the new profession of medicine and public health officials (Foucault, 1978).

The medical, legal, and political establishments adopted positions that nation-states should implement policies to deal with their homosexual populations at about the same time that the Progressive movement was advocating for a more robust government policy to protect the health of the general population from disease (Canaday, 2011). Many medical professionals advocated that policies should not harm or punish homosexuals, but they also favored stopping the spread of homosexuality through various interventions, including hypnosis, testicle transplantation, psychotherapy, lobotomies, aversion therapy with chemicals, and, later, electric shock treatments or electroconvulsive therapy. However, when laws were adopted to address homosexuality, past conceptions of homosexuality as Biblical sin and new conceptions of homosexuality as congenital disease intermixed, and laws proscribing civil penalties like imprisonment for homosexual behavior spread across Western societies (Canaday, 2011). Arguments that homosexuality was not immoral because it was an aspect of a disease, as verified by the psychiatric and medical establishments, became increasingly common until the early 1970s.

In the United States, arguments against homosexuality and homosexuals continued to evolve based on changes in national circumstances and politics. Homosexuality became linked to national security in the 1950s. During the end of the 1940s and 1950s, several dozen or more individuals in the federal government were fired from the federal government for homosexuality. When it was suggested that these individuals could potentially be blackmailed into revealing American secrets by Soviet agents, this argument became a basis for employment discrimination based on sexual orientation in many professions (Johnson, 2004). The 1950s and 1960s seemed to be a peak of mass disapproval of homosexuality, as arguments that homosexuality was sinful, that homosexuality involved sickness, and that homosexuals threatened national security pervaded American culture.

ARGUMENTS FOR THE MORALITY OF HOMOSEXUALITY

A small number of LGB individuals rejected arguments stating that homosexuality was immoral. To the contrary, they contended that legal and unwritten prohibitions on homosexuality were themselves amoral (Garretson, 2018). These counterarguments became much more common after the 1969 Stonewall Riots, which were three days of riots by LGBT people in New York City to protest police raids on the Stonewall Inn, a bar frequented by gay men and transgender people. The riots marked the start of a *mass* LGB social movement that advocates for legal change on homosexuality. In the 1970s, a recognition of large homosexual enclaves in urban areas—communities big enough to be influential in local elections—reduced the social stigma surrounding homosexuality in many major American cities. This freed LGBs and allies living in these regions of the country to challenge claims about the immorality of homosexuality with less fear of being imprisoned, fired, physically assaulted, or socially isolated.

These counterarguments increasingly made their way into the mass media in the 1990s (Brewer, 2008). This likely would not have occurred if not for the intense lobbying by political organizations such as the National Gay and Lesbian Task Force or protests by direct-action organizations such as ACT-UP. ACT-UP formed in response to the AIDS crisis of the 1980s. Many political leaders and elements of the mass media were unwilling to discuss homosexuality prior to the 1990s, despite the astronomical numbers of deaths caused by the spread of the AIDS virus in the gay community. This lack of media attention contributed to a lack of a government response to AIDS. Activism by ACT-UP and other groups from 1987 to 1992 contributed to increased discussion of homosexuality in the mass media, setting the stage for a more robust and two-sided national debate on various aspects of homosexuality, from its morality to whether it was a lifestyle "choice" or a fundamental part of a person's makeup.

The primary counterarguments against prohibitions on homosexuality from the LGB community were that prohibitions on homosexuality violated fundamental American and Western values. Specifically, they contended that prohibitions on homosexuality violated libertarian values—fundamental beliefs that individuals should be allowed to structure their own lives free of legal restraints from the government—and egalitarian values—fundamental beliefs that individuals and social groups should be treated equally by the government and others (Brewer, 2008). Many Americans believe these values to be sacrosanct.

The medical argument that prohibitions on homosexuality helped to insure the health of the public (and thus constituted a public good) had also been fundamentally undermined by the early 1990s. In the 1950s and 1960s, new scientific research cast doubt on the scientific basis for regarding homosexuality as a disease. Most branches of the medical, psychiatric, and scientific establishments repudiated their prior stances stating that homosexuality was an illness and endorsed laws legalizing and destigmatizing homosexuality (Clendinen & Nagourney, 2001). As the

Cold War ended, the rhetorical argument that national prohibitions on homosexuality served national security interests became increasingly difficult to defend. This has, for the most part, left Biblical justifications as the primary justification for claims that homosexuality is immoral.

Although the evidence is more mixed, scientific research in the early 1990s also seemed to suggest that homosexuality (particularly in men) has a firm biological or genetic basis and that, more broadly, sexual orientation is experienced involuntarily. Many proponents of Biblical interpretations of the immorality of homosexuality, however, continue to maintain that individuals are not homosexual for biological reasons but rather choose their sexual orientation or develop it in response to external factors such as bad parenting (Burack, 2008). Some Evangelicals argue further that even if there is a biological basis for homosexuality, it is still a choice to engage in homosexual behavior—a choice that is by their definition immoral. Holders of these views say that because homosexual behavior is chosen, pro-LGB policies are unnecessary and just encourage sinful behavior.

Violations of egalitarian and libertarian norms contained in antigay policies are still justified on the grounds that they protect a public good—in this case the spiritual health of the public and the well-being of children. Some of the latter arguments harken back to old conceptions of homosexuality as pederastic and public safety campaigns depicting child molesters as homosexuals in the 1950s and 1960s. Advocates of specific policies like same-sex adoption point out, however, that studies show that rates of child molestation are actually lower among self-identified lesbians and gays (Herek, 2017).

The public shift in attitudes toward homosexuality is also evident in the decisions that have been handed down by the U.S. Supreme Court over the last three decades. The Supreme Court ruled in 1986 (*Bowers v. Hardwick*) that striking down prohibitions on homosexuality would "cast aside millennia of moral teaching." However, by 2003, the court held that legal bans on homosexuality violated constitutional protections of individual liberty (*Lawrence v. Texas*) and "further no legitimate state interest which can justify its intrusion into the personal and private life of the individual." In 2015, meanwhile, the Court issued its landmark *Obergefell v. Hodges* ruling, which stated that same-sex couples had a constitutional right to marry.

Interestingly, it was perhaps the debate over same-sex marriage that began in the 1990s that made the moral argument in support of homosexuality most prominent. That debate highlighted the moral case for why we should allow people to have their love for another person recognized and protected, regardless of sexual orientation. And during the wave of state constitutional bans on same-sex marriage in the early 2000s, the moral obligation to protect same-sex love was expanded, and opponents of the bans began to publically share visions of same-sex couple families, where children and parents thrived.

CONCLUSION

At the risk of oversimplification, those who argue against the morality of homosexuality tend to focus on specific condemnations in the Bible (and the documents of other faiths) as the primary reason that homosexuality should be regarded as immoral. Those who argue that homosexuality is moral, meanwhile, state that pro-scriptions on homosexuality violate fundamental Western values—those of liberty and equality—and that no objective public good is served by making homosexuality illegal. They contend that legal prohibitions on homosexuality and other anti-gay rights policies are themselves immoral because they needlessly harm LGB people and their families.

Jeremiah Garretson

FURTHER READING

Boswell, John E. 1981. *Christianity, Social Tolerance, and Homosexuality.* Chicago: Chicago Press.

Bowers v. Hardwick, 1986.

Brewer, Paul R. 2008. *Value War: Public Opinion and the Politics of Gay Rights.* Lanham, MD: Rowman & Littlefield.

Burack, Cynthia. 2008. *Sin, Sex, and Democracy: Antigay Rhetoric and the Christian Right.* Albany, NY: SUNY Press.

Canaday, Margot. 2011. *The Straight State.* Princeton, NJ: Princeton University Press.

Clendinen, Dudley, & Adam Nagourney. 2001. *Out for Good: The Struggle to Build a Gay Rights Movement in America.* New York: Simon & Schuster.

Foucault, Michel. 1978. *The History of Sexuality, Vol. 1.* New York: Vintage.

Gallup. 2019. "Gay and Lesbian Rights." Retrieved from http://news.gallup.com/poll/1651/gay-lesbian-rights.aspx

Garretson, Jeremiah. 2018. *The Path to Gay Rights: How Activism and Coming Out Changed Public Opinion.* New York: New York University Press.

Gibson, Michelle A., Jonathan Alexander, & Deborah T. Meem. (2nd ed.). 2013. *Finding Out: An Introduction to LGBT Studies.* Thousand Oaks, CA: Sage Publications.

Haider-Markel, Donald P. 2010. *Out and Running: Gay and Lesbian Candidates, Elections, and Policy Representation.* Washington, DC: Georgetown University Press.

Haider-Markel, Donald P., & Mark Joslyn. 2013. "Politicizing Biology: Social Movements, Parties, and the Case of Homosexuality." *Social Science Journal,* 50(4): 603–615.

Herek, Gregory. 2017. "Facts About Homosexuality and Child Molestation." Retrieved from http://psychology.ucdavis.edu/rainbow/html/facts_molestation.html

Johnson, David K. 2004. *The Lavender Scare: The Cold War Persecution of Gays and Lesbians in the Federal Government.* Chicago: Chicago Press.

Lawrence v. Texas 539 U.S. 558 (2003).

LeVay, Simon. 1996. *Queer Science.* Cambridge, MA: MIT Press.

Mucciaroni, Gary. 2009. *Same Sex, Different Politics: Success and Failure in the Struggles over Gay Rights.* Chicago: University of Chicago Press.

Obergefell v. Hodges 576 U.S. __ (2015).

Pierceson, Jason. 2014. *Same-Sex Marriage in the United States: The Road to the Supreme Court and Beyond.* Lanham, MD: Rowman & Littlefield.

Plato. 1980. *The Symposium.* Cambridge: Cambridge University Press.

Illegal/Undocumented Immigration

Narratives surrounding "illegal" immigration and "illegal" immigrants are tied to moral arguments based on ideological and material conditions. Moral arguments surrounding illegal immigration have strong ties to American criminalization of unauthorized migration and Latinos in particular. Since illegal immigration is a crime, state organizations must create appropriate measures to protect its citizens from potential threats. This moral authority ideology undergirds many efforts to protect the nation against illegality. Moral arguments have also been constructed that tie illegal immigration to immigrant women's sexuality and reproduction. Finally, assessments of the morality of illegal immigration (or "undocumented immigration," the preferred term of advocates for people entering the United States without authorization) have often been linked to varying viewpoints on the fundamental nature of the American identity.

ILLEGALITY AND CRIMINALITY

Debates surrounding "illegal" immigration have a long history, starting in the early 1900s, when increases in immigration contributed to the hardening of white-ethnic and racial categories and led to increased control of immigration flows through executive and legislative action (Ngai, 2004). Immigration policies enacted in the 1920s surrounding border enforcement and visa requirements targeted Mexicans. Later, during the Great Depression, the "illegal immigrant" label was linked to Mexican Americans and to Latinos in general (Chavez, 2013). Since then, the construction of so-called illegal immigration has been tied to changes in unauthorized migration patterns, mostly accelerated by immigration policies in the 1980s and 1990s (Massey, Durand, & Malone, 2002). Prior to the Immigration Reform Control Act (IRCA) of 1986, unauthorized migration was cyclical. Most unauthorized migrants came to the United States to work in seasonal industries such as agriculture and return to Mexico after the working season, but that ended under the original bracero program, started during World War II. Agriculture employers and the U.S. government made significant efforts to recruit temporary farm workers from Mexico to come to the United States and work the fields; the bracero program continued to be extended through 1964. The established pattern of the flow of temporary workers continued through the 1960s and 1970s. However, after IRCA was passed, cyclical migration ended.

IRCA gave some unauthorized immigrants a path to legal residency but made the lives of those who did not qualify for amnesty more difficult. Border crossings became more difficult after IRCA, which authorized increases in the size and enforcement capacities of the Border Patrol and authorized sanctions against employers who hired unauthorized workers, among other things (Massey et al., 2002). In 1996, the Illegal Immigration Reform and Immigrant Responsibility Act (IIRIRA) further heightened border controls and surveillance. It also established 10- to 20-year bars to readmission to any immigrant caught crossing into the United States without proper documentation. As border crossings became more difficult, the unauthorized population began settling in the United States permanently rather than continue the past patterns of cyclical migration between Mexico and the United States. In addition, due to internal enforcement practices authorized under IIRIRA, the unauthorized population became more widely dispersed across the country (Massey et al., 2002).

These changes in migratory patterns came with increased media depictions of "illegal" Latinos (especially men of Mexican descent) as people who engaged in criminal activity in America, including drug dealing, murder, and rape (Chavez, 2013; Sohoni & Sohoni, 2013). News and media coverage depicted flows of immigrants as "dangerous waters"—comparing them to floods and rough seas crashing over the American soil—or as pollutants and spreaders of diseases to U.S. citizens (Santa Ana, 2002). In striking contrast, anti-immigrant mobilizations were often rendered as narratives of "ordinary" Americans attempting to alleviate a "problem" that the government was unwilling or unable to address (Cisneros, 2008). Ideal visions of the United States as a "nation of immigrants" and perceptions of belonging create divides between "us" and "them," contributing to the construction of illegality. And although the criminalization of immigrants is nothing new in the United States—in the past Italians, Irish, Chinese, and Japanese immigrants were also criminalized—today's anti-immigrant connection to illegality is intertwined with moral ideologies and represented in sophisticated media technologies, shaping attitudes and perceptions about unauthorized migration.

PROTECTING THE NATION FROM "BAD HOMBRES"

During the 2016 presidential campaign, Republican nominee Donald Trump declared that "we have some bad hombres here, and we're going to get them out." This was one of many comments Trump made about undocumented immigrants in the months leading up to his election. Many critics of Trump's rhetoric said that the "hombre" quote perfectly exemplifies the racialization and gendering of illegal immigration today. The perception of Latinos as bad, criminals, illegal, and threats follows what Rodriguez and Paredes (2013) call the Moral Authority ideology. Moral

Authority ideology gives the state bureaucracy the responsibility to protect its population and territory from possible threats (Rodriguez & Paredes 2013). Thus agencies such as Border Patrol and Immigration Customs Enforcement (ICE) receive authority and resources to "protect" the nation and its citizens. From 1986, when IRCA was implemented, to 2016, the U.S. government has spent approximately $263 billion in immigration enforcement (American Immigration Council, 2017), much of it to fulfill requirements of new laws and programs (Meissner et al., 2013). The total spending from 1986 to 2012 equals 15 times the budget dedicated to enforcement around the time that IRCA of 1986 was passed, and it exceeds by 25 percent the budgets of the FBI, DEA, U.S. Marshalls Service, the Secret Service, and the Bureau of Alcohol, Tobacco, Fire Arms and Explosives—*combined* (Meissner et al., 2013). The Moral Authority ideology is reinforced by the success of immigration enforcement. As more money is poured into the system, more programs are created to apprehend immigrants at the border and inside the country, which causes more immigrant apprehension, which in turn legitimizes the need for more resources for the apprehension and enforcement programs. This cycle, according to critics, encourages the development of a self-perpetuating bureaucracy (Menjívar & Kanstroom, 2014).

As stated in the Border Patrol mission statement, its goal is to "detect and prevent the illegal entry of aliens into the United States" in order to "to protect our Nation" from "dangerous" people. Immigration enforcement agencies' duties are rooted in moral grounds to protect the country from outsider threats. Thus, for those supporting strong immigration enforcement, the intent of Border Patrol agents is never questioned or perceived as malicious or wrong (Rodriguez & Paredes, 2013). When negative outcomes emerge from immigration enforcement or border patrolling, such as immigrants' deaths or the indefinite separation of families, these are framed by immigration enforcement agencies and Americans who support zero-tolerance responses to illegal/undocumented immigration as "collateral damage" and a small cost to incur in pursuit of the larger mission of protecting the nation. Although the events of 9/11 augmented the Moral Authority ideology, these moral arguments in support of severe penalties for illegal border crossings have been evident since the beginning of the creation of the Border Patrol in the 1920s. The role of the state as protector of its citizens under the Moral Authority Ideology gives bureaucracies the authority to take any measures necessary to achieve its goals.

SEXUALITY AND "ANCHOR" BABIES

Immigrant women's sexuality and fertility are also targeted as grounds of moral concern that contributes to opposition to immigration. Latinas and immigrant women of color are often depicted as hypersexualized, exotic, "on fire," or "spicy" in the media (Chavez, 2013). The perception of Latinas' hypersexuality is linked to ideas of promiscuity and high fertility rates. In particular, Latinas' fertility levels, combined with their alleged promiscuity, are often depicted as alarming and pathological. Immigrant women's fertility is also viewed as a source of possible long-term settlement via "anchor babies"—children who automatically receive U.S.

citizenship because they were born on American soil and who can subsequently be claimed as a relation by parents or other family members seeking citizenship or legal residency in the United States. The anchor baby narrative first emerged in the 1990s, but it was popularized after the terrorist attacks of September 11, 2001, by conservative media figures including Michelle Malkin from Fox News and Lou Dobbs from CNN, both of whom have talked and written about the connection between anchor babies and undocumented migration (Chavez, 2013, 2014).

The anchor baby narrative has fueled anti-immigrant groups' and politicians' demands to change the 14th Amendment, *jus soli*, which guarantees citizenship to those born on U.S. soil (Chavez, 2014). Arguments supporting such changes to the 14th Amendment are based in part on perceptions of morality, with supporters asserting that since undocumented immigrants are unlawfully present in the United States, granting citizenship to their children simply because they were born in America undermines the fairness of rule of law (Motomura, 2012). Supporters also claim that changing the law would remove one of the prime motivations for people from foreign countries to illegally enter the United States. The first attempt at changing *jus soli* for children of undocumented migrants was in the 1990s, and various unsuccessful attempts have been made since that time. However, these efforts have also moved to the state level, with legislative resolutions calling on Congress and the president to act (Chavez, 2014). Supporters of undocumented immigrants and more generous immigration policies, meanwhile, ridicule the whole notion that anchor babies pose a threat to America. They emphasize that while the anchor baby is a common media image, it would be difficult for immigrant women to plan to give birth to an anchor baby because, given current immigration laws, it would take a minimum of 31 years for these women to qualify to apply for a permanent residence based on the citizenship of their baby (Enchautegui & Menjívar, 2015).

THREAT TO THE AMERICAN IDENTITY

Another moral argument legitimating discourses on illegal immigration is the perception held by some Americans that new immigrants, mostly Latinos and Asians, are unable or unwilling to assimilate into an imagined, homogenized U.S. society and culture (unlike European immigrants, past and present). Academic Samuel P. Huntington amplified this view in a 2004 issue of *Foreign Policy* in which he compared Latinos to earlier waves of European immigrants. He argued that Latinos reject American values and norms by forming their own ethnic enclaves and political organizations. Huntington also claimed that Mexicans in particular were aiming for the reclamation or "reconquest" of the Southwestern United States, a territory that was part of Mexico prior to the Treaty of Guadalupe Hidalgo in 1848. These assertions echoed claims Huntington had made in a 2000 article in the *American Enterprise*, in which he claimed that Mexican rapid immigration rates were an "invasion" creating a "threat to American social security" that would ultimately threaten American identity and culture, as well as the future of the country (Chavez, 2014). Sentiments similar to Huntington's have become more visible in American right-wing circles in the 2010s, especially since 2016 when Republican Donald Trump employed similar inflammatory rhetoric throughout that year's presidential campaign.

The perceived threat to the imagined homogenized American culture and identity is based on Classical Assimilation theory, commonly known as the Melting Pot, which follows the view that, as immigrant groups settle in the United States, they are eventually incorporated into the larger society over the course of several generations. However, immigrant incorporation in this view means adopting American Protestant values and norms, an idealized American identity, and speaking English, while simultaneously giving a lower profile to the traditions, languages, identities, cultural norms, and values of ancestral homelands (Chavez, 2014; Menjívar & Kanstroom, 2014).

This view of assimilation ignores whether current citizens are welcoming to immigrants and the potential bias they have on the basis of class, race, gender, sexuality, or skin color. Critics of forced assimilation also contend that this view is dangerous because it provides a pretext of morality from which to create policies that target the values, traditions, and languages of new immigrant groups. For example, the 2010 ethnic studies law (Arizona House Bill 2281) passed in Arizona bans ethnic studies programs. This legislation was widely recognized as targeting Mexican American and Latino studies coursework in K–12 schools. Also, various subnational governments across the country have passed English-as-official-language bills that stigmatize other languages and make government documents available only in English (Workman, 2015).

MORALITY OF "ILLEGAL" IMMIGRATION

Although illegal immigration has been an issue and a topic of debate throughout American history, today, Latinos and Muslims are overwhelmingly depicted as the faces of illegal immigration. In addition, hardline opponents of illegal immigration use imagery describing undocumented immigrants as a threat to national security, a threat to the individual, and a threat to American identity and core values. As a result, the state's actions become rooted in moral ideologies of protection, guardianship of its citizens against "outsiders," legitimating state actions for the "common good," and pushing those considered to be "illegal" immigrants to the outermost margins of society.

Perhaps more than ever before, immigration has been painted as a moral issue by the Republican party, especially with the rise of Donald Trump to the presidency, who campaigned on the threats posed by immigrants in 2016 and who has continued to inflame the issue with false claims that most undocumented immigrants are thieves, murderers, and rapists. But Democrats too have turned to moral narratives, pointing to the immorality of forcing people brought to the United States illegally as children to leave the country and accusing the Trump administration of immoral conduct in its refusal to accept refugees and in its policies of separating undocumented children from their parents at the border.

Andrea Gómez Cervantes

FURTHER READING

American Immigration Council. 2017. *The Cost of Immigration Enforcement and Border Security*. Retrieved from https://www.americanimmigrationcouncil.org/research /the-cost-of-immigration-enforcement-and-border-security

Chavez, Leo R. (2nd ed.). 2013. *Latino Threat: Constructing Immigrants, Citizens, and the Nation*. Redwood City, CA: Stanford University Press.

Chavez, Leo R. 2014. "'Illegality' Across Generations." In Cecilia Menjívar & Daniel Kanstroom (Eds.), *Constructing Immigrant "Illegality,"* 84–110. Cambridge: Cambridge University Press.

Cisneros, J. David. 2008. "Contaminated Communities: The Metaphor of 'Immigrant as Pollutant' in Media Representations of Immigration." *Rhetoric & Public Affairs, 11*(4): 569–602.

Enchautegui, Maria, & Cecilia Menjívar. 2015. "Paradoxes of Family Immigration Policy: Separation, Reorganization, and Reunification of Families Under Current Immigration Laws." *Law & Policy, 37*(1–2): 32–60.

Gonzales, Roberto. 2016. *Lives in Limbo: Undocumented and Coming of Age in America*. Berkeley: University of California Press.

Kanstroom, Daniel. 2007. *Deportation Nation*. Cambridge, MA: Harvard University Press.

Massey, Douglas S., Jorge Durand, & Nolan J. Malone. 2002. *Beyond Smoke and Mirrors*. New York: Russell Sage Foundation.

Meissner, Doris, Donald M. Kerwin, Muzzafar Chishti, & Claire Bergeron. 2013. *Immigration Enforcement in the United States: The Rise of a Formidable Machinery*. Washington, DC: Migration Policy Institute. Retrieved from http://www .migrationpolicy.org/pubs/enforcementpillars.pdf

Menjívar, Cecilia, & Daniel Kanstroom. 2014. *Constructing Immigrant "Illegality."* eBook. New York: Cambridge University Press.

Motomura, Hiroshi. 2012. "Making Legal: The Dream Act, Birthright Citizenship, and Broad-Scale Legalization." *Lewis & Clark Law Review, 16*(4): 1127–1150.

Ngai, Mae N. 2004. *Impossible Subjects: Illegal Aliens and the Making of Modern America*. Princeton, NJ: Princeton University Press.

Rodriguez, Nestor, & Cristian Paredes. 2013. "Coercive Immigration Enforcement and Bureaucratic Ideology." In Cecilia Menjívar & Daniel Kanstroom (Ed.), *Constructing Immigrant "Illegality,"* 63–83. New York: Cambridge University Press.

Santa Ana, Otto. 2002. *Brown Tide Rising*. Austin: University of Texas Press.

Sohoni, Deenesh, & Tracy W. P. Sohoni. 2013. "Perceptions of Immigrant Criminality: Crime and Social Boundaries." *The Sociological Quarterly, 55*: 49–71.

Workman, Romana. 2015. "English-only Movement in the USA—Is There Hope for Language Tolerance?" *Annual of Language & Politics and Politics of Identity, 9*: 131–155.

Minimum Wage

Debates about the minimum wage and proposals to establish a living wage system in the United States have frequently featured a significant moral element. Two moral frames and two moral arguments have frequently been employed in this area by activists, politicians, and public intellectuals. The dominant moral frame in favor of a higher minimum wage is the social contract frame: Its assumption is that those who fulfill their responsibility to society by working hard deserve the pay requisite for a decent life. The property right frame is a second moral frame on the same side of the issue: It calls into question the legitimacy of property holdings, often by highlighting the enormous wealth of the corporations or their owners and sometimes going so far as to imply that it is the workers' work that creates the wealth of the corporations they work for.

The two moral arguments discussed (they are not actually frames but explicit arguments) are both "externality" claims (Stabile, 2008): They both decry cost shifting to third parties by those who shirk their moral obligations, but they take opposite sides of the debate. The corporate cost-shifting argument sees higher minimums and living wages as ameliorating the injustice caused by companies relying upon the taxpayers to keep their employees alive through public assistance programs and by municipalities "subsidizing poverty" by giving incentives to companies that do not pay a living wage. The arbitrary moral burden argument is a moral response to the social contract frame and the corporate cost-shifting argument: If society has a moral obligation to make sure all full-time workers have a decent living, why do only those who hire low-wage labor have the responsibility to pay for society's moral stance, as legitimate as that stance may be?

THE SOCIAL CONTRACT ARGUMENT

The social contract frame holds that everyone has an obligation to work hard and that those who meet this obligation deserve a decent living. This perspective is stated most explicitly by public intellectuals: "[O]ur basic social contract [is to] work hard, be productive, and you and your family can live a decent life with a place to live, food on the table, clothes on your backs, and other necessities" (Ornstein, 2013). As former Clinton Labor Secretary Robert Reich put it, as part of a call for a $15 minimum wage, "People who work full time are fulfilling their most basic social responsibility. As such, they should earn enough to live on" (Reich, 2015). This moral position is central to the rhetorical stance of many advocacy organizations seeking higher minimum wages. "We work hard and we're still stuck in poverty. It's not right. . . . It's time to pay people enough to survive. It's time to pay people what they deserve," argued the Fight for $15 on its website (2017). OUR Walmart, a movement of Walmart employees calling for a $15 wage, argued that "Walmart should honor the hard work and humanity of Associates" and that Walmart workers' "strong work ethic" is not being rewarded with respect from management (2016). This frame is also present in the speeches of prominent politicians who have urged the establishment of a higher national minimum wage. In 2013, President Obama (calling for an hourly minimum wage raise to $9) argued that "no one who works full-time should have to live in poverty." Three years later, Democratic presidential candidate Bernie Sanders echoed that slogan in calling for raising the minimum wage to $15 an hour across the country. The core moral idea serving as the foundation of these utterances is that it is how hard workers work, rather than the value of what they produce or even the fact that they are human beings, that grants workers the right to a certain standard of living.

This frame appeals to a conception of justice that has remained largely unchanged in U.S. public discourse for well over a century. In 1906, Roman Catholic Father John Augustine Ryan published his PhD dissertation, *A Living Wage: Its Ethical and Economic Aspects*, making the moral case for a living wage in the United States. His argument was that all people had an equal right to a "decent livelihood" because God had created the earth to enable His children to live. This right was "suspended" for all who would not work. However, all who did work had a right to demand a decent livelihood from those who controlled nature's resources. Thus the owners of productive resources had a moral obligation to their workers to ensure they were paid enough for a decent life, which included the full development of the human personality for workers and their families, not a bare existence (Snarr, 2011).

Ryan's vision guided the earliest minimum wage legislation in the United States, enacted at the state level in several parts of the country by lawmakers of the so-called Progressive movement between 1912 and 1923, and Ryan's conception of what constituted a living wage was cited by Secretary of Labor Frances Perkins in the rollout of the minimum wage provisions of the Fair Labor Standards Act (FLSA) of 1938. This legislation, although amended many times, is still the basis of today's federal minimum wage. President Franklin Roosevelt's 1937 address to Congress introducing the FLSA echoed Ryan's claim that hard work merited not just survival but a reasonable standard of living: The task was "to bring within the reach of the average man and woman a maximum of goods and of services conducive to the fulfillment of the promise of American life" (1937), which meant social mobility. The American people, said Roosevelt in 1938, demand "respect for the need of all at the bottom to get work—and through work to get a really fair share of the good things of life, and a chance to save and rise." Such rhetoric directly appealed to America's traditional self-image as the land of opportunity.

THE PROPERTY RIGHT ARGUMENT

Whereas the social contract frame focuses on how hard people work, the property right frame focuses on the legitimacy of property holdings. Unlike the social contract frame, the property right frame calls attention to the wealth of the wealthy rather than merely the poverty of the poor; it often makes comparisons between deserving workers and undeserving but wealthy owners, and thus it implicitly asks people to think about who really creates the wealth in the first place.

Examples of this frame are also common in the appeals of the wage movement organizations of recent years. Sometimes they merely point out how wealthy the employers are: "[I]t's not like our employers are struggling—these are multi-billion dollar corporations" (Fight for $15, 2017). At other times, they call attention to both the productivity of the employees and the extreme wealth of the companies they work for: "Walmart is . . . one of the most successful companies in America. We have worked hard to make that a reality. We deserve an opportunity to share in the success" (OUR Walmart, 2016). The property right frame is fundamentally different from the social contract argument in that the former focuses on the property of the owners and sometimes implies that it is the work of workers that produces the owners' property. This can be rather explicit in some movement organization statements, such as this from the Fight for $15: "[L]ow-wage employers everywhere are making billions of dollars in profit . . . while leaving people like us—the people who do the real work—struggling to survive" (2017). Even when the notion that it is the workers who create the wealth is itself absent, this frame often draws such a strong contrast between wealthy owners and poor workers that it invites such thinking, as when Service Employees International Union President Mary Kay Henry described workers fighting for "the basic necessities" as "people who work for the richest corporations in America" (2012).

Politicians also employ this frame, sometimes by calling attention to wealth created by workers that is greater than their pay, as in Representative Keith Ellison's (D-MN) argument: "These people earn every single penny they get. In fact, they earn way more than they get" (2013). At other times, they focus on the recipients of the wealth rather than on the transfer from workers. "There is no justice when all over this country people are working long hours for abysmally low wages," asserted Bernie Sanders, "while 58 percent of all new income being created today goes to the top one percent" (2015). This statement never explicitly says that it is those low-wage workers whose work creates the new income that goes so disproportionately to the top 1 percent, but its framing does encourage such a viewpoint.

The property right frame has been used in U.S. discourse for nearly two centuries. David Walker's *Appeal to the Colored Citizens* (1829) argued that "[t]he greatest riches in all America have arisen from our blood and tears" and thus that it is "our property" (Walker, 1995: 65). As one Reconstruction-era Alabama convention put it, "The property which they hold was nearly all earned by the sweat of *our* brows." Such claims by former slaves were very common during Reconstruction (Foner, 1983: 56).

THE CORPORATE COST-SHIFTING ARGUMENT

One of the most common moral arguments made by proponents of raising the minimum wage is that low-wage companies are simply shifting onto the public the cost of supporting their own workers. As the Fight for $15 put it, employers who pay low wages are "pushing off costs onto taxpayers." When workers can "barely pay our bills and put food on the table," the group declares that the response from McDonald's is, "Go on food stamps" (2017). OUR Walmart decried the need for workers to rely on government assistance (2016). A related argument has been central to the living wage movement since its modern renaissance in 1994 Baltimore: Municipalities that provide incentives to corporations that pay low wages are essentially subsidizing poverty. Thus the central demand of the living wage movement has been for any company doing business with or receiving subsidies from a municipality to pay for higher-than-minimum wages (Snarr, 2011).

THE ARBITRARY MORAL BURDEN ARGUMENT

Politicians who oppose higher wages do not, in the main, rely upon moral arguments. Public intellectuals do, however, and their arguments are often some variant of what is sometimes called the arbitrary moral burden argument. This says that, even if the social contract argument is morally right and workers really do deserve a decent living, this still leaves open the question of who should pay for it and who is to blame for its lack. Because the living wage argument states that full-time workers have a right to a decent living, it "applies with equal moral force to wages as to the costs of food, housing, and fuel, yet its advocates do not critique the sellers of these essentials for their prices. Nor do they criticize businesses for a failure to employ people because they have replaced them with machines" (McMaken, 2015). Thus the reliance of the social contract argument upon a standard of living renders it vulnerable to this counterargument because standards of living are determined by prices as much as by pay. More generally, forcing employers to pay higher wages on the grounds that it is immoral for workers to have low wages is "unfair and wrong" because it amounts to saying, "I believe there is a moral imperative for you to earn more, so I force someone else to pay more. I feel moral while sticking someone else with the bill" (Bandow, 2014).

This argument also works against the corporate cost-shifting argument, producing a conservative argument in favor of public assistance programs rather than higher minimum wages. So, for example, "to make sure that the poor have enough to eat we should be willing to pay the taxes for the SNAP program. Not insist that the money comes out of the pockets of . . . the people who employ minimum wage" workers (Worstall, 2014).

ECONOMIC ARGUMENTS AGAINST AND FOR RAISING THE MINIMUM WAGE

Although conservative philosophers and think tanks have advanced the moral argument against the living wage, conservative and neoliberal politicians have generally favored economic arguments instead. They often turn in particular to an assertion that raising the minimum wage will harm the very people it seeks to help by forcing employers to reduce their workforces or cut other benefits. During their tenures as speakers of the house, Republicans John Boehner and Paul Ryan both made such arguments in response to Obama's 2013 call for a federal $9-an-hour minimum wage, and during the 2016 presidential campaign, Democrat Hillary Clinton used the same argument to defend her support for a $12 rather than a $15 minimum. Arguments that raising wages causes inflation also can be focused on the lowest-paid workers, who are the ones least able to afford higher prices for consumer goods.

Proponents of raising the minimum wage have responded with the economic argument that raising the minimum wage will put more money in the pockets of low-income people who will spend it rather than keeping it in the hands of wealthy businesses who will not. Thus the stimulus effect of a raised minimum wage will counter its tendency to make employers reluctant to hire (Reich, 2015). Some also suggest that a higher minimum wage might enable higher numbers of parents to forego second (or third) jobs and allow them to spend more time with their children, a point of view that overlaps with a morally based "family values" perspective.

CONCLUSION

Given that the social contract frame dominates the *moral* debate about living wages and minimum wages, it is important to recognize its innate conservatism: It does not claim that because the wealth was created by the workers, it belongs to them. Rather, it is the workers' fulfillment of the duty to work that confers upon them the entitlement to a living. When applied to workers in a society where workers do not own their own means of production, the moral obligation to work becomes a moral obligation to serve the owning class and carries the implication that those who choose not to do so are morally deficient. Because it judges workers according to the hard work criterion (which is not applied to owners), it also forms a neat fit with the personal responsibility frame employed to justify the conservative/neoliberal legislation of recent decades, such as the Personal Responsibility and Work Opportunity Reconciliation Act of 1996. It depends upon a strongly procapitalist vision of society as one without fundamental class conflict, a vision implicit in Franklin Roosevelt's initial framing of the issue: "Different from a great part of the world, we in America persist in our belief in individual enterprise and in the profit motive; but we realize we must continually seek . . . opportunities for the little fellow . . . [and] decent wages" (1938). In this vision, what is actually a worker's contract with an employer is transformed into a worker's contract with the rest of society, as if by serving the business owner, the worker were serving the people in general. By contrast, the property right frame, by calling into question the legitimacy of unequal holdings and implicitly raising the issue of who creates the property, has inherently radical, class-conscious implications.

David Brichoux

FURTHER READING

Bandow, Doug. 2014. "The Minimum Wage: Immoral and Inefficient." Cato at Liberty, Cato Institute, January 14.

Boehner, John. 2013. Statement to the Press, February 14. Quoted in Jose Delreal. 2013. "20 Quotes: Politicians on Minimum Wage." *Politico*, December 12. Retrieved from http://www.politico.com/gallery/2013/12/20-quotes-politicians-on-minimum-wage-001347

Convention. 1867. Quoted in Mobile *Nationalist*, May 16. In Eric Foner. 1983. *Nothing but Freedom: Emancipation and Its Legacy*. Baton Rouge: Louisiana State University Press.

DeSilver, Drew. 2017. "5 Facts About the Minimum Wage." *Pew Research Center*, January 4. Retrieved from http://www.pewresearch.org/fact-tank/2017/01/04/5-facts-about-the-minimum-wage

Ellison, Keith. 2013. Interview with Alex Wagner on NOW with Alex Wagner, *MSNBC*, December 5.

Figart, Deborah M. (Ed.). 2004. *Living Wage Movements: Global Perspectives*. New York: Routledge.

Fight for $15. 2017. Organization website. Retrieved from http://fightfor15.org/why-we-strike and http://fightfor15.org/about-us

Foner, Eric. 1984. *Nothing but Freedom: Emancipation and Its Legacy*. Baton Rouge: Louisiana State University Press.

Henry, Mary Kay. 2012. Quoted in Steven Greenhouse. 2012. "With Day of Protests, Fast-Food Workers Seek More Pay." *New York Times*, November 29. Retrieved from http://www.nytimes.com/2012/11/30/nyregion/fast-food-workers-in-new-york-city-rally-for-higher-wages.html

Levin-Waldman, Oren M. 2005. *The Political Economy of the Living Wage: A Study of Four Cities*. New York: M. E. Sharpe.

Luce, Stephanie. 2004. *Fighting for a Living Wage*. Ithaca, NY: ILR Press, Cornell University Press.

McMaken, Ryan. 2015. "The Failed Moral Argument for a 'Living Wage,'" *Mises Institute*, September 4. Retrieved from https://mises.org/library/failed-moral-argument-living-wage

Neumark, David, & William L. Wascher. 2008. *Minimum Wages*. Cambridge and London: MIT Press.

Nordlund, Willis J. 1997. *The Quest for a Living Wage: The History of the Federal Minimum Wage Program*. Westport, CT: Greenwood Press.

Obama, Barack. 2013. State of the Union Address, February 12. Quoted in Jose Delreal. 2013. "20 Quotes: Politicians on Minimum Wage." *Politico*, December 12. Retrieved from http://www.politico.com/gallery/2013/12/20-quotes-politicians-on-minimum-wage-001347

Ornstein, Norm. 2013. "The Moral and Economic Imperative to Raise the Minimum Wage." *The Atlantic*, December 4. Retrieved from https://www.theatlantic.com/politics/archive/2013/12/the-moral-and-economic-imperative-to-raise-the-minimum-wage/282064

OUR Walmart. 2016. Organizational website. Retrieved from http://www.united4respect.org /our_declaration_of_respect and http://www.united4respect.org/15_and_fulltime

Pollin, Robert, Mark Brenner, Jeanette Wicks-Lim, & Stephanie Luce. 2008. *A Measure of Fairness: The Economics of Living Wages and Minimum Wages in the United States*. Ithaca: ILR Press, Cornell University Press.

Pollin, Robert, & Stephanie Luce. 1998. *The Living Wage: Building a Fair Economy*. New York: New Press.

Reich, Robert. 2015. "A $15 Minimum Wage Is the Only Moral Choice." *Salon*, October 20. Retrieved from http://www.salon.com/2015/10/20/robert_reich_a_15_minimum _wage_is_the_only_moral_choice_partner

Rolf, David. 2016. *The Fight for $15: The Right Wage for a Working America*. New York and London: New Press.

Roosevelt, Franklin D. 1937. "Message to Congress on Establishing Minimum Wages and Maximum Hours." May 24. Online by Gerhard Peters & John T. Woolley, The American Presidency Project. Retrieved from http://www.presidency.ucsb.edu /ws/?pid=15405

Roosevelt, Franklin D. 1938. "Fireside Chat." June 24. Online by Gerhard Peters and John T. Woolley, American Presidency Project. Retrieved from http://www.presidency.ucsb .edu/ws/?pid=15662

Rosenblum, Jonathan. 2017. *Beyond $15: Immigrant Workers, Faith Activists, and the Revival of the Labor Movement*. Boston: Beacon Press.

Ryan, John. 1906. *A Living Wage: Its Ethical and Economic Aspects*. New York: Macmillan.

Ryan, Paul. 2013. Interview with Jake Tapper, *CNN*, February 13. Retrieved from http:// cnnpressroom.blogs.cnn.com/2013/02/13/rep-paul-ryan-to-tapper-he-underplayed -the-enormity-of-the-task-before-us-which-is-to-confront-a-debt-crisis

Sanders, Bernard. 2015. Campaign website. Retrieved from https://berniesanders.com/press -release/sanders-addresses-justice-and-morality-at-liberty-university

Snarr, C. Melissa. 2011. *All You That Labor: Religion and Ethics in the Living Wage Movement*. New York and London: New York University Press.

Stabile, Donald R. 2008. *The Living Wage: Lessons from the History of Economic Thought*. Northampton: Edward Elgar.

Walker, David. [1830] 1995. *Appeal to the Colored Citizens of the World, But in Particular, and Very Expressly, to Those of the United States of America*. New York: Hill & Wang.

Waltman, Jerold. 2000. *The Politics of the Minimum Wage*. Urbana and Chicago: University of Illinois Press.

Waltman, Jerold L. 2004. *The Case for the Living Wage*. New York: Algora Publishing.

Worstall, Tim. 2014. "The Moral Case Against Raising the Minimum Wage." *Forbes*, March 6. Retrieved from https://www.forbes.com/sites/timworstall/2014/03/06/the -moral-case-against-raising-the-minimum-wage/#cae5bbe7df83

Obesity

Moral arguments are used to mobilize groups in many social debates. Moral frames generate support from the public without the need for complicated explanations or technical expertise. Furthermore, tying morality to an issue sparks passionate reactions from those who find the values in keeping with their own code of conduct. The topic of obesity in the United States likewise generates deep feelings from the public. Issue frames are often created to support deep-seated public values or are used as a means of targeting a base of support. There are policy implications associated with each frame and with the inherent assumption made about overweight people in our society.

The infusion of religious values into society has been common throughout the span of history. As far back as the medieval Catholic Church, religious leaders remarked on social issues. This has included warnings about excessive weight. The church associated corpulence with the deadly sins of gluttony and avarice. Adam and Eve's fall was said to bring sin into the world. Gluttony was viewed as one of the seven deadly sins because of its association with animal impulses. Indulging in excess indicated a lack of reason and self-restraint. Gluttony was said to be a "gateway drug" to other sins.

The word "diet" in Greek can be translated into "way of living" (Oliver, 2005: 64). To avoid the sin of gluttony, the faithful were to fast and avoid lavishness. Ascetic monks took this to an extreme as a show of devotion to God. Fleeing to deserts or other places of solitude, they rejected the things of the world. Popes and priests also condemned overeating for its association with wealth and power. Being overweight was a sign of avarice because only the elite could afford food enough to spare. By rejecting the signs of wealth, religious leaders showed their autonomy. Protestants likewise discouraged weight as sin. Since fatness symbolized the political elites of the day, Protestants saw thinness as a way of showing resistance and moral fortitude.

Traditional morality, based on Judeo-Christian moral beliefs, has influenced political values in the United States, including liberty, work ethic, and individualism. It is a combination of these values that have contributed to a frame of thinking of obesity as a preventable health risk. This frame centers focus on individual habits and therefore puts responsibility squarely on the shoulders of the overweight. A lack of successful weight loss must be blamed on a lack of self-discipline, work ethic, or responsible behavior. This way of thinking became the norm as obesity started receiving more attention by political elites and the media.

The number of overweight Americans started to rise sharply in the 1980s, and experts began warning of an obesity crisis by the early 1990s. A focus on reforming individual behavior become especially prevalent in the early 2000s when public health experts, the medical industry, and the media started framing obesity as an epidemic. In 2001, the U.S. Department of Health and Human Services released a surgeon general's report wherein they claimed that the numbers of overweight and obese Americans had reached epidemic levels (Office of the Surgeon General, 2001).

The dire message from the surgeon general sparked interest in the media. The mass media have played a role in framing obesity as an issue of personal responsibility by drawing on antiobesity research in their reporting. Antiobesity activists are those who focus their work on obesity as a serious public health problem. Since the early 2000s, the media have spread the message that obesity was an epidemic. They interviewed antiobesity health officials and researchers to provide support. Most public health experts were more than willing to work with the media to spread the news that personal changes are necessary.

Viewing obesity as an epidemic stemming from risky or excessive behavior puts weight gain in a similar category as smoking, drinking, or gambling. Traditional morality rejects these risky behaviors as sinful. This view is also consistent with the ideals of upward mobility. Being in good physical shape is associated with economic success and demonstrates a willingness to self-improve. Thus, maintaining a healthy weight has itself become a moral good. Culture has been adapting to this morality and pressure to diet, and cultivating a certain body type is rampant.

In response to the antiobesity movement, a rights-based movement promoting "fat acceptance" has emerged. This movement draws on a different moral foundation to focus its activism. The change in focus from traditional to secular morality generates a completely different narrative about obesity. Although those promoting this view of obesity are less likely to explicitly reference religious morality, the connection to secular morality is still important to consider because adherents are fighting against discriminatory attitudes and behavior. Secular morality draws upon many similar themes as traditional morality, such as the Ten Commandments and the Golden Rule, but it differentiates itself by focusing on values that promote a better existence in the here and now. The political values of equality, tolerance, and fairness are key principles for "fat acceptance." Advocates argue that obesity is a type of body diversity among people, linking weight to other genetic characteristics such as gender and race.

Activists in the fat acceptance camp reject the notion that obesity is an epidemic. Rather, they point to the genetic and biological bases of obesity. These scholars and activists think that weight obsession, not obesity is the real problem (Saguy & Riley, 2005: 874). The focus on obesity as an epidemic is said to have led to *fat phobia* in society. Indeed, some suggest that discrimination based on weight is the last acceptable prejudice in society (Haider-Markel & Joslyn, 2018). There is a concern that, by primarily focusing on individual responsibility, we have added to the psychological and social stress placed on the overweight.

Overweight children and adolescents have struggled with body image and self-esteem. This in turn leads to an increased likelihood of developing eating disorders or depression. Those viewing obesity through a secular moral frame fear that overweight children are not developing friendships normally because of the stigma associated with their weight. Romantic relationships are likewise effected. Preoccupation with standards of beauty artificially generated by advertisers, movie producers, and the like promote feelings of insecurity and unattractiveness. This can be especially true for the overweight. However, looking at obesity as diversity is a strategy to create a wider range of what is considered beautiful.

Discrimination in the workplace is another major concern. If overweight individuals are viewed as lazy, gluttonous, or irresponsible, then employers will be less likely to hire them. This is especially the case when the job calls for manual labor. Promotions, especially into executive positions, become less likely either because the overweight are ignored or because they themselves do not think they deserve it. Discrimination might also occur among employees, creating an unsafe environment. Women face an even greater chance of workplace discrimination because society is generally harsher toward overweight women.

Antiobesity elites and researchers, as well as those in support of a personal responsibility frame, are skeptical of these critiques. Fat acceptance is tantamount to accepting bad behavior, according to antiobesity activists like Michael Fumento: "The fat acceptance people . . . have turned what had been two of the Seven Deadly Sins—sloth and gluttony—into both a right and a badge of honor. . . . That's a sin in and of itself" (Fumento, 1997: 130).

Another group driven by secular morality has emerged criticizing the biology-based obesity frame. This group focuses on the impact of the environment on obesity. They worry about exacerbating stigma by promoting that the overweight are inherently different from "healthy" people. Since biology is often seen as immutable, the genetic approach can create pessimism and a sense of helplessness. Finally, the biological approach creates apathy toward health policy and other nonbiological efforts because they are not seen as being capable of having a meaningful effect.

Despite their criticism of the genetic approach, those favoring a look at the "food environment" share the secular moral foundation. They too worry about equality and tolerance but are more concerned with protecting the obese from the food industry and persuasive advertising. Overweight individuals are seen as victims of big business and other geographic and economic factors outside their control but within the purview of government policy.

The activists engaged in this battle often use the same evidence, framed differently, to support their respective claims. For instance, research has shown that overweight people tend to be downwardly mobile economically from their parents (Goldblatt, Moore, & Stunkard, 1965: 1043), and fatness tends to be associated with lower socioeconomic status (Sobal & Stunkard, 1989: 260). Does this show that overweight individuals struggle with taking on personal responsibility, or could it be that the overweight are less likely to attend college due to discrimination? Another explanation could be that because parents have bought into a traditional value system, they are less likely to pay for their child's educational expenses

(Crandall, 1991: 607–609). Right or wrong, political elites have proposed policy solutions based on both of these morality frameworks.

Depending on the value system adopted and on the attribution and frame utilized, different policy remedies naturally follow due to an intangible link between morality and attribution. They each provide a way to bring meaning into the world. A link between partisan and ideological preference, moral beliefs, and attributions (frames) can be seen across a variety of social issues. Conservatives have been shown to make individual-level attributions based on poverty and homosexuality and when considering support for capital punishment. Liberals, on the other hand, are far more likely to make situational claims that focus on the environment people are in (Haider-Markel & Joslyn, 2018).

When it comes to health policy surrounding obesity, ideology and partisanship have had mixed results. It could be that conservatives were more likely to have anti-fat attitudes, but this could be the result of a correlation with orthodox beliefs. Researchers have found that, contrary to what most health experts believe, Americans are not seriously concerned about obesity (Oliver & Lee, 2005: 923). Ideology and partisanship, therefore, are not good predictors of attitudes on obesity policy. The morality an individual conscribes to and the framework adopted are much better determinants. By understanding the moral arguments made by different groups, we gain greater understanding of the policy solutions they support.

By asserting that obesity is a form of diversity akin to race, gender, or disability, "fat acceptance" activists bring attention to the need for diversity training, greater social tolerance, and less discrimination based on weight. As a group, they are the least focused on policy. However, they support antidiscrimination laws, efforts to accommodate the overweight in public spaces, and other policies that effect how people are treated in society. A focus on changing workplace discrimination has also been made in recent years.

It has been those supporting "personal responsibility" and the effect of the environment that have been arguing over policy goals. As support mounts on both sides, groups try to persuade political elites to adopt policy in alignment with their frameworks and moral codes. Status quo proponents have been in favor of the antiobesity movement, as they have received most of the attention from public health officials, the medical community, and the media. The personal responsibility narrative has also been successfully tied to other morality policies including smoking, alcohol consumption, and gambling. The public is most familiar with this frame.

In response to this public view, health advocates and urban planners likewise blame television, cars, and urban sprawl for eliminating the need for exercise. Since health is a personal responsibility, policies supporting exercise have been a staple. City planners and other local officials and administrators have rushed to make their cities biking and walking friendly. Beautification projects have been utilized to make exercising more appealing, and parks have been developed to create a public space away from electronic screens. Schools across the United States have observed national "no TV" and "screen-free" weeks, designed to get children away from their electronics. First Lady Michelle Obama also took up the charge with her 2010 Let's Move campaign. Although the first lady's program had many other elements that included health awareness and ensuring access to healthy and affordable food, a large focus was on encouraging children to exercise.

Another policy prescription embedded with moral implications is the so-called sin tax—a tax on items considered undesirable or harmful to society. These taxes can be imposed on a wide range of good and services deemed by some to be harmful to communities, including cigarettes, liquor, and pornography. Sin taxes specifically crafted to combat obesity, mostly the sugar in soda, have been adopted in several cities across the United States. One of the most famous cases was over New York City Mayor Michael Bloomberg's 2012 proposal to ban sweetened drinks of more than 16 ounces. After the soda companies filed a lawsuit, Manhattan Supreme Court Justice Milton Tingling overturned the ban. However, other cities like Philadelphia, San Francisco, and Seattle have passed laws taxing sugar-sweetened soft drinks and other beverages at a higher rate.

Taxes on soda and other sweets are supposed to discourage people from excessively eating unhealthy food by consuming less of it as the cost increases. However, some worry that the result will constitute an unfair economic burden on the overweight as well as low income people, who disproportionality pay more taxes as a portion of their income. Some analysts also assert that sin taxes have very little effect on changing behavior, though other experts believe that they can be an effective driver of societal change.

Those supporting an environmental approach to policy focus on reforming businesses. Extra large portion sizes at restaurants and supermarkets, and super sized value meals at fast food chains have turned these establishments into villains. Works like Eric Schlosser's (2001) *Fast Food Nation* and Morgan Spurlock's influential documentary "Super-Size Me" have helped to place pressure on the food industry. The publicity helped to prompt law professors, as well as other legal experts, to bring lawsuits against fast-food restaurants for contributing to obesity. In response, McDonald's, as well as other companies, rolled out calorie transparent menus and healthy options for sides and drinks to try to curtail the negative attention. Advertising companies also have taken some of the heat for the consistency and persuasiveness of their marketing campaigns.

Finally, campaigns to address so-called food deserts have received increased support from a broad array of lawmakers and activists concerned with poverty and nutrition, especially in urban centers and rural areas. The Centers for Disease Control and Prevention (CDC) defines food deserts as areas that lack access to affordable fruits, vegetables, whole grains, low-fat milk, and other foods that make up the full range of a healthy diet (CDC, 2012). Some Americans live in communities and locations where the only easily accessible food comes from fast-food restaurants. A lack of options makes living a healthy lifestyle difficult, even if an individual really wants to lose weight.

Bronson P. Herrera

FURTHER READING

Centers for Disease Control and Prevention (CDC). 2012. "A Look Inside Food Deserts." Retrieved from https://www.cdc.gov/features/FoodDeserts/index.html
Crandall, Christian S. 1991. "Do Heavyweight Students Have More Difficulty Paying for College?" *Personality and Social Psychology Bulletin, 17*: 606–611.

Fumento, Michael. 1997. *The Fat of the Land: Our Health Problem Crisis and How Over-weight Americans Can Help Themselves.* New York: Penguin.

Goldblatt, Phillip B., Mary E. Moore, & Albert J. Stunkard. 1965. "Social Factors in Obesity." *Jama, 192*: 1039–1044.

Haider-Markel, Donald P., & Mark R. Joslyn. 2018. "'Nanny State' Politics: Causal Attributions About Obesity and Support for Regulation." *American Politics Research, 46*(2): 199–216.

New York Daily News. 2013. "Judge Halts Bloomberg's Large Soda Ban One Day Before It's Set to Go into Effect." Retrieved from http://www.nydailynews.com/new-york /bloomberg-soda-ban-national-article

New York Times. 2012. "Health Panel Approves Restriction on Sale of Large Sugary Drinks." Retrieved from http://www.nytimes.com/2012/09/14/nyregion/health -board-approves-bloombergs-soda-ban.html

Office of the Surgeon General. 2001. "The Surgeon General's Call to Action to Prevent and Decrease Overweight and Obesity." Retrieved from https://www.ncbi.nlm.nih .gov/books/NBK44206

Oliver, J. Eric. 2005. *Fat Politics: The Real Story Behind America's Obesity Epidemic.* New York: Oxford University Press.

Oliver, J. Eric, & Taeku Lee. 2005. "Public Opinion and the Politics of Obesity in America." *Journal of Health Politics, Policy and Law, 30*: 923–954.

Rasmussen, David W. 2019. "The Rights/Development Nexus: Sen, Olson, and the Obesity Rights Movement." *Social Science Quarterly.* https://doi.org/10.1111/ssqu.12577

Saguy, Abigail C., & Kevin W. Riley. 2005. "Weighing Both Sides: Morality, Mortality, and Framing Contests over Obesity." *Journal of Health Politics, Policy and Law, 30*: 869–923.

Schlosser, Eric. 2001. *Fast Food Nation: The Dark Side of the All-American Meal.* New York: Houghton Mifflin Harcourt.

Sobal, Jeffery, & Albert J. Stunkard. 1989. "Socioeconomic Status and Obesity: A Review of the Literature." *Psychological Bulletin, 105*: 260.

Spurlock, Morgan. 2004. *Super Size Me.* Documentary Film. New York: Hart Sharp Video.

Whitehouse. 2016. "About Let's Move." Retrieved from https://letsmove.obamawhitehouse .archives.gov.

Organ Donation

Organ transplantation is one of medicine's greatest achievements. Since the first successful human kidney transplant in 1954, extraordinary progress has been made in reducing the likelihood that an organ is rejected, the preservation of tissue and organs, surgical techniques, and the organization and management of organ procurement and distribution. As a result, every year, thousands of patients with an organ that is failing or that has been damaged by injury or disease receive a replacement organ recovered from a deceased donor or given by a living donor. The clinical benefits of organ transplantation provide strong grounds in favor of this practice. Yet this "miracle" is steeped in ethical issues and controversy. In 1966, the first major international conference focusing on the ethical problems of organ donation and transplantation was held in London. Conference attendees discussed a set of critical ethical questions that very early on emerged among the transplant community and beyond. Is it ethical to cause unnecessary harm to a person so that another can receive a new organ? How should we make sure that a person's decision to donate is free from coercion? What definition of death should be adopted so that organs can be ethically removed from a body before they become unviable? Should we allow organ donors to receive financial compensation? In the following several decades, these critical ethical issues have animated a lively and often heated debate, and they still inspire ongoing controversies among very vocal actors and groups, including ethicists, philosophers, surgeons, and other health care professionals, patient and donor advocates, and lawmakers.

A "BASIC QUALITATIVE SHIFT" IN PHYSICIANS' AIMS

Dr. Joseph Murray, who performed the first successful kidney transplant, confessed to being deeply troubled by the ethical problem of removing an organ from a healthy person, even if doing so would save another person's life. Murray's concern illustrates one of the core ethical tensions that would underlie several of the subsequent debates and controversies, the dichotomy between deontological ethical foundations—in this case, adhering to the "first do no harm" imperative—and a consequentialist approach according to which the morality of an act depends on its consequences and that therefore may allow someone to be harmed if that implies a greater benefit for someone else. Embracing organ transplantation required, in Dr. Murray's words, "a basic qualitative shift" in physicians' aims (quoted in Jonsen, 2012: 264). The clinical success of transplantation also forced debates within religious traditions such as Christianity and Judaism that for centuries had prohibited "mutilations" of otherwise healthy bodies. As scholar Albert Jonsen has pointed out, the shift that occurred produced a "reconceptualization of transplantation from 'mutilation' to 'donation,'" an "act of virtue" consistent with the "highest moral priority to the saving of life" (Jonsen, 2003).

THE "DEAD DONOR RULE" AND CONTROVERSIES OVER THE DEFINITION OF DEATH

Although healthy people have two kidneys and can live with only one, the donation of vital organs such as the heart, the entire liver, or both kidneys are admissible only from deceased donors. The so-called dead donor rule, that is, the deontic principle according to which it is morally wrong to cause a person to die by removing organs, has been a cornerstone in the ethics of organ transplantation since the beginning. Prior to advances in pulmonary and cardiac support devices, an individual was considered dead after cardiopulmonary arrest. In 1968, an ad hoc committee chaired by Henry Beecher at Harvard Medical School suggested revisions to the definition of death that would allow recovering organs from individuals who have suffered devastating neurological damage but whose organs are still viable enough to be transplanted.

The 1981 Uniform Determination of Death Act formally codified into law the "brain death" criterion, according to which "we recognize as dead an individual whose loss of brain functions is complete and irreversible" (quoted in Barclay, 1981). According to philosopher Peter Singer, the brain death criterion represented a fundamental shift in our conception of life and death: "[W]e can now take warm pulsating human beings, declare them dead . . . and cut out their hearts and other organs" (Singer, 1994). Although the brain death criterion appears to be broadly accepted in the transplant community, the concept has been challenged on ethical grounds.

Some philosophers and bioethicists such as Robert Veatch have argued that the current criterion is too restrictive and that individuals (or their surrogates) who have expressed a wish to give their organs should be allowed to donate even when the loss of brain function is not complete, as long as they are in a state of permanent unconsciousness (Veatch, 1989). Building their argument upon the principle of respect for autonomy and the individual's rights to die in a dignified way and donate their organs, Jan Bollen and coauthors have suggested that organ donation could be combined with euthanasia (Bollen et al., 2016). The main argument against these ideas is that they would violate the dead donor rule because organs would be obtained from patients who are not yet dead.

Another set of arguments opposing brain death criteria challenge its basic premise that the cessation of brain function equates to the death of a person. The prominent neurologist Alan Shewmon argued that "the integrative functions of the brain . . . are not strictly necessary for, much less constitute, the life of an organism as a whole" and that "the body without brain function is surely very sick and disabled, but not dead" (Shewmon, 2001). In a 2003 article, Robert Truog and Walter Robinson wrote that the concept of cerebral death "fails to correspond to any coherent biological or philosophical understanding of death" (Truog & Robinson, 2003). If these objections are accepted, they imply that the brain death criterion violates the dead donor rule. Some, including Robert Truog and Franklin Miller, have suggested that we should simply abandon the dead donor rule because "the rule has provided misleading ethical cover that cannot withstand careful scrutiny" (Truog & Miller, 2008).

The lack of consensus about both the definition of death and the criteria to be used to determine when a person should be considered dead led bioethicists Robert Veatch and Lainie Ross to propose yet another solution. They have argued that, although society should establish a default rule, individuals should be given the possibility to choose among the various possible definitions of death that corresponds to their religious, spiritual, or cultural beliefs (Veatch & Ross, 2016: 13). In this spirit, the states of New Jersey and New York recognize religious or conscientious exceptions to standard death determination.

THE QUESTION OF CONSENT

Consistent with the prevailing view that organ donation fosters socially important values such as altruism and benevolence, the 1968 Uniform Anatomical Gift Act (UAGA) established that competent adults who have received and understand all the relevant information may consent to have their organs donated after their death; moreover, the removal of organs for donation could be authorized by designated family members. Since 1968, the UAGA has been periodically revised to accommodate developments in medicine and transplantation. Some critical ethical tensions have emerged after the latest revision in 2006, which introduced more limits to family members overriding their loved one's consent to donate. Critical and palliative care physician Michael DeVita and bioethicist Arthur Caplan have criticized the 2006 revision of UAGA, arguing that "it prioritizes care for the potential donor organs over care and comfort for the dying person" (DeVita & Caplan, 2007: 876). These tensions are part of a broader debate regarding how consent to donate organs postmortem should be expressed. In the United States, UAGA prescribes that consent must be given explicitly, implying that in the absence of a valid explicit expression of consent, the default is that the person does not wish to donate organs.

Some ethicists, however, argue that explicit consent is not necessary for organ donation. In a 1983 article that generated much discussion, Arthur Caplan argued in favor of a regime where everyone is assumed to be willing to donate their organs upon their death, unless the person or their family has explicitly objected (Caplan,

1983). Caplan asserted that because the majority of Americans are in favor of donating their organs, an "opt-out" system would result in more transplants and in more lives saved while still respecting individual preferences. Some have taken an even stronger stance, arguing that the moral imperative to save lives implies that it is immoral to decline consent for donating one's organs. Critics of presumed consent have vigorously pushed back, arguing that opt-out regimes violate the fundamental ethical principles of respect for autonomy and personal integrity and that they are too coercive. The ethics committee of the U.S. Organ Procurement and Transplantation Network (OPTN) reported in 1993 that "it is unadvisable to pursue the policy of presumed consent" and that "the policy stands to contradict a profound respect a majority of Americans reserve for the value of individualism" (Dennis, 1994: 17). There have been several attempts to introduce presumed consent in the United States, including in Virginia in 1981, in California and New York in 2010, in Colorado and Pennsylvania in 2011 and 2014, respectively, and in Connecticut and Texas in 2017. All of these attempts failed because they are perceived to be contrary to the American ethical, religious, and legal tradition, especially concerning individuals (Samuel, 2017).

The ethical principle of respect for autonomy inspires also the requirement that living donor consent should be informed and free from coercion or undue influence. Although there is full agreement on the principles, some have expressed concern that the principles might not be always receiving full actual application. In particular, consent might not be fully informed due to the scarcity of comprehensive longitudinal studies on the long-term effects of organ donation on the donor's health and financial outcomes. Also, choices might be manipulated by specific ways in which information and requests are framed. Moreover, donors who are biologically or otherwise related to the patient might be effectively coerced into consenting to donate by social or self-generated pressure; the ethical concern that consent must be free from coercion is so strong that transplant teams may provide a "medical excuse," that is, a statement indicating the person's actual or even fictitious unsuitability to donate.

COMPENSATING ORGAN DONORS?

At the end of 2017, UNOS data indicate that about 115,000 patients were waiting for an organ in the United States, up from 84,000 in 2000. This trend indicates a large and growing gap between the demand for organs and the available supply. Between 5,000 and 10,000 patients every year drop out of the waiting list because they either die or are too sick to receive a transplant. One of the most ethically contested policy solutions to the organ shortage is allowing organ donors to receive financial compensation. Currently, the 1984 National Organ Transplant Act (NOTA) prohibits the transfer of human organs for "valuable consideration," punishing violators with fines and prison time. In fact, the two core ethical principles that inspired NOTA are that organs should always be donated and that no financial compensation can be given to donors (except to cover travel, lost wages, and medical costs). Economist and Nobel laureate Alvin Roth includes the sale of organs among so-called repugnant transactions, that is, exchanges that somebody would like to engage in but that third parties consider immoral and wish to prohibit (Roth, 2007). Opponents of compensating organ donors argue that the practice would run counter to the principles of volunteerism and "gift relationship" on which the U.S. organ procurement and distribution system is founded. More specifically, opposition to incentives rests on concerns of exploitation, coercion, distributive justice, and violation of human dignity from the "commodification" of the human body (Satz, 2010). In the words of transplant surgeon Francis Delmonico and coauthors, "[Payments are] ethically unacceptable . . . despite the purported benefits of such a sale for both the buyer and the seller. . . . Fundamental truths of our society, life and liberty, should not have monetary price" (Delmonico et al., 2002: 1189). Economics Nobel laureate Gary Becker and coauthor Julio Elias have suggested that a payment of $15,000 would eliminate the kidney shortage. Becker and Elias take a fundamentally utilitarian perspective and argue that payments would be ethically justified because they would potentially be saving thousands of lives while providing poor individuals with resources (Becker & Elias, 2007).

A consequentialist approach founded on the ethical value of saving lives is indeed the main argument adopted by proponents of payments to donors. Sally Satel, a psychiatrist, a recipient of two kidney transplants, and a longtime proponent of compensating organ donors, argues that if altruism is the only incentive we provide to donors, it means that thousands will die every year waiting for a kidney (Satel, 2008). Recent studies aim to better characterize Americans' ethical views toward organ donor payments and other morally repugnant transactions. One of the goals of these studies is to determine whether the ethical concerns regard aspects that could be potentially addressed with appropriate policy design (e.g., a government agency could compensate donors and ensure that organs are distributed according to need and not income) or whether instead the opposition is deontological (e.g., Americans might believe that paying donors is wrong because it violates human dignity). In recent years, the opposite positions have found some middle ground in recognizing that donating an organ should not leave the donor worse off. In fact, some suggest a moral obligation covering the donor costs of travel, lodging, medical expenses, lost wages, and costs for dependent care (Delmonico et al., 2015).

REFORMS MUST OVERCOME MORAL REPUGNANCE

Arguably the most significant innovation in the organ transplant sphere in the past decade is represented by so-called kidney exchange. In such an exchange, an incompatible donor–recipient pair is matched to another pair for a "swap," whereby each donor gives a kidney to the other pair's recipient; a single, nondirected donation may also start a "chain" of exchanges. Although participants in a kidney exchange enjoy mutual benefits, the transaction has not raised moral objections. In fact, the act of Congress that in 2007 amended NOTA to clarify the legality of "human paired donations" passed without any opposition. The success of kidney exchanges, which currently account for over 10 percent of living-donor kidney transplants in the United States, illustrates the importance of innovations that overcome constraints posed by ethical concerns.

Mario Macis

FURTHER READING

Barclay, W. R. 1981. "Guidelines for the Determination of Death." *JAMA*, *246*(19): 2194.

Barker, C. F., & J. F. Markmann. 2013. "Historical Overview of Transplantation." *Cold Spring Harbor Perspectives in Medicine*, *3*(4): a014977.

Beauchamp, T. L., & J. F. Childress. 2001. *Principles of Biomedical Ethics*. New York: Oxford University Press.

Becker, G. S., & J. J. Elias. 2007. "Introducing Incentives in the Market for Live and Cadaveric Organ Donations." *The Journal of Economic Perspectives*, *21*(3), 3–24.

Bollen, J., R. Ten Hoopen, D. Ysebaert, W. van Mook, & E. van Heurn. 2016. "Legal and Ethical Aspects of Organ Donation After Euthanasia in Belgium and the Netherlands." *Journal of Medical Ethics*: medethics-2015.

Caplan, A. L. 1983. "Organ Transplants: The Costs of Success." *Hastings Center Report*, *13*(6): 23–32.

Delmonico, F. L., R. Arnold, N. Scheper-Hughes, L. A. Siminoff, J. Kahn, & S. J. Youngner. 2002. "Ethical Incentives—Not Payment—for Organ Donation." *N Engl J Med*, *346*(25): 2002–2005.

Delmonico, F. L., D. Martin, B. Domínguez-Gil, E. Muller, V. Jha, A. Levin, G. M. Danovitch, & A. M. Capron. 2015. "Living and Deceased Organ Donation Should Be Financially Neutral Acts." *American Journal of Transplantation*, *15*(5): 1187–1191.

Dennis, J. M., P. Hanson, & R. M. Veatch. 1994. "An Evaluation of the Ethics of Presumed Consent and a Proposal Based on Required Response." *UNOS Update*, *10*(2): 16–21.

DeVita, M. A., & A. L. Caplan. 2007. "Caring for Organs or for Patients? Ethical Concerns About the Uniform Anatomical Gift Act (2006)." *Annals of Internal Medicine*, *147*(12): 876–879.

Durand, C. M., D. Segev, & J. Sugarman. 2016. "Realizing HOPE: The Ethics of Organ Transplantation from HIV-Positive Donors." *Annals of Internal Medicine*, *165*(2): 138–142.

Gentry, S., E. Chow, A. Massie, & D. Segev. 2015. "Gerrymandering for Justice: Redistricting US Liver Allocation." *Interfaces*, *45*(5): 462–480.

Goodwin, M. 2006. *Black Markets: The Supply and Demand of Body Parts*. Cambridge: Cambridge University Press.

Healy, K., & K. D. Krawiec. 2017. "Repugnance Management and Transactions in the Body." *American Economic Review*, *107*(5): 86–90.

Johnson, E. J., & D. Goldstein. 2003. "Do Defaults Save Lives?" *Science*, *302*(5649): 1338–1339.

Jonsen, A. R. 2012. "The Ethics of Organ Transplantation: A Brief History." *Virtual Mentor*, *14*(3): 264.

Jonsen, A. R. 2003. *The Birth of Bioethics*. New York: Oxford University Press.

Lavee, J., T. Ashkenazi, G. Gurman, & D. Steinberg. 2010. "A New Law for Allocation of Donor Organs in Israel." *The Lancet*, *375*(9720): 1131–1133.

Leider, S., & A. E. Roth. 2010. "Kidneys for Sale: Who Disapproves, and Why?" *American Journal of Transplantation*, *10*(5): 1221–1227.

Liverman, C. T., & J. F. Childress. (Eds.). 2006. *Organ Donation: Opportunities for Action*. Washington, DC: National Academies Press.

Potts, M., P. A. Byrne, & R. G. Nilges. (Eds.). 2001. *Beyond Brain Death: The Case Against Brain Based Criteria for Human Death*. Boston: Kluwer Academic.

Rees, M. A., T. B. Dunn, C. S. Kuhr, C. L. Marsh, J. Rogers, S. E. Rees, A. Cicero, L. J. Reece, A. E. Roth, O. Ekwenna, & D. E. Fumo. 2017. "Kidney Exchange to Overcome Financial Barriers to Kidney Transplantation." *American Journal of Transplantation, 17*(3): 782–790.

Roth, A. E. 2015. *Who Gets What—and Why*. New York: Houghton Mifflin Harcourt.

Roth, A. E. 2007. "Repugnance as a Constraint on Markets." *Journal of Economic Perspectives, 21*(3): 37–58.

Samuel, L. "To Solve Organ Shortage, States Consider 'Opt-out' Organ Donation Laws." *Stat News*, July 6. Retrieved from https://www.statnews.com/2017/07/06/opt-solution-organ-shortage

Sandel, M. J. 2012. *What Money Can't Buy: The Moral Limits of Markets*. New York: Macmillan.

Satel, S. L. (Ed.). 2008. *When Altruism Isn't Enough: The Case for Compensating Kidney Donors*. Washington, DC: AEI Press.

Satel, S., & D. C. Cronin. 2015. "Time to Test Incentives to Increase Organ Donation." *JAMA Internal Medicine, 175*(8): 1329–1330.

Satz, D. 2010. *Why Some Things Should Not Be for Sale: The Moral Limits of Markets*. New York: Oxford University Press.

Shewmon, D. A. 2001, January. "The Brain and Somatic Integration: Insights into the Standard Biological Rationale for Equating 'Brain Death' with Death." *The Journal of Medicine and Philosophy: A Forum for Bioethics and Philosophy of Medicine, 26*(5): 457–478.

Singer, P. 1994. *The Oxford Reader on Ethics*. New York: Oxford University Press.

Starzl, T. E. 2000. "History of Clinical Transplantation." *World Journal of Surgery, 24*(7): 759–782.

Truog, R. D., & W. M. Robinson. (Eds.). 2003. "Role of Brain Death and the Dead-donor Rule in the Ethics of Organ Transplantation." *Critical Care Medicine, 31*(9): 2391–2396.

Truog, R. D., & F. G. Miller. 2008. "The Dead Donor Rule and Organ Transplantation." *New England Journal of Medicine, 359*(7): 674–675.

Veatch, R. M. (rev. ed.). 1989. *Death, Dying, and the Biological Revolution*. New Haven, CT: Yale University Press.

Veatch, R. M., & L. F. Ross. 2016. *Defining Death: The Case for Choice*. Washington, DC: Georgetown University Press.

Weir, R. F. (Ed.). 1998. *Stored Tissue Samples: Ethical, Legal, and Public Policy Implications*. Iowa City: University of Iowa Press.

Wolstenholme, G. E. W., & M. O'Connor. (Eds.). 1966. *Law and Ethics of Transplantation*. London: J & A Churchill.

Police Use of Force

The President's Task Force on 21st Century Policing, appointed in 2014 by President Barack Obama to study policing, was a response to increased public anger and media scrutiny concerning the use of force by law enforcement, especially in interactions with African American individuals and communities. As the Task Force noted, however, the use of force by the police is not in itself misconduct. In fact, the use of force, even lethal force, may be both legally and ethically justified in the protection of the public. Understanding the distinction between moral responsibility and culpability in a particular incidence of lethal force is determined by the policy on the use of force and the validity of the rationale for using force. For example, an officer may be morally responsible for the use of force but not to blame based on the physical threat a suspect posed. The officer's use of force in the performance of law enforcement duties may also be found to be legally justified if enacted in accordance with policy. However, the validity of the rationale and the estimation of threat are subject to a considerable degree of interpretation. Democratic policing is paradoxical in that force is used to maintain peace. Therefore it is highly problematic if the lives at hand are not equally valued.

Many studies over the years have demonstrated that the protection provided by the police is not applied equally across all communities. A 2015 report by Amnesty International demonstrates the increasing rate of the use of force by police officers in the United States and highlights a pattern of racial disparities in deadly force exercised by the police. Black people experienced lethal force at a rate of 7.69 per million Americans in 2015 and 6.66 per million Americans in 2016. The lethal force rate for Hispanic/Latino/a people was 3.45 per million Americans in 2015 and 3.23 per million in 2016. In 2015, 5.49 Native American people per million were killed by U.S. police and 10.13 per million in 2016, a rate that doubled over the course of a single year (an increase attributed to amplified clashes between law enforcement and environmental activists on Native America reservation lands). Meanwhile, 2.95 per million white people in 2015 and 2.9 per million white people in 2016 were killed by police. The lowest rate of lethal force reported during this period is for Asian/Pacific Islanders, 1.34 per million in 2015 and 1.17 per million in 2016. In addition, 15- to 34-year-old black males were nine times more likely to be subject to lethal force than other Americans in 2016 (Swain & McCarthy, 2017). Other research utilizing mortality data suggests that the federal government significantly underreports incidents of lethal force (Feldman et al., 2017).

CONTINUUM OF FORCE

Given moral and legal concerns about the use of force by law enforcement, police departments follow a use of force continuum—policies that guide officers in the use of force. Officer training conditions officers to estimate and respond with a level of force deemed appropriate in a given circumstance based on an escalating series of actions. These strategies range from the mere presence of an officer exerting authority by verbal command to deadly force. The use of force policies and rates vary considerably across law enforcement agencies. A 2011 study of deadly force by the police found that citizen injury rates in less than lethal interactions with the police range from 17 to 64 percent; meanwhile, the officer injury rate when less than lethal force is applied varies from 10 to 20 percent (Bulman, 2011).

Organized movements aimed at restraining the police use of force argue that physical force is too often used and more likely to be wielded against nonwhites. They identify several policies that have the potential to constrain the use of force and reduce harm, and they outline what are referenced as "meaningful protections against police violence" (Nix et al., 2017). The policies they specify are as follows:

- De-escalation required
- Continuum of force policy and training
- Banning of chokeholds and strangleholds
- Warning before shooting required
- hooting at moving vehicles restricted
- All other means exhausted before lethal force is justified required
- Duty to intervene
- Comprehensive reporting required

They contend that police departments that are more restrictive of the use of force have fewer incidents of police violence and that this also results in fewer incidents of violence toward the police.

WHO IS BEING POLICED?

When considering the appropriateness of force and the validity of threat assessments, mental health and race are principal factors. If some segments of the population are disproportionately subjected to police surveillance and the use of force, the moral support for using force to protect citizens is weakened. Ample research suggests that police use of force is more likely when police encounter persons with mental health issues or individuals who are members of racial and ethnic minority groups (see, e.g., Nix et al., 2017).

A 2015 report by the Treatment Advocacy Center argues that, partly as a result of cuts to the mental health treatment hospital system dating back to the 1980s, 1 out of every 10 law enforcement responses address a person in mental health crisis, and one-fourth of the fatal encounters with police end the life of a person with mental illness (Fuller at al., 2015). Research suggests that police officers are now the most likely to deal with mental health emergencies and are the main sources of referral to treatment. In fact, evidence suggests that people with mental health issues face a risk six times greater than the general public of deadly force at the hands of police. A 2016 American Public Health Association study is one of many such research projects documenting how African Americans are at increased risk of victimization by both police and criminal predators (Buehler, 2017; Ochs, 2011). Furthermore, "get tough" policies and "hot spots" policing contribute to officer misconduct and focus police efforts on communities of color, particularly low-income communities (Epp et al, 2014; Walker & Archbold, 2019).

Police actions have far-ranging implications and can affect tensions in communities, trigger riots, impose substantial costs on people, and shape perceptions of democratic values. Many observers believe, however, that the political incorporation of black people in local politics reduces the frequency and severity of use-of-force incidents, reduces policing costs, mitigates legal risks, and enhances the legitimacy of law enforcement (Ochs, 2011). They assert that black mayors change how police interact with the black community, implement policies more responsive to black communities, and hold police administrations accountable to the concerns of black communities in a manner that engenders trust, credibility, and legitimacy and that enhances black satisfaction with public services. Similarly, minority representation on city councils can improve trust in government and contribute to the legitimacy of the law and of law enforcement in so-called majority–minority communities.

Hubert Blalock's (1965) racial threat hypothesis posits a curvilinear relationship between population demographics and policies and practices of social control. The fear of crime is associated with the subpopulation deemed "other" or threatening, irrespective of the actual instances of criminal behavior. As the subpopulation grows and is perceived (at least in some quarters) as a threat to the existing social order, policies and practices are likely to become more oppressive up to the point at which the subpopulation is able to exert a meaningful degree of influence over policy. Absent adequate restraints, a considerable degree of force is more likely to be used to maintain order. And unstable social conditions are created when myths of "criminal" minorities pervade community perceptions and restrict economic and educational opportunities. These unstable social conditions are navigated by the police, and their actions determine the boundaries of inclusion and exclusion.

The differential crime hypothesis claims that blacks are subject to the law more often because they are more criminal. This speculation regarding the likelihood of criminal behavior mistakes the history of oppression in the United States with the character of its subjects. During the course of American history, the law has frequently been used to subjugate black people, from the period of enslavement, to Jim Crow, and to contemporary efforts to undermine or suppress voting rights. Black people are still significantly more likely to be stopped and searched by the police while walking, biking, or driving despite the fact that they are considerably less likely to be in violation of the law (Epp et al., 2014). Policies like "hot spot" policing are likely to amplify racially biased patterns of policing based on faulty assumptions about criminal tendencies.

The community violence thesis is another way of understanding how police–public interactions shape the relative risk of lethal force. Poverty isolation and racial segregation are structural inequalities with complex implications for people living in such communities. Some argue that police violence is a response to higher rates of violence in some communities. Certainly, those communities deserve police protection as much as any other in a democratic society. At the same time, communities that are densely populated, that lack economic and educational opportunities, and where incidents of domestic violence are often more commonly reported to the police represent threats to the community, as well as presenting some of the most difficult challenges for police work.

Historically, movements aimed at addressing the immorality of the disproportionate execution of deadly force (such as Black Lives Matter) have been met with considerable resistance from law enforcement agencies as well as from sectors of the public whose primary sympathies lie with the police. The desire to be "tough on crime" and to engage in a War on Drugs through the 1980s and 1990s has ensured that the dominant message is that people suspected of violating the law deserve harsh treatment.

REFORMS AND CONCLUSION

We grant the state the authority to exercise the legitimate use of violence to protect citizens and to maintain social order. As such, the legitimate use of force by the state is morally justified. Police officers and other law enforcement officials thereby morally use force in the name of the state when they are protecting citizens. However, the police use of force can be immoral if it is inequitable. The evidence suggests that may be the case in the United States, inspiring calls for reforms of policing.

A number of innovations, social trends, and variations across contexts affect lethal force. Body-worn cameras (BWCs) are among the more recent trends in the waves of reforms aimed at policing. Some argue that body cameras protect the police and the public by documenting encounters between them. However, there are a few challenges. First, cameras present a single, narrow lens on an incident. Second, technology can fail, and/or officers can forget or fail to turn the cameras on. Third, there are important bureaucratic concerns regarding how body cameras may be implemented in line with civil service protections. Fourth and most critically, body cameras are effective at reducing explicit bias but may in fact increase cognitive errors resulting from implicit bias. Indeed, a recent study found that those viewing bodycam footage versus those viewing patrol car footage of the same real-life incidents were less likely to place blame on the officer (Turner et al., 2019). In other words, body cameras alone will not address biased patterns in deadly force. The implication is that bias—perhaps often implicit bias—exists in policing and that training must be implemented to reduce such bias and restore equity. Many police departments, including the Las Vegas, Nevada, police department, have implemented implicit bias training. The implementation of the training has been associated with a decline in police use of force. Likewise, crisis intervention training (CIT) is one measure to address the criminalization of people with mental health issues and to direct these people to resources for help rather than sending them to jail. CIT programs have been implemented in limited ways in many cities across the United States, and preliminary evidence suggests that the safety of the police and of the public are positively impacted by CIT training.

Holona LeAnne Ochs

FURTHER READING

Alexander, Michelle. 2010. *The New Jim Crow*. New York: New Press

Balko, Radley. 2014. *Rise of the Warrior Cop*. New York: Public Affairs.

Blalock, Hubert M. 1965. *Toward a Theory of Minority Group Relations*. New York: Capricorn Books

Buehler, James W. 2017. "Racial/Ethnic Disparities in the Use of Lethal Force by US Police, 2010–2014." *American Journal of Public Health, 107*(2): 295–297.

Bulman, Philip. 2011. "Police Use of Force." *National Institute of Justice Journal, 267*: 4–11. Washington, DC. Retrieved from https://www.nij.gov/journals/267/pages /use-of-force.aspx. Cite last visited 11/1/17

"The Counted: People Killed by Police in the U.S." 2019. *The Guardian*, January 10. Retrieved from https://www.theguardian.com/us-news/ng-interactive/2015/jun/01 /the-counted-police-killings-us-database

Epp, Charles, Steven Maynard-Moody, & Donald Haider-Marke. 2014. *Pulled Over: How Police Stops Define Race and Citizenship*. Chicago: University of Chicago Press.

Feldman, J. M., S. Gruskin, B. Coull, & N. Krieger. 2017. "Correction: Quantifying Underreporting of Law-Enforcement-Related Deaths in United States Vital Statistics and News-Media-Based Data Sources: A Capture-Recapture Analysis." *PLOS Medicine, 14*(10): e1002449

Fridell, Lorie A. 2016. "Racial Aspects of Police Shootings: Reducing Both Bias and Counter Bias." *Criminology & Public Policy, 15*(2): 481–489.

Fuller, Doris A., H. Richard Lamb, Michael Biasotti, & John Snook. 2015. *Overlooked in the Undercounted: The Role of Mental Illness in Fatal Law Enforcement Encounters*. Retrieved from https://www.treatmentadvocacycenter.org/storage/documents /overlooked-in-the-undercounted.pdf

Goff, P., & K. Kahn. 2012. "Racial Bias in Policing: Why We Know Less Than We Should." *Social Issues and Policy Review, 6*(1): 177–210.

Jacobs, David. 1998. "The Determinants of Deadly Force: A Structural Analysis of Police Violence." *American Journal of Sociology, 103*(4): 837–862.

Lawrence, Regina G. 2000. *The Politics of Force*. Berkeley: University of California Press.

Miller, Seumas. 2016. *Shooting to Kill*. New York: Oxford University Press.

Nix, Justin, Bradley Campbell, Edward Byers, & Geoffrey Alpert. 2017. "A Bird's Eye View of Civilians Killed by Police in 2015." *Criminology & Public Policy, 16*(1): 309–340.

Ochs, Holona LeAnne. 2009. "Public Participation in Policing: The Impact of Citizen Oversight on the Incidence of Lethal Force over Time in the Largest U.S. Cities." *Justice Research and Policy, 11*(1): 105–140.

Ochs, Holona LeAnne. 2011. "The Politics of Inclusion: Black Political Incorporation and the Incidence of Lethal Force." *Journal of Ethnicity in Criminal Justice*, *9*(3): 238–265.

Rothstein, Richard. 2017. *The Color of Law*. New York: Norton.

Swain, John, & Ciara McCarthy. 2017. "Young Black Men Again Face Highest Rate of US Police Killings in 2016." *The Guardian,* January 8. Retrieved from https://www.theguardian.com/us-news/2017/jan/08/the-counted-police-killings-2016-young-black-men

Turner, Broderick L., Eugene M. Caruso, Mike A. Dilich, & Neal J. Roese. 2019. "Body Camera Footage Leads to Lower Judgments of Intent Than Dash Camera Footage." *Proceedings of the National Academy of Sciences.* https://doi.org/10.1073/pnas.1805928116

Walker, Samuel E., & Carol A. Archbold. 2019. *The New World of Police Accountability*. New York: Sage.

Wood, Jennifer D., & Amy C. Watson. 2017. "Improving Police Interventions During Mental Health-Related Encounters: Past, Present and Future." *Policing and Society*, *27*(3): 289–299.

Pornography

The legal history of pornography in the United States is intimately tied to, yet not exhausted by the discourse surrounding obscenity and free speech. Yet beyond the issue of whether pornographic material is protected speech are issues of harm, exploitation, and discrimination.

PORNOGRAPHY AND OBSCENITY

The First Amendment states: "Congress shall make no law . . . abridging the freedom of speech, or of the press." Yet there are exceptions. Speech that is "directed to inciting or producing imminent lawless action and is likely to incite or produce such action" is not protected, as noted in *Brandenburg v. Ohio* (1969). Beyond these limited restrictions, the Supreme Court has also carved out an exception for obscene material.

The first federal law restricting obscene material was the Comstock Act. Passed in 1873 by the 42nd Congress, this act restricted the trade, possession, manufacture, and distribution of "obscene" materials and materials of an "immoral nature." The ability of the government to regulate such material went unquestioned until *Roth v. United States* (1957). In Roth, the Supreme Court addressed the constitutionality of 18 U.S.C. 1461, a 1948 law based on the Comstock Act that made punishable the mailing of "obscene, lewd, lascivious, or filthy" materials.

Justice William Brennan, delivering the opinion of the Court, claimed that the First Amendment does not protect "obscene" speech. As justification, he offered a brief history of state and federal laws that prohibited various forms of speech, from obscenity to blasphemy. Brennan concluded that the First Amendment was never meant to protect every utterance. Its ostensible purpose is to assure the "unfettered interchange of ideas for bringing about political and social changes desired by the people." Thus, exceptions to First Amendment protections apply to those ideas or expressions that do not possess "redeeming social importance." Obscenity is unprotected, according to Brennan, since it is not valuable. Thus, the *Roth* opinion carved out an exception to First Amendment protections: Obscenity is not protected.

Justice Brennan offered the following definition of obscenity in *Roth*: "The standard for obscenity . . . is whether, to the average person, applying contemporary community standards, the dominant theme of the material, taken as a whole, appeals to prurient interest." Brennan's intention was to offer a definition that was neither too broad nor too narrow. Brennan wanted to include all and only obscene material. Brennan was sensitive to the problem that a vague, evaluative definition, such as that offered in *Roth,* could lead to overbroad applications, undue suppression of free speech, and perhaps even violation of fair notice, and he tried to be as precise as possible. He was clear that obscenity and sex were not synonymous. Material is not obscene merely by virtue of being sexually explicit. He did not want to suppress legitimate contributions to public discourse.

The problems the *Roth* decision created were numerous, however, and the Court spent the next 16 years wrestling with them. The definition was adapted as new cases were adjudicated. In *Jacobellis v. Ohio* (1964), the Court claimed obscene materials must be "utterly without redeeming social importance." The justices labored for years with defining obscenity, with Justice Potter Stewart famously claiming in exasperation in a concurring opinion in *Jacobellis* that "I know it when I see it."

In the early 1970s, the Court revisited the issue of obscenity in a pair of rulings, *Miller v. California* (1973) and *Paris Adult Theatre I v. Slayton* (1973). In *Miller*, the Court offered new guidelines for the determination of obscenity. The new guidelines consisted of three criteria for the determination of obscenity:

> a) whether 'the average person, applying contemporary standards' would find that the work, taken as a whole, appeals to the prurient interest . . . b) whether the work depicts or describes, in a patently offensive way, sexual conduct specifically defined by the applicable state law; and c) whether the work, taken as a whole, lacks serious literary, artistic, political, or scientific value.

In response to *Miller*, Justice Brennan had a change of heart and in *Paris Adult Theatre I v. Slayton* recanted his support for the Court's definition and application of obscenity standards. He claimed that this new standard, particularly the claim that a work merely needs to be shown to lack "serious" value, causes the statute to be overbroad and so suppresses a great deal of what ought to be protected expression. In addition, this standard failed "to provide adequate notice to persons who are engaged in the type of conduct the statute could be thought to proscribe" and invited the "arbitrary and erratic enforcement of the law." Brennan concluded, "[I]n absence of some very substantial interest in suppressing such speech, we can hardly condone the ill effects that seem to flow inevitably from the effort." These concerns continued to guide the legal discourse over pornography and obscenity.

PORNOGRAPHY AND HARM

In 1986, during the Presidency of Ronald Reagan, Attorney General Edwin Meese's commission on pornography released its final report. The commission considered several categories of pornography, including pornography denoted "sexually violent," "non-violent depicting degradation, domination, subordination, or humiliation," and "non-violent and non-degrading." The findings were as follows. With regard to the first two categories of sexually explicit material, it was found that viewers exposed to such material demonstrated "attitudinal changes." According to Meese's commission, "The attitudinal changes are numerous. Victims of rape or other forms of sexual violence are likely to be perceived by people so exposed as more responsible for the assault, as having suffered less injury, and as having been less degraded as a result of the experience." In addition, they are "likely to see the rapist or other sexual offender as less responsible for the act and as deserving of less stringent punishment." Finally, viewing such materials leads to "a greater acceptance of the 'rape myth' in its broader sense—that women enjoy being coerced into sexual activity, that they enjoy being physically hurt in sexual context." Works denoted "non-violent and non-degrading" failed to show a similar impact on viewers (Downs 1987).

The question in terms of governmental regulation is whether pornography crosses over from being mere speech to conduct, that is, does it incite violence or immanent lawless action? Can a causal link be demonstrated between the consumption of pornography and sexually violent, criminal behavior? Here the commission was clear: "We have not found . . . that the images people are exposed to are a greater cause of sexual violence than all or even many other possible causes." So, although the attitudinal changes are worrisome, and perhaps some connections between "substantial exposure" to this kind of material and sexual violence or coercion may be possibly determinable—so much so that the commission described pornography as "on the whole harmful to society"—the causal connection is not significant enough to warrant the regulation of pornography (Attorney General's Commission on Pornography, 1986). But public safety and health concerns do not end at sexual violence.

In 1983, Harold Freeman, president of the Hollywood Video Production Company, was arrested and prosecuted for five counts of pandering during production of his adult film, *Caught from Behind, Part II* (one count for each of the actresses hired to perform in the film). In 1988, his case was brought before the California Supreme Court. His conviction was overturned when the Court ruled that paying acting fees to perform in an adult film was not pandering.

The issue raised in *People v. Freeman* was whether the sexual conduct in pornographic films is protected by the First Amendment or whether it qualifies as sex for remuneration—in which case the conduct is prostitution, and the procuring of such services qualifies as pandering. The Court concluded that the fee paid was for acting services, and since the act itself—sex between consenting adults—"when considered aside from the payment of the acting fees [is] itself lawful," no lewd act was performed and so no pandering. In addition, "[T]he fact that the People concede that a film identical to that in this case could be made lawfully if the performers were not paid also belies the asserted 'public health' interest." Thus, *People v. Freeman* established that pornographic films are not forms of prostitution and that the production of such films does not pose a public health risk. The Court noted: "[T]he prosecution . . . under the pandering statute must be viewed as a somewhat transparent attempt at an 'end run' around the First Amendment and the state obscenity laws." The Court further asserted that should such a prosecution have been successful, the impact on speech would have been significant. They noted, "[T]o subject the producer and director of a nonobscene motion picture depicting sexual conduct to prosecution and punishment . . . would rather obviously place a substantial burden on the exercise of protected First Amendment rights." Insofar as there is no harming of public morals or public health interest, and the actions are not in themselves illegal, the production of a pornographic film is not an illegal act, nor does it include the illegal acts of pandering or prostitution.

However, debates about the nature and character of pornography continued to rage, especially with the rise of the Internet, which greatly expanded access to pornography. In 1996, Congress passed the Communications Decency Act (CDA), which, among other things, criminalized the transmission of materials that were "obscene or indecent" to persons known to be under 18. The regulation of "indecent" materials was challenged in *Reno v. American Civil Liberties Union* (1997), and there the Court ruled that the statute in question was overbroad. An additional law, the Child On-line Protection Act (COPA) of 1998, also sought to regulate the dissemination of pornographic material online. Drawing on the three-part test for obscenity set forth in *Miller v. California* (1973), COPA defined "material that is harmful to minors" as:

> any communication, picture, image, graphic image file, article, recording, writing, or other matter of any kind that is obscene or that—(A) the average person, applying contemporary community standards, would find, taking the material as a whole and with respect to minors, is designed to appeal to, or is designed to pander to, the prurient interest; (B) depicts, describes, or represents, in a manner patently offensive with respect to minors, an actual or simulated sexual act or sexual contact, an actual or simulated normal or perverted sexual act, or a lewd exhibition of the genitals or post-pubescent female breast; and (C) taken as a whole, lacks serious literary, artistic, political, or scientific value for minors.

However, COPA was immediately challenged in the courts. A court issued a preliminary injunction barring the enforcement of COPA because, as Attorney General John Ashcroft himself admitted in a 2002 writ of certiorari to the U.S. 3rd Circuit Court of Appeals, "it concluded that the statute was unlikely to survive strict scrutiny." The Third Circuit ultimately found that COPA's use of "contemporary community standards" to identify material harmful to minors was overbroad. The concern was predicated on the use of the Miller standards, specifically reliance on contemporary community standards, which the Court maintained would vary so greatly among communities as to leave the law unacceptably vague and ultimately force producers of online materials to abide by the standards of the nation's most conservative communities.

A similar issue resurfaced in 2005 in *Nitke v. Gonzalez* (2005), in which the obscenity component of the CDA was challenged for being overbroad, with plaintiffs citing the Miller standards as cause for concern. In this case, the District Court rejected the plaintiff's claim that contemporary community standards deviated significantly among communities, thus making the law overbroad in application. In 2006, the Supreme Court affirmed the decision. A successor to these laws, the Children's Internet Protection Act (CIPA) of 2000, tied federal funding to K–12 schools and libraries based on their use of Internet filters restricting access to various content—including obscene material as defined in Miller. This law was challenged but deemed constitutional insofar as it related to funding. Yet the most significant legal challenge to pornography stems from the claim that pornography is akin to discrimination.

PORNOGRAPHY AND GENDER DISCRIMINATION

Scholar Catharine MacKinnon has suggested that pornographers should be liable to civil suits. Her argument is that pornography is gender discrimination, and so it should be actionable as a violation of women's civil liberties.

Catharine MacKinnon's basic claim is that pornography "eroticizes hierarchy, it sexualizes inequality. . . . It institutionalizes the sexuality of male supremacy, fusing the eroticization of dominance and submission with the social construction of male and female" (MacKinnon, 1995: 59–60). She asserts that pornography creates a hierarchy of inequality and perpetuates a culture that excuses and rationalizes sexual aggression and dominance. Pornography bolsters sexual discrimination.

This approach doesn't rely on a contentious claim that pornographic material is not protected by the First Amendment. In fact, this position can presume that pornography is protected speech and argue for its suppression based on the fact that the First Amendment is not absolute. This position also does not rely on the link between porn and violence.

In 1983, feminist law professor Catharine MacKinnon and radical feminist Andrea Dworkin drafted an amendment to the Minneapolis Civil Rights ordinance that would construe pornography as gender discrimination. One year later, the Indianapolis City and County Council adopted a similar law. It was challenged in court and ruled unconstitutional by the Seventh Circuit Court of Appeals. The ordinance in question contained prohibitions on trafficking pornography, coercing others into performances, and forcing porn on anyone. Pornography was defined as:

> The graphic sexually explicit subordination of women, whether in pictures or in words, that also includes one or more of the following: (1) women are presented as sexual objects who enjoy pain or humiliation; or (2) women are presented as sexual objects who experience sexual pleasure in being raped; or (3) women are presented as sexual objects tied up or cut up or mutilated or bruised or physically hurt, or as dismembered or truncated or fragmented or severed into body parts; or (4) women are presented as being penetrated by objects or animals; or (5) women are presented in scenarios of degradation, injury abasement, torture, shown as filthy or inferior, bleeding bruised, or hurt in a context that makes these conditions sexual; or (6) women are presented as sexual objects from domination, conquest, violation, exploitation, possession, or use, or through postures or positions of servility or submission or display.

Writing for the Seventh Circuit, Justice Easterbrook declared the ordinance "unconstitutional." He argued that First Amendment protections to speech apply regardless of moral content. The federal government must remain neutral with respect to the content of speech. In this ordinance, given the definition of pornography, the court ruled that this ordinance sought to establish "an 'approved' view of women" and open up offenders to prosecution. In addition, the court noted that, even though it is most likely true that pornography affects its consumers, this is true of all speech; should that fact alone allow for governmental regulation, free speech would cease to exist. Thus the ordinance was struck down.

In a similar vein, in 1992 the Canadian Supreme Court, in *R v. Butler* (1992), interpreted Canadian antiobscenity laws to apply to "degrading" and "dehumanizing" depictions of women. Degrading and dehumanizing materials were deemed to fail the community standards test, and the moral corruption implicit therein was acknowledged to have a detrimental effect on society, in this case, a discriminatory effect on women. As one author noted, "Obscenity in Canada is now about gender equity" (Scales, 2007). In this case, the Canadian court decided to remove protections to speech when they functioned in a way that discriminated against women as well as other minority groups, following a rationale similar to hate speech laws found in Britain, such as the Public Orders Act of 1936, Race Relations Acts of 1965 and 1976, and the Public Order Act of 1986 (Easton, 1994). These laws restrict speech and make it prosecutable when its intent is to incite racial hatred or it has the effect of causing animus resulting in demonstrable harm. Pornography, it has been argued, is equally as harmful and functions as incitement to sexual hatred (Itzin, 1992: 585). However, in the United States, pornography is still protected speech insofar as it is nonobscene.

Jacob M. Held

FURTHER READING

American Psychological Association, Task Force on the Sexualization of Girls. 2007. *Report of the APA Task Force on the Sexualization of Girls*. Washington, DC: American Psychological Association. Retrieved from www.apa.org/pi/wpo/sexualization.html *R v. Butler*, 1992 1 S.C.R. 452.

Brandenburg v. Ohio, 1969.

Coleman, Lindsay, & Jacob Held (Eds.). 2014. *The Philosophy of Pornography: Contemporary Perspectives*. Lanham, MD: Rowman & Littlefield.

Dines, Gail. 2010. *Pornland: How Porn Has Hijacked Our Sexuality*. Boston: Beacon Press.

Downs, Donald. 1987. "The Attorney General's Commission and the New Politics of Pornography." *American Bar Foundation Research Journal, 12*(4): 641–679.

Downs, Donald Alexander. 1989. *The New Politics of Pornography*. Chicago: University of Chicago Press.

Dwyer, Susan (Ed.). 1995. *The Problem of Pornography*. Belmont, CA: Wadsworth.

Easton, Susan M. 1994. *The Problem of Pornography: Regulation and the Right to Free Speech*. New York: Routledge

Giesberg, Judith. 2017. *Sex and the Civil War: Soldiers, Pornography, and the Making of American Morality*. Chapel Hill: University of North Carolina Press.

Itzin, Catherine. 1992. "Pornography and Civil Liberties: Freedom, Harm, and Human Rights." In Catherine Itzin (Ed.), *Pornography: Women, Violence, and Civil Liberties: A Radical View*, 1–27. Oxford: Oxford University Press.

Jacobellis v. Ohio, 1964.

Kendrick, Walter. 1996. *The Secret Museum: Pornography in Modern Culture*. Berkeley: University of California Press.

Langton, Rae. 2009. *Sexual Solipsism: Philosophical Essays on Pornography and Objectification*. Oxford: Oxford University Press.

MacKinnon, Catharine A. 1995. "Frances Biddle's Sister: Pornography, Civil Rights, and Speech." In Susan Dwyer (Ed.), *The Problem of Pornography*, 55–70. Belmont, CA: Wadsworth.

MacKinnon, Catharine. 1996. *Only Words*. Cambridge, MA: Harvard University Press.

Maitra, Ishani, & Mary Kate McGowan (Eds.). 2012. *Speech & Harm: Controversies over Free Speech*. Oxford: Oxford University Press

McElroy, Wendy. 1995. *XXX: A Woman's Right to Pornography*. New York: St. Martin's Press.

Nussbaum, Martha C. 1999. *Sex and Social Justice*. New York: Oxford University Press.

Roth v. United States, 1957.

Scales, Ann. 2007. "Avoiding Constitutional Depression: Bad Attitudes and the Fate of Butler." In Drucilla Cornell (Ed.), *Feminism and Pornography*, 349–392. Oxford: Oxford University Press.

Soble, Alan. 2002. *Pornography, Sex and Feminism*. Amherst, NY: Prometheus Books.

Strossen, Nadine. 2000. *Defending Pornography: Free Speech, Sex, and the Fight for Women's Rights*. New York: New York University Press.

Poverty and Social Welfare

Since the advent of pensions for Civil War veterans, governments within the United States have taken steps to alleviate poverty for Americans. Moral considerations have been central in the debate over poverty and the necessity for government intervention to assist those in poverty. On the one hand, government assistance to the poor is viewed as a moral obligation consistent with most major religions, including Christianity. On the other hand, some attributions for poverty suggest that individual moral failings bring about poverty and that the poor therefore do not deserve to be helped.

A 2015 report by the National Low-Income Housing Coalition (NLIHC) illustrates the challenges faced by people attempting to move out of poverty in the United States. While people working 48–125 hours per week at the minimum wage rate just to afford a one-bedroom apartment struggle across every state, Puerto Rico, and Washington, D.C., notions of dependency, fraud, and exploitation used to justify control over "the poor" persist. Indeed, the neoliberal perspective that began to emerge on the political left during the 20th century favored a version of free-market capitalism where the economy could be shaped by influencing the labor market, which includes socially controlling the population, especially the poor, through government welfare programs and the criminal justice system. In this paternalistic perspective, the poor are weak but undeserving, and those opposed to generous government assistance capitalize on stereotypes, such as the racialized "welfare queen" that has more children to collect more social welfare benefits, as presented by Newt Gingrich in the 1990s.

Another form of the paternalistic perspective suggests that the poor are morally weak and that government assistance creates harm. Mary Theroux, researcher at the Independent Institute, claimed, in response to state legislative attempts to strengthen social welfare programs, that welfare programs "handicap people from learning to take care of their families and help them have a better life than they do" (Cadelgo, 2015).

Antipoverty advocates have long challenged welfare reform policies aimed at managing family size among people living in poverty. They have increasingly been joined by those who disagree with the way that such laws often attempt to limit family size while simultaneously limiting birth control access. Assistance is denied or reduced in 46 states when family size increases while receiving welfare benefits. Two states offer vouchers but no further cash assistance for additional children, and two other states provide flat grants regardless of family size. States have also recently been entertaining laws that make eligibility for welfare contingent upon drug screenings but do not necessarily offer or refer to treatment. These laws illustrate the logic of a desire to control "undeserving" people in poverty by managing their lives and were a central aspect of welfare reform efforts in the 1990s.

Many welfare stories told in the United States begin with or use the establishment of the welfare state in the United States as the touchstone. This state-centric view often uses indicators of well-being but fails to capture the evolution of practices that frame choice in the U.S. context. Social policy evolved through relationships between public authority and the people living within the territory under that authority. Welfare systems are, in essence, rituals that express and reinforce the boundaries of inclusion and the behaviors believed to promote certain values. Welfare practices categorize and sort people based on a view that suggests whether or not a person in poverty is dependent and deserving.

THEORETICAL APPROACHES

There are four distinct theories regarding the shape, design, formulation, and implementation of social policy. Each theory is distinct in terms of the causal relationships between poverty and economic development, the location of intervention efforts, and the prescriptions for intervention.

Social needs theory describes welfare policy as a function of demographic and economic conditions. It has its roots in psychology, specifically Abraham Maslow's hierarchy of needs, as detailed in his 1954 book *Motivation and Personality*. From this perspective, physiological needs are essential to survival, and higher-order needs cannot be achieved without the achievement of basic needs. Although humans are conceived of as having a basic desire for self-actualization, it is contingent upon basic needs being satisfied. Consequently, welfare policies are considered more or less progressive based on the extent to which they might address higher-order needs. However, it is important to note that recent cross-cultural research suggests that people can have strong social relationships and achieve self-actualization even when basic needs are not met. Perhaps more importantly, the notion of self-determination accommodates the neoliberal logic concerning both economic self-determination and paternalistic notions that social status is a function of character. The primary limitation of social needs theory is the deterministic approach that undermines the agency required for self-determination and the fundamental attribution error that is the faulty logic assigning behavior to character rather than to circumstance.

Subjugation theory identifies the heart of social policy in the class, race, and gender categories that assign social status and regulate political power. The highly influential book *Contract and Domination* (2007) by Carole Pateman and Charles Mills illustrates that there are at least two perspectives on domination. One perspective, argued by Mills, contends that although class, race, and gender have been central tenets of subjugation in contracting, contract theory offers some liberty between parties engaged in a contract. Contracts have come to define the disarticulated provision of welfare in the United States. If Charles Mills is correct, the neoliberal economic logic of a social welfare contract offers opportunities, contingent upon the privileges of gender, race, and class. However, if Carole Pateman is correct, social welfare contracts are structured, and the patterns and practices of governance are ordered according to race, gender, and class in order to maintain the status quo. In this case, we can see the government agreeing to provide benefits to the poor but only on the condition that the poor agree to being controlled, through welfare limits, drug tests, and work requirements, among other demands. In this case state antipoverty policy meets a moral obligation to help the poor but also gains control over those citizens whom it might not otherwise have.

Moralistic theories describe welfare policies as reflections of social values or attribute social problems to moral negligence. Distinctions between morality and immorality from this perspective are determined primarily by the emotional response to the experience. Alternatively, some view morality as relative and the determination of moral facts to be bound by human understanding, affected in large part by human emotion. Paternalistic influences on welfare politics come from both camps.

Elements of each of these theories are evident in the devolved and contractual nature of welfare policy in the United States. However, an examination of the evolution of welfare politics demonstrates that the manipulation of aspects of all these perspectives mobilizes different groups. The common theme is a story of subjugation of welfare recipients by promoting racial, gender, and class stereotypes regarding the needs and morality of the poor.

WAR ON POVERTY

Over the 50 years that we have been fighting the War on Poverty in the United States, the battlefields have shifted several times. President Lyndon Johnson's 1964 State of the Union speech defined poverty as a national problem but notably referenced state and local coordination and intergovernmental collaboration as essential for an effective attack. He then went on to describe our obligation to fight in battlefields in every private home and public office. Johnson proposed joint federal and local efforts using better education, job training, homes, health care, and better job opportunities as the weapons of war. The welfare discourse itself has changed very little, but there have been significant shifts in the authorities armed to regulate antipoverty efforts. The conflict itself is repeatedly about what is better and for whom.

The private or public nature of the problem of poverty remains a point of controversy, and the battlefields cross all sectors—public, private, and nonprofit. Yet a degree of consensus has formed, confining the conflict space to debates over the appropriate market solutions for what are widely believed to be private or individual initiatives. This consensus around the neoliberal ideal about poverty means that anything perceived or effectively defined as an attack on business is also perceived as restricting opportunities for people trying to move out of poverty.

Privatization is the weapon of choice in the regulation of opportunity within the current welfare context. Privatization refers to three distinct mechanisms diffusing the government monopoly on social services: (1) vouchers, (2) welfare transfers to the private sector (e.g., Work Opportunity Tax Credits [WOTC]), and (3) contracting out the provision of social service. It also reflects the extent to which poverty has come to be defined as an individual problem for which the promotion of business is the purported solution.

The progressive story line about welfare devolution and privatization is that opportunities for integrating people living in poverty into economic and social systems are maximized by the "flexibilities" of devolution and the "choices" it allows for in the market. The conservative story line is that devolution affords states greater flexibility in regulating people living in poverty so that institutional stability is not compromised. These intertwined story lines allow policy makers to claim they are taking the moral high ground in addressing poverty.

As the nonprofit sector becomes increasingly politicized, extremely wealthy philanthropists have engaged in public battles over the value of social wealth, or the value of resources a person has to meet individual social and emotional needs. In a July 26, 2013, *New York Times* article, Peter Buffet calls for a reexamination of humanism. He cautions against charitable organizations that are overly concerned with the return on investment (RoI) for their programs rather than with investment in ideas that change the processes that feed growing inequalities. Many of the editorial responses to Buffet's article defend the neoliberal rationale for charitable giving and social entrepreneurship, calling for an understanding of the appropriate balance between individual and social objectives in microfinance and economic development.

CONCLUSION

Poverty and attempts to reduce it have always been informed by moral understanding in American politics. However, notions of what is morally right in attempting to address poverty have become increasingly polarized. Morally based arguments have been embedded in fostering the view that those receiving government assistance are "undeserving" and "deviant" and that their use of government programs must therefore be tightly regulated.

We now know that individual participation in these restrictive programs that are meant to alleviate poverty tends to decrease the likelihood of participation in politics or civic organizations (Soss, Fording, & Schram, 2011). This means that the voices of those who have been in poverty and who have received government assistance are less likely to be heard by elected representatives making policy decisions. As such, most current social welfare programs serve to marginalize lower-class citizens politically, which may foster the growing economic inequality within our system. In short, poverty may become even more entrenched as private interests are distanced from people with little political power and low social status.

Holona LeAnne Ochs

FURTHER READING

Bolton, Megan, Elina Bravve, Emily Miller, Sheila Crowley, & Ellen Errico. 2015. "Out of Reach." Report by the National Low-Income Housing Coalition. Washington, DC. Retrieved from http://nlihc.org/sites/default/files/oor/OOR_2015_FULL.pdf

Cadelgo, Christopher. 2015. "California Legislator Says 'Welfare Queen' Law Has Got to Go." *Sacramento Bee*, February 22. Retrieved from https://www.sacbee.com/news/politics-government/capitol-alert/article10966202.html

Hall, Peter Dobkin. 2002. "Philanthropy, the Welfare State, and the Transformation of America's Public and Private Institutions, 1945–2000." In Lawrence Friedman & Mark McGarvie (Eds.), *Charity, Philanthropy, and Civility in American History.* Cambridge: Cambridge University Press.

Hall, Peter Dobkin. 2006. "A Historical Overview of Philanthropy, Voluntary Associations, and Nonprofit Organizations in the United States, 1600–2000." In Walter W. Powell & Richard Steinberg (Eds.), *The Nonprofit Sector.* New Haven, CT: Yale University Press.

Heclo, Hugh. 2001. "The Politics of Welfare Reform." In Rebecca Blank & Ron Haskins (Eds.), *The New World of Welfare.* Washington, DC: Brookings.

Herrick, John M., & Paul Stuart. 2005. *Encyclopedia of Social Welfare History in North America.* New York: Russell Sage.

Hilliard, David, & Cornell West. 2008. *The Black Panther Party: Service to the People Programs.* Albuquerque: New Mexico University Press.

Jordan-Zachery, Julia S. 2009. *Black Women, Cultural Images, and Social Policy.* New York: Routledge.

Katz, Michael. 1989. *The Undeserving Poor: From the War on Poverty to the War on Welfare.* New York: Pantheon.

Katz, Michael. 1996. *In the Shadow of the Poorhouse: A Social History of Welfare in America.* New York: Basic.

Maslow, Abraham H. 1954. *Motivation and Personality.* New York: Harper.

Mettler, Suzanne. 2018. *The Government–Citizen Disconnect.* New York: Russell Sage Foundation.

Mink, G., & R. Solinger. 2003. *Welfare: A Documentary History of U.S. Policy and Politics.* New York: New York University Press.

Nadasen, Premilla. 2004. *Welfare Warriors: The Welfare Rights Movement in the United States.* New York: Routledge.

Ochs, Holona L. 2015. *Privatizing the Polity.* Albany, NY: SUNY Press.

Ore, Tracy. 2003. *The Social Construction of Difference and Inequality.* New York: McGraw-Hill.

Pateman, Carole, & Charles Mills. 2007. *On Contract and Domination.* New York: Polity.

Piven, Frances Fox, & Richard A. Cloward. 1971. *Regulating the Poor: The Functions of Public Welfare.* New York: Vintage Books.

Skocpol, Theda. 1995. *Protecting Soldiers and Mothers: The Political Origins of Social Policy in the United States.* Cambridge: Harvard University Press.

Smith, Rogers. 1993. "Beyond Tocqueville, Myrdal, & Hartz: The Multiple Traditions in America." *American Political Science Review,* 87(3): 549–566.

Soss, Joe, Richard Fording, & Sanford Schram. 2011. *Disciplining the Poor: Neoliberal Paternalism and the Persistent Power of Race.* Chicago: University of Chicago Press.

Verney, Kevern, & Lee Sartain (Eds.). 2009. *Long Is the Way and Hard: One Hundred Years of the NAACP.* Little Rock: University of Arkansas Press.

Prayer and Religious Observance

There are three major frameworks for understanding debates about the legislation of prayer and religious observance in the United States. The Judeo-Christian heritage frame appeals to a common sense of history, while the social integration frame appeals to sociology. Both of these frameworks can be supported by people of faith and people with no religious beliefs because they argue for the social and moral good, not the supernatural power of public displays of religion. The third justification for publicly supported prayer and religious observance—the Psalm 33 framework—is a uniquely conservative Christian perspective, though it also welcomes Jewish supporters. People arguing for public observations of religion can choose elements of these frames to use in different debates—for example, debates about prayer in public schools or about the display of Christmas nativity scenes on government property.

At a time when religious conservatives are overrepresented among political conservatives, appeals to religion can have significant electoral consequences. For example, during his 2016 quest for the Oval Office, Republican Donald Trump repeatedly stated that if he won the election, "We're going to start saying 'Merry Christmas' again." Trump was specifically referencing what Fox News and other conservative voices in American life have described as a War on Christmas, a reference to the move among retailers and government agencies to be inclusive in holiday decorating and holiday greetings by using the words Happy Holidays or Season's Greetings to wish people well. Supporters of these nondenominational statements say that they reflect the reality that many Americans hold beliefs about religions that don't leave them with any religious attachment to Christmas. They also assert that such forms of agreement are entirely appropriate, given the U.S. Constitution's explicit language regarding the importance of separating church and state and not favoring one religious faith over another.

But some conservative Christians argue that this trend reflects a disturbing larger movement away from Christian teachings that has been detrimental to American society. They object to the idea of placing Christmas alongside Hanukkah, Kwanzaa, and the winter solstice, as if all the winter holidays were equally important in

American history and culture. They heard Trump's call to reinstate "Merry Christmas" as a recognition that American Christianity, as conservative Christians understand it, has been diminished by multiculturalism, political correctness, and government overreach, common targets of political conservatives' ire. As Trump told a conservative Christian audience in a closed-door meeting in June 2016, "[A]ll of your leaders are selling Christianity down the tubes, selling the evangelicals down the tubes, and it is a very, very bad thing that is happening." He told the crowd that, as president, he would ensure that their kind of Christianity got the respect to which it was entitled. Such promises affirm a particular conservative Christian version of a perceived decline in American greatness—that America was founded as a Christian nation, with high levels of religiosity throughout U.S. history, government-sanctioned expressions of faith, and laws that aligned with traditional Christian values but that over time, especially since the 1960s, America has been abandoning those Christian foundations.

For politically and theologically conservative Christians, that declension from a "city upon a hill"—where the rest of the world can look to see a society organized upon Biblical tenets—to our present falling/fallen state has been hastened by a variety of legal defeats: the 1925 Scopes Monkey Trial and subsequent battles over the teaching of evolution; *Engel v. Vitale*, the 1962 Supreme Court case in which the Court ruled mandatory prayer in public school was unconstitutional; *Abington School District v. Schempp*, the 1963 Supreme Court decision that found mandatory devotional Bible reading to be unconstitutional; and *McCreary County v. ACLU*, a 2005 Supreme Court case in which the majority decided that courtroom displays of the Ten Commandments were unconstitutional on separation-of-church-and-state grounds.

APPEAL TO HISTORY: THE JUDEO-CHRISTIAN HERITAGE FRAME

Conservative American Christians embraced the term "Judeo-Christian" in the 1980s to mobilize the politically conservative Jews, a move that inspired many conservative Christians to refine their theology to allow space for politically conservative Jews to be part of their vision of American history and future. In an effort to create a "Judeo-Christian heritage," they have ignored long-standing anti-Semitism within Christianity and American history, instead focusing on the common texts—and, more importantly, conservative politics—that conservative Christianity and Judaism share.

Indeed, the appeal to the Judeo-Christian heritage is less an appeal directly to religious tradition or Scripture and more an appeal to a historical sense that the nation was "founded upon" Judeo-Christian "values" or "ideals." Historians of religion have repeatedly argued that the United States was less "Christian," by measures such as church attendance, than the Judeo-Christian heritage frame suggests. This frame argues that public religious traditions that venerate a common history (even for those who do not personally identify with it) provide a common language, moral heroes (such as Washington, who "could not tell a lie," and Honest Abe Lincoln), and a set of experiences.

Calls to honor America's Judeo-Christian heritage take many forms, from President Ronald Reagan's Proposition 5018, which made 1983 The Year of the Bible, to efforts to name the Bible as the official state book in Louisiana (2014), Mississippi (2015), and Tennessee (2016). Such calls to commemorate this imagined heritage have created a marketplace for consumers who are invested in the idea that America was founded as a New Jerusalem, a model of Christian government. Their work includes libraries of books seeking to prove that the colonists and founders were Christians and that U.S. laws are rooted in Judaism and Christianity, not English common law. Though these latter arguments have been rebutted by historians, they continue to appear in homeschooling curricula, sermon series, radio broadcasts, and Christian tourism information.

Although each of these endeavors to promote America's Judeo-Christian heritage positions America as unique in world history and deserving of public honor, and recognition proponents are not content to leave Judeo-Christianity in the past. Contemporary calls to commemorate and honor this heritage are often paired with efforts to reinforce Biblical norms (as interpreted through conservative evangelical Protestantism) as law, as Judeo-Christian heritage proponents believe was done in the past.

APPEAL TO SOCIOLOGY: SOCIAL INTEGRATION FRAME

Sacred traditions may be invented precisely for the purpose of uniting a nation. In his 1863 Thanksgiving Proclamation, Lincoln called upon Americans to celebrate the last Thursday of November as a "day of Thanksgiving and Praise to our beneficent Father who dwelleth in the Heavens"—but his impulse was not merely worship. He also urged those gathering around the family dinner table to "fervently implore the interposition of the Almighty Hand to heal the wounds of the nation and to restore it as soon as may be consistent with Divine purposes to the full enjoyment of peace, harmony, tranquility and Union." This prayer is only partly an appeal to God for national healing; it is also an appeal to Americans to join together in a religious rite to create that healing.

Indeed, from the social integration perspective, the details of the deity are irrelevant; what is important is that people are joining together in the public expression of faith. This may be seen as so important that it is mandatory either in law or in practical terms. The inclusion of "In God We Trust" on currency, for example, provides a small but frequent reminder that "we" are doing this act (trusting God) together. The insertion by Congress of "Under God" into the Pledge of Allegiance in 1954 was a similar effort to generate social cohesion against the atheism of the Soviet Union. The issue was less about God and more about coercing integration through the public performance of religiously infused rituals. For this reason, defenders of public prayer and the observation of religion have not always insisted that such expressions be uniquely Christian (or vaguely Judeo-Christian) so much as that they must be religious in some way—echoing President Dwight Eisenhower's words delivered to Freedoms Foundation in New York City in 1952: "Our government has no sense unless it is founded in a deeply felt religious faith, and I don't care what it is."

A social integration framework can be stretched to include any religious orientation that supports the American system of politics, economics, and social organization, for in this framework the functioning of these systems is the *point* of religion. Indeed, in the majority opinion in *Marsh v. Chambers* in 1983, Chief Justice Burger waved away the importance of prayers as a religious expression. For a chaplain on the payroll of a government to invoke "divine guidance on a public body" during a legislative session was not, he argued, establishing a religion; instead, "it is simply a tolerable acknowledgement of beliefs widely held among the people of this country." In short, what mattered for the Court was not the content of the belief but that the practice of opening government business with prayer united people in action.

In *Town of Greece v. Galloway* (2014), the Supreme Court took this logic further, deciding that public prayer in government spaces must mean something *other than* what those engaging it as religious believers intend it to mean. Here, the Supreme Court allowed public prayer to open a local government meeting because it served as a "recognition" of the long-standing belief among many Americans that such prayer is "consistent with a brief acknowledgement of their belief in a higher power." From a social integration perspective, the Court said that public prayer used for "permissible ceremonial purpose" connects Americans to one another through the ritual of prayer and ". . . invoking spiritual inspiration . . . without directing any religious message."

APPEAL TO RELIGIOUS BELIEF: THE PSALM 33 FRAME

While both the Judeo-Christian heritage and social integration frames allow publicly supported expression of religion, they do not satisfy the desire of some religious believers to ground religious expression in religious belief. While the Supreme Court has generally said that religious expressions can stand *because* they are sociological, not supernatural, in nature, those who adopt the Psalm 33 frame say that such religious expressions *only work* because the faithful are intervening with God on behalf of the nation.

This frame looks to Puritan John Winthrop's encouragement to his fellow colonists that they were to establish a "city on a hill," which adherents understand to be a nation with laws that accord with conservative Christianity. Indeed, proponents of this framework argue that this is the only way to ensure the continuance of God's protection of the nation e. As the psalmist writes in Psalm 33, "Blessed is the nation whose God is the LORD." Those who adopt the Psalm 33 framework call on America to "bless God" if it hopes to be favored by God in return. National tragedies, such as the September 11 attacks and Hurricane Katrina, are interpreted as signs of God's displeasure with a nation that is failing to maintain its place as a "city on a hill" and is thus losing God's blessing.

Although the First Amendment seems to circumvent theocracy, Psalm 33 adherents argue that all people, including non-Christians, are under God's dominion, of which the U.S. government is merely a small part. Any effort to deny or reject the rule of God results in natural social decay and supernatural punishment.

Thus, even non-Christians are forced to obey God. Laws against liquor sales, blue laws prohibiting Sunday sales, and other laws restricting behavior based on Judeo-Christian morality ensure that even those who are not believers are obeying.

People who argue that all rights are "endowed" on people by their Creator (who in the Judeo-Christian heritage frame is the Judeo-Christian deity) also assert that those who do not recognize this Creator thus cannot have these rights. This argument has been invoked in efforts to prevent the building of mosques, with opponents claiming that Islam is not a religion and that Muslims, since they did not participate in the signing of the Constitution, do not get to enjoy the right to the free exercise of religion guaranteed in the First Amendment.

In the Psalm 33 framework, the particulars of religious faith—a conservative Judeo-Christian faith—matter; respect for religious diversity does not unify Americans but merely incites God's wrath. One conservative Christian protestor expressed this worldview when a Hindu religious leader, Rajan Zed, led the opening U.S. Senate prayer for the first time in 2007. The protestor interrupted the prayer by shouting, "Lord Jesus, forgive us, Father, for allowing the prayer of the wicked, which is an abomination in your sight" (Huntington, 2007). He then invoked the commandment, shared by Jews and Christians, that "[y]ou shall have no other gods before you," to criticize Hinduism as polytheistic and thus outside of the Judeo-Christian tradition. In this view, non-Judeo-Christians are not merely threatening to America's social fabric, heritage, and morality; they are threatening the nation's very existence.

CONCLUSION

Close readings of the many legislative and court efforts to advance or prevent the legislation of prayer and other expressions of religion in the public sphere reveal a diverse set of tactics, sometimes in tension with one another even as they are also used simultaneously. A court may decide that religious expressions supported with taxes are acceptable because they express beliefs long held by Americans—but also that the content of beliefs are irrelevant. Supporters of state-sponsored religion may argue that religion holds Americans together but also that some religious Americans may not be included in public expressions. Courts and legislative bodies continue to argue about whether the Establishment Clause of the First Amendment applies to government entities beyond Congress or whether individual states can establish official religions.

Such arguments will continue if present trends continue and the percentage of self-described traditionalists and conservative Christians in America shrinks, replaced by increasingly irreligious Americans who see religious diversity, like other kinds of diversity, as a national strength, not as cause for God's wrath; mandatory religious participation as coercion, not religious freedom; religiously inspired laws as oppression, not heritage; and the use of tax money to support others' religious expressions as a violation of their individual moral codes—or, as early American Baptist Roger Williams argued, "There is no prudent Christian way of preserving peace in the world but by permission of differing consciences."

Rebecca Barrett-Fox

FURTHER READING

Abington School District v. Schempp, 1963.

Bindewald, Benjamin J., & Suzanne Rosenblith. 2015. "Addressing Orthodox Challenges in the Pluralist Classroom." *Educational Studies: A Journal of the American Educational Studies Association, 51*: 497–509.

Castle, Jeremiah J. 2015. "The Electoral Impact of Public Opinion on Religious Establishment." *Journal for the Scientific Study of Religion, 54*: 814–832.

Engel v. Vitale, 1962.

Foster, Gaines M. 2003. *Moral Reconstruction: Christian Lobbyists and the Federal Legislation of Morality, 1865–1920.* Chapel Hill: University of North Carolina Press.

Grzymala-Busse, Anna. 2015. *Nations Under God: How Churches Use Moral Authority to Influence Policy.* Princeton, NJ: Princeton University Press.

Huntington, Doug. 2007. "Protestors Interrupt Senate's First Hindu-led Prayer." *The Christian Post*, July 14. Retrieved from http://www.christianpost.com/news/protestors-interrupt-senate-s-first-hindu-led-prayer-28443/

Jones, Jeffery Owen. 2003. "The Man Who Wrote the Pledge of Allegiance." *Smithsonian Magazine*, November. Retrieved from http://www.smithsonianmag.com/history/the-man-who-wrote-the-pledge-of-allegiance-93907224/

Kosek, Joseph Kip (Ed.). 2017. *American Religion, American Politics: An Anthology.* New Haven, CT: Yale University Press.

Lynerd, Benjamin T. 2014. *Republican Theology: The Civil Religion of American Evangelicals.* New York: Oxford University Press.

Matzke, Nicholas J. 2016, January. "The Evolution of Antievolution Policies After *Kitzmiller Versus Dover.*" *Science, 351*: 28–30.

McCreary County v. ACLU, 2005.

Shapiro, Adam R. 2013. *Trying Biology: The Scopes Trial, Textbooks, and the Antievolution Movement in American Schools.* Chicago: University of Chicago Press.

Smith, Rodney K. 1983. "Justice Potter Stewart: A Contemporary Jurist's View of Religious Liberty." *North Dakota Law Review*: 183.

Solomon, Stephen D. 2007. *Ellery's Protest: How One Young Man Defied Tradition and Sparked the Battle over School Prayer.* Ann Arbor: University of Michigan Press.

Town of Greece v. Galloway, 2014.

Willett, Jennifer Beck, Bernie Goldfine, Todd Seidler, Andy Gillentine, & Scott Marley. 2014. "Prayer 101: Deciphering the Law—What Every Coach and Administrator Should Know." *Journal of Physical Education, Recreation & Dance, 85*: 15–19.

Williams, Daniel K. 2010. *God's Own Party: The Making of the Christian Right.* New York: Oxford University Press.

Religious Freedom

People find deep personal satisfaction and meaning in their religious beliefs and practices, and some argue that they have a natural right to follow these impulses. Denying one the opportunity to express their deepest yearnings is harmful and morally problematic. Meanwhile, governments are obligated to protect the natural rights and liberties of all. Oftentimes, religious liberty and equality clash, and the state cannot always resolve the conflict by showing a blind preference for one over the other. Although most agree that, in some instances, a state has to protect its citizens from some forms of religion, they disagree about when it is in the interest of all to do so.

THE RELIGIOUS FREEDOM RESTORATION ACT

Two Native Americans who worked as counselors for a drug rehabilitation organization in 1982 were fired for ingesting peyote—an illegal hallucinogenic drug. When they applied for unemployment benefits, the State of Oregon denied the claim on the grounds that they had been dismissed for "misconduct." The two sued the State, arguing that their consumption of the illegal narcotic was part of a religious ritual and should not be considered misconduct. The case went before the U.S. Supreme Court, which ruled against the defendants in the 1990s. In the majority opinion, Justice Antonin Scalia wrote that an individual's religious beliefs do not excuse them from compliance with an otherwise valid law prohibiting such conduct. In other words, if the government passes a law, people must obey that law even if it conflicts with their religious beliefs.

In response, Congress passed the Religious Freedom Restoration Act (RFRA) of 1993. This law prohibits any agency, department, or official of the United States or any state from substantially burdening a person's exercise of religion unless there is a demonstrable compelling government interest *and* it is the least restrictive means of furthering that interest.

The limits of this law were tested in 1997 when the Archbishop of San Antonio was denied a permit to expand his church into a historic preservation district located in Boerne, Texas. Flores sued the city of Boerne on the grounds that the city was violating his rights under RFRA. After hearing arguments in the case, the U.S. Supreme Court ruled that RFRA was not a proper exercise of Congress's enforcement power because it contradicts vital principles necessary to maintain the separation of powers and the federal–state balance. In short, because Congress had not demonstrated widespread religious discrimination, it could not rely on the same principles used to defend the Voting Rights Act of 1965 as justification for RFRA. If religious organizations or individuals wanted the same protections from their respective states that RFRA offers at the federal level, they would have to get states to pass their own religious freedom laws.

RELIGIOUS FREEDOM RESTORATION IN THE STATES

Only two states (Connecticut and Rhode Island) had their own versions of RFRA laws on the books before *City of Boerne v. Flores*. Within three years of that decision, nine more states had passed some form of RFRA, but there is nearly a 10-year gap before most of the other states began passing state-level RFRA legislation. With the exception of Missouri (2003) and Virginia (2007), no other states passed RFRA bills until after 2009. This is approximately the same time that courts began rejecting claims of discrimination on the basis of religious morality and were overturning various laws defining marriage as a union as solely between one man and one woman. As such, some believed that states were passing RFRA legislation not out of concern for religious minorities but as a means to allow some people to deny legal same-sex marriage.

When the Arizona state legislature passed a bill in 2014 expanding the scope of their previous RFRA, business leaders openly urged Republican Governor Jan Brewer to veto the legislation. They argued that the legislation was not necessary for protecting religious liberty: rather it was a veiled attempt to support people who did not want to provide services to openly gay individuals. Eventually, Governor Brewer (who had previously supported the bill) decided to veto SB 1062. Similarly, after Republican Governor Mike Pence signed Indiana's RFRA into law in 2015, many organizations cancelled conventions, cities and states issued travel bans to the State of Indiana, and nine CEOs from Indiana's largest businesses sent a letter opposing the new law. In response, Governor Pence and the GOP-controlled Indiana legislature modified the legislation.

RELIGIOUS FREEDOM AS A GUISE FOR DISCRIMINATION

The dominant view among those who oppose "religious freedom" laws is that the term has become a code for intolerance. Scholar Randall Ballmer (2014), for example, argues that the religious right was founded on opposition to racial desegregation, not abortion. After the *Brown v. Board of Education* decision in 1954 made it unlawful for public schools to racially segregate students, many Southerners founded private religious schools that perpetuated racial segregation. In the early 1970s, the federal government began denying tax-exempt status to any segregated schools in the United States. Some of these schools argued that these actions violated their freedom of religion. When the IRS rescinded the tax exemption for Bob Jones University in 1976, many Christian leaders decided to politically organize to protect themselves from further antireligious government action (Ballmer, 2014).

Many critics see the present struggle for religious freedom as the continuation of this movement that began to oppose racial equality. The religious right has a long history of opposing gender and racial equality and presently opposes legislation expanding protections based on sexual orientation and gender identity. However, many religious groups are not aligned with the religious right and have supported expanded civil liberties for minority groups in America. For example, black Protestant churches were an integral part of the Civil Rights movement and have been the means through which many government programs have helped the poor. As such, when religious groups affiliated with the religious right warn that religious liberty is under attack, many are unsympathetic.

In 2013, Elane Photography in New Mexico was sued for refusing to take photos at a commitment ceremony for two women. One law in New Mexico prohibits public accommodations from discriminating against people based on their sexual orientation. Another—the New Mexico Religious Freedom Restoration Act— prohibits the state from passing laws that force people to violate their religious beliefs. The New Mexico Supreme Court ruled that a commercial photography business is subject to antidiscrimination provisions *and* that the state's RFRA was not applicable because the incident involved two private parties—not the government. Incidents like this are commonly cited as evidence that religious freedom in America is under attack. Advocates of religious liberty argue that the government should not force people to violate their conscience and to provide business services to people who are behaving in ways that they regard as immoral. This position has been criticized by observers who contend that many of the same religious groups that were willing to put up with racial and gender inequality in American society were now arguing that their own rights had been violated. Indeed, Andrew Lewis (2017) argues that religious conservatives have turned the "rights" arguments of the American left to their advantage in trying to protect their rights to reject anything that conflicts with their deeply held religious morals.

After the Supreme Court legalized same-sex marriage in all 50 states in 2015 (*Obergefell v. Hodges*), many government officials argued that RFRA protections allowed them to deny marriage licenses to same-sex couples. Mississippi passed a law that provided religious protections for marriage beliefs. A county clerk in Kentucky, Kim Davis, refused to issue marriage licenses to same-sex couples. The U.S. District found that she had violated the law and ordered her to begin issuing marriage licenses. Davis refused to comply and was sent to jail for several days until she agreed to comply with the court order by allowing her deputy clerks to conduct marriages on her behalf. Those who want to see a firm separation between church and state in America see these events as evidence that religious believers do not actually want freedom to practice their religion; they want to impose their own views on the rest of the world. They want freedom to discriminate against others based on their religious beliefs.

Others argue that the belief that religious freedom is under attack is a fictional-ized attempt to reconcile the fact that one's views are becoming less popular. Scholar Jay Michaelson (2015) argues that Christianity is losing ground in America because of the number of scandals involving religion. Several sex scandals involving Evangelical leaders, the Catholic clergy, and reality television stars espousing Christian morals have caused public distrust in organized religion. Rather than accepting this as the cause for the erosion of religion in American life, Michaelson and other critics claim that religious Americans have created a mythical war against religion. If the decline of Christianity is caused by a war on religion, the trend can be reversed by winning the war. Michaelson argues that the so-called War on Christmas mythology is one manifestation of this phenomenon. The fact that more and more people celebrate a cultural as opposed to religious version of Christmas, in which Santa Claus and a Christmas tree are more representative of the season than Jesus in a manger, is due to there simply being fewer practicing Christians in America. Instead of acknowledging this reality, many Christians believe that secularists are forcing their particular religious faith off the American stage.

RELIGIOUS FREEDOM AS A TARGET OF ATTACK

The alternative view is that religion is good for society. Some argue that a religion-based morality is necessary for democracies to function properly. In churches, people are taught from a young age to voluntarily obey the law, to respect other people's property, and to refrain from stealing or lying. People follow these rules because they have come to believe that even if the police or court systems don't catch them when they break a law, God will catch them and hold them account-able. Some morality psychologists argue that religious belief has been an impor-tant component of human evolution. They cite historical examples of secular and religious societal groups in support of this assertion. Religious groups have tended to fare better than their secular counterparts because, in these small societies, group interests can be subsumed to individual interests. Individual group members tend to place their own self-interest below the interest of the group. It is difficult to suf-ficiently monitor and punish freeloading, so groups need people to voluntarily sac-rifice their own interests for the good of the group on occasion. Religious groups can do this more easily than secular groups. When people believe that an all-knowing Deity is both monitoring all behavior and punishing those who shirk, they are more likely to adhere to unenforceable societal norms.

Others argue that it is important to protect religious freedom because people derive deep personal satisfaction and meaning from religious behaviors and prac-tices. One of the reasons that religion has played some role in human experience from virtually the beginning of recorded history is that people enjoy religion. Some even argue that religion is a fundamental characteristic of human nature. Recently, neuroscientists conducted functional magnetic resonance imaging (fMRI) scans of individual's brains while they were engaged in a variety of tasks. They wanted to identify the regions of the brain associated with empathetic behavior. In a series of experiments, Anthony Ian Jack and his colleagues (2016) found that faith and reason activate different neural pathways. In addition, those who were more religious were significantly more religious, while atheists were less empathetic. They conclude that when society emphasizes only analytic reasoning and scientific belief, it compromises the ability to cultivate the kind of thinking that leads to social or moral insight. As such, religious freedom is a moral and political good because the right to hold religious belief and put it into practice is fundamental to what it means to be human. "If we cannot live according to our judgements about what is most important in human life, and our part in some greater scheme of things, we are not really free to live our lives as we wish" (Trigg, 2013: 18).

Proponents of religious liberty argue that the discrimination frame makes it difficult for people to openly express their religious beliefs. They see a double standard in the position that opponents of religious liberty often take. In their view, liberals are not opposed to the government imposing values on people; they regularly support government control over diet, exercise, parenting, sex, and race—and express outrage with resistance or noncompliance with their agenda. These critics contend that what liberals really want is to remove all dissenting views from the public forum and treat religious views as no more credible than racist sentiments.

In September 2016, the U.S. Commission on Civil Rights issued a report called *Peaceful Coexistence: Reconciling Non-Discrimination Principles with Civil Liberties*. The chair of the committee, Martin Castro, wrote:

> The phrases 'religious liberty' and 'religious freedom' will stand for nothing except hypocrisy so long as they remain code words for discrimination, intolerance, racism, sexism, homophobia, Islamophobia, Christian supremacy or any form of intolerance. Religious liberty was never intended to give one religion dominion over other religions, or a veto power over the civil rights and civil liberties of others. However, today, as in the past, religion is being used as both a weapon and a shield by those seeking to deny others equality.

A coalition of religious leaders from Jewish, Islamic, and Christian faiths were appalled by these statements in the report and issued an open letter asking President Barack Obama and other congressional leaders to denounce this view of religious freedom. President Obama never made a public statement about the report.

In a forum organized in recognition of the 25th anniversary of the 1993 RFRA, a group of religious leaders and scholars met to discuss the current state of religious liberty in America. Many expressed concern about whether the debate could be resolved amicably. Marc Stern, general counsel for the American Jewish Committee, stated:

> When I was young, we thought of religious liberty as, 'I don't have to agree with you, but I have to agree to let you live your life.' . . . The debate is now, 'Do I think what you're doing is right?' . . . For neither side should that be a winning proposition. But that is the way the battle is now shaping up. (BJC Staff Reports, 2013)

Discussions about religious liberty are now about deciding the correct view. At the same symposium, Dahlia Lithwick, senior editor and legal correspondent for *Slate* magazine, argued that the media have polarized the debate over religious liberty (BJC Staff Reports, 2013).

Religious freedom continues to struggle to find a balance in a polarized political environment. Today even members of the U.S. Supreme Court are so isolated in their social groups that people on one side of the issue do not even know people who have views on the opposing side of the issue. This contributes to the new forum in which religious liberties are discussed. One side cannot take seriously the claim that people are genuinely concerned about protecting their own religious liberties (and not simply hiding homophobia) because nonreligious and religious Americans associate with one another less often and in less meaningful ways than in past generations. One way forward, at a minimum, would include more respect and civil discourse.

Matthew R. Miles

FURTHER READING

Balmer, Randall Herbert. 2007. *Thy Kingdom Come: How the Religious Right Distorts the Faith and Threatens America: An Evangelical's Lament.* New York: Basic Books.

Balmer, Randall Herbert. 2014. "The Real Origins of the Religious Right." *Politico Magazine*, May 27.

BJC Staff Reports. 2013. "A Day of Reflections on RFRA and Religious Freedom." December 11. Retrieved from https://bjconline.org/a-day-of-reflections-on-rfra-and-religi ous-freedom

Castro, Martin R., Patricia Timmons-Goodson, Roberta Achtenberg, Gail L. Heriot, Peter N. Kirsanow, David Kladney, Karen K. Narasaki, & Michael Yaki. 2016. *Peaceful Coexistence: Reconciling Non-discrimination Principles with Civil Liberties.* U.S. Commission on Civil Rights.

City of Boerne v. Flores, 1997.

Galen, Luke W. 2012. "Does Religious Belief Promote Prosociality? A Critical Examination." *Psychological Bulletin*, *138*(5): 876.

Gervais, Will M, Azim F Shariff, & Ara Norenzayan. 2011. "Do You Believe in Atheists? Distrust Is Central to Anti-atheist Prejudice." *Journal of Personality and Social Psychology*, *101*(6): 1189.

Gill, Anthony James. 2008. *The Political Origins of Religious Liberty.* Cambridge Studies in Social Theory, Religion, and Politics. Cambridge and New York: Cambridge University Press.

Grim, Brian J., & Roger Finke. 2011. *The Price of Freedom Denied: Religious Persecution and Conflict in the 21st Century*, Cambridge Studies in Social Theory, Religion and Politics. New York: Cambridge University Press.

Haidt, Jonathan. 2013. *The Righteous Mind: Why Good People Are Divided by Politics and Religion.* New York: Vintage.

Hurd, Elizabeth Shakman. 2015. *Beyond Religious Freedom: The New Global Politics of Religion.* Princeton, NJ: Princeton University Press.

Jack, Anthony Ian, Jared Parker Friedman, Richard Eleftherios Boyatzis, & Scott Nolan Taylor. 2016. "Why Do You Believe in God? Relationships Between Religious Belief, Analytic Thinking, Mentalizing and Moral Concern." *PloS One*, *11*(3): e0149989.

Jelen, Ted G. 2010. "Religious Liberty as a Democratic Institution." In Derek Davis (Ed.), *The Oxford Handbook of Church and State in the United States*, xv, 575. New York: Oxford University Press.

Johnson, David, & Katy Steinmetz. 2015. "This Map Shows Every State with Religious-Freedom Laws." *Time*, April 2.

King, Robert. 2015. "RFRA: Boycotts, Bans and a Growing Backlash." *Indianapolis Star*, April 2.

Lewis, Andrew R. 2017. *The Rights Turn in Conservative Christian Politics: How Abortion Transformed the Culture Wars*. New York: Cambridge University Press.

Lori, William E., Gérald J. Caussé, Hamza Yusuf Hanson, Charles Haynes, Russell Moore, Leith Anderson, Ron Sider, III Frank Madison Reid, Anuttama Dasa, Gregory John Mansour, Kit Bigelow, Mohamed Magid, Nathan J. Diament, Eugene F. Rivers III, Jacqueline C. Rivers, & Thomas Farr. 2016. "Open Letter: Asks US Government to Reject Report That Stigmatizes Religious Americans." Retrieved from https://newsroom.churchofjesuschrist.org/article/interfaith-coalition-president-congress-biased-religious-liberty-report?__prclt=cD5DApZi.

Merrill, Laurie, & Russ Wiles. 2014. "Arizona Business Groups Overwhelmingly Opposed to SB 1062." *The Arizona Republic*, February 21.

Michaelson, Jay. 2015. "The Religious Right Is Right to Be Scared: Christianity Is Dying in America." *The Daily Beast*, December 26. Retrieved from http://www.thedailybeast.com/articles/2015/12/26/the-religious-right-is-right-to-be-scared-christianity-is-dying-in-america.html

Norenzayan, Ara, & Azim F Shariff. 2008. "The Origin and Evolution of Religious Prosociality." *Science*, *322*(5898): 58–62.

Obergefell v. Hodges, 2015.

Shariff, Azim F., Aiyana K. Willard, Teresa Andersen, & Ara Norenzayan. 2016. "Religious Priming: A Meta-analysis with a Focus on Prosociality." *Personality and Social Psychology Review*, *20*(1): 27–48.

Smith, Steven D. 2014. *The Rise and Decline of American Religious Freedom*. Cambridge, MA: Harvard University Press.

Stavrova, Olga, & Pascal Siegers. 2013. "Religious Prosociality and Morality Across Cultures How Social Enforcement of Religion Shapes the Effects of Personal Religiosity on Prosocial and Moral Attitudes and Behaviors." *Personality and Social Psychology Bulletin*: 0146167213510951.

Stern, Marc, & Dahlia Lithwick. 2013. "Free Religion in a Diverse Society: Current and Future Challenges." *Newseum* (video). Retrieved from https://www.youtube.com/watch?v=WtfCagMOJiA

Toft, Monica Duffy, Daniel Philpott, & Timothy Samuel Shah. 2011. *God's Century: Resurgent Religion and Global Politics*. New York: W. W. Norton.

Trigg, Roger. 2013. *Equality, Freedom, and Religion*. New York: Oxford University Press.

Reproductive Services and Infertility

Shortly before midnight on July 25, 1978, Lesley and Peter Brown welcomed their daughter Louise Joy Brown to the world. Weighing in at 5 pounds, 12 ounces, this baby girl born at Oldham and District General Hospital in Manchester, England, appeared to be like any other healthy baby girl. However, as the world's first "test tube baby," Louise Brown ushered in a new era of reproductive services available to people suffering from infertility. While Louise Brown served as evidence of the potential for reproductive services to help people grow their families, these services also brought about intense moral and legal debates about topics such as when life begins, gay and single parenting, the commodification of babies, and even eugenics.

According to the Centers for Disease Control and Prevention (CDC), approximately 12 percent of women and 8 percent of men in the United States have sought treatment for infertility, which is defined as the inability to conceive after 12 months of unprotected intercourse. Infertility services can include a variety of treatments including drug therapy, intrauterine insemination (also known as artificial insemination), surgeries to remove blockages, and assisted reproductive technologies (ARTs) such as in vitro fertilization (IVF) or surrogacy.

PLAYING GOD

Throughout history and even today, segments of the population believe that utilizing reproductive services to conceive children is unnatural. Opponents of reproductive services claim that circumventing the natural conception process is akin to playing God and that using fertility technologies is going against God's will. Others view reproductive services, especially ones that utilize donor eggs or sperm, as vulgar, and some critics have even asserted that the use of donor sperm for artificial insemination is the same as committing adultery.

The moral argument that fertility doctors are playing God is supported by several doctrinal interpretations published by prominent religious organizations. For

instance, the Catholic Church has taken a clear stance on the morality of any reproductive service that replaces the marital act or introduces third-party gamete
(sperm and egg) donations. In 2009, the United States Conference of Catholic Bishops (USCCB) approved a document outlining the church's stance toward the use
of reproductive technologies. In this document, the USCCB clearly summarizes
that reproductive technologies that replace the marital act are immoral. The USCCB
does, however, specify that certain types of reproductive services that enhance
reproduction through the marital act can be acceptable. The conference specifically
mentions fertility treatments, such as surgeries to remove fallopian tube blockages,
hormonal regimens, or other treatments that restore reproductive health, as actions
that can be considered moral. Dr. John M. Haas, president of the National Catholic
Bioethics Center, summarized the church's stance by saying, "Engendering children
is a cooperative act between husband, wife, and God himself. Children, in the final
analysis should be begotten not made" (Haas, 1998: 30).

In contrast to the Catholic Church's strong stance against ARTs, other denominations and religious traditions have taken more favorable positions based on biblical teachings that frame procreation as an obligation ordained by God. In fact,
the Old Testament of the Bible is filled with examples of individuals who utilized
alternative means to bear children, including the use of surrogates and herbal fertility enhancements. The Presbyterian Church, the United Methodist Church, the
United Church of Christ, and the Episcopal Church are examples of denominations
that have crafted doctrinal statements embracing the use of certain ARTs. Other
denominations, such as the Lutheran Church, take a more cautious approach, calling for further study and prayerful consideration. Despite different doctrinal
approaches to reproductive services, most religious organizations encourage those
dealing with surrogacy to be mindful of the moral considerations that are inherent
in fertility treatments, including the sanctity of life and the sacredness of the human
body. Many of the documents adopted by church organizations recommend seeking guidance from spiritual leaders as they make difficult choices about growing
their families. The conflicting messages from different religious organizations only
adds to the morality debate surrounding use of reproductive services.

EXCESS EMBRYOS

Another moral controversy surrounding ARTs stems from the fact that use of
these procedures often results in excess embryos being produced. ARTs are very
expensive, and in order to reduce costs, to improve the chances of conception, and
to reduce the number of treatments on the body, doctors often recommend harvesting more gametes than may be immediately needed. Because there are difficulties in
successfully storing eggs, fertility experts recommend fertilizing eggs and storing the resulting embryos. Doctors then use IVF to implant a small number of
embryos at a time, hoping that there is at least one successful implantation leading
to a healthy pregnancy and eventually a live birth. For a variety of reasons including a successful pregnancy, those undergoing fertility treatments sometimes end
their treatments before utilizing all their embryos. Moral controversy arises over

what should be done with these excess embryos, and the moral cleavage ultimately comes down to the question of when life begins.

There are a variety of options for how to accommodate excess embryos. In order to maintain their viability for future use, embryos are frozen and stored in cryogenic storage facilities. Storage can be quite costly, and as time progresses, available storage space decreases. The question then turns to how long embryos should remain in storage and what should happen when storage space is no longer available.

A significant portion of the population believes that life begins at conception and therefore that embryos should not be destroyed. This viewpoint leaves little room for compromise as there are limited options for handling excess embryos that align with the value placed on life. The only options are to either store excess embryos indefinitely or to allow embryos to be adopted by couples undergoing IVF treatment. Each option presents its own set of counterarguments. First, some argue that indefinite storage in a cryogenic facility does not properly honor the sanctity of human life and that, just as destroying an embryo would be ending human life, indefinite storage would stunt human life. The adoption of excess embryos has been offered as an alternative solution, but opponents argue that biological parents might have little input on who adopts their embryos—and that this option opens the door for gay couples to become parents, a scenario seen as unacceptable by some social conservatives.

In recent years, those who argue that life begins at conception have lobbied state governments to pass bills or to make constitutional amendments that legally recognize embryos as human life, with all the same rights bestowed on humans such as the right to life, liberty, and property. These efforts have been labeled personhood initiatives, and while they have been supported by a variety of individuals across the United States, they have been championed primarily by Personhood USA, an organization formed in 2008 and based in Denver, Colorado. But although Personhood USA has fought for these initiatives to be introduced and adopted across the United States, few such initiatives have been introduced—and none have passed—as of mid-2018. It should be noted, however, that while they have not passed specific personhood initiatives, Kansas and Missouri do have personhood language included in other legislation on their books. In addition, on April 25, 2017, the Alabama legislature voted to place a personhood amendment initiative on the November 6, 2018, ballot. This initiative was approved by 59 percent of voters and amends the Alabama constitution to recognize the sanctity of unborn life.

Although personhood initiatives have the support of many pro-life individuals, they have nonetheless caused a split within the pro-life movement. One concern about these initiatives is the impact they could have on the availability of reproductive services. Despite being considered one of the strongest pro-life states in the United States, Mississippi's personhood amendment failed on November 8, 2011, with 58 percent of the population voting against the state constitutional amendment to recognize embryos as persons. This amendment was defeated, in part, due to grassroots efforts and a social media campaign led by Atlee Breland, a Christian, pro-life woman. Breland, who utilized IVF to conceive her twin daughters, argued that the amendment had the potential to impact the availability of fertility treatment for couples needing assistance to grow their families. Breland is not the only person to voice concerns about the dampening effect of personhood initiatives on reproductive services. A variety of organizations in support of reproductive services, including the National Infertility Association, the Center for Reproductive Rights, and the Society for Assisted Reproductive Technology, argue that giving embryos personhood status could make fertility doctors legally and criminally liable for embryos that are not transferred to a womb or that do not result in a live childbirth. While groups like Personhood Alliance argue that medical professionals would not be criminally liable for accidental or natural embryo death, there is currently no legal precedent on these issues.

The debates on the legal status of embryos have also fueled the debate over stem cell research in the United States. Opponents of human embryonic stem cell research argue that this line of research destroys human life. Proponents argue in favor of the life-saving potential of this form of research. A September 2007, the Pew Research Center poll revealed that the nation was quite divided on the issue of stem cell research, with 51 percent of respondents in favor and 35 percent in opposition (Pew Research Center, 2009). However, by 2017 a Gallup poll showed an increase in support, with 61 percent supporting human embryo stem cell research (Jones, 2017).

Aligning with the opponents of stem cell research, President George W. Bush signed an executive order in 2001 that banned federal dollars from being spent on embryonic stem cell research involving newly destroyed embryos. On March 9, 2009, President Barack Obama signed Executive Order 13505, lifting this ban. Obama's order did not address the legislative ban that disallows federal research funding from being spent on creating new stem cell lines, but it did allow federal monies to be spent on researching stem cell lines not previously created using federal dollars. In 2018, the Donald Trump administration halted federal agencies from acquiring new fetal tissue and began reviewing fetal tissue research. While these federal actions appear to be contradictory and complicated, researchers argued that the lifting of the ban could result in medical breakthroughs and cures to a variety of diseases.

CREATING NONTRADITIONAL FAMILIES

Deciding who is worthy of using reproductive services and how reproductive services should be used is another moral debate that has emerged. As demonstrated by several of the doctrinal statements released by religious organizations, many believe that reproduction should take place only within the confines of traditional, legal, heterosexual marriage and that those who deviate from that prescription are behaving immorally. As such, there has been opposition to the use of reproductive services by gay couples and single women. Those who argue that gay couples and single women should not be able to utilize reproductive services have seen some support for their position in the form of state laws governing insurance coverage of fertility treatments. For instance, five states—Arkansas, Hawaii, Maryland, Rhode Island, and Texas—have laws that allow those who are not legally married to be excluded from having fertility treatments covered by insurance. These laws specifically target those who are unmarried, but they were also applied to gay couples whose marriages were not legally recognized until the Supreme Court case *Obergefell v. Hodges* (2015). Arkansas, Hawaii, Maryland, and Texas also exclude individuals who use donor gametes in their fertility treatments. While these particular laws could impact a variety of individuals seeking fertility treatment, opponents argue that the laws devalue the rights of those seeking to create nontraditional families, especially gay couples who have no other choice but to utilize at least one donor gamete.

Not only do current debates address who should have access to reproductive services, but they also consider how individuals should utilize these technologies, especially considering the practice of multiple embryo implantations. The topic of multiple implantations begets two moral arguments. The first debate concerns selective reduction. In order to increase the likelihood of a successful pregnancy, fertility doctors often implant multiple embryos into the womb, and this can sometimes result in a multiple pregnancy. Because carrying multiples to full term can be difficult, doctors sometimes recommend selective reduction, which involves terminating one or more fetuses. This option is usually considered only when there are three or more fetuses or when the pregnancy is considered high risk. Because the process involves the termination of a fetus, it is also sometimes called selective abortion, making the moral argument obvious.

The second moral argument that arises from multiple embryo implantation occurs when individuals choose to purposefully implant multiple embryos in an attempt to increase the chances of birthing multiples. The most famous example of this occurring happened in January 2009 when Nadya Suleman, also known as Octomom, gave birth to eight babies, which she had conceived using IVF and a sperm donor. Suleman, a single woman who already had six children, was criticized for purposefully having so many babies at once. Adding to the criticism was the fact that Suleman was a college student receiving public assistance. Organizations such as the American Society for Reproductive Medicine and the Medical Board of California claimed that implanting so many embryos at once violated professional and ethical standards, putting the babies and the mother at risk due to the potential medical complications of multiples, such as premature birth, low birth weight, and high-risk pregnancy. The controversy surrounding Suleman garnered so much attention that in 2009, two states, Georgia and Missouri, introduced legislation to limit the number of embryos that could be implanted during one IVF cycle. Neither of these bills was adopted. The debate over multiple embryo transfers continues, however, and multiple countries, including the United Kingdom, Australia, and Canada, have approved regulations limiting the number of embryos that can be transferred at one time.

NEW TECHNOLOGIES, NEW DEBATES

As technology continues to advance, new morality debates are continually being introduced. Once such debate centers on the issue of so-called designer babies. The term "designer baby" refers to the idea that parents, through the technology of gene manipulation, may someday be able to custom-create their offspring to have certain genetic traits and qualities. Scientists seem to agree that the technology is nowhere close, despite recent advancements, to being able to accommodate this level of gene manipulation. In August 2017, however, researchers at the Oregon Health and Science University revealed that they had successfully developed and tested a technique to repair a gene mutation that is the source of heart conditions in multiple human embryos. This discovery has reopened the debate about gene manipulation being used to create designer babies. While having the option to have children free of defect and full of talent and beauty sounds good to some, others worry that this technology could lead to ideas of creating a race of "ideal" humans, also sometimes referred to as eugenics. Although the science to create designer babies has not yet caught up to the debate about the possible immoral uses of the technology, the National Academy of Sciences and the National Academy of Medicine have endorsed research on gene manipulation in human embryos but have restricted that endorsement to research aimed only at averting disease and disability. Members of several advocacy groups for people with disabilities have criticized this type of research as discriminatory in nature. Disability advocates argue that since the ultimate goal is to decrease or eliminate populations with certain disabilities such as dwarfism or Down syndrome, research into and use of genetic altering related to disability suggests that disabled people are somehow "less than" or not equal to nondisabled people.

Another scientific advancement on the horizon that has sparked moral debate is the development of an artificial womb. In April 2017, a team of scientists published research that revealed the development of an artificial womb that successfully gestated a lamb that lived for four weeks after being born. While this technology is not yet available for human trial, scientists are already discussing and debating the implications for human births. This technology has the potential to help premature babies survive outside their mothers' wombs in order to give couples new ways to conceive and perhaps even to address the issue of unwanted pregnancy. Like other types of reproductive services, though, morality and ethical concerns have been raised about this research, such as questions about who should be able to access this technology and the ethical implications of conceiving outside the confines of traditional, heterosexual marriage.

Kellee J. Kirkpatrick

FURTHER READING

Associated Press. 2009. "'Octomom' Spawns Legislation Limiting Embryo Implants." *CBCNews*. Retrieved from http://www.cbc.ca/news/technology/octomom-spawns -legislation-limiting-embryo-implants-1.864774

Belluck, Pam. 2017. "Gene Editing for 'Designer Babies'? Highly Unlikely, Scientists Say." *New York Times*. Retrieved from https://www.nytimes.com/2017/08/04/science/gene -editing-embryos-designer-babies.html?mcubz=0&_r=0

CBSNews. 2009. "Obama Ends Stem Cell Research Ban." *CBSNews*. Retrieved from https://www.cbsnews.com/news/obama-ends-stem-cell-research-ban

Centers for Disease Control and Prevention. 2017. "Reproductive Health: Infertility FAQs." Retrieved from https://www.cdc.gov/reproductivehealth/infertility/index.htm

Haas, John M. 1998. "Begotten Not Made: A Catholic View of Reproductive Technology." United States Conference of Catholic Bishops. Retrieved from http://www.usccb.org/issues-and-action/human-life-and-dignity/reproductive-technology/begotten-not-made-a-catholic-view-of-reproductive-technology.cfm

Heidt-Forsythe, Erin. 2018. *Between Families and Frankenstein: The Politics of Egg Donation in the United States.* Oakland: University of California Press.

Jones, Jeffrey M. 2017. "American Hold Record Liberal Views on Most Moral Issues." *Gallup Social & Policy Issues,* May 11. Retrieved from https://news.gallup.com/poll/210542/americans-hold-record-liberal-views-moral-issues.aspx

Kirkpatrick, Kellee J. 2017. "The 'Not Yet Pregnant': The Impact of Narratives on Infertility Identity and Reproductive Policy." In Brian Attebery, John Gribas, Mark K. McBeth, Paul Sivitz, & Kandi Turley-Ames (Eds.). *Narrative, Identity, and Academic Community in Higher Education,* 111–128. New York: Routledge.

Klitzman, Robert. 2016. "Deciding How Many Embryos to Transfer: Ongoing Challenges and Dilemmas." *Reproductive BioMedicine and Society Online, 3*(December 2016): 1–15.

Legislative Tracker. 2017. "Personhood." Retrieved from https://rewire.news/legislative-tracker/law-topic/personhood

Obergefell v. Hodges, 2015.

Partridge, Emily A., Marcus G. Davey, Matthew A Hornick, Patrick E. McGovern, Ali Y. Mejaddam, Jesse D. Vrecanak, Carmen Mesas-Burgos, Aliza Olive, Robert C. Caskey, Theodore R. Weiland, Jiancheng Han, Alexander J. Schupper, James T. Connelly, Kevin C. Dysart, Jack Rychik, Holly L. Hedrick, William H. Peranteau, & Alan W. Flake. 2017. "An Extra-uterine System to Physiologically Support the Premature Lamb." *Nature Communications, 8*: 1–15.

Pew Research Center. 2009. "Stem Cell Support." *Pew Research Center.* Retrieved from http://www.pewresearch.org/fact-tank/2009/03/09/stem-cell-support

Rao, Radhika. 2015. "How (Not) to Regulate Assisted Reproductive Technology: Lessons from 'Octomom.'" *Family Law Quarterly, 49*(1): 135–147.

Religious Institute. 2009. *A Time to Be Born: A Faith-Based Guide to Assisted Reproductive Technologies.* Westport, CT: Religious Institute. Retrieved from http://religiousinstitute.org/a-time-to-be-born

United States Conference of Catholic Bishops. 2009. "Life-Giving Love in an Age of Technology." *United State Conference of Catholic Bishops.* Retrieved from http://www.usccb.org/beliefs-and-teachings/what-we-believe/love-and-sexuality/life-giving-love-in-an-age-of-technology.cfm

Woliver, Laura R. 2002. *The Political Geographies of Pregnancy.* Urbana: University of Illinois Press.

Right to Die/Physician-assisted Suicide

Fall 2017 marked the 20th year of legalization of the Death with Dignity Act in the state of Oregon. The Act refers to a procedure by which decisionally capable patients diagnosed with a terminal illness with a life expectancy of six months or less can request a prescription from a qualified physician to end their lives in a humane and dignified manner. The legal permission for physicians to participate in the hastening of death of a terminally ill patient was in its inception referred to as physician-assisted suicide, although it is more commonly known now as physician assistance in death or physician aid-in-dying and occasionally as medically assisted death. The differences in nomenclature are not free of value assumptions; however, conceptually "physician-assisted suicide" or "physician-assisted death" is distinguished from (1) procedures in which patients might exercise a legal and ethical right to decline or withdraw medical life support (such as a ventilator or feeding tubes), the cessation of which will most likely bring about their death, and (2) procedures in which a physician directly administers a lethal pharmacological agent into a patient's bloodstream with the intention of bringing about their death, a process frequently designated as active euthanasia.

The legal and ethical legitimacy of refusal or cessation of life support was established in the United States in the 1970s and 1980s in a series of influential court cases, and statutes in every state permit patients to compose advance directives that document their wishes regarding end-of-life treatments. Physician administration of euthanasia is not legal anywhere in the United States, although it is permitted in several European countries, such as the Netherlands, Belgium, and Switzerland, and more recently has been accepted in Canada. In contrast to both of these processes, physician-assisted death is in a legal liminal or ambiguous status. Since legalization in Oregon in 1997, legalization modeled after the Oregon statute has occurred in five other states: Washington (2008), Montana (2008), Vermont (2013), California (2015), and Colorado (2016). Terminally ill patients in each of these states have a more expanded set of legal rights about end-of-life options than persons who reside in other states, though there is no legal right to the administration of euthanasia anywhere in the United States.

LEGALIZATION ARGUMENTS

Patient Rights. A primary rationale for the passage of the Oregon statute that legalized physician-assisted death was respect for patients' claims of autonomy and self-determination. Autonomy- or rights-based arguments continue to be the foundational philosophical and ethical appeal for legalization in current debates. This argument begins by observing that there is legal recognition, supported by ethical principles, of substantive patient rights to decline or discontinue medical treatment with the expectation that death will be the most likely outcome of treatment cessation. The law, medical professionalism, ethical theories, and most religious traditions support a patient's *negative* right of noninterference pertaining to decisions to forgo medical treatment at the end of life. This right of noninterference is grounded in patient claims of bodily integrity, autonomy, and moral authority over decisions regarding health care, as well as the invasive nature of various medical procedures necessary to sustain life.

The legalization argument then builds on currently established patient rights of decision making in end-of-life care and expands the scope of such rights to encompass a right to assistance in hastening death through a prescription from a qualified physician. There is certainly controversy over whether the assertion of a *positive* right to assistance in dying is the moral and legal equivalent of the established negative right to noninterference in dying. Proponents of legalization see the positive right to assistance as implicit in and an extension of the negative right, while opponents, such as current Supreme Court Justice Neil Gorsuch, see a radical discontinuity between the two kinds of rights claims and contend a positive right to assistance in dying needs a separate and independent justification. It is important to note that the right to physician assistance does not entail a "duty" to exercise the right either to obtain a prescription or to ingest the medication following the dispensation of the prescription. The cumulative data from Oregon indicates that in about 65 percent of patients who receive a prescription use it to end their lives; in the remaining 35 percent of patients, the medication functions more as form of psychological assurance about control over dying or the patient dies of other causes (Oregon Death with Dignity Act, 2019).

A related rationale for legalization draws on the rights of all persons in a liberal, pluralist society to make choices that are central to self-understanding and self-identity, meaning, and dignity. Two interrelated points are made in this claim. The first concerns the scope and content of personal rights. In this view, the question of the manner of dying is not solely about exercising a negative or positive right about medical treatment but rather concerns a deeply personal and intimate interpretation of ultimate or existential concern. These ultimate concerns include finding meaning in one's life and in the personal encounter with one's own mortality, and they extend to considerations of personal dignity. Though clearly intertwined with understandings of personal identity, a dignified death on this argument typically entails dying in a manner consistent with the values and relationships by which one has lived and avoiding profound diminishments of self that may be brought on by experiences of dependency and concerns about becoming a burden for familial caregivers.

The second aspect of this claim addresses the nature of the fair or minimally just society. A liberal, pluralist society committed to the protection of respect for autonomy, the equality of persons, and the promotion of fairness will not permit authoritarian views of either the good life or the good death to be imposed on its citizens. An account of the good life and the dignified death are determinations left to individuals in the context of their own families and moral communities. It follows that the minimally just society will give wide discretion to personal choice about the manner of dying consistent with considerations of public well-being and professional integrity. This means that legal restrictions on dying that may infringe on a person's view of their dignity, or that otherwise reflect a philosophic, political, professional, or religious interpretation of a good or dignified death, are paternalistic and unjustified.

Professional Responsibility. A third rationale for legalization of physician-assisted death focuses less on the patient's right of self-determination and more on the background conditions of the terminal condition of the patient and the participation of the physician in light of professional, ethical, and legal imperatives of medicine to provide care that prevents harm and relieves patient pain and suffering. These moral commitments to the physical and emotional welfare of patients help establish the uniqueness of the medical vocation in contrast to other professions such as law or education. Given both the physical pain and the emotional and spiritual suffering attendant upon terminal illness, as well as various deprivations the patient might experience, such as limited mobility or diminished interaction in the world, including with loved ones, the vocational argument affirms that physicians have an inherent responsibility, grounded in the ethical principle of beneficence, to provide treatments that alleviate pain or suffering and an equally compelling commitment, grounded in the virtues of compassion and presence, to provide forms of comfort care that assure meaningful quality of life even at the end of life.

There is little disagreement about these commitments as defining features of the medical profession and of medical ethics. The controversial question in this regard is whether this general responsibility of a physician to promote patient welfare, including the compassionate relief of pain and suffering, requires a specific form of action, namely, the writing of a prescription for a lethal medication that a patient can choose to ingest or not. Most physician advocates of legalization tend to portray physician assistance in this setting as a *last resort* when other alternatives, such as the cessation of treatment or increased doses of sedatives including palliative sedation, that manifest the commitment of physician beneficence are unlikely to bring about the end desired by both the physician and patient. All state statutes legalizing physician assistance in death indicate that the attending physician has a duty to inform the patient of alternatives such as hospice care and comfort care; in practice, however, hospice care may be understood as complementary to a patient's request for a prescription to end life rather than as an alternative.

Even if there is a compelling philosophical, ethical, and even religious argument from beneficence and compassion that can support legalization of physician-assisted death, the legal status of such an argument is disputed. The legal statutes on physician-assisted death ground the practice in the patient's right of self-determination and do not mention the patient's experience of pain, suffering, or deprivation. (The European countries that permit both assisted dying and physician euthanasia do indicate that patient conditions of unrelieved and protracted suffering can be occasion for medical assistance in death.) The state statutes also affirm that there is no legal duty of a health care professional or institution (e.g., a hospital) to participate in the patient's request for a medication to end life. Physicians do refuse to participate, and if this is the case, it seems hard to defend the proposition that the general obligation of compassionate physician beneficence implies the specific means of relieving pain, suffering, and deprivations by a lethal medication. However, as with other contexts of conscientious refusals in medicine, even if such a commitment is not assumed as binding on every professional, it can still have a morally binding status on the profession as a whole.

RETENTIONIST ARGUMENTS

There are several arguments in support of retaining current legal prohibitions on physician assistance in the death of a terminally ill patient. The first of these arguments is embedded in various religious traditions that suggest legalized physician assistance of death would violate the religious and social commitment to the sanctity of human life. This perspective supports professional claims of conscientious objection and is certainly relevant for the policy debate over legalization.

The broader value of the sanctity of human life is, for some persons—particularly those within the professional traditions of medicine—reflected in the prohibition against physicians providing deadly drugs expressed in the classical version of the Hippocratic Oath (ca. fourth century BCE). The Hippocratic prohibition doesn't address the matter of legalization per se and may actually presuppose legalization, but it does address the professional integrity of physicians whose participation in physician-assisted death would seem to violate the Hippocratic commitment. However, the classical version of the Hippocratic Oath is no longer taken by medical professionals, and contemporary professional oaths, such as the Declaration of Geneva (revised 2017), affirm a general professional commitment to respect human life without dictating specific prohibitions and elevate responsibility for patient health and well-being as the primary professional consideration. In short, 21st-century physicians have no professional responsibility to follow the Hippocratic Oath of the fourth century BCE.

Critiques of the Autonomy Argument for Legalization. Other arguments for retaining the legal prohibitions are frequently direct counters to many of the legalization arguments. Some leading physicians argue that the argument for respecting patient self-determination cannot have general applicability because terminally ill patients who express requests to end their life are vocalizing concerns from a place of profound personal vulnerability that is influenced by loneliness and depression. These background circumstances that attend terminal illness can mean the patient is experiencing a condition of impaired judgment that would call into question the informed and voluntary patient choice presumed in the legalization argument. This retentionist critique of patient autonomy observes that the state statutes legalizing assisted death leave the assessment of depression or impaired judgment up to the attending physicians, who may lack the requisite professional expertise to request a psychiatric or palliative care consult for the patient. Moreover, none of the state statutes make such a consultation mandatory, and empirical evidence indicates the rate of referrals for psychiatric evaluation of terminally ill patients who are requesting physician-assisted death is low (about 5 percent of patients in Oregon who receive a prescription) and has declined considerably over the years.

Two kinds of legalization arguments are presented against this critique. First, there are clear instances in public literature, documentaries, and patient narratives where patients who request medication to end life are acting autonomously and with full awareness. The most prominent exemplar is the 2014 case of Brittany Maynard, a 29-year-old woman diagnosed with a progressive form of brain cancer who moved from California to Oregon to ensure that she could have access to a prescription to end her life. Second, most patients who request physician assistance in death are enrolled in hospice care programs (approximately 87.5 percent in Oregon), which means a premium is placed on ensuring the high quality of holistic care, not treatment confined solely to physical symptoms.

A second retentionist criticism of the autonomy-based arguments for legalization focuses less on the circumstances of individual patients and more on what is perceived to be the inexorable moral logic of the self-determination position. If respect for patient rights of choice about ending life is to be the primary ethical consideration for legalization, there is nothing in principle to preclude a practice of legalized physician-assisted death from expanding into a practice of physician-administered euthanasia. Furthermore, it is unclear why the moral logic of autonomy wouldn't also include nonterminal patients, who may be suffering from psychic distress, in the demographics of persons who should have access to a physician's assistance in dying. If these kinds of expansions seem implausible or are dismissed as invalid "slippery slope" conjectures, retentionist arguments observe that European nations and Canada already accept physician-administered euthanasia as well as physician-assisted death for both terminally ill persons and some persons with nonterminal conditions. The moral logic of autonomy inevitably expands beyond a confined practice of physician-assisted death.

Critiques of the Professional Responsibility Argument for Legalization. Critics of legalization also find that physician (and pharmacist) participation in a patient request for hastened death manifests a compromise of professional integrity. The professional commitment to beneficence and compassion presumes an understanding of health care professions as engaged fundamentally in the work of healing, in caring when curing is not possible, and in the presence for and nonabandonment of vulnerable patients. Writing or dispensing a prescription to end life at the patient's choice is considered by critics to reflect a professional role as a skilled technician rather than a commitment to be a compassionate healer. Such critics, supported by assessments from specialists in palliative care and hospice care, also contend that virtually all pain experienced by terminally ill patients is treatable and manageable by different medications and forms of symptom relief. There is then no dispute that physicians and other health care professionals are under a professional and ethical imperative to relieve patient pain and suffering; the claim rather is that physicians who are committed to the principles of palliative and hospice care are so proficient in palliation that a legalized practice of physician-hastened death is not medically necessary.

Retentionist positions also reject two theses of moral equivalence presented by advocates. The first such thesis, as previously delineated, claims there is no moral distinction between a negative and a positive right. The second thesis claims that there is moral equivalence either between treatment withdrawals or refusals and interventions or assistance by physicians to hasten death or between allowing someone to die and medical killing. Many legalization advocates contend that, once a determination is made that a seriously ill patient is incurable and death is a matter of time, regardless of treatment interventions, the means by which death is brought about—the cessation of treatment or the prescription of a medication (or physician administration of medication)—are not different morally. The retentionist response to this equivalence argument commonly appeals to a difference recognized in both ethics and the law regarding the intentionality of an action, sometimes formalized as the *rule of double effect*. Physicians justify stopping medical treatment not because they intend for the patient to die but because good medicine requires forgoing invasive and medically pointless interventions, or they justify providing pain medication in a dosage amount that may accelerate the dying process because the underlying intention is to relieve patient pain, while the patient's death is an unintended secondary outcome. When a physician prescribes or administers a lethal medication, by contrast, the retentionist claim is that such action displays an integrity compromising intention of bringing about the patient's death.

Despite divisive philosophical and ethical argumentation that is reflected in the legal liminality of physician-assisted death in many states, there are shared commitments to enhancing patient control over the dying process and to affirming the importance of a dignified death for all persons. This is manifested through expansive patient rights regarding completion of advance directive documents, generally recognized claims for treatment cessation, and the incorporation of palliative care methods in medical practice. There is also a very compelling societal emphasis on the centrality of hospice care programs as the ideal venue for terminally ill patients to experience their dying no matter the underlying legal context.

Courtney S. Campbell

FURTHER READING

Aviv, Rachel. 2015. "The Death Treatment." *The New Yorker*, June 22. Retrieved from http://www.newyorker.com/magazine/2015/06/22/the-death-treatment

Battin, Margaret P., Rosamond Rhodes, & Anita Silvers. 1998. *Physician Assisted Suicide: Expanding the Debate*. New York: Routledge.

Campbell, Courtney S. 2014. "Moral Meanings of Physician-Assisted Death for Hospice Ethics." In Timothy W. Kirk & Bruce Jennings (Eds.), *Hospice Ethics: Policy and Practice in Palliative Care*, 223–249. New York: Oxford University Press.

Chell, Byron. 2014. *Aid in Dying: The Ultimate Argument*. North Charleston, SC: CreateSpace Publishing.

Cholbi, Michael J. (Ed.). 2017. *Euthanasia and Assisted Suicide: Global Views on Choosing to End Life*. Santa Barbara, CA: Praeger.

Compassion and Choices. Retrieved from https://www.compassionandchoices.org

Emanuel, Ezekiel J. 1997. "Whose Right to Die?" *The Atlantic*, March. Retrieved from http://www.theatlantic.com/magazine/archive/1997/03/whose-right-to-die/304641

Foley, Kathleen, & Herbert Hendin (Eds.). 2002. *The Case Against Assisted Suicide: For the Right to End-of-Life Care.* Baltimore: Johns Hopkins University Press.

Gawande, Atul. 2014. *Being Mortal: Medicine and What Matters in the End.* New York: Metropolitan Books.

Gorsuch, Neil M. 2006. *The Future of Assisted Suicide and Euthanasia.* Princeton, NJ: Princeton University Press.

Hedberg, Katrina, & Craig New. 2017. "Oregon's Death with Dignity Act: Twenty Years of Experience to Inform the Debate." *Annals of Internal Medicine, 167*: 579–583.

Moreno, Jonathan (Ed.). 1995. *Arguing Euthanasia: The Controversy over Mercy Killing, Assisted Suicide and the "Right to Die."* New York: Simon & Schuster.

Oregon Death with Dignity Act. 2019. *2018 Data Summary.* Retrieved from https://www.oregon.gov/oha/PH/PROVIDERPARTNERRESOURCES/EVALUATIONRE SEARCH/DEATHWITHDIGNITYACT/Documents/year21.pdf

Quill, Timothy E. 2008. "Physician-assisted Death in the United States: Are the Existing 'Last Resorts' Enough?" *Hastings Center Report, 38*: 17–22.

Richardson, Peter. 2010. *How to Die in Oregon.* Documentary film. Clearcut Productions. Retrieved from www.howtodieinoregon.com

"The Right to Die." 2015. *Economist*, June 27. Retrieved from http://www.economist.com /news/leaders/21656182-doctors-should-be-allowed-help-suffering-and -terminally-ill-die-when-they-choose

Somerville, Margaret A. 2014. *Death Talk: The Case Against Euthanasia and Physician-Assisted Suicide.* Montreal: McGill-Queens University Press.

Sumner, L. Wayne. 2017. *Physician-assisted Death: What Everyone Needs to Know.* Oxford: Oxford University Press.

Same-Sex Marriage

The political debate over same-sex marriage is primarily a fight over morality. On one side of the debate, in opposition to same-sex marriage, are two types of moral arguments. First are religious-based arguments that either emphasize the sinfulness of same-sex relationships or that relate to the "naturalness" of heterosexual, monogamous marriage, grounded in traditional gender roles. The second moral argument is more secular, emphasizing the alleged role of same-sex marriage in the overall decline of marriage as an important social institution. On the other side, proponents of same-sex marriage emphasize moral values associated with liberal constitutionalism and the equal dignity of same-sex relationships and same-sex families. Finally, critics of same-sex marriage from the left argue that liberal proponents of same-sex marriage are too morally conservative in privileging traditional notions of marriage and asking for access to a historically immoral institution—one that oppresses women and imposes oppressive norms that limit family diversity.

The modern debate over same-sex marriage in the United States began in the wake of a 1993 decision of the Supreme Court of Hawaii that provisionally held that the state constitution, which banned gender discrimination, required the legal recognition of same-sex relationships. This led to a national debate, as states generally recognize the marriages performed in other states. Thus, this court decision set off a decades-long debate about the morality of marriage. Ultimately, the morality of liberal constitutionalism prevailed when the United States Supreme Court legalized same-sex marriage nationwide in 2015, but this was a late resurgence of this moral frame, as the debate was dominated by conservative morality for decades.

MORALITY AND OPPOSITION TO SAME-SEX MARRIAGE

Discussions of the morality of same-sex marriage are connected to discussions about the morality of sexual diversity more generally. When proponents of same-sex marriage advocate for legalization, opponents tap into deep cultural, religious, and legal condemnation of same-sex intimacy. Laws outlawing same-sex intimacy existed in every state in the mid-20th century, and they were not deemed unconstitutional by the U.S. Supreme Court until 2003. In fact, the Supreme Court put its stamp of approval on these laws in 1986 in the case of *Bowers v. Hardwick*, invoking historical hostility toward and moral condemnation of same-sex intimacy to defend them against a constitutional challenge. As Chief Justice Warren Burger declared: "Decisions of individuals relating to homosexual conduct have been subject to state intervention throughout the history of Western civilization. Condemnation of those practices is firmly rooted in Judeo-Christian moral and ethical standards" (196). While in reality these laws were aimed more broadly at nonprocreative forms of sexual activity, regardless of the gender of those involved, Burger's statement accurately reflects the moral position on the question of sexual intimacy of opponents of lesbian and gay rights broadly and of same-sex marriage in particular. As Burger's statement also indicates, much of this moral condemnation derived from interpretations of sexual morality from religious texts, asserting the "sinfulness" of same-sex intimacy.

This was also a powerful political frame for activist opponents of same-sex marriage, especially in the 1990s and 2000s. Explicit theological appeals were made to citizens during campaigns over popular initiatives to ban same-sex marriage and other forms of recognition in state constitutions. In Hawaii, the Catholic and Mormon Churches were politically active and successful in campaigning against same-sex marriage, as they were in 2004 in several states, and in 2008, when California voters narrowly enacted Proposition 8, a constitutional ban on same-sex marriage in the state. They were eventually joined by conservative Protestant churches of the Religious Right. Religious activists and voters from the Religious Right often went further than merely condemning sexual minorities as sinful. They also portrayed sexual minorities as a threat to society by portraying homosexuality as a disease (despite being not deemed so by the medical community since 1973) and sexual minorities as spreaders of disease, a legacy of the homophobia of the AIDS crisis of the 1980s and 1990s.

Reflecting this approach, the 2010 Texas Republican Party Platform included the following illustrative language:

> We support the definition of marriage as a God-ordained, legal and moral commitment only between a natural man and a natural woman, which is the foundational unit of a healthy society. . . . We affirm that the practice of homosexuality tears at the fabric of society, contributes to the breakdown of the family unit, and leads to the spread of dangerous, communicable diseases. Homosexual behavior is contrary to the fundamental, unchanging truths that have been ordained by God . . . and shared by a majority of Texans.

The platform called for the recriminalization of same-sex intimacy along with its opposition to same-sex marriage. In the debate over the last state constitutional ban on same-sex marriage enacted before the Supreme Court invalidated these bans, a pastor in North Carolina preached a sermon calling for sexual minorities to be housed in concentration camps where they would eventually die, thus removing homosexuality and bisexuality from society. When Hawaii debated and enacted a same-sex marriage law in 2013, opponents engaged in a "citizens' filibuster" with 1,000 citizens voicing their opinion, most of them in opposition. Many of the talking points were provided by conservative churches, and much of the testimony echoed the same themes as the Texas platform: sin, social decline, and disease.

A similar moral critique of same-sex marriage derived from a movement in legal and political philosophy of the last several decades called the New Natural Law. Advocates of this approach include the philosophers John Finnis and Robert George. This approach to philosophy is derived from Catholic teachings on sexual morality first defined by the philosopher and theologian Thomas Aquinas. Aquinas attempted to merge Catholic religious doctrine with the political philosophy of the classical political philosopher, Aristotle. Aristotle is known for an approach to philosophy that is teleological, that is, focused on the purpose, or *telos*, of an object or institution. In his famous work *Politics*, Aristotle argued that marriage existed for the purpose of human procreation because heterosexual sex has the potential to create a pregnancy. This was the "nature" of sex, not something that merely brings pleasure or an intimacy among individuals. Thus, the New Natural Law theorists, like the Catholic Church, view the "complementarity" of male and female genitalia as signaling their moral use: for procreation within a heterosexual marriage. Because same-sex marriage opposes this "natural" order of things, it must be opposed under this moral framework.

Robert George applied this morality to his leadership of the group, the National Organization for Marriage, a leading anti–same-sex marriage activist organization. George is a cofounder of the organization and served as the chair of its board of directors. In 2009, he coauthored the *Manhattan Declaration*, a document designed to unify conservative religious opposition to same-sex marriage and abortion. This declaration drew heavily from the New Natural Law. The document invokes natural law analysis to defend its opposition to same-sex marriage, referring to heterosexual marriage as an "objective reality" (reflecting an Aristotelian approach). The document argues "that marriage is made possible by the sexual complementarity of man and woman, and that the comprehensive, multi-level sharing of life that marriage is includes bodily unity of the sort that unites husband and wife biologically as a reproductive unit" (Manhattan Declaration, 2009: 6). The document also argues that this view of marriage is reflected in the fact that many faiths view marriage as a sacrament.

A final moral approach in opposition to same-sex marriage is more secular and is derived from an intellectual tradition known as neoconservatism. Starting in the 1960s and 1970s, neoconservative thinkers were focused on the role that laws, policies, and social norms and values played in what they saw as social decline. In particular, they focused on the increasing rate of out-of-wedlock births in the United States. This phenomenon was also taking place in other countries, but the neoconservatives were focused mostly on the reasons for the shift in America. They argued that excessively generous social welfare policies, lax divorce laws, and changing cultural views about parenthood and marriage were driving social decline, as evidenced by the rise in out-of-wedlock births. Beyond changing the laws and policies governing marriage and divorce, they advocated for a strong role for religious teachings that supported the traditional heterosexual, two-parent family. Some leading voices in this camp, like Gertrude Himmelfarb, argued that single mothers should be shamed for their decisions, as single mothers had been back in Victorian

England. The neoconservative argument against same-sex marriage is that it will lead to a further decline of marriage as an institution, which in turn will exacerbate various social ills.

Neoconservative author and activist David Blakenhorn turned to advocacy against same-sex marriage after decades of writing and activism concerning what he saw as the decline of fatherhood. He became such a prominent anti–same-sex marriage activist that he was called to be a witness in the federal trial over Proposition 8 on the side of those defending the measure. He testified about his concerns regarding same-sex marriage and family decline, asserting that marriage was a fragile institution and that any changes would further weaken it (the *Manhattan Declaration* also presents this argument). Remarkably, however, just a few years later, he announced his support for same-sex marriage in a *New York Times* editorial. Although he still had concerns about the state of the institution of marriage, he viewed many of his fellow same-sex marriage opponents as utilizing homophobia and hostility toward sexual minorities in their arguments. Blakenhorn's change of heart has been cited by some observers as evidence that the neoconservative opposition was never as strong as the theological opposition. Religious- and New Natural Law–based opponents maintain their strong moral stance against same-sex marriage.

THE MORALITY OF LIBERAL CONSTITUTIONALISM

The moral framework utilized by advocates of marriage equality has been grounded in the notion that the values of individual dignity and equality embodied in provisions of the U.S. and state constitutions protect and support the rights of same-sex couples to form relationships and have those relationships and families promoted and protected by policy and law. Over the course of several decades, activists convinced lawmakers and judges to move beyond the religious-/tradition-/harm-based view of sexual minorities and to embrace the new, constitutionally driven moral frame of dignity and equality.

Evan Wolfson was a leading advocate and activist for same-sex marriage. Deeply involved in litigation and grassroots activism since Hawaii (and even before), he also founded a leading advocacy group: Freedom to Marry. In a blueprint for the movement that he wrote in 2001, he framed the moral argument in the following manner:

> [W]e need to communicate resonant portrayals that show how the exclusion of gay people from marriage has a real and detrimental impact on children, families, and society; how withholding marriage does injustice and cruel harm to lesbian and gay seniors; how the United States is lagging behind other countries; how separate and unequal treatment is wrong; and why the government should not interfere with same-sex couples who choose to marry and share fully and equally in the rights, responsibilities, and commitment of civil marriage. (Wolfson, 2001: 36–37)

Wolfson changed the framing of the issue from harm to society stemming from sexual diversity to harm to same-couples and their families stemming from discrimination. He also invoked a leading principle of 20th-century constitutional morality, the immorality of "separate and unequal treatment." Finally, Wolfson, tapped into the powerful American value of libertarianism by calling for the government not to interfere with same-sex relationships, while at the same time advocating for their recognition by the state.

An important shift in the debate over the morality of marriage equality occurred a few years after Wolfson's blueprint appeared. In the landmark case of *Lawrence v. Texas* (2003), the Court issued a 6–3 decision that removed the moral condemnation of sexual minorities in *Bowers* and turned the Court's moral voice clearly in the direction of approval of same-sex relationships. As Justice Anthony Kennedy stated in the majority opinion, "When sexuality finds overt expression in intimate conduct with another person, the conduct can be but one element in a personal bond that is more enduring. The liberty protected by the Constitution allows homosexual persons the right to make this choice." This opinion was cited in November 2003 when the first state supreme court decision mandated same-sex marriage (in Massachusetts). The implications of these decisions were not lost on the leading voice on the U.S. Supreme Court in favor of the *Bowers* approach to the morality of sexual diversity. Justice Antonin Scalia accused Kennedy of paving the way for the Court's eventual endorsement of marriage equality.

After over a decade of activism and litigation following the broad moral outline articulated by Wolfson, the Supreme Court fully embraced the morality of liberal constitutionalism when it found a constitutional right to same-sex marriage in 2015. As Justice Kennedy declared in *Obergefell v. Hodges*:

> It is now clear that the challenged laws [prohibiting same-sex marriage] burden the liberty of same-sex couples, and it must be further acknowledged that they abridge central precepts of equality. Here the marriage laws enforced by the respondents are in essence unequal: same-sex couples are denied all the benefits afforded to opposite-sex couples and are barred from exercising a fundamental right. Especially against a long history of disapproval of their relationships, this denial to same-sex couples of the right to marry works a grave and continuing harm. The imposition of this disability on gays and lesbians serves to disrespect and subordinate them. And the Equal Protection Clause, like the Due Process Clause, prohibits this unjustified infringement of the fundamental right to marry. (Slip Opinion, 2014: 22)

When same-sex couples first applied for marriage licenses in the early 1970s, they were essentially laughed out of court, given the negative moral frame concerning sexual minorities represented in *Bowers*. Indeed, the Supreme Court held that the Constitution offered no protections for these couples. However, decades of grassroots and legal activism designed to change this moral frame were successful.

THE MORAL CRITIQUE OF SAME-SEX MARRIAGE FROM THE LEFT

An additional moral frame in this legal and policy debate derives from feminist morality. Under this moral framework, marriage is seen as a historically patriarchal institution in which generations of women have faced oppression and violence. In the contemporary setting, in which some of this oppression has been alleviated, viewing marriage and thus a family as a relationship that includes two parents (opposite-sex or same-sex) limits the types of families sanctioned and supported by society and the state. It also reinforces traditional gender roles. This moral stance led many in the LGBT rights movement to oppose the embrace of marriage equality as a central goal of the movement. Rather than ask for inclusion into the institution of marriage, advocates of this perspective call for a broadening of the definition of family to many nontraditional forms and an elimination of the link between two-person marriages and the benefits of the welfare state, such as Social Security, health care, and tax benefits. As stated by law professor Nancy Polikoff, a leading advocate of this moral position, the movement for same-sex marriage "positions the gay rights movement on the wrong side of the culture war over acceptable family structures. . . . The civil rights victory of marriage for those gay and lesbian couples who seek it may come at the expense of law reforms benefiting a wider range of families" (Polikoff, 2008: 98).

This position points in the direction of greater appreciation and protection for family diversity, but it has struggled to gain traction in the U.S. debates over same-sex marriage. The less radical approach of liberal constitutionalism has been a more influential frame, indicating the presence of a broader moral conservatism in the United States about marriage. For instance, in many European countries and Canada, the legal recognition of cohabiting heterosexual couples served as the starting point for discussion about the legal protections for same-sex couples. However, in the United States, these policies never gained traction due to the elevated moral position of marriage in the culture and public policy.

Jason Pierceson

FURTHER READING

Babst, Gordon A., Emily R. Gill, & Jason Pierceson (Eds.). 2009. *Moral Argument, Religion, and Same-Sex Marriage*. Lanham, MD: Lexington Books.
Ball, Carlos Al (Ed.). 2016. *After Marriage Equality: The Future of LGBT Rights*. New York: New York University Press.
Bamforth, Nicholas C., & David A. J. Richards. 2008. *Patriarchal Religion, Sexuality, and Gender: A Critique of the New Natural Law*. New York: Cambridge University Press.
Blakenhorn, David. 2012. "How My View on Gay Marriage Changed." *New York Times*, June 22. Retrieved from http://www.nytimes.com/2012/06/23/opinion/how-my-view-on-gay-marriage-changed.html.
Bowers v. Hardwick 478 U.S. 186 (1986).
Fejes, Fred. 2008. *Gay Rights and Moral Panic*. New York: Palgrave Macmillan.
George, Robert, et al. 2009. "The Manhattan Declaration: A Call to Christian Conscience." Retrieved from http://manhattandeclaration.org/man_dec_resources/Manhattan_Declaration_full_text.pdf
Haider-Markel, Donald P. 2001. "Policy Diffusion as a Geographical Expansion of the Scope of Political Conflict: Same-sex Marriage Bans in the 1990s." *State Politics and Policy Quarterly*, *1*(1): 5–26.
Lawrence v. Texas 539 U.S. 558 (2003).
Manhattan Declaration. (2009). *Manhattan Declaration: A Call of Christian Conscience*. Retrieved from https://www.manhattandeclaration.org/
Mucciaroni, Gary. 2009. *Same Sex, Different Politics: Success and Failure in the Struggles over Gay Rights*. Chicago: University of Chicago Press.

Obergefell v. Hodges 576 U.S. ___ (2015).

Pierceson, Jason. 2014. *Same-Sex Marriage in the United States: The Road to the Supreme Court and Beyond.* Lanham, MD: Rowman & Littlefield.

Polikoff, Nancy. 2008. *Beyond (Straight and Gay) Marriage.* Boston: Beacon.

Slip Opinion. 2014. "Supreme Court of the United States, Syllabus." *Obergefell et al. v. Hodges, Director, Ohio Department of Health, et al.* Retrieved from https://www.supremecourt.gov/opinions/14pdf/14-556_3204.pdf

Texas Republican Party Platform. 2010. Retrieved from https://static.texastribune.org/media/documents/FINAL_2010_STATE_REPUBLICAN_PARTY_PLATFORM.pdf

Wolfson, Evan. 2001. "All Together Now (A Blueprint for the Movement)." *The Advocate,* September 11: 34–37.

Second Amendment (Right to Bear Arms)

The full text of the Second Amendment to the United States Constitution reads: "A well regulated militia being necessary to the security of a free state, the right of the people to keep and bear arms shall not be infringed." Yet just what "the right of people to keep and bear arms" means in terms of policy remains a contentious issue. On the one hand, advocates for gun rights have long argued that the Second Amendment franchises an individual's right to keep and bear arms, entailing minimal (or even no) governmental oversight on private gun ownership. On the other hand, proponents for gun control contend that the Second Amendment franchises a collective right to firearm ownership originally intended to prevent Congress from legislating away state-level self-defense in the form of citizen militias and that private firearm ownership is subject to regulation. These competing interpretations of the Second Amendment generally reflect the two prevalent paradigms on gun rights and gun control in the United States. Yet within these two paradigms are moral and political arguments to which advocates and interest groups appeal.

ADVOCATES FOR GUN RIGHTS

A number of organizations and individuals advocate for gun rights in the United States, and not all of them operate in the same political arena. For instance, organizations like the Federalist Society and the Second Amendment Society have worked within the judicial branch to enhance gun rights by producing legal research and court briefs with the intent to shape judicial opinions that can set legal presidents interpreting gun rights as an individual right. But the most visible advocacy for gun rights comes from state and national member-based advocacy groups, the most notable of which is the National Rifle Association (NRA). The NRA is comprised of around 5 million members, has chapters in every state, spends millions of dollars on lobbying and electioneering, and possesses a professional media production studio that produces content for both gun rights advocates and apolitical gun owners. The NRA is the flagship organization for gun rights in the United States, and as such many of the moral and political arguments made by the NRA are the most visible and emphasized ones heard in American political discourse.

Perhaps the most common argument from groups like the NRA is that gun rights are an individual right enshrined in the Constitution, not unlike the right to free speech or the right to peacefully assemble. This argument of gun rights as a Constitutional right is only partially an appeal to the legality of gun rights; it also seizes on the idea of the United States as a "city on a hill" and "the land of the free." It also attributes the defense of private gun rights as a moral duty to the Founding Fathers of the nation, who were supremely wise to protect such rights in a founding document. Likewise, many gun rights activists believe a Constitutional right to bear arms serves as a check on governmental power, arguing that an armed populace cannot be oppressed. This constitution-based case for gun rights also forms the basis for many other gun rights–related arguments, such as the right of self-defense and the right to participate in firearm-related commerce. For gun rights activists, the idea of self-defense is synonymous with gun rights, which is in turn synonymous with the Constitution. Likewise, the idea that one must purchase a firearm in order to become a gun owner underlies the importance of firearm commerce as a constitutional right. Adherents of this view believe that one cannot suggest that restrictions on the ability to engage in firearm dealing do not touch upon the Constitutional right to own a gun because as long as a right to own a gun exists, there inherently must be the right to sell and/or acquire guns. In short, the moral appeal to the constitutionality of gun rights in the United States is a centerpiece to many of the rights-based arguments that many gun rights activists and advocacy groups use.

GUN RIGHTS AND AMERICAN SELF-IMAGE

A second argument often used by gun rights advocates relies on appeals to traditional American values of self-reliance and rugged individualism. Gun rights advocates often appeal to these traditional values by noting the historical role of firearms in activities ranging from hunting (essential to pioneer survival) to wars of self-defense and territorial expansion. The continuing popularity of shooting sports and the perceived moral imperative of being able to personally protect one's home and family from criminal victimization are an extension of these traditional values. At the same time, appeals to these "traditional American" values sometimes malign (either implicitly or explicitly) advocates of gun control as perhaps less "American" than those supporting gun rights. These values of self-reliance are also present in arguments around the need for people to be self-reliant with regard to potential criminal victimization, with mottos such as, "A gun in the hand is better than a cop on the phone."

A third argument for gun rights appeals to the differences between decent law-abiding people with guns and lawbreakers with guns. Gun rights advocates often frame these arguments around the notion that gun laws are by definition violated by criminals, and therefore people who own guns and follow the law are a non-problem. On the other hand, people who are willing to break the law will have little incentive to follow any gun control laws, and therefore gun control will only take guns away from law-abiding citizens who should have the right to be armed against criminal threats. The safety and law-abiding citizen argument also argues that when more law-abiding citizens are armed, it may even deter crime as criminals will face greater odds of armed resistance. Thus, there can be a moral imperative for people to legally carry firearms if they are allowed to do so, and "good guys" with guns can help prevent crime.

ADVOCATES FOR GUN CONTROL AND THEIR MORAL ARGUMENTS

Turning to the side of gun control, a number of organizations and individuals are also dedicated to advocating and promoting new regulations for firearms. The first organizations dedicated to gun control advocacy emerged in the wake of progressive social movements from the 1960s and the passage of the Gun Control Act in 1968. In 1974, both the Nation Council to Control Handguns and the National Coalition to Ban Handguns were founded and evolved over time to become the Brady Campaign to Prevent Gun Violence and the Coalition to Stop Gun Violence (CSGV). However, these organizations have never been able to achieve the same level of popular support or membership levels that the NRA has. But in 2014 a new organization emerged called Everytown for Gun Safety, which combined a grassroots organization called Mom's Demand Action with a coalition of political leaders called Mayors Against Illegal Guns founded by the billionaire and former New York City Mayor Michael Bloomberg. Everytown for Gun Safety stands out from the Brady Campaign and the CSGV because it combines both a large grassroots membership presence with a well financed political organization to lobby for gun control for the first time in the United States. In the short time that Everytown for Gun Safety has existed, though, it has managed to score some significant political victories in recent elections for gun control that bode well for the organization's future.

Arguments put forth by gun control advocates often rely on themes of safety and democratic values to make the moral case of gun control. A common argument for gun control often rests on the notion that public opinion generally endorses new gun control laws and that a democratic society should implement policies that reflect this public opinion. At the same time, gun control advocates argue that, when public opinion is not reflected in policy, democratic values have been betrayed by special interest groups imposing minority beliefs upon a majority that should not abide by such views. An example of this is the case of universal background checks (a policy that requires one to undergo a background check prior to any firearm purchase), which a large majority of Americans support regardless of their position on gun rights but which is opposed by organizations like the NRA. For gun control advocates, the fact that such a policy has widespread public support yet is not reflected in policy represents a miscarriage of democracy.

Similarly, gun control advocates often argue that democratic values are threatened when local and municipal governments are unable to implement gun control policies because of state or federal policies that protect gun rights. An example of this can be seen in state-level preemption laws, which prevent local and municipal governments from enacting firearm policies that conflict with state law. A preemption law may state that firearm laws are the purview of the state and that therefore cities cannot enact their own firearm laws, which can effectively prevent cities from enacting policies that they feel are needed to protect public safety. Appealing to the idea of home rule for local governments, gun control advocates claim that local governments should be able to democratically implement the laws they feel they need for firearm safety and that policies preventing this from happening are both undemocratic and serve the interest of overly powerful groups such as the NRA.

Another argument for gun control rests on appeals to public health. Such arguments posit that firearm prevalence is intrinsically linked to firearm violence and that, in order to reduce such violence, it is important to reduce the general prevalence of and access to firearms. These arguments do not distinguish between "good guys" with guns and "bad guys" with guns but rather put forth the idea that firearms are a vector for injury that can be controlled, not unlike a disease. This argument is particularly salient given that the United States has both the highest rates of firearm injury and violence and civilian firearm ownership of any Western democratic nation (Hemenway, 2006). This argument also relies on the idea that an immoral consequence of America's widespread firearm ownership is an unparalleled rate of firearm deaths and tragedies, such as mass shootings and suicides that occur because the opportunity for such outcomes is more likely given such high rates of firearm ownership (Reeping et al. 2019).

The final argument for gun ownership discussed here is that of gun control as crime control. Unlike the public health arguments that attempt to emphasize the role of firearms as a vector of violence, gun control advocates argue that there are "bad guys" who should not have access to guns and that gun control legislation will make it harder for them to obtain and use such weapons in crime. A policy closely related to this argument is, again, universal background checks, which would eliminate the practice of background-check-free sales at gun shows or by private sellers. For gun control advocates, the implementation of new gun laws requiring background checks for sales has the potential to catch and prevent those prohibited from gun ownership from obtaining a gun, which will reduce crime (not only because it prevents would-be criminals from getting guns but also because these people are committing crimes just by obtaining guns that they shouldn't have access too). Likewise, gun control advocates will point out that many policy proposals they present are often endorsed by law enforcement agencies, suggesting again that "good guys" support the idea of gun control to prevent "bad guys" from using guns.

The debate on the Second Amendment in the United States is relatively new, given the fact that the amendment itself is 225 years old. In 1934, the very first federal gun control laws emerged with the National Firearms Act, which put a prohibitive stamp tax of $200 (a value today of over $3,600) on machine gun sales. But it wasn't until the late 1960s and 1970s that the first major debates emerged between the dedicated gun rights and gun control groups. Following the wave of high-profile political assassinations on President John F. Kennedy (1917–1963), Martin Luther King Jr. (1929–1968), Robert F. Kennedy (1925–1968), and Malcolm

X (1925–1965), political will to pass new control laws was incredibly high. In response, Lyndon B. Johnson (1908–1973) passed the Gun Control Act of 1968, which created a national licensing system for gun dealers, banned the mail-ordering of firearms, and required a serial number for all new firearms made or imported. After the passage of the Gun Control Act, many gun rights supporters began to push groups like the NRA to more vigorously advocate gun rights and to push back against gun control policies. This change was new for the NRA, which, prior to 1968, was relatively apolitical and primarily served as a resource for sport shooters and conservationists. In 1977, NRA members voted at their annual meeting in Cincinnati to oust the old leadership that was fighting for gun rights and instead replaced them with more radical leadership dedicated to fighting gun control. Since then, the NRA has been a vanguard for gun rights.

In 1994, both the Federal Assault Weapons Ban (FAWB) and the Brady Bill were passed. The FAWB expired in 2004, but for the 10 years it was enacted, it restricted the sale of assault weapons and may have contributed to a decline in violent crime across the nation over the past 20 years. Similar arguments could be made for the Brady Bill, which created the National Instant Background Check System that is now used by all federally licensed firearm dealers when they sell a firearm to a customer. In 2006, the arguably biggest change to gun rights occurred with the Supreme Court ruling of *District of Columbia vs. Heller. Heller* was the first time the Supreme Court ruled that the Second Amendment was a protection of the individual right to own a gun rather than a collective right of the states to have militias. In practice, the *Heller* decision overturned a handgun ban in Washington, D.C., which had long been a thorn in the side of gun rights activists, and effectively ruled it unconstitutional for local or state governments to deny access or ownership to common types of firearms like handguns or long guns (but not for more dangerous weapons like machine guns). In short, the past 20 years has been a time of expansion for gun rights all across the United States, with many states enacting new laws allowing the issuance of concealed carry permits and court rulings like *Heller.* However, organizations like Everytown for Gun Safety represent a revitalization for gun control advocacy over older groups like the CSGV and the Brady Campaign. But whether Everytown can maintain its momentum against the organizational skills, resources, and persistence of the NRA and its allies remains to be seen.

Trent Steidley

FURTHER READING

Cagle, M. Christine, & J. Michael Martinez. 2004. "Have Gun, Will Travel: The Dispute Between the CDC and the NRA on Firearm Violence as a Public Health Problem." *Politics & Policy, 32*(2): 278–310.

Carlson, Jennifer. 2015. *Citizen-Protectors: The Everyday Politics of Guns in an Age of Decline.* New York: Oxford University Press.

Cook, Philip J., & Kristin A. Goss. 2014. *The Gun Debate: What Everyone Needs to Know.* Oxford: Oxford University Press.

District of Columbia vs. Heller, 2008.

Dowler, Kenneth. 2002. "Media Influence on Attitudes Toward Guns and Gun Control." *American Journal of Criminal Justice, 26*(2): 235–247.

Downs, Douglas. 2002. "Representing Gun Owners Frame Identification as Social Responsibility in News Media Discourse." *Written Communication, 19*(1): 44–75.

Gahman, Levi. 2014. "Gun Rites: Hegemonic Masculinity and Neoliberal Ideology in Rural Kansas." *Gender, Place & Culture, 22*(9): 1203–1219.

Goss, Kristin A. 2008. *Disarmed: The Missing Movement for Gun Control in America.* Princeton, N.J.: Princeton University Press.

Haider-Markel, Donald P., and Mark R. Joslyn. (Guest Eds.). 2017. *Special Issue: Gun Politics. Social Science Quarterly.* Hoboken, NJ: Wiley-Blackwell, *98*(2): 377–512.

Haider-Markel, Donald P., & Mark R. Joslyn. 2001. "Gun Policy, Opinion, Tragedy, and Blame Attribution: The Conditional Influence of Issue Frames." *The Journal of Politics, 63*(2): 520–543.

Hemenway, David. 2006. *Private Guns, Public Health.* Ann Arbor: University of Michigan Press.

Holbert, R. Lance, Dhavan V. Shah, & Nojin Kwak. 2004. "Fear, Authority, and Justice: Crime-related TV Viewing and Endorsements of Capital Punishment and Gun Ownership." *Journalism & Mass Communication Quarterly*, 81(2): 343–363.

Joslyn, Mark R., Donald P. Haider-Markel, Michael Baggs, & Andrew Bilbo. 2017. "Emerging Political Identities? Gun Ownership and Voting in Presidential Elections." *Social Science Quarterly, 98*(2): 382–396.

Kleck, Gary, Marc Gertz, & Jason Bratton. 2009. "Why Do People Support Gun Control? Alternative Explanations of Support for Handgun Bans." *Journal of Criminal Justice, 37*(5): 496–504.

Melzer, Scott. 2009. *Gun Crusaders: The NRA's Culture War.* New York: New York University Press.

Merry, Melissa K. 2016. "Constructing Policy Narratives in 140 Characters or Less: The Case of Gun Policy Organizations." *Policy Studies Journal, 44*(4): 373–395.

Reeping, P. M., M. Cerdá, B. Kalesan, D. J. Wiebe, S. Galea, & C. C. Branas. 2019. "State Gun Laws, Gun Ownership, and Mass Shootings in the US: Cross Sectional Time Series." *British Medical Journal, 364*: 1542–1545.

Smidt, Corwin D. 2012. "Not All News Is the Same Protests: Presidents, and the Mass Public Agenda." *Public Opinion Quarterly, 76*(1): 72–94.

Spitzer, Robert J. 2012. *The Politics of Gun Control.* Boulder, CO: Paradigm Publishers.

Steidley, Trent, & Cynthia G. Colen. 2016. "Framing the Gun Control Debate: Press Releases and Framing Strategies of the National Rifle Association and the Brady Campaign." *Social Science Quarterly.* doi:10.1111/ssqu.12323

Stroud, Angela. 2016. *Good Guys with Guns: The Appeal and Consequences of Concealed Carry.* Chapel Hill: University of North Carolina Press Books.

Sex Education in Public Schools

Since the 1910s, public schools have been a hotbed for morally framed policy debates, and since the 1960s and 1970s, sexual education in public schools has become a major point of contention in these larger curricular conflicts. Sexual education can be broken into three basic types: comprehensive, abstinence-based, and abstinence-only. Comprehensive sexual education is instruction that includes information on the use of contraceptives and other types of birth control methods, the prevention of sexually transmitted diseases (STDs), and human development, reproduction, and sexuality. Abstinence-based sexual education is focused on instructing students that abstinence is the only way to prevent pregnancy and sexually transmitted disease but may include additional instruction on other topics, such as pregnancy prevention, reproduction, human development, and sexuality. Abstinence-only education is instruction that only instructs students on the virtues of abstinence; no other topics are covered.

The differences in these types of sexual education instruction can be traced back to the moral arguments leveled against comprehensive sexual education programs in public schools. These moral objections center on three larger ideas: abstinence until marriage, relationships being between one woman and one man, and parental control. First, parents, religious leaders, and religious groups contend that since the Bible states that individuals should remain abstinent from (or not engage in) sex prior to marriage, schools should teach students only to avoid sexual encounters before marriage. Furthermore, they argue that teaching about contraceptives and the prevention of sexually transmitted diseases encourages students to engage in sexual activity (Deckman, 2004). Second, beyond objections to the instruction on contraceptives and disease prevention, religious individuals and groups protest any instruction of human development and sexuality that includes sexual orientation and gender identity. Finally, like other morally based objections to public school policies, parents contend that they alone should have control over the content of their child's education and that if the school is doing any kind of sexual education, it should follow the moral views held by the parents and promote the concept of the traditional family that is presented in religious doctrine (Deckman, 2004; Reich,

2002; Wilcox & Robinson, 2011). For these parents, any sexual instruction that is not abstinence-only is encouraging immorality and encroaching on their rights to morally instruct their children (Deckman 2009; Reich 2002; Wilcox and Robinson 2011).

THE RISE OF SEXUAL EDUCATION IN PUBLIC SCHOOLS

The 1960s and 1970s were a period marked with cultural change. Younger individuals were starting to question traditional social norms and engage in sexual activity outside of traditional moral guidelines touted by their parents and wider American society. There was a rise in sexual relationships and cohabitation outside of marriage, along with a growing alarm about youth engagement in sexual activity and concerns about homosexuality. In response to these larger societal changes, schools introduced sexual education lessons to inform youth about pregnancy, sexually transmitted diseases, contraceptives, and abortion. When some religious parents became aware that schools were teaching their children about sex, they challenged these programs as infringements on their authority to instruct their children in matters of morality and sexual activity. They were, however, in the minority at the time, and local school districts continued offering sexual education courses (Doan & McFarlane, 2012).

As conservative religious parents became more politically organized and active throughout the 1980s and 1990s, many focused their anti–sex education efforts on grassroots mobilization and winning local school board elections. At the local level, their efforts paid off with the ouster of school board members who were supportive of the sex education curriculum. Religiously motivated parents began to run for office and often were elected to local school boards, usually running as Republicans in sleepy races, and pushed for the removal of sexual education curriculum. After some victories at the local level, the sex education issue became more prominent at the national level and gained key conservative political allies, such as President Ronald Reagan and Senators Orin Hatch (R-Utah) and Jeremiah Denton (R-Alabama). One result of the growing strength of the movement was the Adolescent Family Life Act (AFLA) of 1981, which provided money for schools and community programs that promoted chastity, self-discipline, and abstinence until marriage (Arsneault, 2001; Deckman, 2004). Despite the growing prominence of abstinence-only programs, however, states continued to provide sex education programs and HIV/AIDS prevention instruction in public schools (Doan & McFarlane, 2012).

MOVING TOWARD ABSTINENCE-ONLY EDUCATION

Throughout the 1980s and 1990s, the overall influence of the religious movement grew, and alongside that growth, abstinence-only education gained prominence as the governmentally supported means to educate youth about sex. The next major victory for religious conservatives came in 1996 with the passage of a welfare reform law that included a provision allocating $50 million per year to states to promote abstinence-only education. In addition, stipulations were added that required programs utilizing the welfare reform and AFLA funds to abide by eight federal guidelines defining abstinence-only education (Vergari, 2000). The guidelines required that programs:

> [h]ave as its exclusive purpose teaching the social, psychological, and health gains to be realized by abstaining from sexual activity; teach abstinence from sexual activity outside marriage as the expected standard for all school-age children; teach that abstinence from sexual activity is the only certain way to avoid out-of-wedlock pregnancy, sexually transmitted diseases, and other associated health problems; teach that a mutually faithful, monogamous relationship in the context of marriage is the expected standard of sexual activity; teach that sexual activity outside the context of marriage is likely to have harmful psychological and physical effects; teach that bearing children out-of-wedlock is likely to have harmful consequences for the child, the child's parents, and society; teach young people how to reject sexual advances and how alcohol and drug use increases vulnerability to sexual advances; teach the importance of attaining self-sufficiency before engaging in sexual activity. (Title V, Section 510 of the Social Security Act)

The result of this legislation and funding stipulation was a large growth in state implementation of abstinence-only education programs (Collins et al., 2002). While the AFLA was the first legislation to provide funding for abstinence-only education, the new legislation was far more specific about what programs could and could not say to youth, and it provided a much larger block grant for states (Doan & McFarlane, 2012).

Following on the heels of the 1996 legislation, Congress passed the Community-Based Abstinence Education (CBAE) program in 2000. Similar to the programs that proceeded it, the CBAE stipulated that organizations utilizing the funds must abide by the eight guidelines defining the scope of abstinence-only education. In contrast to previous legislation, however, this new program did not allocate funds to states to distribute to schools and community organizations (Doan & McFarlane, 2012; Santelli, 2006). The absence of funds stemmed from a concern that states were not using the funds specifically for abstinence-only education and instead were using monies for loosely affiliated programming (Doan & McFarlane, 2012). Instead of allowing states to distribute funds as they see fit, the CBAE program instead bypasses states and allocates monies directly to community= and school-based organizations. Furthermore, organizations that accept CBAE monies must target programs toward 12- to 18-year-olds and cannot provide any information about safe sex or contraceptives—regardless of whether they are using non-CBAE monies (Santelli, 2006). In 2007, Congress added further restrictions to the Title V welfare reform funds and stipulated that curricula must discourage the use of contraceptives. Throughout the two terms of George W. Bush's administration (2001–2009), the national government increased its influence on sexual education curricula, and abstinence-only education and programming grew.

THE REJECTION OF ABSTINENCE-ONLY EDUCATION

Although morally motivated parents and officials were successful in passing federal policies mandating strict abstinence-only education, much of the public opposed morally based abstinence-only programming, and states began to reject the federal funds. First, a survey done by researchers at the Annenberg Public Policy Center found that while the public expressed overwhelming support for programs that teach abstinence along with other prevention measures, only about one-third of the public actively supported abstinence-only sex education programs—and about half of the respondents were outright opposed to abstinence-only education (Bleakley, Hennessy, & Fishbein, 2006). By 2009, half of the states had rejected the Title V funds. One of the primary drivers of these rejections was the publication of research showing that abstinence-only education was not working; studies indicated that there were no differences in sexual activity between youth who went through an abstinence-only education program and those who did not (Trenholm et al., 2008). Furthermore, reports from various states indicated that abstinence-only education might be doing harm by, for example, not educating youth about pregnancy and disease prevention (SIECUS, 2010). Beyond the question of the results of abstinence-only education, states also rejected the funds due to a lack of administrative capacity to manage the programs and a disagreement with the ideological and moral principles behind the programs (Doan & McFarlane, 2012; SIECUS, 2010).

CURRENT APPROACHES TO SEX EDUCATION

Although the Title V funding program expired in 2009, during the debate over the Affordable Care Act (ACA) of 2010, conservative members of Congress were able to add in funding for the Title V abstinence-only program (SIECUS, 2011). Once again, the legislation allocated $50 million per year to states via block grants and stipulated that funded programs must promote abstinence and cannot include other topics such as contraception. However, alongside the revival of abstinence-only education, the ACA also created the Personal Responsibility Education Program (PREP), which allocates $55 million per year in grants to states. This program requires education about abstinence and contraceptives as a means to prevent pregnancy and sexually transmitted diseases, as well as instruction on relationships, development, and other life skills (SIECUS, 2011). States have the opportunity to apply for both grant programs, and as of 2011, 45 states applied for PREP funds and 34 applied for Title V funds (SIECUS, 2011).

Andrea Vieux

FURTHER READING

Arsneault, Shelly. 2001. "Values and Virtue: The Politics of Abstinence-only Sex Education." *American Review of Public Administration, 31*(4): 436–454.

Bleakley, Amy, Michael Hennessy, & Martin Fishbein. 2006. "Public Opinion on Sex Education in US Schools." *Archives of Pediatrics and Adolescent Medicine, 160*: 1151–1156.

Collins, Chris, Priya Alagiri, Todd Summers, & Stephen F. Morin. 2002. "Abstinence Only vs. Comprehensive Sex Education: What Are the Arguments? What Is the

Evidence?" Policy Monograph Series. AIDS Research Institute. University of California, San Francisco. March.

Deckman, Melissa M. 2004. *School Board Battles: The Christian Right in Local Politics.* Washington, DC: Georgetown University Press.

Doan, Alesha E., & Jean Calterone Williams. 2008. *The Politics of Virginity: Abstinence in Sex Education.* Westport, CT: Praeger.

Doan, Alesha, & Deborah R. McFarlane. 2012. "Saying No to Abstinence-only Education: An Analysis of State Decision-making." *Publius: The Journal of Federalism, 42*(4): 613–635.

Reich, Rob. 2002. "Testing the Boundaries of Parental Authority over Education: The Case of Homeschooling." In Stephen Macedo and Yael Tamir (Eds.), *Moral and Political Education,* 275–313. New York: New York University Press.

Santelli, John S. 2006. "Abstinence-only Education: Politics, Science, and Ethics." *Social Research, 73*(3): 835–858.

SIECUS (Sexuality Information and Education Council of the United States). 2010. "A History of Federal Funding for Abstinence-only-until-marriage Programs." (Fiscal Year 2010 edition). Retrieved from www.siecus.org

SIECUS (Sexuality Information and Education Council of the United States). 2011. "State by State Decisions Fiscal Year 2011 Edition: The Personal Responsibility Education Program and Title V Abstinence-Only Program." (Fiscal Year 2011 edition). Retrieved from www.siecus.org

Title V Section 510 (b)(2)(A–H) of the Social Security Act.

Trenholm, Christopher, Barbara Devaney, Kenneth Fortson, Melissa Clark, Lisa Quay, & Justin Wheeler. 2008. "Impacts of Abstinence Education on Teen Sexual Activity, Risk of Pregnancy, and Risk of Sexually Transmitted Diseases." *Journal of Policy Analysis and Management, 27*(2): 255–276.

Vergari, Sandra. 2000. "Morality Politics and Educational Policy: The Abstinence-only Sex Education Grant." *Educational Policy, 14*(2): 290–310.

Wilcox, Clyde, & Carin Robinson. (4th ed.). 2011. *Onward Christian Soldiers? The Religious Right in American Politics.* Boulder, CO: Westview Press.

Sin Taxes

As the 20th-century Austrian economist Joseph Schumpeter wrote, taxes "are one of the best starting points for an investigation of society" (Schumpeter, 1919: 101). Taxes are a particularly incisive lens when it comes to investigating the prevailing moral values of a given society. Whom to tax and what to tax often come down to moral and political concerns rather than purely economic considerations. Nowhere is this more apparent than in debates surrounding sin taxes. A sin tax refers to a specific type of excise tax levied on items generally regarded as being harmful or undesirable. Taxes levied specifically on alcohol or tobacco, for instance, are considered sin taxes. Sin taxes function morally as "symbolic expressions of disapproval" (Carruthers, 2016: 2570); that is, they signal that certain commodities and behaviors are socially stigmatized and may attempt to incentivize people to abandon such behaviors. However, different frames get deployed to respond to that stigmatization.

EVOLUTION OF SIN TAXES IN AMERICA

The attention given to sin taxes among the media, the public, and academics has increased in recent years as reliance on these taxes has also increased. However, sin taxes are not new. Excise taxes have always been politically divisive since the first excise tax in England was levied in 1643 on items such as beer, ale, and cider. The introduction of the excise tax was a "landmark in the history of British political theory and practice" because "never, within memory, had the poor, the propertyless, and the disenfranchised been taxed for support of the government" (Slaughter, 1986: 17). The reactions to the British excise tax varied, though; for both the supporters and the opposition, arguments utilized both economic and moral justifications. For some of the supporters of the new excise taxes, the argument was that this type of tax was the most morally defensible tax because it was "voluntary." The voluntary nature of an excise tax lay in the assumption that people had a choice in "how much they paid by how much they consumed," and supporters further argued that it was "good policy to tax people's vices and might actually result in more temperate consumption of evil spirits and tobacco" (Slaughter, 1986: 18). Opponents of the new excise taxes, on the other hand, denounced the new tax as "morally offensive" because it increased the tax burden on the poor and had the potential to hurt farmers and small producers of taxed products (Slaughter, 1986: 17). The dislike of the new tax led to a number of riots and attacks on tax collectors following its implementation.

Many of these same moral and political frames carried over to America when, in 1791, Secretary of the Treasury Alexander Hamilton proposed an excise tax on whiskey distilled in America. The so-called whiskey tax was proposed to help the new U.S. government pay for the war debt. However, like the British excise, the whiskey tax proved to be immediately unpopular. For those opposed to the tax, "Most . . . could agree that an excise was 'odious, unequal, unpopular, and oppressive'" (Slaughter, 1986: 87). For those in support of the tax, the hope was that the tax would limit negative behavior: "The heart of moral support for the excise came from those concerned about the harmful effects of drink on the physical and mental well-being of the nation's imbibers" (Slaughter, 1986: 88). The animosity toward the government for introducing the whiskey tax continued to fester and eventually turned into a popular rebellion lead by farmers in Pennsylvania. In 1794, farmers and other tax rebels marched on the house of John Neville, the local tax collector, and set fire to his house. This event caused Washington to send in over 12,000 militia to quell the uprising. The riots, in the long run, were successful, and in 1802, under Thomas Jefferson, the United States repealed the whiskey tax, along with all other "internal" (meaning excise) taxes in favor of "external" (meaning tariffs on imports) taxes. The United States maintained its no-internal-tax policy until the Civil War when, due to the pressure to raise money to fund the army, the government reintroduced a variety of excise taxes (Huret, 2014: 3). By 1900, the federal government received 43 percent of its revenue through excise taxes (Mehrotra, 2013: 7). However, federal reliance on excises dropped after 1913 when the income tax was passed. For instance, in 1920, excise taxes made up just 7 percent of federal government revenue, while income taxes made up 66 percent (Mehrotra, 2013: 7).

Although the federal government now receives less from this type of tax, the same is not true of state and local governments. Subfederal governments' reliance on sin taxes has continued to increase in recent decades. Prior to the early 1910s, states relied almost exclusively on local property taxes to fund local government. However, as the property tax increased to fund more services, it became a burden on farmers who began to form populist parties that advocated for diversifying the kinds of taxes levied (McNall, 1988). As a result of the political pressure, states began to tax sales and incomes, though sin taxes still remained low. For instance, in 1913 taxes on alcohol sales accounted for 0.7 percent of total state revenue and tax revenues on tobacco were zero, but by 1934 alcohol accounted for 1.8 percent and tobacco accounted for 0.7 percent (Carruthers, 2016: 2576). That percentage continued to gradually increase for the remainder of the 20th century and into the early years of the current century. In 2014, for example, 3.4 percent of all local and state taxes derived from tobacco products, and 1.3 percent came from alcohol products.

Of course, there is great variation among states with the distribution of sin taxes. For instance, Missouri has the lowest tax on cigarettes at only $0.17 per pack, while in Arizona it is $2 a pack. Additionally, more things now fall under the umbrella of sin taxes. For instance, in 2007 Texas introduced a "pole tax" of $5 for strip club patrons (Morse, 2009). Several states also have excise taxes on gambling, and debate has been growing about whether and how states should consider taxing e-cigarettes and vaping. Some cities have also passed laws to tax soda and other sugary drinks to combat obesity, a tax that has come to be known as a fat tax. In 2014, Berkeley, California, implemented America's first soda tax; it was quickly followed by Philadelphia, San Francisco, and several other U.S. cities.

MORAL CATEGORIZATION OF SIN TAXES

Part of the reason for the proliferation of sin taxes is their moral categorization. It is worth noting here that the definition and categorization of what is considered sinful enough to be subjected to a sin tax change over time. In this way, sin taxation directly reflects American morality on a variety of issues. For instance, while cigarettes, alcohol, and gambling are commonly sin-taxed behaviors today, during the New Deal era, "discussions of luxury taxes depended on the perceived status of various goods" (Carruthers, 2016: 2570). However, many of the same debates remain regardless of the item being taxed. Politically, these taxes are relatively easy to pass because of the moral frames they carry with them. They allow governments to raise revenue "without also arousing the ire of voters" (Johnson & Meier, 1990: 577). As such, arguments about the morality and efficacy of sin taxes continue to be important. While the debates surrounding the earliest excise taxes, such as the whiskey tax, are not directly comparable to present discussions, many of the moral frames and arguments used at that time still inform today's debates.

The first moral framing employed in support of imposing sin taxes is the view that they deter or reduce harmful behavior. There's an epigram often attributed to Ronald Reagan: "If you want less of something, tax it." This aphorism has come to underlie the logic of sin taxes. If you want people to stop smoking, raise taxes on cigarettes, and people will make the calculation that the pleasure they receive from smoking is no longer worth the cost. This argument is staunchly couched in the neoclassical economic views of human behavior as well as the role of public finance. In the neoclassical frame, taxes are utilized primarily to correct for externalities (McCaffery & Slemrod, 2006: 6). However, "Government today acts to modify behaviors, not as an unavoidable by-product of its usual tasks, such as taxation, but purposefully in response to a perceived need to induce people to behave more 'appropriately'" (McCaffery & Slemford, 2006: 5). Thus, in the realm of public policy, behavioral economics has started to gain influence (Oliver, 2015).

Behavioral economics utilizes the field of psychology to help explain people's economic behaviors. The public policy use of sin taxes in particular has been buoyed by the field of behavioral economics, particularly the concept of nudging, which refers to "any factor that significantly alters the behavior of Humans" (Thaler & Sunstein, 2008: 8). Policy makers have thus started to use taxes as a way to nudge people into making better choices (or to avoid making bad ones). This is particularly on display in the realm of public health where sin taxes are used to deter negative health behaviors such as smoking or excessive alcohol consumption. However, some see nudging as a form of government paternalism or even social engineering.

Evidence of the effectiveness of sin taxes to curb negative behaviors is somewhat mixed. For instance, in Berkley, after the implementation of the soda tax, consumption of sugary drinks did drop dramatically. In the first year of the tax, consumption of sugary drinks dropped 21 percent, and consumption of water increased 63 percent (Falbe et al., 2016). However, when it comes to taxes on cigarettes, the evidence is less convincing. While cigarette taxes do, on average, show a decrease in smoking, it's often a small, statistically insignificant amount (Callison & Kaestner, 2014). Despite their mixed track record, these taxes take up a great amount of policy maker's attention.

The second major moral frame, however, is the view of sin taxes as punitive and regressive; that is, this type of tax disproportionately impacts the poor over the rich. Sin taxes are doubly regressive in a way. On the one hand, they're regressive because they are a form of sales tax, and sales taxes are, by their nature, regressive. On the other hand, they're also regressive because the types of behaviors that sin taxes target are often clustered among low-income people. For instance, "Cigarette expenditures as a share of income are 3.2% in the bottom quartile of the income distribution, but are only 0.4% of income in the top quartile" (Gruber & Koszegi, 2004). However, not all sin tax behaviors are like this. Research has shown that, while low-income people are more likely to engage in heavy drinking, people with higher incomes tend to drink much more frequently (Cerdá, Johnson-Lawrence, & Galea, 2011).

It is easy to see why these taxes would be attractive to policy makers. A tax that purports to help reduce a negative behavior while also raising revenue to help society pay for the cost of that negative behavior seems like a win-win. Because the state gains revenue from sinful behavior, often states spend sin tax revenue in a somewhat penitent manner; that is, the money from sin taxes is often earmarked for funding socially positive programs, like school programs, for instance. Of course, the irony built into this arrangement is that the stream of revenue generated by the sin tax would ideally dry up eventually as negative behavior, such as smoking, eventually ceased. There are also questions about the moral position these taxes put the government in. Is it moral for the state to draw revenue from behaviors that are addictive or potentially addictive?

MORAL DIMENSIONS OF SIN TAXES

Sin taxes can also serve a legitimating function. Sin taxes, while taxing socially undesirable activities, still tax legal activity and not illegal activities. Distillers and brewers, for instance, consented to alcohol taxes, which "gave state and federal governments a good fiscal reason not to follow the prohibitionists and completely prohibit alcohol" (Carruthers, 2016: 2572). An arguably similar strategy is at work with the legalization of marijuana in the United States. One of the most persistent arguments by advocates of legalization is that governments should legalize it in order to tax it. In this case, advocates were essentially asking for their product to be taxed in order to legitimize it as well as draw the state into a lucrative revenue stream. Colorado, which legalized recreational marijuana in 2014, taxes the substance at the state's 2.9 percent sales tax, a 10 percent marijuana sales tax, a 15 percent marijuana excise tax—all this in addition to local sales and marijuana taxes (Colorado Department of Revenue, n.d.). And in 2016 Colorado brought in over $1 billion dollars in new tax revenue (Huddleston, 2016). The additional revenues brought in by marijuana taxes have been used primarily in schools. Indeed, the first $40 million in marijuana excise tax revenue is earmarked specifically for school construction (Silbuagh, 2015).

The morality of sin taxes remains contested even as their usage increases. However, these moral consternations tap into a long thread of moral concerns in American history and culture. It is doubtful that policy makers will ever strike the right balance between alleviating the regressive nature of sin taxes while trying to encourage healthful behaviors. However, it's clear that moral concerns continue to drive this debate.

Daniel R. Alvord

FURTHER READING

Callison, Kevin, & Robert Kaestner. 2014. "Do Higher Tobacco Taxes Reduce Adult Smoking? New Evidence of the Effect of Recent Cigarette Tax Increases on Adult Smoking." *Economic Inquiry, 52*(1): 155–172.

Carruthers, Bruce G. 2016. "The Semantics of Sin Tax: Politics, Morality, and Fiscal Imposition." *Fordham Law Review, 84*(6): 2565–2582.

Cerdá, Magdalena, Vicki D. Johnson-Lawrence, & Sandro Galea. 2011. "Lifetime Income Patterns and Alcohol Consumption: Investigating the Association Between Long- and Short-term Income Trajectories and Drinking." *Social Science & Medicine, 73*(8): 1178–1185.

Colorado Department of Revenue. n.d. "Marijuana Tax Data." Retrieved from https://www .colorado.gov/pacific/revenue/colorado-marijuana-tax-data

Falbe, Jennifer, Hannah R. Thompson, Christina M. Becker, Nadia Rojas, Charles E. McCulloch, & Kristine A. Madsen. 2016. "Impact of the Berkeley Excise Tax on Sugar-sweetened Beverage Consumption." *American Journal of Public Health, 106*(10): 1865–1871.

Gruber, Jonathan, & Botand Koszegi. 2004. "Tax Incidence When Individuals are Time-consistent: The Case of Cigarette Excise Taxes." *Journal of Public Economics, 88*: 1959–1987.

Haile, Andrew J. 2009–2010. "Sin Taxes: When the State Becomes the Sinner." *Temple Law Review, 82*(4).

Huddleston, Tom, Jr. 2016. "Colorado Topped $1 Billion in Legal Marijuana Sales in 2016." *Fortune*, December 13. Retrieved from http://fortune.com/2016/12/13/colorado -billion-legal-marijuana-sales

Huret, Romain D. 2014. *American Tax Resisters*. Cambridge, MA: Harvard University Press.

Johnson, Cathy M., & Kenneth J. Meier. 1990. "The Wages of Sin: Taxing America's Legal Vices." *Western Political Quarterly, 43*(3): 577–595.

McCaffery, Edward J., and Joel Slemrod, eds. 2006. *Behavioral Public Finance*. Washington, SC: Russell Sage Foundation.

McNall, Scott G. 1988. *The Road to Rebellion*. Chicago: University of Chicago Press.

Mehrotra, Ajay K. 2013. *Making the Modern American Fiscal State*. New York: Cambridge University Press.

Meier, Kenneth J. 1994. *The Politics of Sin: Drugs, Alcohol and Public Policy*. New York: M. E. Sharpe.

Morse, Rachel E. 2009. "Resisting the Path of Least Resistance: Why the Texas 'Pole Tax' and the New Class of Modern Sin Taxes are Bad Policy." *Boston College Third World Law Journal*, *29*(1): 189–221.

Oliver, Adam. 2015. "Nudging, Shoving, and Budging: Behavioural Economic-Informed Policy." *Public Administration*, *93*(3): 700–714.

Schumpeter, Joseph A. 1919. "The Crisis of the Tax State." In R. Swedberg (Ed.), *The Economics and Sociology of Capitalism*, 99–140. Princeton, NJ: Princeton University Press.

Silbaugh, Larson. 2015. "Distribution of Marijuana Tax Revenue." Colorado Legislative Council Staff. Issue Brief Number 15-10, July. Retrieved from https://leg.colorado.gov/sites/default/files/15-10_distribution_of_marijuana_tax_revenue_issue_brief_1.pdf

Slaughter, Thomas P. 1986. *The Whiskey Rebellion: Frontier Epilogue to the American Revolution*. New York: Oxford University Press.

Tatalovich, Raymond, & Byron W. Daynes. 2011. *Moral Controversies in American Politics*. New York: M. E. Sharpe.

Thaler, Richard H., & Cass. R. Sunstein. 2008. *Nudge: Improving Decisions About Health, Wealth, and Happiness*. New York: Penguin Books.

Surveillance

Persistent surveillance has become a ubiquitous feature of modern American life. With a looming "War on Terror" and rapid technological development, a significant change of course is unlikely in the foreseeable future. This issue is often portrayed in a partisan light, but narrowly focusing on "right versus left" obscures the cross cutting moral foundations of the debate over surveillance—a debate that cuts to the core of our national ethics. What are the limits of state power and the bounds of citizenship? How much control should private companies have over our personal information and consumer options? Is privacy a fundamental human right or a luxury attached to one's social status? These are difficult questions without clear answers, but understanding their moral foundations and implications is essential to making progress in any public debate.

"Security" has become the watchword of the post-9/11 era. Nation-states, companies, and even individuals are turning to sophisticated surveillance technologies to monitor threats of terrorism and to attempt to identify and control potentially harmful or destructive behavior. Revelations in the summer of 2013 by Edward Snowden, however, a former Central Intelligence Agency (CIA) employee and National Security Agency (NSA) subcontractee for Dell and Booz Allen, both intensified and complicated debates over national security and privacy. Snowden revealed new details of a sprawling government surveillance apparatus that collects and analyses millions of e-mails, text messages, and phone calls every day. Once this information was released to the press, it became clear that the NSA and other national intelligence agencies operate an extensive domestic and international dragnet that collects both communications metadata (the sender/receiver as well as time-stamps of communications) and sometimes the contents of these communications. Snowden's revelations are arguably one of the most significant disclosures of classified material since the release of the Pentagon Papers in 1971.

The fallout from Snowden's disclosures was considerable. In the United States, the political discourse over the revelations was surprisingly nonpartisan. Congressional Democrats' and Republicans' responses were split: Republican House Speaker John Boehner joined Democrat Dianne Feinstein in calling Snowden a traitor, while Democratic Civil Rights pioneer John Lewis called him a "hero" who was appealing to a "higher law," joining Republican Rand Paul in comparing his actions to those of famous civil dissidents like Ghandi and Martin Luther King Jr. These kinds of strange bedfellows were evident in the public reaction as well, as Snowden's revelations brought together left-wing intellectual Noam Chomsky and conservative commentator Glenn Beck in praising Snowden's actions.

Why were reactions to Snowden's leaks so mixed and seemingly contradictory? Portraying debates over mass surveillance exclusively as a political issue masks a more fundamental examination about the morality of surveillance itself and the importance of personal and data privacy as a human right. In short, debates over surveillance strike at the core of contradictory American morality politics, one that is not easily mapped onto a simple partisan grid. The moral debates over mass surveillance practices can be broken down into three broad assertions frequently voiced by proponents of such surveillance:

1. "If you're not doing anything wrong, you have nothing to worry about."
2. "Extensive surveillance is a necessary trade-off for national security."
3. "Surveillance gives us more of what we want and less of what we don't."

These arguments tap into moral frameworks that span traditional political positions and parties and are thus difficult to elucidate by focusing strictly on political ideologies. Fierce debates over these assertions provide a window into the complex moral underpinnings of the contemporary political debate over 21st-century government and corporate surveillance.

"IF YOU'RE NOT DOING ANYTHING WRONG, YOU HAVE NOTHING TO WORRY ABOUT"

Public figures from former President George W. Bush to Google CEO Eric Schmidt have used this phrase—or some version thereof—to justify government and corporate surveillance alike. Cryptographer and computer security and privacy specialist Bruce Schneier (2006) cites this kind of assertion as "the most common retort against privacy advocates." Though the phrase has been dubiously attributed to members of the Nazi regime, a variant of it more likely originated with muckraking journalist Upton Sinclair in an account of the Haymarket bombings. The British government even used it in the media campaign they launched in connection with the massive expansion of their CCTV program (Solove, 2011). The argument is relatively straightforward and hinges on the belief that surveillance should be permissible, if not justified, for anyone who is not engaged in some type of malfeasance or criminal activity. Why would you insist on privacy unless you're doing something you shouldn't be doing in the first place? The value of transparency is the operative concept in this argument—if a child insists that no one should look under his bed or a spouse puts her phone or computer under password protection, the immediate assumption is likely be that they are doing something they would not like others to know about. The argument is thus inherently a moral one.

Legal scholar Daniel Solove points out one difficulty with this argument: It is based on the idea that privacy is based on the notion of hiding something. The argument "myopically views privacy as a form of secrecy" rather than, among other things, a right to free, unencumbered space for thought and reflection. Solove (2011: 27) continues that understanding privacy in a more multifaceted and nuanced way "demonstrates that the disclosure of bad things is just one among many difficulties caused by government security measures." Such difficulties lie in aggregation, exclusion, secondary use, and distortion—all of which result in a multifaceted but limited view of the person themselves.

Another retort to the nothing-to-hide argument is that privacy protects one from the effects of power differentials inherent within surveillance practices. Surveillance presumes a watcher and a watched, each of whom has needs and interests that are presumably at odds with one another. The protection of privacy is about the creation and maintenance of a power-free zone for those being watched. Schneier (2006) wrote in *Wired* magazine, "Privacy protects us from abuses by those in power, even if we're doing nothing wrong at the time of surveillance." Private spaces are spaces where one can retreat, rest, and reflect, without fear of reprimand or judgment. "We do nothing wrong when we make love or go to the bathroom. We are not deliberately hiding anything when we seek out private places for reflection or conversation. We keep private journals, sing in the privacy of the shower, and write letters to secret lovers and then burn them." Privacy, Schneier argued, "is a basic human need."

Commentator and social media researcher danah boyd (2013) connects the idea of surveillance with social inequality, asking whether, for instance, it is okay for state surveillance to disproportionately target minority groups or those otherwise disadvantaged. To create and maintain such a zone of privacy within an increasingly surveilled society can require resources—financial, political, and cognitive—that disproportionately inhere with majority groups. danah boyd (2013) links such privilege to systemic social inequalities, noting that what we deem "suspicion" often inheres disproportionately within such minority groups. As boyd puts it, "Is your perception of your safety worth the marginalization of other people who don't have your privilege?"

"EXTENSIVE SURVEILLANCE IS A NECESSARY TRADE-OFF FOR NATIONAL SECURITY"

As previously noted, "security" has become the organizing principle of domestic policy since 9/11 (Monahan, 2010). One common argument in support of mass government surveillance post-9/11 is that such an extensive monitoring apparatus is a regrettable but necessary trade-off for national security in the fight against asynchronous enemies and the threat of "terror." This argument is often espoused by politically conservative groups and commentators who say that the nature of the War on Terror is one that demands an extensive and flexible government surveillance apparatus to combat a threat that is continually evolving in its tactics and capabilities for harm. Public concern reflects this sentiment. A recent Pew Research poll indicated that just under half of Americans say the U.S. government has "not gone far enough to protect our country," while only a third feel the government has "gone too far in restricting civil liberties." Moreover, the trend has been consistent over time. With the exception of a brief reversal following the Snowden leak, the percentage of Americans advocating for more security has been higher than those advocating for more privacy (Raine, 2016).

The Snowden leaks of 2013 brought these arguments to the fore. Legal analyst and national security expert Glenn Sulmasy (2013) stated on CNN, "What might have been reasonable 10 years ago is not the same any longer. The constant armed struggle against the jihadists has adjusted our beliefs on what we think our government can, and must, do in order to protect its citizens." Fighting terrorism—by its very nature as a diffused and global threat—is different from fighting a war against a nation-state and "requires new ways and methods of gathering information. As technology has increased, so has our ability to gather valuable, often actionable, intelligence." Self-radicalized and so-called homegrown terrorists are another worry, and catching them necessarily requires "collections of U.S. citizens' conversations with potential overseas persons of interest." Gerald Walpin, writing for the conservative *National Review*, agreed. Echoing the nothing-to-hide argument, Walpin (2013) stated that the collection of metadata is necessary but, in fact, does not go far enough. "Our intelligence people know phone numbers or area codes used by terrorists in various world locations," he observed, speaking of the bulk collection of such information by the National Security Agency.

> Wouldn't you want our intelligence services to know who in the United States called those numbers and area codes and to examine the information to determine whether those calls were innocent or not? I certainly would. If this program had been applied to identify the Boston bombers, that attack could have been prevented.

Despite Gerald Walpin's dubious counterfactual assertions that the NSA's programs could have prevented the 2013 Boston Marathon Bombing (they were in place at the time of the bombing, and the bombers themselves were largely self-radicalized and not part of established terrorist networks), the arguments clearly indicate the belief that there is an irreconcilable tension between privacy and security. Privacy advocates and political liberals counter these claims with several positions. Their first rebuttal is that the trade-off itself is a false dichotomy. As Solove (2011: 34) puts it, "Sacrificing privacy doesn't automatically make us more secure" and "not all security measures are invasive of privacy." After 9/11, plane cockpit doors were required to be locked before take-off, a measure that certainly increased security without sacrificing much privacy. While certainly most Americans would be willing to make some commonsense trade-offs between privacy and security, the portrayal of the dichotomy as an "all-or-nothing" trade-off misses the point. Second and perhaps more fundamentally, the idea of "national security" can be stretched in myriad ways to justify any number of activities. Solove continues that it is often difficult to distinguish "threats to national security" from what we might deem ordinary crime. "National-security threats are a form of crime," he observes. "They are severe crimes, but the rules for investigating ordinary crime are designed to regulate government information gathering no matter how grave the particular crime might be." Finally, others have suggested that, once put in place, surveillance techniques and programs tend to expand beyond the bounds of their original intent and mission, a phenomenon known as surveillance creep, which is sometimes encouraged by greater efficiency and reduced costs (Barnard-Wills, 2012).

"SURVEILLANCE GIVES US MORE OF WHAT WE WANT AND LESS OF WHAT WE DON'T"

Another significant arena of mass surveillance is in the area of the marketing and sales of goods and services, with much of this activity taking place on the Internet. A leading market research firm predicted that by 2016 e-commerce and online retail sales in the United States would reach close to $300 billion, with consumers' average yearly online spending estimated to be $1,738 per person. With so much at stake, e-commerce companies engage in various so-called data mining techniques to identify, track, and collect large amounts of information on potential customers. The goal of all this "dataveillance" is to target desirable prospects for highly individualized courting and to turn the unpredictable consumer into a responsive customer (Clarke, 1994). Proponents of data mining argue that this strategy is a more efficient way to address customer demand, to lower prices, and to increase company profits. For example, marketing firms may use historical data to predict customer response to ad campaigns, promotional marketing, and the like. By targeting specific individuals based on personalized profiles, consumers are offered products and services that they are more likely to be interested in rather than being overwhelmed by irrelevant and extraneous advertising. The search engine Google, for example, encourages users to contribute to "ad personalization" by providing personal profile information and topics of interest so that the company can show users ads of interest to them. But data mining strategies have appeared in other sectors as well. In banking and finance, data collected on a customer's prior financing behavior is used to build models to customize future loans and rates, while the close monitoring of credit card use helps banks detect possible fraud. In the health care sector, administrators use data mining techniques to identify and monitor high-risk patients and chronic diseases and to design the right interventions, find best practices, and decide on the most effective treatments.

Government agencies can also use "transactional" data mining information—collected both by industry and by its own operations—to look for patterns of criminal activity such as tax fraud, as well as to investigate patterns of behavior that might suggest terrorist activities.

Yet detractors of data mining and Big Data analytics contend that such techniques and systems are designed to engage in forms of "social sorting," which may be inherently biased and discriminatory. That is, not only should some dataveillance practices be considered as potential threats to individual privacy and civil liberties, but, from a sociological perspective, they may operate as a powerful means of creating and reinforcing social differences and enhancing the life chances of some while diminishing those of others (Lyon, 2002). With banks, insurance companies, and large employers deploying these data, one's access to quality health services, to a competitive mortgage rate, to knowledge about educational opportunities, even to landing a job may depend on the quality of one's "digital DNA." Various forms of so-called "web lining and digital discrimination may help to reinforce existing social and economic inequalities. For example, some "data brokers" can produce "e-scores," an algorithmic-generated assessment of your likelihood of spending money on certain goods and services. The score is a product of a person's occupation, salary, home value, as well as spending and shopping habits. Once tagged with a low e-score or other low desirability category, someone may find it exceedingly difficult to shed that classification since the very opportunities not offered might be the ones that permit a person to move out of these classifications. Although the scores may be helpful for companies, as one journalist put it, "[T]hey may send some consumers into a downward spiral, locking them into a world of digital disadvantage." Frank Pasquale, a professor at Seton Hall University School of Law, says, "I'm troubled by the idea that some people will essentially be seeing ads for subprime loans, vocational schools and payday loans while others might be seeing ads for regular banks and colleges, and not know why" (Singer, 2012).

Alexander J. Myers and William B. Staples

FURTHER READING

Barnard-Wills, David. 2012. "Epistemology of Creep." *Surveillance and Identity: Research into Surveillance and Identity Issues*, May 21. Retrieved from http://surveillantidentity.blogspot.com/2012/05/epistemology-of-creep.html

Boyd, Danah. 2013. "The Problem with the 'I Have Nothing to Hide' Argument." *Dallas News*, June 14. Retrieved from http://www.dallasnews.com/opinion/commentary/2013/06/14/danah-boyd-the-problem-with-the-i-have-nothing-to-hide-argument

Clarke, Roger. 1994. "Dataveillance by Governments: The Technique of Computer Matching." *Information Technology & People*, 7(2): 46–85.

Greenwald, Glenn. 2014. *Nowhere to Hide: Edward Snowden, the NSA, and the U.S. Surveillance State*. New York: Metropolitan Books.

Lyon, David. 2002. *Surveillance as Social Sorting: Privacy, Risk, & Digital Discrimination*. New York: Routledge.

Lyon, David. 2015. *Surveillance After Snowden*. Malden, MA: Polity.

Monahan, Torin. 2010. *Surveillance in the Time of Insecurity*. New Brunswick, NJ: Rutgers University Press.

Raine, Lee. 2016. "The State of Privacy in Post-Snowden America." Pew Research Center. Retrieved from http://pewrsr.ch/2cRz16m

Schneier, Bruce. 2006. "The Eternal Value of Privacy." *Wired*, May 18.

Schneier, Bruce. 2015. *Data and Goliath: The Hidden Battles to Collect Your Data and Control Your World*. New York: W. W. Norton.

Singer, Natasha. 2012. "Secret E-scores Chart Consumers' Buying Power." *New York Times*, August 18. Retrieved from http://www.nytimes.com/2012/08/19/business/electronic-scores-rank-consumers-by-potential-value.html?pagewanted=all

Solove, Daniel J. 2011. *Nothing to Hide: The False Tradeoff Between Privacy and Security*. New Haven, CT: Yale University Press.

Staples, William G. 2013. *Everyday Surveillance: Vigilance and Visibility in Postmodern Life*. Lanham, MD: Rowman & Littlefield.

Sulmasy, Glenn. 2013. "Why We Need Government Surveillance." CNN, June 10. Retrieved from http://www.cnn.com/2013/06/10/opinion/sulmasy-nsa-snowden

Walpin, Gerald. 2013. "We Need NSA Surveillance." *National Review*, August 16. Retrieved from http://www.nationalreview.com/article/355959/we-need-nsa-surveillance-gerald-walpin

Terrorism and Counterterrorism

After the September 11 attacks in 2001, President George W. Bush declared that the United States needed to engage in a War on Terror. Upon invoking this course of action, Bush called this a fight of freedom versus fear, justice versus cruelty, and suggested that God was on the side of the United States in the fight to come. While there are few moral absolutes, many people view the world in similar black-and-white terms—living in a world of good versus evil, where right and wrong are both clear and distinct. Acts of terrorism are regarded by the overwhelming majority of people as clear violations of morality, but is there no exception for terrorism? Is terrorism rooted in evil? What if the perpetrators believe that the potential ends justify the means? Does it depend on the cause or issue to which the people engaging in these acts are dedicated? Does it matter if the victims are civilians or agents of the government? After all, violent acts taken by political radicals, abolitionists, antiabortion activists, neo-Nazis, and environmental activists have all been placed under the umbrella of terrorism—but people have a wide range of opinions about the legitimacy of these actors and their methods.

THE IMPORTANCE OF LANGUAGE

In order to explore the moral questions related to terrorism, we must first define it. Definitions and indeed all language have consequences. As one may observe, definitions have an important role to play in our broader understanding of terrorism, but the language used to describe the phenomenon is already value laden (Gearty, 2004). Conor Gearty (2004) suggests that the language we use is already attached to our views of morality; for instance, we call perpetrators terrorists. Terrorism, he argues, is a method, not a label for a group or individual. It is a method that is sometimes employed to achieve a given end. It is not a personal characteristic. We label perpetrators in order to attach a negative, or evil, connotation to them, regardless of circumstance. Moreover, those who battle perpetrators are called counterterrorists, setting up the simple, familiar image we have of good versus evil.

Walter Enders and Todd Sandler (2000) define terrorism as "the premeditated use or threat of violence by individuals or subnational groups to obtain a political or social objective through intimidation of a large audience beyond that of the immediate victims." This definition suggests that both a threat and an act of violence may be labeled terrorism, that an objective may be either social or political, and that a perpetrator may be acting alone or within a group. It does not suggest that who the victims are matters or that that the victims are the primary target; rather, the effect of the attack on a broader scale is what is of consequence. This definition is making a broader statement about terrorism, that its goals are vast and not limited to the immediate effects of attacks. It is a display of power, one that perpetrators hope will lead to concessions in their favor.

On the other hand, Boaz Ganor (2010) suggests that what distinguishes terrorists from other rebel groups is their deliberate targeting of civilians. This distinction implicitly attaches innocence to the victims. However, one could make the argument that civilians may still be perceived as complicit. For example, J. Robert Oppenheimer was not a member of the military, but he steered the effort that created the atomic bomb. He was a civilian, but would one consider an attempt on his life still equally immoral? Is he equally innocent? Moreover, terrorism occurs more frequently in democracies, and if democracies are directed by the people, are the people also responsible for the policies that may have led the perpetrators to commit acts of terror?

Walter Enders and Todd Sandler's (2000) definition is frequently used in academic literature, but it is not the same definition that the federal government uses. The Department of Defense (DOD) defines terrorism as "the unlawful use of violence or threat of violence, often motivated by religious, political, or other ideological beliefs, to instill fear and coerce governments or societies in pursuit of goals that are usually political." This definition brings in an additional component: legality. By this definition, states are exempt from guilt as they have the authority to use force. Furthermore, this definition does not declare a target, leaving the victims of the attack all equally innocent. Given that the War on Terror is guided by the DoD, their definition is especially significant. The absence of a target, namely noncombatants, is especially poignant as it suggests that attacks on the military may still be considered acts of terror. This is not unprecedented. On October 23, 1983, Marine barracks in Beirut were attacked by Hezbollah; a truck bomb was detonated and killed over 200 people. This attack was widely referred to as an act of terror.

EXAMINING "INNOCENCE"

The concept of innocence may appear simplistic; we generally agree that attacking a child in a public square is a moral travesty, but do we consider an attack on a military location as fair? Do we think an act of violence is still an act of terror when an oppressor is attacked?

Consider the Oklahoma bombing; on April 19, 1995, Timothy McVeigh and Terry Nichols bombed the Murrah Federal Building in Oklahoma City. This terrorist attack was fueled by antigovernment sentiment. The blast was deadly, and among those killed were children in the building's second-floor day care. This instance of terrorism appears like a clear moral violation; it was indiscriminate and perpetrated against noncombatants, as it killed 168 people, including children, and created millions of dollars in property damage to the building and surrounding areas.

Now consider the Palestinian fight against Israeli occupation, specifically during President Yasser Arafat's term. After a failed campaign by Arab allies in 1967 to reclaim Palestinian lands, President Arafat became a "reluctant terrorist" (Gearty, 2004) as he sought to continue the fight for liberation. In doing so, he became a supporter of more isolated attacks; given the asymmetrical nature of the conflict, this was his only perceived recourse (Gearty, 2004). One could say that this instance is less clear. Some scholars argue that there is an "oppressed exception" (Coady, 2004), where conventional considerations of terrorism should be set aside. If we classify a fight against an oppressor as terrorism, how may oppressed groups ever gain their freedom or rights?

Finally, consider the retaliation. C. A. J. Tony Coady (2004) notes that in response to the acts of violence committed by the Palestinians against the Israelis, Israel also attacked civilian Palestinian areas, with disproportionate force. However, Israel is a recognized state and therefore granted authority to use force. States can also perpetrate acts of terror; Coady (2004) calls this "bent" morality, where a state creates an exceptional justification or "supreme emergency license" for a given circumstance. Supreme emergency allows states to bend their morality, as it is not always utilitarian in quashing conflict but does not extend to the perpetrators, even oppressed ones.

President Bush framed the War on Terror as good-versus-evil conflict, but are all these circumstances so clear? Morality is relative, and while many of us may agree on what constitutes good or evil, there is no universal consensus on morality or innocence.

ARE TERRORISTS SIMPLY INSANE?

Terrorism may appear to be a belligerent, ad hoc method of gaining a given goal, but some experts have argued that it is rational and, in some cases, even born of perceived necessity. Although conventional wisdom may assume that terrorists are insane and even uneducated, the empirical research suggests otherwise. Scholars have found that perpetrators are generally not poor, and they are generally well educated; they note that the makeup of Hezbollah, for example, is more educated and less poor than the general population in Lebanon (Kruger & Malečková, 2003). Ethan Bueno de Mesquita (2005) suggests that this is due to a selection effect. Terrorist groups vet the applicants and select the more educated, less poor candidates given their higher level of ability and skills. This further suggests the calculating, strategic nature of groups committing terrorism. With these studies in mind, one must consider that perpetrators are not behaving randomly. Their behavior is a means to an end. The actions they take, although shocking and reprehensible to the great majority of people, have in many cases been long considered and planned, with an end political goal usually in mind.

STATE BIAS

States have legitimacy, whereas nonstate actors do not. States are a part of the international community, and they are endowed and entitled to certain rights, including the authority to use force. States' use of force against destabilizing nonstate actors within their borders does not violate international norms or laws. However, those nonstate actors are violating the law. Regardless of their cause, they are labeled and vilified. Consider the Irish Republican Army (IRA) in Northern Ireland. The Irish people were historically persecuted by the British government, and they wanted autonomy, to be separate and speak their own language and to practice their religion. Is the IRA rebellion terrorism? Meanwhile, Hitler and Stalin were both recognized leaders of their states, and they committed acts that one could classify as terrorism—but we do not generally label it as such. Why not? Is it because we have a different set of terms—even a different language—that we use when referencing state actors who carry out vicious atrocities?

States do not always directly commit acts of terror; they also sponsor them. The attack on the Marine barracks in Beirut in the 1980s, for example, was perpetrated by Hezbollah, a group that has traditionally been revered by the Southern Lebanese population. Hezbollah is a classic example of the saying that "one man's freedom fighter is another man's terrorist." It also is a group well-known for receiving financial and other help from the government of Iran (Byman & Kreps, 2010).

Our understanding has not evolved fast enough to cope with the modern age of terrorism. States are still considered principal actors, even when nonstate actors have emerged as key players on both the domestic and the international levels. For example, Just War theory, the guiding theory of conflict among states, does not extend to nonstate actors. Just War theory depends on established distinctions, one of which includes the distinction between state actors and nonstate actors (Sussmann, 2013). Another distinction is that of war and peace; if a state is not formally declared as a party to an international war but is still being bombarded with frequent domestic terror attacks, is it still at peace (Sussman, 2013)? Would 9/11 not be considered an act of war even though it was perpetrated by a nonstate actor? Distinction between peace and war is now more complex. In the modern era of persistent terrorist attacks, can we truly claim a state of peace? These assumptions make Just War theory incapable of adequately processing terrorism in the modern era.

CONCLUSION

Reactions to acts of terror stem from our understanding of what terrorism is. If we perceive military targets as fair targets, then we would not view the 1983 Beirut attack as terrorism, but if we perceive that all people are potential victims of attacks, then we would view it as such. Definitions matter greatly, but given the lack of consensus on definitions, discussing terrorism and morality is especially challenging. There is no universal moral compass, and therefore any considerations pertaining to morality are relative. As this chapter has discussed, context and nuance can potentially challenge our views regarding just and unjust attacks.

Although perpetrators have grievances and perceive acts of terror as the means to achieve their goals, they fail to understand that their methods deafen their message to the broader public. Terrorists may face injustice, but their tactics travel further than their objectives or motives. We do, however, need to take great care when assigning labels to perpetrators; oppressed people rebelling against tyrannical regimes should not be delegitimized and discredited by being carelessly labeled as terrorists.

Ranya Radhi Ahmed

FURTHER READING

Abadie, Alberto, & Sofia Dermisi. 2008. "Is Terrorism Eroding Agglomeration Economies in Central Business Districts? Lessons from the Office Real Estate Market in Downtown Chicago." *Journal of Urban Economics, 64*(2): 451–463.

Bueno de Mesquita, Ethan. 2005. "The Quality of Terror." *American Journal of Political Science, 49*(3): 515–530.

Byman, Daniel, & Sarah E. Kreps. 2010. "Agents of Destruction? Applying Principal–agent Analysis to State-sponsored Terrorism." *International Studies Perspectives, 11*(1): 1–18.

Coady, C. A. J. Tony 2004. "Terrorism, Morality, and Supreme Emergency." *Ethics, 114*(4): 772–789.

Crenshaw, Martha. 1981. "The Causes of Terrorism." *Comparative Politics, 13*(4): 379–399.

Crenshaw, Martha. 2000. "The Psychology of Terrorism: An Agenda for the 21st Century." *Political Psychology, 21*(2): 405–420.

De Mesquita, Ethan Bueno. 2005. "Conciliation, Counterterrorism, and Patterns of Terrorist Violence." *International Organization, 59*(1): 145–176.

De Mesquita, Ethan Bueno. 2005. "The Quality of Terror." *American Journal of Political Science, 49*(3): 515–530.

Enders, Walter, & Todd Sandler. 2000. "Is Transnational Terrorism Becoming More Threatening? A Time-Series Investigation." *Journal of Conflict Resolution, 44*(3): 307–332.

Gassebner, Martin, & Simon Luechinger. 2011. "Lock, Stock, and Barrel: A Comprehensive Assessment of the Determinants of Terror." *Public Choice, 149*(3–4): 235.

Ganor, Boaz. 2010. "Defining Terrorism: Is One Man's Terrorist Another Man's Freedom Fighter?" *Police Practice and Research, 3*(4): 287–304.

Gearty, Conor. 2004. "Terrorism and Morality." *Whitehall Papers, 61*(1): 19–27.

Gurr, Ted R. 2015. *Why Men Rebel*. New York: Routledge.

Kaplan, Jeffrey. 2010. *Terrorist Groups and New Tribalism: The Fifth Wave of Terrorism*. New York: Routledge.

Khatchadourian, Haig. 1988. "Terrorism and Morality." *Journal of Applied Philosophy, 5*(2): 131–145.

Krueger, Alan B., & Jitka Malečková. 2003. "Education, Poverty and Terrorism: Is There a Causal Connection?" *The Journal of Economic Perspectives, 17*(4): 119–144.

Pape, Robert A. 2003. "The Strategic Logic of Suicide Terrorism." *American Political Science Review, 97*(3): 343–361.

Piazza, James A. 2009. "Is Islamist Terrorism More Dangerous? An Empirical Study of Group Ideology, Organization, and Goal Structure." *Terrorism and Political Violence, 21*(1): 62–88.

Piazza, James A. 2011. "Poverty, Minority Economic Discrimination, and Domestic Terrorism." *Journal of Peace Research, 48*(3): 339–353.

"President Bush Addresses the Nation." 2001. *Washington Post*, September 20. Retrieved from http://www.washingtonpost.com/wp-srv/nation/specials/attacked/transcripts/bushaddress_092001.html

Primoratz, Igor. 1990. "What Is Terrorism?" *Journal of Applied Philosophy*, *7*(2): 129–138.

Primoratz, Igor. 1997. "The Morality of Terrorism." *Journal of Applied Philosophy*, *14*(3): 221–233.

Rapoport, David, & Yonah Alexander. 1989. *The Morality of Terrorism*. New York: Elsevier.

Shanahan, Timothy. 2008. *Provisional Irish Republican Army and the Morality of Terrorism*. Edinburgh: Edinburgh University Press.

Sussmann, Naomi. 2013. "Can Just War Theory Delegitimate Terrorism?" *European Journal of Political Theory*, *12*(4): 425–446.

Victoroff, Jeff. 2005. "The Mind of the Terrorist: A Review and Critique of Psychological Approaches." *Journal of Conflict Resolution*, *49*(1): 3–42.

Torture and Extreme Interrogation Techniques

The United States government long felt pressure to prevent terrorist attacks, but the September 11, 2001, attacks forced the realization that America was an active target of aggression. On that date, 2,996 people were killed when four commercial flights leaving the East Coast were hijacked by members of the Islamic terrorist group, al-Qaeda. The terrorists flew two planes into the north and south World Trade Center towers in New York City, another plane into the Pentagon (United States Department of Defense building) in Arlington, Virginia, and crash-landed the last plane into a field in Shanksville, Pennsylvania.

Following this unprecedented attack on United States soil, the George W. Bush administration faced the great burden of providing the American public with the assurance that the nation was resilient and safe and that the Bush administration would take the necessary steps to prevent any future attacks and to bring anyone associated with the attack—including Osama bin Laden and other al-Qaeda leaders—to justice. In the face of this pressure, the administration issued a Memorandum Regarding Standards of Conduct for Interrogation that outlined what "enhanced interrogation" techniques the government could administer when interrogating or otherwise attempting to extract information from suspected terrorists. These legal justifications for enhanced interrogation (which critics characterized as a euphemism for torture) would be later referred to as the Torture Memos when they were leaked to the press.

When the extreme interrogation tactics where publicized in news media reports, a fierce debate broke out about the tactics employed by the Bush administration. The Obama administration joined with key Congressional allies, including Republican Senator John McCain, a Vietnam War prisoner of war (POW) who had endured torture at the hands of his captors, to argue that the enhanced interrogation techniques approved by the Bush administration constituted immoral behavior that could be classified as torture. They asserted that by sanctioning such techniques for the first time in U.S. history, America had damaged the country's ability to stand on the international moral high ground. When the American public and broader government officials became aware of these enhanced interrogation tactics, questions about what constituted moral and ethical treatment of suspected terrorists further intensified.

RESPONSIBILITY TO PROTECT

Following the September 11 attacks, Republican President George W. Bush addressed the nation in an effort to put its citizens at ease. After reminding the country of all the heroic acts that took place on that day, he reassured the nation: "Our first priority is to get help to those who have been injured, and to take every precaution to protect our citizens at home and around the world from further attacks." This would not be an easy task, and the Bush administration felt tremendous pressure to do everything in its power to prevent any additional terrorist attacks. Part of that prevention involved finding suspected terrorists and getting information from them as quickly as possible to break down the terrorist networks and foil any future attacks.

John Yoo, the deputy assistant attorney general for the Bush administration, soon went to work drafting memos that outlined how enhanced interrogation techniques could be used by the Department of Defense and the Central Intelligence Agencies to secure information from suspected terrorists. Two clinical psychologists, James E. Mitchell and John Bruce Jessen, were contracted by the CIA to use their knowledge and skills to create tactics for breaking the detainees and getting them to share intelligence with the interrogators. The men devised a list of what they believed were appropriate means to obtain information, and those tactics were used by interrogators, including Mitchell and Jessen, on detainees. They believed these tactics were firmly within the bounds of international agreements on the treatments of detainees, and they claimed they designed them to not be excessively cruel or degrading.

In a deposition tape, Jessen said that they did not want to have to use these tactics, but they were critical toward obtaining necessary information. In those same depositions, Mitchell argued they were not "breaking new ground" but were instead using established techniques (Fink, Browne, & Reneau, 2017). According to Jessen, they were also told by CIA supervisors that "every day a nuclear bomb was going to be exploded in the United States" and that if they stopped the practices, "it was going to be my fault if I didn't continue" (Maizland, 2017).

Of course, the line between what is considered acceptable treatment of a detainee and what crosses into being thought of as torture is a matter of moral interpretation. The U.S. government is formally against the use of torture. When constructing the list, Mitchell and Jessen were tasked with creating a delicate balance between what would be firm enough to break the detainee and what would go too far and be considered torture. When the United Nations passed an international treaty called the Convention Against Torture in 1985 to uphold the human rights of combatants, the United States saw it as a moral obligation to sign on to the treaty to guide their interrogation practices. The agreement states that for an act to be considered torture, "it must be equivalent in intensity to the pain accompanying serious physical injury, such as organ failure, impairment of bodily function, or even death" (U.S. Department of Justice Office of Legal Council, 2002: 1). One of the main goals of interrogation is to mentally break detainees to make them succumb to the authority of the interrogator. Given that objective, moral parameters are also placed to ensure that those interrogated do not have lasting mental harm. The tactics are therefore limited in that they cannot pose:

> threats of imminent death; threats of inflicting the kind of pain that would amount to physical torture; infliction of such physical pain as a means of psychological torture; use of drugs or other procedures designed to deeply disrupt the senses, or fundamentally alter an individual's personality; or threatening to do any of these things to a third party. (U.S. Department of Justice Office of Legal Council, 2002: 1)

The Justice Department used these guidelines to ensure that the tactics devised allowed the interrogators to try to extract information from detainees while in their view still upholding moral and ethical standards.

Mitchell and Jessen's interrogation program detailed several options that the U.S. Justice Department felt were within these moral standards considering the pressing need for intelligence and the U.N. agreement. The men approved methods like sleep deprivation, walling, exposure to extreme heat or cold, and simulated drowning. When detailing these methods, the CIA shows the delicate balance between physical intimidation and ensuring the safety of the detainee. For example, Mitchell describes walling: "The interrogator pulls the individual forward and then quickly and firmly pushes the individual into the [flexible] wall. It is the individual's shoulder blades that hit the wall. During this motion, the head and neck are supported with a rolled hood or towel" (Maizland, 2017). Mitchell described this practice as being "discombobulating, not painful" and likens it to being on an amusement ride in how it makes the detainee feel dizzy (Fink, Browne, & Reneau, 2017). These enhanced interrogation methods were used on approximately 40 detainees over the course of the War on Terror carried out by the Bush administration at various secret prisons (mostly operated by the CIA), also referred to as black sites, around the world.

The CIA's acting general counsel during the time of the enhanced interrogation program, John Rizzo, shared his insights on the necessity of carrying out the methods. In a Frontline interview, Rizzo stressed that the methods were not used "rashly or even enthusiastically" (Khan, 2011). Instead, Rizzo stated, "Measures like this were the only possible effective way to glean from these high-value detainees, these psychopathic, remorseless killers, possible information about the next imminent attack upon the homeland" (Khan, 2011). Rizzo admitted that the mistake was not the immorality of using the enhanced interrogation techniques but rested instead in not adequately communicating to Congress the necessity of their use.

ENHANCED INTERROGATION TECHNIQUES CONSIDERED TORTURE

Within days of taking office, President Barack Obama officially announced the United States would no longer use the enhanced interrogation methods. The Senate was also in the midst of what would become a five-year investigation into the interrogation tactics carried out at the black sites. By December 2012, the Senate Intelligence Committee Report on CIA Torture was completed; months later, a summary report was released to the public. As more details emerged about the practices that took place at these secret CIA prisons, both the morality and the effectiveness of the tactics were strongly challenged.

The report provided details on the interrogation methods, which were rooted in the Cold War–era tactics that U.S. trainers used to prepare military personnel at high risk for capture. Charles A. Morgan III, a Yale University faculty member and expert psychiatrist on posttraumatic stress disorder, worked closely with the Survival Evasion, Resistance, and Escape (SERE) program, which prepares American military members for how to survive in the case of capture. Upon learning of America's enhanced interrogation program, he stated his shock and disappointment about America's use of Soviet Union–style torture tactics. He said, "How did something used as an example of what an unethical government would do become something we do?" (Shane, 2007). This sentiment was also shared by the new administration. President Obama spoke out openly against these tactics, describing them as "brutal" and stated they "constituted torture in my mind" (Vaidyanathan, 2014). He felt it was imperative to have the Senate release the report with the hope that the transparency and admittance of wrongdoing would help prevent these acts from reoccurring.

The Senate report detailed the methods designed by Mitchell and Jessen, who were paid $81 million for their work (Fink, 2017). The report showed that the program produced very little usable intelligence and declared that traditional interrogation techniques were found to be far more effective. It was also found that some of the detainees were either (1) farmers with no knowledge of any terrorist organizations or plots or (2) low-level members who simply were not high enough in the organization to have access to the information the interrogators sought. Lastly, the methods themselves were questioned. It emerged that the two men's descriptions of the methods did not necessarily accurately depict how the tactics were carried out, nor did they include all the tactics used including sexual humiliation, rectal fluid resuscitation, and rectal feeding. The moral line was also crossed when it was revealed that threats of sexual abuse and murder had been made toward detainees' family members. These threats constituted clear violations of the United Nations Convention Against Torture agreement.

Two former detainees, Suleiman Salim and Mohamed Ben Soud, and Gul Rahman, the nephew of Obaidullah who died while in prison, sued Mitchell and Jessen for the unethical treatment they endured while in captivity. In those deposition tapes, the men describe in detail their experiences at the hands of the interrogators. The governmental actors, like Jose Rodriguez, former head of the CIA Counterterrorism Center, downplayed the harm in the tactics used, for example likening the use of placing detainees in stressful positions to that of a workout at the gym. The detainees, however, told of a very different experience and of lasting physical and psychological damage. When asked about the use of waterboarding, a simulated drowning technique long considered to be a torture technique, Mitchell said that he thought it could be safely administered and that he did not know if it was painful but instead destressing. In past interviews, Mitchell made earlier claims counter to this statement and said that if choosing between having your legs broken and waterboarding, he felt most people would choose having their legs broken (Fink & Risen, 2017). In August 2017, the lawsuit was settled in favor of the detainees, and the government was forced to payout an undisclosed amount to the men (Fink, 2017).

Throughout Sen. John McCain's career, he consistently advocated against torture and the use of enhanced interrogation techniques. He even went against his Republican party colleagues in endorsing the Senate report on the former interrogation program. His own five-and-a-half-year experience as a tortured prisoner of war during the Vietnam War allowed him to provide personal insights on the subject. In addition to his stance that the intelligence gained from using torture will likely be "intentionally misleading" in order to get the captors to stop, he believes "the use of torture compromises that which most distinguishes us from our enemies, our belief that all people, even captured enemies, possess basic human rights" (Chandler, 2014). McCain does not believe that the argument raised that torture was used to "serve the greater good" is convincing and instead charged that "they stained our national honor, did much harm and little practical good" (McCain, 2014). He claimed that the question about whether the tactics used were moral was not one that should be linked to our enemies but instead rested on us. He said our standards for imprisonment must be higher because "it's about who we were, who we are, and who we aspire to be. It's about how we represent ourselves to the world" (McCain, 2014). In 2015, Senator McCain and Senator Diane Feinstein successfully introduced language into the National Defense Authorization Act for Fiscal Year 2016 that explicitly barred American officials from using violence in interrogations or the use of waterboarding.

CONCLUSION

The debate over the moral and ethical treatment of suspected terrorist combatants is riddled with complexities. While America agreed to join with other nations around the world in the United Nations Convention against Torture agreement, where the line is drawn between appropriate means of coercion and what constitutes torture is still contentious. This turned more pressing as the United States government focused on preventing future terrorist plots following the September 11, 2001, attacks. President George W. Bush's administration felt great pressure to protect the American people and, in response, developed the enhanced interrogation program. As time passed without another major attack on American soil, the sense of urgency dissipated, and information began to emerge about our practices. During this same time, the Obama administration, Congress, and the American public were made aware of the extreme methods used at these secret prisons to extract information. Those responsible for the design and implementation of the enhanced interrogation program maintained the necessity of the tactics used to protect further loss of life and stressed the need to keep America safe by obtaining information from suspected terrorists. Nevertheless, the Obama administration ended the practices, insisting that they violated the moral and ethical standards our nation upholds.

Downplaying moral concerns over torture as political correctness during the 2016 presidential campaign, Republican Donald Trump promised to bring back enhanced interrogation techniques and perhaps even take more extreme steps, such as killing the families of terrorists. Since taking office, Trump has argued that "torture works." However, many Republican leaders have rejected Trump's proposals. The Trump administration issued a draft executive order in 2017 that called for a review of the possibility of using enhanced interrogation techniques again, as well as secret detention centers. Trump also signed an executive order stating that the detention facility in Guantanamo Bay, Cuba, would remain open. Even with Trump's refuted claims about the effectiveness and justifiability of torture in protecting Americans, and the appointment of advisors and officials that appear to support the use of torture techniques, no publically available information suggests that the administration has officially shifted direction away from the Obama administration's stance on torture.

Whitney L. Court

FURTHER READING

Barnes, Jamal. 2017. *A Genealogy of the Torture Taboo*. London: Routledge.

Bernstein, Jay M. 2015. *Torture and Dignity: An Essay on Moral Injury*. Chicago: University of Chicago Press.

Bush, George W. 2001. "Address to the Nation on the September 11 Attack." September 11. Retrieved from https://georgewbush-whitehouse.archives.gov/infocus/bushrecord /documents/Selected_Speeches_George_W_Bush.pdf

Chandler, Adam. 2014. "This Is How a Prisoner of War Feels About Torture." December 9. Retrieved from https://www.theatlantic.com/politics/archive/2014/12/John-Mccain -Speech-Senate-Republican-CIA-Torture-Report/383589

Danner, Mark. 2009. "US Torture: Voices from the Black Sites." April 9. Retrieved from http://www.nybooks.com/articles/archives/2009/apr/09/us-torture-voices-from -the-black-sites/?pagination=false

Fink, Sheri. 2017. "Settlement Reached in C.I.A. Torture Lawsuit." August 17. Retrieved from https://www.nytimes.com/2017/08/17/us/cia-torture-lawsuit-settlement.html ?rref=collection%2Ftimestopic%2FCentral%20Intelligence%20Agency&action =click&contentCollection=timestopics&region=stream&module=stream_unit &version=latest&contentPlacement=1&pgtype=collection

Fink, Sheri, Malachy Browne, & Natalie Reneau. 2017. "C.I.A. Torture: Interrogating the Interrogators." June 21. Retrieved from https://www.nytimes.com/video/us /100000005176335/cia-torture-interrogating-the-interrogators.html

Fink, Sheri, & James Risen. 2017. "Psychologists Open a Window on Brutal C.I.A. Interrogations." June 21. Retrieved from https://www.nytimes.com/interactive/2017/06 /20/us/cia-torture.html

Haider-Markel, Donald P., & Andrea Vieux. 2008. "Gender and Conditional Support for Torture in the War on Terror." *Politics & Gender*, 4(1): 5–33.

Khan, Azmat. 2011. "John Rizzo: CIA's Enhanced Interrogation "Necessary and Effective." September 13. Retrieved from http://www.pbs.org/wgbh/frontline/article/john -rizzo-cias-enhanced-interrogation-necessary-and-effective

Leidner, Bernhard, Peter Kardos, & Emanuele Castano. 2018. "The Effects of Moral and Pragmatic Arguments Against Torture on Demands for Judicial Reform." *Political Psychology*, 39(1): 143–162.

Maizland, Lindsay. 2017. "The CIA's Torture Program as Explained by the Psychologies Who Designed It." June 21. Retrieved from https://www.vox.com/world/2017/6/21 /15845896/cia-torture-program-psychologists-testimony-jessen-mitchell

McCain, John. 2014. "Floor Statement by Senator John McCain on Senate Intelligence Committee Report on CIA Interrogation Methods." December 9. Retrieved from https://www.mccain.senate.gov/public/index.cfm/press-releases?ID=1a15e343 -66b0-473f-b0c1-a58f984db996

Moore, Alexandra S., & Elizabeth Swanson (Eds.). 2018. *Witnessing Torture: Perspectives of Torture Survivors and Human Rights Workers*. New York: Springer.

Pfiffner, James P. 2009. *Torture as Public Policy: Restoring US Credibility on the World Stage*. New York: Routledge.

Shane, Scott. 2007. "Soviet-style 'Torture' Becomes 'Interrogation.'" *New York Times*, June 3. Retrieved from https://www.nytimes.com/2007/06/03/weekinreview/03 shane.html

United States Department of Justice Legal Counsel. 2002. "Memorandum Regarding Standards of Conduct for Interrogation." August 1. Retrieved from https://www.justice .gov/olc/file/886061/download

Vaidyanathan, Rajini. 2014. "CIA Report Sparks Prosecution Calls." December 10. Retrieved from http://www.bbc.com/news/av/world-us-canada-30408565/cia-int errogations-report-sparks-prosecution-calls

Transgender Issues

Popular culture has embraced transgender issues over the past decade, and support for the community continues to grow as exposure and awareness of the transgender experience increases. Members of the lesbian, gay, bisexual, and transgender (LGBT) community all share the experience of facing conflict grounded in moral concerns regarding gender norms and expectations from traditional society. Public opinion is largely in favor of and knowledgeable about lesbian, gay, and bisexual (LGB) people, but support for transgender individuals continues to lag behind (Lewis et al., 2017). Additional logistical concerns also arise for this segment of the LGBT population that lead to intense conflict between society's conception of what "male" and "female" include. The use of morality frames will continue for years to come, particularly due to the rise of Religious Freedom Restoration Acts, increased concern for values with the rise of culture wars (Haider-Markel & Taylor, 2016), and the polarization of political parties over support for the LGBT issues (Taylor, Lewis, & Haider-Markel, 2018).

Morality frames range from concern for individual safety to religious liberty to concerns for women and children. Opponents of transgender protections typically rely on biblical guidance on sexual behavior and expressions of concern about the potential harm to women and children of transgender-inclusive policies. For instance, Ted Cruz voiced the concern raised by many social conservatives that transgender-inclusive laws place "little girls alone in a bathroom with grown men." Advocates of transgender protections are often unable to shift discourse away from these frameworks to more practical concerns. Yet they have realized successes in increasing protections for transgender individuals in hate crime policy, as well as reform in health care treatment and curbing police abuse by appealing to moral concerns about the value of human life. Often these frames come from actual experiences, that is, from real-life stories about the tragic deaths of various transgender individuals.

Opponents of protections for transgender individuals originally grounded their stance in expressions of concern for the morality of transgender individuals. Protesters questioned what sort of behavior transgender people would engage in if they were allowed into various gendered spaces. These accusations are still sometimes heard. However, opponents of transgender rights have refined their position and brought new arguments to the fore in recent years. As the reach of LGBT nondiscrimination legislation continues to expand and advocates gain support, opponents voice their concern by leveling arguments that orbit around freedom of religion and the potential for unknown threats that might yet emerge from integration of transgender individual into American society. The freedom of religion argument—that being forced to accept that transgender individuals could constitute a violation of the tenets of one's faith—proved effective in several policy areas and has led to the rise of Religious Freedom Restoration Acts, while concern for unknown threats allows opponents to continue to assert that biological men will take advantage of transgender protections to harm defenseless women and children. Attempts by LGBT advocates to shift dialogue away from this frame when speaking about gendered public spaces, such as bathrooms and changing rooms, often continues to fail. Yet transgender advocates have effectively marshaled arguments in other areas, such as hate crimes policy, health care coverage, and employment rights that frame transgender individuals as deserving of the same basic rights that their fellow citizens enjoy.

The "bathroom issue" is the most famous conflict regarding transgender politics. Time and time again, comprehensive nondiscrimination bills that address a number of issues, such as employment, housing, and health care, inevitably raise concerns over the use of single-gender facilities. In a number of instances, debate over this issue has caused the entire policy making process to stall. Conflict regarding which bathroom transpeople can use has become particularly contentious in recent years. An added element is the rise of Religious Freedom Restoration Acts. These pieces of legislation have been crafted to allow companies the right to refuse service to individuals based on their religious beliefs. Religious liberties frequently come up in discourse, but government cannot refuse providing assistance to transcitizens on the basis of their gender identity alone (Taylor, 2007). Government must allow transgender individuals to access bathrooms, so much of the debate centers on *which bathroom* is right for the individuals. Also with it come hypothetical concerns regarding men claiming a female identity for the sole purpose of sexually harassing women and young girls. Some of the opponents rely more on the fear that biological men will take advantage of these transgender protections for their own ill intent.

Opponents of transgender individuals in bathrooms and gendered facilities frequently use morality-based arguments to halt debate on nondiscrimination policies. These arguments typically revolve around (1) the immorality of those who change their gender, (2) the effect on other individual or corporate religious rights, and (3) protecting women and young girls from a perceived but unrealized threat. Users of these morality frames emphasize how the presence of transgender individuals make others feel or impact others, while advocates, unable to change the rhetoric among participants, frequently present their side of the argument using a similar moral logic regarding how transgender people are made to feel when they are not allowed to have their gender identity recognized in public settings. Religion in politics plays a very important role in discussion of the first two concerns. Many sects of Christianity recognize only an individual's birth sex and view changing one's gender as an affront to God (Macgillivray, 2008), so they see society as a whole as being threatened by transgenderism.

The dominant and most effective morality-based argument (in terms of influencing public opinion) utilized by antitransgender voices concerns the safety of young girls and women in the bathroom if transgender individuals are permitted to use the same facilities. They assert that the *wrong* person will abuse these policies in order to threaten helpless females. Allowing transgender individuals to enter the bathroom, they say, could lead to sexual misconduct by men who falsely claim transgender status to prey on victims. The early variant of this argument focused on arguments that the policy would give transgender individuals opportunities to perpetrate sexual assault, but more modern arguments steer slightly away from this. Even staunch opponents of transgender protections, such as spokesman Greg Scott for the Alliance Defending Freedom, acknowledge that the majority of transgender individuals do not misuse facilities. But they assert that citizens should still be wary of these policies because they enable biological men to enter into women-only facilities to molest females. This refinement proves even more effective as support for the transgender community increases because it still allows for alarm for women and children without targeting transgender individuals specifically. In July 2016, Idaho police arrested a transgender woman for voyeurism, which further added fuel to the fire. This is the only documented incident to ever occur in U.S. history, but this event was seized on by opponents.

Proponents of nondiscrimination bills find the antitransgender morality frame hard to overcome. Appeals to shift the frame from an immoral one to a practical or one that focuses on a morally based protransgender rights largely fail. One common response by advocates is that transgender individuals used bathrooms without harm for decades. In fact, many transgender men (female to male) continue to use the men's restroom in North Carolina, despite the law requiring them to use the women's facilities, because of the potential harm that *could come to them*. Another argument put forward is that by requiring transgender individuals to go into the bathroom of their birth sex, government really is requiring transgender men to use female facilities. Transgender advocates disagree over deploying this tactic in debate. Some believe that such arguments hurt the long-term goals of creating safe spaces for transgender individuals because they do not discard the scare tactic that opponents turn to involving transgender women. Others argue that this response serves as a reminder that transgender men exist and that discourse is myopic because it does not consider the full implications of the legislation.

Transgender youth in schools is an interesting case because both sides lean heavily on morality based arguments. One defining feature of morality policy is that one side of the argument uses a moral framework to advance their side of the argument (Gusfield, 1963). However, both sides of the debate about transgender students argue in the interest of children—just different children. The Department of Education contributed to the discussion when it stated in 2016 that schools "generally must treat transgender students consistent with their gender identity" as an extension of sex-based protections provided under Title IX (U.S. Department of Education, 2016). Presently, litigation is under way in several state and federal courts across the country regarding transgender student access to educational facilities (Transgender Law Center, 2016). In fact, in November of 2016, the Supreme Court agreed to take up a case against a Virginia school board that denied a transgender teenage boy from using male facilities. The student, Gavin Grim (*G. G. v. Gloucester County School Board*), has since graduated from high school, and the case was returned to a lower court in 2018 for further consideration. The primary interest of advocates on both sides of the debate raise concerns regarding the potential threats to children when transgender students need to access single-gender facilities.

Similar to other policy areas, the side opposed to protections for transgender individuals typically centers on the alleged negative effect of various transgender acceptance policies in schools on women and children, in this case female children. Many of the arguments against allowing transgender individuals from using gendered facilities present the scenario of a grown male showering with young female children, but this appeal gains less traction than the public accommodations example because both of the individuals are students. Also, many citizens are aware of or sympathetic to the bullying and harassment that transgender students face in schools. Other morality frames that are drawn on are reminiscent of the opposition to allowing LGB teachers to work in school systems.

Focus on the Family's website stresses the organization's belief that allowing transgender students to use facilities consistent with their gender identity, rather than birth sex, places an undue burden on cisgender students and infringes upon the religious rights of parents to teach or not teach their children about gender and sexuality. Opponents argue that the schools are endorsing a lifestyle that is against parents' religious beliefs by allowing transgender students, often labeled as confused, to use facilities consistent with their gender identity (Macgillivray, 2008).

Transgender advocates assert that we have a moral obligation to protect transgender students. There is also the added element of concern for transgender students in regard to bullying and violence against sexual minority groups. The National Transgender Discrimination Survey (National Center for Transgender Equality [NCTE], 2012: 4) found that many transgender students face "harassment (78%), physical assault (35%) and sexual violence (12%); harassment was so severe that it led almost one-sixth (15%) to leave school." Moral arguments center on society's obligation to help all children and ensure that they have equal access to education. Public approval is generally more accepting of LGB individuals than transgender people, but calls to protect these at-risk students continue to gain support.

Transgender students tend to confront greater harassment and barriers to completing their education than their LGB or cisgender peers (NCTE, 2012). Gender-neutral bathrooms are typically available but are often located in inconvenient areas for students. Additionally, advocates argue that refusing to let transgender students access gendered facilities continues their disassociation from their peers and perpetuates the idea that transgender individuals are "others" or "outsiders" in society as a whole (McKinney, 2005). This disconnect with their peers leads to higher levels of depression and has resulted in a string of highly publicized suicides in the 2010s by transgender youth suffering from harassment and depression due, in part, to isolation from their peers. The general consensus recognizes the need to protect these students; however, the solutions proposed by socially liberal and conservative people differ considerably.

Although opponents of transgender inclusiveness usually rely on morality frameworks to advance their arguments, this same approach proved effective for early efforts of transgender advocacy. One particularly effective morality frame asserts that transgender individuals have an inherent *right to life*. Normally, right to life is championed by prolife advocates in debates surrounding abortion, but this is a broader framework that repeatedly comes up when discussing the death penalty, war, health care, and the role of government in society. This moral doctrine, in its most basic form, argues that individuals have an intrinsic "right not to be killed or allowed to die" (Feinberg, 1978: 94).

The 1990s brought with it two of the first instances where Americans were harshly introduced to the struggles of transgender individuals' right to life: (1) the murder of Brandon Teena in 1993 and (2) the refusal of emergency medical care for Tyra Hunter in 1995—a refusal that ultimately resulted in Tyra's death. Brandon Teena was a transgender man who was murdered by two former friends after they learned of his transgender status. Prior to his death, he was assaulted and raped by his former friends, which led to a series of mishandlings from health care providers and law enforcement officials that included loss of evidence, as well as an investigative focus on Brandon's identity and behavior rather than on evidence regarding the murder. Tyra Hunter's death also demonstrates the daily problems that transgender individuals face. She was a passenger in a car accident, but because of her anatomy, first responders mocked her and refused to treat her at the scene. The hospital is alleged to have provided subpar care that led to her death. She died of internal bleeding, which is highly treatable if responded to quickly.

These events, along with the highly publicized and brutal 1998 murder of gay college student Matthew Sheppard from the University of Wyoming, caused a groundswell of support for LGBT people's right to life in the late 1990s and early 2000s. Policy makers across the states and in Congress responded to the many problems that arose in these instances in order to address treatment of all patients irrespective of their sexual orientation or gender identity, complaints of rape, and assault from gay and transgender citizens and to raise awareness regarding other transgender issues. These high-profile deaths led more people to view transgender concerns as not a lifestyle or fringe issue but rather as examples of heteronormative biases depriving people of their right to life.

This framework of a right to life arises in many ways. It is particularly effective because it allows advocates to shift attention away from the typical discourse that focuses on protecting children or debating whether gender is immutable. The right to life is one that proponents of American ideals and even religious texts support across the board, so advocates win support by building an argument that draws on ways that transgender individuals suffer and sometimes die from a range of policies. For instance, access to health care, beyond just receiving emergency services, is a matter of life or death for transgender individuals. Even transgender people with insurance face barriers to health care, such as medical providers refusing to provide treatment or insurance companies denying coverage of life-threatening illnesses. The Obama administration finalized a rule in 2016 on Section 1557 of the Affordable Care Act that prevents insurance companies from categorically excluding all transition-related health care (U.S. Department of Health & Human Services, 2016). While advocates of transgender rights described this change as a step forward, they noted that health care providers can still refuse treatment for those whose lives are not in imminent danger on the grounds of religious freedom. Transgender advocates successfully used similar right-to-life or right-to-live decently arguments in discourse on rights of employment, housing, those incarcerated, and homeless youth.

CONCLUSION

Morality frames repeatedly enter the debate on transgender issues. Opponents of transgender protections cite freedom of religion and concern for defenseless women and children to support their side of the argument. Once discourse moves to these frames, it proves difficult to shift attention to more practical concerns regarding the intent of the policy. However, concepts of morality underpin many of the arguments leveled by supporters of transgender rights as well. In the case of education policy, we see two competing interests—protecting cisgender families and their beliefs and defending transgender students from harassment to ensure they have the opportunity to pursue an education. Transgender advocates also frequently employ a so-called right-to-life framework predicated on the idea that while not everyone supports transgender individuals, the right to life, liberty, and the pursuit of happiness is one of the most basic American ideals. Due to the successes for both sides in positioning their perspectives as ones based on deeply felt moral values, morality frameworks are likely to continue to dominate the discourse on transgender issues for years to come.

Mitchell Sellers

FURTHER READING

Button, James W., Barbara A. Rienzo, & Kenneth D. Wald. 1997. *Private Lives, Public Conflicts: Battles over Gay Rights in American Communities.* Washington, DC: CQ Press.

Centers for Disease Control and Prevention. 2016. *Health Risks Among Sexual Minority Youth.* August 11. Retrieved from http://www.cdc.gov/healthyyouth/disparities/smy .htm

Chokshi, Niraj. 2016. *Transgender Woman Is Charged with Voyeurism at Target in Idaho.* July 14. Retrieved from http://www.nytimes.com/2016/07/15/us/target-transgender -idaho-voyeurism.html

Currah, Paisley, Richard M. Juang, & Shannon Minter. 2006. *Transgender Rights.* Minneapolis: University of Minnesota Press.

Davis, Heath Fogg. 2017. *Beyond Trans: Does Gender Matter?* New York: New York University Press.

Feinberg, Joel. 1978. "Voluntary Euthanasia and the Inalienable Right to Life." *Philosophy & Public Affairs,* 7(2): 93–123.

G. G. v. Gloucester County School Board, 2017.

Gusfield, Joseph R. 1963. *Symbolic Crusade: Status Politics and the American Temperance Movement.* Chicago: University of Illinois Press.

Haider-Markel, Donald P. 1999. "Morality Policy and Individual-level Political Behavior: The Case of Legislative Voting on Lesbian and Gay Issues." *Policy Studies Journal*, *27*(4): 735–749.

Haider-Markel, Donald P., & Mark R. Joslyn. 2013. "Politicizing Biology: Social Movements, Parties, and the Case of Homosexuality." *The Social Science Journal*, *50*(4): 603–615.

Haider-Markel, Donald P., & Jami Kathleen Taylor. 2016. "Two Steps Forward, One Step Back: The Slow Forward Dance of LGBT Rights in America." In Carlos A. Ball (Ed.), *After Marriage Equality: The Future of LGBT Rights*, 42–72. New York: New York University Press.

Lewis, Daniel, Andrew Flores, Donald P. Haider-Markel, Patrick Miller, Barry Tadlock, & Jami K. Taylor. 2017. "Degrees of Acceptance: Variation in Public Attitudes Toward Segments of the LGBT Community." *Political Research Quarterly*, *70*(4): 861–875.

Macgillivray, Ian K. 2008. "Religion, Sexual Orientation, and School Policy: How the Christian Right Frames Its Arguments." *Educational Studies*, *43*(1): 29–44.

McKinney, Jeffrey S. 2005. "On the Margins: A Study of the Experiences of Transgender College Students." *Journal of Gay & Lesbian Issues in Education*, *3*(1): 63–76.

Mooney, Christopher Z., & Mei-Hsien Lee. 1995. "Legislative Morality in the American States: The Case of Pre-*Roe* Abortion Regulation Reform." *American Journal of Political Science*, *39*(3): 599–627.

Mucciaroni, Gary. 2011. "Are Debates About 'Morality Policy' Really About Morality? Framing Opposition to Gay and Lesbian Rights." *Policy Studies Journal*, *39*(2): 187–216.

Mucciaroni, Gary. 2008. *Same Sex, Different Politics: Success and Failure in the Struggles over Gay Rights*. Chicago: University of Chicago Press.

National Center for Transgender Equality (NCTE). 2012. *National Transgender Discrimination Survey*. August 11. Retrieved from http://www.transequality.org/issues/resources/national-transgender-discrimination-survey-full-report

Stryker, Susan. 2008. *Transgender History*. Berkeley, CA: Seal Press.

Taylor, Jami K. 2007. "Transgender Identities and Public Policy in the United States: The Relevance for Public Administration." *Administration & Society*, *39*(7): 833–856.

Taylor, Jami K., & Donald P. Haider-Markel. 2014. *Transgender Rights and Politics: Groups, Issue Framing, and Policy Adoption*. Ann Arbor: University of Michigan Press.

Taylor, Jami Kathleen, Daniel C. Lewis, & Donald P. Haider-Markel. 2018. *The Remarkable Rise of Transgender Rights*. Ann Arbor: University of Michigan Press.

Taylor, Jami K., Daniel C. Lewis, Matthew L. Jacobsmeier, & Brian DiSarro. 2012. "Content and Complexity in Policy Reinvention and Diffusion Gay and Transgender-Inclusive Laws Against Discrimination." *State Politics & Policy Quarterly*, *12*(1): 75–98.

Teich, Nicholas. 2012. *Transgender, 101: A Simple Guide to a Complex Issue*. New York: Columbia University Press.

Transgender Law Center. 2016. *Youth Legal & Policy Work*. Retrieved from http://transgenderlawcenter.org/legal/youth

U.S. Department of Education. 2016. Retrieved from http://www.ed.gov/news/press-releases/us-departments-education-and-justice-release-joint-guidance-help-schools-ensure-civil-rights-transgender-students

U.S. Department of Health & Human Services. 2016. "Nondiscrimination in Health Programs and Activities, 81 Fed. Reg. 31375-31473 (May 18, 2016)." https://www.federalregister.gov/documents/2016/05/18/2016-11458/nondiscrimination-in-health-programs-and-activities.

Selected Bibliography

Abramowitz, Alan I., & Kyle L. Saunders. 2008. "Is Polarization a Myth?" *The Journal of Politics*, *70*(2): 542–555.

Barker, David C., & Christopher Jan Carman. 2012. *Representing Red and Blue: How the Culture Wars Change the Way Citizens Speak and Politicians Listen*. New York: Oxford University Press.

Barker, David C., Jon Hurwitz, & Traci L. Nelson. 2008. "Of Crusades and Culture Wars: 'Messianic' Militarism and Political Conflict in the United States." *The Journal of Politics*, *70*(2): 307–322.

Ben-Yehuda, Nachman. 1990. *The Politics and Morality of Deviance: Moral Panics, Drug Abuse, Deviant Science, and Reversed Stigmatization*. Albany, NY: SUNY Press.

Bishop, Bill. 2009. *The Big Sort: Why the Clustering of Like-minded America Is Tearing Us Apart*. New York: Houghton Mifflin Harcourt.

Burns, Gene. 2005. *The Moral Veto: Framing Contraception, Abortion, and Cultural Pluralism in the United States*. New York: Cambridge University Press.

Busby, Joshua W. 2010. *Moral Movements and Foreign Policy*. New York: Cambridge University Press.

Chapman, Roger, & James Ciment. 2014. *Culture Wars in America*. Lanham, MD: M. E. Sharpe.

Coady, C. Anthony J. 2008. *Messy Morality: The Challenge of Politics*. New York: Oxford University Press.

Critcher, Chas. 2008. "Moral Panic Analysis: Past, Present and Future." *Sociology Compass*, *2*(4): 1127–1144.

Easterly, Bianca. 2019. *The Chronic Silence of Political Parties in End of Life Policymaking in the United States*. Lanham, MD: Lexington Books.

Etzioni, Amitai. 2018. "Moral Dialogs." *The Social Science Journal*, *55*(1): 6–18.

Etzioni, Amitai. 1988. *Moral Dimension: Toward a New Economics*. New York: Free Press.

Fiorina, Morris. 2017. *Unstable Majorities: Polarization, Party Sorting, and Political Stalemate*. Stanford, CA: Hoover Press.

Fiorina, Morris P., Samuel A. Abrams, & Jeremy C. Pope. 2008. "Polarization in the American Public: Misconceptions and Misreadings." *The Journal of Politics*, *70*(2): 556–560.

Gates, Henry Louis, Jr., Anthony P. Griffin, Donald E. Lively, & Nadine Strossen. 1996. *Speaking of Race, Speaking of Sex: Hate Speech, Civil Rights, and Civil Liberties.* New York: New York University Press.

Goode, Erich, & Nachman Ben-Yehuda. 2010. *Moral Panics: The Social Construction of Deviance.* New York: John Wiley & Sons.

Gottlieb, Roger S. 2019. *Morality and the Environmental Crisis.* New York: Cambridge University Press.

Gray, Margaret. 2013. *Labor and the Locavore: The Making of a Comprehensive Food Ethic.* Berkeley: University of California Press.

Green, John Clifford, James L. Guth, & Corwin E. Smidt. 1996. *Religion and the Culture Wars: Dispatches from the Front.* Lanham, MD: Rowman & Littlefield.

Grummel, John A. 2008. "Morality Politics, Direct Democracy, & Turnout." *State Politics & Policy Quarterly*, 8(3): 282–292.

Gusfield, Joseph R. 1996. *Contested Meanings: The Construction of Alcohol Problems.* Madison: University of Wisconsin Press.

Gusfield, Joseph R. 1986. *Symbolic Crusade: Status Politics and the American Temperance Movement.* Champaign-Urbana: University of Illinois Press.

Gusfield, Joseph R. 1984. *The Culture of Public Problems: Drinking-driving and the Symbolic Order.* Chicago: University of Chicago Press.

Gusfield, Joseph R. 1967. "Moral Passage: The Symbolic Process in Public Designations of Deviance." *Social Problems*, 15(2): 175–188.

Gusfield, Joseph R. 1955. "Social Structure and Moral Reform: A Study of the Woman's Christian Temperance Union." *American Journal of Sociology*, 61(3): 221–232.

Haider-Markel, Donald P., Jami Taylor, Andrew Flores, Daniel Lewis, Patrick Miller, & Barry Tadlock. 2019. "Morality Politics and New Research on Transgender Politics and Public Policy." *The Forum.* https://doi.org/10.1515/for-2019-0004

Hartman, Andrew. 2015. *A War for the Soul of America: A History of the Culture Wars.* Chicago: University of Chicago Press.

Heichel, Stephan, Christoph Knill, & Sophie Schmitt. 2013. "Public Policy Meets Morality: Conceptual and Theoretical Challenges in the Analysis of Morality Policy Change." *Journal of European Public Policy*, 20(3): 318–334.

Heineman, Kenneth J. 1998. *God Is a Conservative: Religion, Politics, and Morality in Contemporary America.* New York: New York University Press.

Hunter, James Davison. 1992. *Culture Wars: The Struggle to Control the Family, Art, Education, Law, and Politics in America.* New York: Basic Books.

Hurka, Steffen, Christian Adam, & Christoph Knill. 2017. "Is Morality Policy Different? Testing Sectoral and Institutional Explanations of Policy Change." *Policy Studies Journal*, 45(4): 688–712.

Knill, Christoph. 2013. "The Study of Morality Policy: Analytical Implications from a Public Policy Perspective." *Journal of European Public Policy*, 20(3): 309–317.

Kreitzer, Rebecca J. 2015. "Politics and Morality in State Abortion Policy." *State Politics & Policy Quarterly*, 15(1): 41–66.

Lakoff, George. 2010. *Moral Politics: How Liberals and Conservatives Think*. Chicago: University of Chicago Press.

Layman, Geoffrey C. 1999. "'Culture Wars' in the American Party System: Religious and Cultural Change Among Partisan Activists Since 1972." *American Politics Quarterly*, *27*(1): 89–121.

Layman, Geoffrey C., & Thomas M. Carsey. 2002. "Party Polarization and 'Conflict Extension' in the American Electorate." *American Journal of Political Science*, *46*(4): 786–802.

Levendusky, Matthew. 2009. *The Partisan Sort: How Liberals Became Democrats and Conservatives Became Republicans*. Chicago: University of Chicago Press.

Lindaman, Kara, & Donald P. Haider-Markel. 2002. "Issue Evolution, Political Parties, and the Culture Wars." *Political Research Quarterly*, *55*(1): 91–110.

MacCallum, Gerald Cushing. 1993. *Legislative Intent and Other Essays on Law, Politics, and Morality*. Madison: University of Wisconsin Press.

Meier, Kenneth J. 1994. *The Politics of Sin: Drugs, Alcohol and Public Policy*. Armonk, NY: M. E. Sharpe.

Miles, Andrew, & Stephen Vaisey. "Morality and Politics: Comparing Alternate Theories." *Social Science Research*, *53*(1): 252–269.

Moellendorf, Darrel. 2014. *The Moral Challenge of Dangerous Climate Change: Values, Poverty, and Policy*. New York: Cambridge University Press.

Mooney, Christopher Z. 2000. "The Decline of Federalism and the Rise of Morality-Policy Conflict in the United States." *Publius* (Winter–Spring): 171–188.

Mooney, Christopher Z. 1999. "The Politics of Morality Policy: Symposium Editor's Introduction." *Policy Studies Journal*, *27*(4): 675–680.

Mooney, Christopher Z., & Richard G. Schuldt. 2008. "Does Morality Policy Exist? Testing a Basic Assumption." *Policy Studies Journal*, *36*(2): 199–218.

Mucciaroni, Gary. 2011. "Are Debates About 'Morality Policy' Really About Morality? Framing Opposition to Gay and Lesbian Rights." *Policy Studies Journal*, *39*(2): 187–216.

Oldmixon, Elizabeth Anne. 2005. *Uncompromising Positions: God, Sex, and the U.S. House of Representatives*. Washington, DC: Georgetown University Press.

Patton, Dana. 2007. "The Supreme Court and Morality Policy Adoption in the American States." *Political Research Quarterly*, *60*(3): 468–488.

Permoser, Julia Mourão. 2019. "What Are Morality Policies? The Politics of Values in a Post-Secular World." *Political Studies Review*. https://doi.org/10.1177/1478929918816538

Perry, Michael J. 1990. *Morality, Politics, and Law*. Oxford: Oxford University Press on Demand.

Pierce, Patrick A., & Donald E. Miller. 2004. *Gambling Politics: State Government and the Business of Betting*. Boulder, CO: Lynne Rienner.

Posner, Richard A. 1992. *Sex and Reason*. Cambridge, MA: Harvard University Press.

Posner, Richard A., & Katharine B. Silbaugh. 1996. *A Guide to America's Sex Laws*. Chicago: University of Chicago Press.

Sandel, Michael J. 2005. *Public Philosophy: Essays on Morality in Politics*. Cambridge, MA: Harvard University Press.

Schecter, David L. 2005. "Legislating Morality Outside of the Legislature: Direct Democracy, Voter Participation and Morality Politics." *The Social Science Journal*, *46*(1): 89–110.

Sharp, Elaine B. 2005. *Morality Politics in American Cities*. Lawrence: University of Kansas Press.

Simmons, Randy T., Ryan M. Yonk, & Diana W. Thomas. 2011. "Bootleggers, Baptists, and Political Entrepreneurs: Key Players in the Rational Game and Morality Play of Regulatory Politics." *The Independent Review*, *15*(3): 367–381.

Smith, T. Alexander, & Raymond Tatalovich. 2003. *Cultures at War: Moral Conflicts in Western Democracies*. Peterborough, ON: Broadview.

Stone, Christopher D. 2010. *Should Trees Have Standing? Law, Morality, and the Environment*. Oxford: Oxford University Press.

Stone, Christopher D. 2003. "Do Morals Matter—The Influence of Ethics on Courts and Congress in Shaping US Environmental Policies." *Environs: Environmental Law & Policy Journal*, *27*: 13–52.

Tatalovich, Raymond, Byron W. Daynes, & Theodore J. Lowi. (4th ed.). 2014. *Moral Controversies in American Politics*. New York: Routledge.

Wagner, David, & Jennifer Barton Gilman. 2012. *Confronting Homelessness: Poverty, Politics, and the Failure of Social Policy*. Boulder, CO: Lynne Rienner.

Zimmerman, Jonathan. 2002. *Whose America? Culture Wars in the Public Schools*. Cambridge, MA: Harvard University Press.

About the Editor and Contributors

EDITOR

DONALD P. HAIDER-MARKEL is Professor of Political Science at the University of Kansas. He has authored or coauthored several books, over 70 refereed articles, and more than a dozen book chapters in a range of issue areas, including civil rights, politics in the culture wars, criminal justice policy, counterterrorism, race and inequality, and environmental policy.

CONTRIBUTORS

RANYA RADHI AHMED, PhD, is a senior information officer at the SAMS Foundation, Washington, D.C.

MAHALLEY D. ALLEN is professor, legal studies coordinator, and chair in the Political Science and Criminal Justice Department at California State University, Chico.

DANIEL R. ALVORD is a PhD candidate in sociology at the University of Kansas. He is a qualitative researcher motivated by questions of political ideology and political processes, specifically, understanding various expressions of contemporary conservative politics in the United States.

REBECCA BARRETT-FOX is an assistant professor of sociology, Arkansas State University. She is the author of *God Hates: Westboro Baptist Church, American Nationalism, and the Religious Right.*

BRANDON BRETL is a PhD candidate and Nona Tollefson Fellow in the School of Education, University of Kansas, Lawrence. His research asks questions about the various ways social and cultural contexts can influence cognitive development and vice versa, especially related to science education and beliefs about science.

DAVID BRICHOUX, PhD, is an instructor of political science at the University of Kansas, Lawrence.

COURTNEY S. CAMPBELL is the Hundere Professor in Religion and Culture, Philosophy Department, and has previously served as chair of the Philosophy Department and as director of the Program for Ethics, Science, and the Environment at Oregon State University.

CAROLINA COSTA CANDAL is a doctoral candidate in the Department of Political Science at the University of Kansas, Lawrence.

WHITNEY L. COURT is assistant professor of political science at the College of Saint Benedict and Saint John's University.

JEREMIAH GARRETSON is assistant professor of political science, California State University, East Bay.

ANDREA GÓMEZ CERVANTES is University of California President's Postdoctoral Fellow at UCLA and begins her appointment as assistant professor in the Department of Sociology at Wake Forest University in the Fall of 2020.

JACOB M. HELD is associate professor of philosophy and director of the UCA Core (General Education) at the University of Central Arkansas. He is a philosophical generalist who pursues any and all philosophical issues that he finds pertinent to crafting a praiseworthy life.

BRONSON P. HERRERA is assistant professor of political science at Northwest Missouri State. He teaches and conduct research on public opinion and public policy.

TERILYN JOHNSTON HUNTINGTON is assistant professor of political science, Indiana University of Pennsylvania. She studies political theory and international relations.

MICHAEL D. JONES is associate professor in the School of Public Policy, Oregon State University. His research focuses on the role and influence of narrative in public policy processes, outcomes, and science communication.

ALEXANDER JORGENSEN is a political science instructor at Winona State University.

J. ROBERT KENT is adjunct researcher in the Department of Special Education and adjunct research associate in American Studies at the University of Kansas. He researches and writes on social thought and disability issues.

KELLEE J. KIRKPATRICK is assistant professor of political science at Idaho State University. Her research agenda examines issues of women's health and reproductive policy and specifically focuses on questions that concern how and why governments regulate private, social issues.

MARIO MACIS is associate professor in the Carey Business School, Johns Hopkins University. His areas of interest include morally controversial transactions.

ELIZABETH MEITL is a teacher and PhD candidate in the Special Education Department in the School of Education at the University of Kansas, Lawrence. Her research and work are focused on creating and implementing policies and strategies intended to foster inclusive educational environments.

MATTHEW R. MILES is professor of political science at Brigham Young University, Idaho. His research agenda explores the interaction between individual traits and institutional arrangements. He examines how individual attributes interact with institutions to influence political attitudes, beliefs, and behaviors.

ALEXANDER J. MYERS is a PhD student in sociology, University of Kansas, Lawrence.

ROBERT J. NORRIS is assistant professor in criminology, law, and society, George Mason University. His research interests revolve around change—how reform happens and how it is shaped by social, cultural, political, and legal factors. Much of his work focuses specifically on wrongful convictions and miscarriages of justice.

HOLONA LEANNE OCHS is associate professor of political science, Lehigh University. Her research interests include poverty and inequality.

HOLLY L. PETERSON is assistant professor at the University of South Alabama.

JOHNATHAN C. PETERSON is assistant professor of government, Palo Alto College, Texas.

JASON PIERCESON is professor of political science, University of Illinois Springfield. His teaching and research focus on public law, the legal and political issues relating to sexuality and gender, and political theory.

STEPHEN P. SCHNEIDER is a PhD candidate in the Department of Political Science at the University of Nebraska–Lincoln. His research interests fall under the umbrella of political psychology and biopolitics.

MITCHELL SELLERS is a visiting assistant professor at Tulane University. His research interests fall broadly into the field of state politics and policies, in addition to executive–legislative relations. He specializes in American politics, research design, statistics, and public policy.

KARRIE A. SHOGREN is professor and senior scientist at the School of Education, Special Education, and the Life Span Institute, and codirector, Kansas University Center on Developmental Disabilities, University of Kansas.

THOMAS M. SKRTIC is the Williamson Family Distinguished Professor of Special Education, School of Education at the University of Kansas.

BONNIE B. STABILE is director, Master of Public Policy Program and research assistant professor, Schar School of Policy and Government, George *Mason* University. She is coeditor of *World Medical & Health Policy.*

WILLIAM B. STAPLES is professor of sociology, University of Kansas. His research and teaching investigate surveillance in the current era.

TRENT STEIDLEY is assistant professor, Department of Sociology and Criminology, University of Denver.

JAMES W. STOUTENBOROUGH is assistant professor at Idaho State University and senior research fellow in the Institute for Science, Technology, and Public Policy at Texas A&M University. His research interests include public policy, state politics, public opinion, and political psychology with a substantive interest in science and technology issues like climate change, water, and renewable energy.

STEVEN SYLVESTER is assistant professor in the History & Political Science Department at Utah Valley University. His research interests primarily focus on state and health policy examining health care implementation and autism.

STEVEN E. TORRENTE teaches political science at the Metropolitan State University of Denver. He researches torture, conflict, and other phenomena at the intersection of politics and ethics.

ABIGAIL VEGTER is a PhD student in political science at the University of Kansas, Lawrence.

ANDREA VIEUX is assistant professor of political science at Johnson County Community College.

Index